The People's State

The People's State
East German Society from Hitler to Honecker

Mary Fulbrook

Yale University Press
New Haven and London

For information about this and other Yale University Press publications, please contact:
U.S. Office: sales.press@yale.edu   yalebooks.com
Europe Office: sales @yaleup.co.uk   www.yalebooks.co.uk

Set in Minion by Northern Phototypesetting Co. Ltd, Bolton
Printed in Great Britain by St Edmundsbury Press Ltd, Bury St Edmunds

ISBN 0–300–10884–2

Library of Congress Control Number 2005932990

A catalogue record for this book is available from the British Library

10 9 8 7 6 5 4 3 2 1

Contents

Illustrations

Plates

1. Chess championship in the 'Maxim-Gorki House of German–Soviet Friendship', Scherwin, November 1953

2. Russian soldier and German child at the Soviet War Memorial in Treptow Park, May 1952

3. Poster advertising the 'Second Congress of Young Activists' in Erfurt, April 1949

4. Young Pioneers and leaders on a 'tourism' training camp, August 1955

5. Entrance to the 'Eisenhüttenkombinat' works in 'Stalinstadt', May 1953

6. The Krupp works in Magdeburg, May 1951

7. A 'Machine and Tractor Station', March 1960

8. A sign celebrating the compulsory collectivisation of independent peasants into 'LPGs', spring 1960

9. Election slogan for Volkskammer elections of November 1958

10. Leipzig shop window, April 1961

11. Street corner scene before the Wall, in Bernauerstraße, Berlin

12. Bernauerstraße as barbed wire is unrolled, 13 August 1961

13. Women receiving paramilitary training in the 'Society for Sport and Technology', August 1967

14. Members of a 'youth brigade', August 1970

15. Female operators of combine harvesters, July 1975

16. Medical education for international students, Quedlinburg, March 1973

Photographs are reproduced here courtesy of the Bundesarchiv Koblenz, with the exception of images 7–12, which are courtesy of the photographer, Hans-Joachim Helwig-Wilson.

Tables   *page*

Figures

Preface

In the mid-1990s, I was intrigued by the comments made by a tour guide at Colditz Castle, an intelligent and educated young woman, metaphorically one of 'Honecker's children' – a product of the German Democratic Republic (GDR). She continued unselfconsciously to reproduce GDR historical interpretations and related vocabulary (such as the alleged 'liberation' of East Germans by Soviet troops), even in talks to western visitors several years after unification. When I asked her about her experiences and life before 1989, she protested repeatedly that it was possible to lead 'a perfectly normal life' ('ein ganz normales Leben') in the GDR. This is an assertion that I have met with repeatedly since then, among East German friends and acquaintances, and among interviewees in the 'five new *Länder*' (as the area of the former GDR is often termed); and East German students attending UCL (University College London) often tell me that they have been shocked by reports in the press and history books about how 'bad' their 'dictatorship' was – a sharp contradiction to their own memories of happy childhoods and the 'perfectly normal lives' led by their parents, friends and relatives.

Yet such professions of 'normality' have to be set against the many other stories: of those who had to make agonising choices that resulted in stigmatisation, loss of a career, imprisonment or involuntary exile; of those whose lives were blighted by the loss of friends and relatives who fled to the West, or who were unable to visit places of interest and see people who were important to them; of those who constantly trod a fine line between saying what they really thought and saying what they thought the teacher, the factory works manager, the trade union or Party functionary would want to hear them say. Even without exaggerating the significance of the secret police, or Stasi, for the millions of East Germans who never overstepped the political mark, there was enough to feel oppressed by and to complain about in a state in which even a sudden consignment of bananas could be a major event and cause of mass excitement.

It is the latter, more sombre, aspects of life in an enclosed dictatorship, crawling with Soviet tanks, with a landmark Wall and a failing economy, which have to date received the greatest attention in the literature on the GDR. Political repression and opposition are central themes, as are popular protests and, eventually, the successful revolution of 1989. But it is equally important to understand what the structures and experiences of life were like for the vast numbers of East German citizens who did not hit up uncomfortably against the 'limits of the state', and who saw their lives – whether at the time, or with the partially nostalgic spectacles of hindsight – as interesting, varied and full of educational, career and leisure opportunities. We also have to understand how it was that many East Germans felt, at least at certain times, that it was possible to take initiatives, raise their voices, and contribute to the building of a better future within 'actually existing socialism'.

In short, there are conflicting narratives here, and the latter narrative – that of 'perfectly ordinary lives' – has been drowned out by the narratives of power and oppression or, when heard, rapidly rejected as a form either of political apologetics or retrospective nostalgia. But it seems to me that if we are to gain any form of adequate historical understanding of what is often too readily dismissed as the 'second German dictatorship', the conflicting narratives need deeper exploration: it is important to try to comprehend how both were possible. We have to try to understand how a set of social and political arrangements that appear not merely unacceptable, but even bizarre and unintelligible to many outside observers as well as internal opponents, could appear 'perfectly normal' to many who grew up within the parameters of this state. We have to try to understand how such a sense of 'normality' was – arduously – constructed over time, and how, in the process, the very constitution of social groups and collective patterns of attitude and behaviour shifted and changed.

We also have to explore just how far the structures of East German society were transformed over the forty years of separation from the West following the collapse of Nazi Germany. East German society was very different in 1989 from German society under Hitler, from the apparent 'achievements' and triumphalism, and the racism, murderous brutality and ruins, of the Nazi peacetime and wartime years from 1933 to 1945. To understand the history of the GDR is both to place it in a line of historical continuity with this shared German past and also to explore just how much had changed – just how far *Ossis*, or 'easterners', differed from their predecessors under Nazi rule – and why these changes had occurred. And, as many commentators noted with a degree of surprise at the time, the *Ossi* who swarmed across the Wall in the euphoria of November 1989 turned out to be very different in all manner of ways from the *Wessis*, or West German citizens of the Federal Republic of Germany. It is important to gain a deeper understanding of these differences than what is available in the jokes and stereotypes surrounding unification. The East German past is as much a part of the history of today's Federal Republic of Germany as that of West Germany, which has tended to loom far larger in public perceptions of 'German history'.

This book is not a political tract. My concern is neither to denounce nor defend the now defunct GDR: I have no personal axes to grind.

Why should one have to say this explicitly? Because so much of the historical writing on the GDR has been overtly or implicitly politicised, written to condemn or to exculpate, to 'overcome' or 'come to terms with', the curious legacies of the GDR. Any historical reconstruction of a relatively recent past is at least to some extent about people who are still alive and who have a stake in the way their lives and actions are (mis)represented. Interpretations of recent or 'contemporary' history are therefore almost inevitably controversial with respect to evaluations of the ways in which people still living have acted in the past. And when what we are dealing with is a communist dictatorship that was founded on the ruins of Hitler's Third Reich and which ultimately collapsed and was subsumed into its erstwhile arch-enemy, the capitalist democratic Federal Republic of Germany, controversies over morality, complicity and guilt are likely to involve a high level of emotion. Representations of this controversial past are almost inevitably closely related to political and moral positions, and are bound to raise considerable hackles in some quarters.

Part of my purpose in this book is to provide an empirically founded alternative interpretation to one such highly politicised model of the GDR: that of totalitarianism. But I do this not because (as some commentators will no doubt wish to argue) I am allegedly an 'old leftie' nostalgically hankering after some mythical past, or yearning for a rose-tinted picture of what might have been, but rather – more mundanely – because as a professional historian and scholar with a social science background I think the totalitarian approach simply does not capture adequately the empirical realities of life in the GDR. As much recent research has begun to demonstrate, a more comprehensive exploration of GDR social history reveals a greater complexity and a more diverse range of experiences and ways of living than the simple black-and-white vocabulary of Cold War castigation can comprehend or portray.

To emphasise the dichotomous poles of state and society, power and oppression, is to impose a template highlighting the ways in which the GDR differed from Western models of democracy, and this is a template that, while perhaps important for some in political debates, screens out much of historical interest and importance about the far more complex realities of the GDR. Many books on the GDR produced in the early years after the fall of the Wall focused, with justification, on the clearly dictatorial features of the East German communist regime. These restrictive, limiting, oppressive features are clearly central. But the vast tracts that lay behind, beyond, were for some considerable time less well explored. More recently, the German historiographical landscape has been littered with exceedingly well-researched and detailed analyses of particular periods, themes and questions. Yet little has as yet emerged by way of overall synthesis of the wider patterns of the social history of the GDR.

This book thus arose from the desire to understand better the ways in which many East Germans felt it was possible to lead quite 'normal' lives in the GDR, and to explore the ways in which implicit conceptions of 'normality' developed with wider changes in social structure and experience. Such exploration suggests we need new ways of thinking about the interrelations between political processes and social change in the GDR than the old dualistic models of state versus society, regime versus people, can allow. I have thus sought in this book, through exploration of what seem to me to be key aspects of GDR social history, to suggest some ways out of the over-politicised debates of the first decade after German unification and towards a more adequate understanding of the complex history of Germany's 'five new *Länder*'.

The breadth of focus needed to present a new approach to understanding GDR history in this wider perspective has necessarily been at the expense of depth in specific areas. I have been able to benefit from, and have tried to synthesise, some of the great wealth of specialist research that has been appearing in quite startling quantities over the last few years in the better-trodden areas of East German social history, and I have been able to rely extensively on such secondary sources on many topics. I have also used a range of primary sources – much more so in some areas than others – in part to try to gain a better understanding of particular issues and questions that have been less well covered in the available secondary literature, and in part to gain a sense of how the structures and institutions that are relatively well described in the secondary literature were actually experienced by people at the time. These sources range from those dealing with individuals who were perceived as 'problems' – cases to be reported on and dealt with by the relevant authorities – and reports of 'special incidents' ('besondere Vorkommnisse'), to wider surveys and overviews of the arguably 'silent majority' of the population who made their lives in less contentious ways. I have also made use of the innumerable letters from ordinary citizens to various authorities (the so-called

'Eingaben der Bürger') that have been assiduously stored in the federal archives and which have provided extraordinary insights not only into the kinds of problems faced by people, but also into the ways in which they perceived their rights, and the types of rhetoric they used to try to deal with their situation. The overall aim is to present a coherent overview of the distinctive patterns and development of East German society that manages to do justice both to a wide range of lived experiences and to the underlying structures of which contemporaries may well have been unaware. This general aim has determined the somewhat varied means, as far as choice of primary and secondary material is concerned.

This book is, thus, about the ways in which most East Germans lived their lives, under changing conditions, over the decades from the collapse of Hitler's Third Reich through to the collapse of the GDR. It is about how the very patterns of birth, health and illness, consumption, love and death were both affected by and constituted the history of the GDR; about the ways in which the GDR was not merely a communist state in a Cold War context, but also a modern industrial society facing familiar economic challenges, participating in wider patterns of globalisation and cultural and social change, albeit through a distinctive institutional and political framework; and about the ways in which it is not possible adequately to understand GDR history in the terms of dichotomous notions of regime versus people, or inherited conceptual vocabularies such as that of 'class'. It has therefore required not merely a sampling of the voluminous and formidable legacies of the East German archives, but also considerable rethinking of approaches and frameworks of analysis.

The book aims thus not so much (or merely) to develop an explicit theoretical critique of Cold War approaches, but rather (or rather more) to replace them with empirically founded new ways of thinking about the social history of the GDR, which cannot be simply reduced to the 'effects' of high politics and policies. I hope that the broad approach I develop here is also of wider significance for placing GDR history both in the longer sweep of twentieth-century German history and in the wider context of later twentieth-century European history, both east and west, and in the process helps to lift it out of a narrow specialist ghetto behind its own invisible historical Wall.

Acknowledgements

I am extremely grateful to the Arts and Humanities Research Board (now Arts and Humanities Research Council) of the UK, which has most generously supported my research over several years, both with an earlier period of research leave, and in funding a wider collaborative project on 'The "Normalisation of Rule"? State and Society in the GDR 1961–1979', the other strands of which have greatly stimulated and informed my thinking while completing the final manuscript of this particular work. I am also very grateful to the German Academic Exchange Service (DAAD) and to the Dean's Fund of the UCL Faculty of Arts and Humanities for research grants that helped to finance periods of travel and research in Germany.

I would like particularly to thank colleagues at the Zentrum für Zeithistorische Forschung, Potsdam, for their many institutional initiatives and cooperation, as well as frequent stimulating exchanges of views with individual colleagues both current and former, particularly Arnd Bauerkämper, Konrad Jarausch, Monika Kaiser, Christoph Kleßmann, Thomas Lindenberger, Siegfried Lokatis and Martin Sabrow. My thanks are due also to the very helpful staff of the Bundesarchiv in Berlin, where much of the archival research was carried out; and to the staff of the former Zentralinstitut für Jugendforschung in Leipzig, most particularly Barbara Bertram who very kindly donated a whole boxful of GDR sociological literature that, for all the obvious limitations occasioned by the constrained environment in which it was produced, is of far greater continuing interest than is often recognised. Individual colleagues, students and friends have also assisted (whether they are aware of it or not!) in countless ways in the development of this book, in this particular shape, through their comments, conversations and insights over the years. Ian Kershaw gave me the wise advice to send most of my theoretical and historiographical references to the footnotes. Alf Lüdtke has always been a source of inspiration. Mark Hewitson has listened with characteristic patience and good humour to my repeated doubts about how to deal with the material. A number of former and present doctoral students, many of whom are now colleagues, have accompanied and influenced my own thinking over the years. I am particularly grateful to Jeannette Madarász, who has been a constant discussion partner through the writing of this book and who very kindly took the time to read through and comment on a full draft; I have also much appreciated stimulating discussions with Mark Allinson, Angela Brock, Mark Fenemore, George Last, Esther von Richthofen, Corey Ross, Merrilyn Thomas, Damian mac con Uladh and Dan Wilton. All translations from German sources, unless explicitly stated otherwise, are my own. Needless to say, I also bear full responsibility for the remaining inadequacies of this text. Robert Baldock and Peter Robinson proved remarkably patient and supportively non-interventionist with the very slow birth of this book through what were some difficult years for me in a variety of ways. My warmest gratitude also to Marianne Wagner-Reinecke and (sadly, the late) Hans-Peter Reinecke, for their incredible hospitality and friendship during trips to Berlin.

Finally, my deepest thanks to my family – Julian, Conrad, Erica and Carl – who have always been such wonderful companions.

Chapter One

Introduction: The people's paradox

When in November 1989 the Berlin Wall fell, Westerners were aghast at the state of East Germany: the crumbling housing; the pot-holed, cobbled roads; the brown coal dust and chemical pollution in the industrial centres of the south; the miserable offerings in the shops; the relative paucity and poor quality of consumer goods; and the ubiquitous, spluttering, Trabant or 'Trabi' cars. Western condemnation of the failing economy was more than matched by condemnation of the repressive political system. The people, whose well-being was allegedly so dear to the regime, were walled into their own country, with hundreds of miles of inner-German border guarded by watchtowers, tanks, vicious dogs, a wide strip of mined no-man's-land and a larger guarded hinterland; their capital city was divided and they were prevented from entry into the Western (capitalist, democratic) half by the Berlin Wall. Their human rights in terms of freedom of movement and freedom of expression and association were dramatically restricted, and an extensive system of internal surveillance and suppression through the secret State Security Service (Staatssicherheitsdienst, or Stasi), complemented the activities of the regular police, military forces and border guards. Once the figures on paper were revealed, immediate impressions were confirmed: the economy was heading rapidly towards bankruptcy. In short, the GDR had neither political legitimacy nor economic viability.

And yet, once historians, sociologists and political scientists started to write about East Germany under communist rule, protesting voices began to be raised. Faced with accounts of repression, complicity and collusion, former citizens of the GDR claimed that their own memories and experiences told them otherwise. Their own biographies did not seem to fit easily within the bleak picture of oppression and fear. Most East Germans did not feel that they had spent up to four decades of their lives trembling in 'inner emigration', or conspiratorially plotting against the regime, or making a pact with the Red

Devil for private advancement. Life for most people in the GDR was simply not (or not for most people, most of the time) the way it was described in black-and-white characterisations of 'Germany's second dictatorship'. The GDR was not the equivalent, albeit under different ideological colours, of the Nazi Third Reich. The experience of East German citizens was far more complex: the distinctions between a brutal repressive state and a subordinate, repressed, or complicit society could not be drawn so neatly.

Herein lies the paradox, the question that is at the heart of this book. A massive disjuncture appears to have opened up between analyses of the dictatorial political system of the defunct GDR, on the one hand, and the experiences, perceptions and memories of many of those who lived through it, on the other. The institutionalised denial of human rights was given literally concrete embodiment in the shape of the Wall; yet even so, for long stretches of time – more in some periods than others – the GDR came to appear quite 'normal', taken for granted, among large numbers of its citizens. The undoubtedly dictatorial political system was 'carried' by the active participation of many of its subjects. It is the purpose of this book to explore in more detail the character of 'normal lives' in the East German dictatorship.

History and memory

For forty years the communist Socialist Unity Party (SED) ruled over a rump state – that part of defeated Nazi Germany that had come under Soviet control at the end of the Second World War. At first tentative – called by the West a 'provisorium' or 'the Zone' – a separate East German state became an ever more accepted fact of the post-war division of Europe. By the late 1960s, refusal to acknowledge the existence of a separate German state (under the so-called Hallstein doctrine) was clearly no longer a tenable position. Following the *Ostpolitik* of West German Chancellor Willy Brandt, the GDR's existence was begrudgingly accepted by the West; and, for all the peculiarities in the relations between the two German states, to all intents and purposes through most of the 1970s and '80s the GDR became an apparently permanent feature of the geopolitical landscape. Within the GDR, new generations grew to maturity who had known nothing else; those who remembered an undivided Germany, those socialised in Imperial Germany, the Weimar Republic or the Third Reich, became an ever-dwindling minority of the population. The GDR began to be taken for granted, both within and without. 'Normalisation' was reflected, too, in academic writing on the GDR, which by and large adopted a more sober tone than that of the early years.[1]

With the dramatic collapse of communism in 1989, all this changed – not only, and very obviously, in respect of present realities, but also in terms of prevailing perceptions of the past. Denunciations of an illegitimate dictatorship were unleashed again in full fury. A media feeding frenzy erupted as newspapers, magazines and television shows scrambled for the latest revelations on who had been an 'unofficial collaborator' (*Inoffizielle Mitarbeiter*, or IM) or informer for the hated Stasi. The slightest taint was sufficient to destroy relationships, topple careers or blight lives. Debates raged over the problems of bringing to justice through the law courts those who had been responsible for a system of injustice – a repressive system symbolised by the 'order to shoot' any citizen who sought to escape across the 'Iron Curtain' or the Berlin Wall.[2] The parliament of the newly united and enlarged Federal Republic of Germany instigated an extraordinarily thorough investigation, with two lengthy parliamentary 'commissions of inquiry' (*Enquêtekommissionen*) into the character of the East German dictatorship, involving both experts and witness testimonies.[3] Both scholars and journalists became fascinated by the repression of human rights, the infiltration of the Churches and the everyday malign and sinister activities of the Stasi.[4] And academic interpretations were fractured and coloured by their political implications, from denunciation, through the quest for a more neutral understanding, to pleas for exoneration and exculpation.

But beyond all this turmoil, this heated ferment of debate, lay the largely inarticulate voices of those East Germans who had lived through it all and found little that reflected their own experiences, that touched a chord with their own lives, perceptions and aspirations, in the babble of accusations and denials, prosecutions and protests. Many East Germans were surprised and shocked to hear the revelations of corruption, to learn the extent of Stasi infiltration. And they were baffled by the analyses of the political scientists who told them they had been victims or, worse, accomplices in a dictatorship comparable with that of Hitler. Many thought, by contrast, that they had been able to lead what they considered to be 'perfectly ordinary lives' – or, to use the German expression, 'ein ganz normales Leben' – in the GDR. Little over a decade after the GDR had been dealt the double death blow of 'gentle revolution' in autumn 1989 and unification with the West in 1990, a 'memory boom' was under way, with GDR products, GDR design and aspects of GDR everyday life enjoying a massive posthumous renaissance.

It may of course be objected that this perception of normality is a retrospective projection, a symptom of 'ostalgia' (*Ostalgie*) – nostalgia for the good times in the East German past, a sentiment flowering only under the conditions of upheaval and uncertainty in the difficult years after formal political unification. There is, of course, an element of truth in this. In a situation of high unemployment, of even higher general anomie, there will of course be a yearning for at least some of the security and certainties of the old regime, however compromised and constraining. But there is more to it than merely rosy memories. Even if one discounts entirely the dubious evidence of hindsight, there is much by way of pre-1989 evidence to suggest that all was not quite as clear-cut as it is sometimes depicted. The East German dictatorship was one that managed to involve large numbers of its citizens in its political structures and processes. One in five adults became a member of the SED. An astonishing number appear to have been willing to act as unofficial informers for the Stasi. Nearly all working adults were members of the state trade union organisation, the Freier Deutscher Gewerkschaftsbund (FDGB). The vast majority of young people were members of the state youth organisations under the Freie Deutsche Jugend (FDJ). And, by the 1970s, despite continuing grumbling over all manner of specific irritations and shortages, there is much evidence to suggest that there was widespread acceptance of the general parameters of life, that this was simply the 'way things were'. For long stretches of time, the GDR functioned not primarily through the overt exercise of coercion – although (again paradoxically) the apparatus of coercion and covert capacity for repression was growing exponentially – but rather through some form of internalisation of, or willingness to play by, the unwritten 'rules of the game'.

These 'rules of the game' were of course not internalised overnight. The early years in particular were characterised by very obvious repression, the wilful exercise of 'political justice' and widespread experience of brutality and force. The replacement of the Nazi dictatorship by a communist dictatorship – with a very different ideology and in principle far more humanistic set of goals, yet with a comparable disregard for individual human rights and liberal notions of freedom – was for millions of Germans a traumatic experience. But this experience was to some degree class-specific, and highly variable according to political and moral standpoint. The imposition of the East German dictatorship was particularly unpleasant for people from upper-class, bourgeois and professional backgrounds, and also for Christians and others with explicit moral and political disagreements with the new regime. People from working-class or peasant backgrounds, people who were not direct targets of repression, and people with strong left-wing sympathies, by contrast, often found new opportunities in the post-war upheavals, or at least were able to grumble and get by without being any more adversely affected than they had been during the previous decades. These were decades, it should be remembered, which had even in peacetime been characterised by horrendous inflation, mass unemployment, political violence, repression of independent political parties and trade unions, and in which ordinary workers were nearly always on the receiving end of orders. Moreover, whatever people's experiences in the early years of the GDR, over time new generations came to maturity who were in many ways products of the regime, used to living by its rules and agreeing with many of the aims in principle, if not the realities in practice, of 'actually existing socialism'. This is not to suggest that everything was wonderful in the GDR, about which both many jokes and far more savage critiques were made at the time and since; but it is to suggest that the experiences of East Germans were highly varied, with some suffering far more than others, and some a great deal more enthusiastic and willing than others. There was some genuine basis in the realities of a selectively recalled past to provide material for nostalgic memories after unification. Most importantly, it is to suggest that the history of East German society cannot be adequately understood purely within the parameters of a top–down political and institutional history.

The transformation of German society

East German social history is the key to understanding the paradox of history and memory. It is not a mere adjunct to political history, or an interesting sideline, or an antiquarian rag-bag of the flotsam and jetsam of everyday life for nostalgia addicts, but rather it is fundamental and integral to developing a more adequate interpretation of GDR history as a whole.

In the process of trying to achieve the Marxist vision of an egalitarian society, East German communists pursued radical policies, effecting a major social revolution, often wholly against the wishes of those members of the population who found their previous interests, freedom and material well-being adversely affected. This social revolution was not, and was not intended to be, democratic in the Western sense of having the implied consent of a majority of the population (if only in being able periodically to vote an unpopular government out of power). The transitional stage of transformation to communism had inevitably, on the Marxist view, to be undemocratic: it had of necessity to be a stage of the 'dictatorship of the proletariat', since the attempts of the oppressed classes to overthrow an unequal and unjust society would inevitably provoke protest and active opposition from the previously rich and powerful, now at risk of being ousted from their positions of privilege. But the proletariat might still be suffering from 'false consciousness' arising from generations of exposure to the ideology of the ruling classes, and thus might well not consciously recognise what was in their own long-term best interests. So, on the Marxist-Leninist version, the transitional period was in effect one of the 'dictatorship of the vanguard party'. The leading communist party's historic mission was to act on behalf of the oppressed classes, whether or not they liked what was being done in their name. The end, in this world-view, clearly justified the means.

Hence the transformation of East German society was pushed through by force. A war-ravaged population – those who had survived twelve years of Nazi rule, six years of which had been characterised by death and destruction at the front, shortages, air-raids and eventual occupation at home – faced a new and arguably even more interventionist regime of a very different ideological persuasion. The constant haemorrhage from East to West Germany of people who were variously persecuted, disadvantaged, or sought pre-emptive escape from the new economic and political policies logically led to the effective incarceration of the entire population behind the ever more fearsome 'Iron Curtain' and, from 1961, the Berlin Wall. In face of all manner of problems, the SED continued to struggle mightily to achieve its conception of the perfect society, periodically revising its own strategies and labels for the alleged 'stage' that had been reached. In the process, the overall shape of East German society was dramatically transformed. Radical policies were introduced to transform society in the desired directions. But one cannot write East German social history simply and only in terms of communist intentions, explicit policies and domestic resistances.[5]

Some social changes in the GDR were clearly the direct results of communist policies. A combination of successive economic reforms and political pressures led to a radical transformation of the socio-economic structure: the abolition of major private ownership in industry and finance was effected very soon after the war, and the collectivisation of agriculture effectively completed by 1961. At the same time, the 'bourgeoisie' was transformed from the old propertied or professional middle classes into a state-dependent socialist 'intelligentsia'. However, many changes were a result of quite other factors outside the control of the SED. Of crucial importance were long-term socio-economic trends, continued industrialisation and urbanisation, and the imperatives of economic competition, within the constraints of the Soviet bloc, on international markets. Wider processes of change – the unintended impact of aspects of industrialisation, urbanisation, globalisation of communications and culture; the economic strains of defence expenditure in a Cold War context; and the lures of consumerism – constantly deflected these policies into unexpected developments. The partly self-contradictory Enlightenment aspirations embodied in Marxist thought – that the Party could understand, intervene and guide the 'Course of History' – proved impossible to realise in a divided world in which capitalism in the West, for all its periodic wobbles and crashes, showed little sign of succumbing to fatal collapse under the weight of its supposedly inevitable contradictions.

Nor did influence run in only one direction. SED policies were affected not only by the dictates and limits set by external parameters (the Soviet Union, the Cold War), but also by pressures and inputs from below and considerations with respect to a variety of social groups. The notion of an implicit 'social contract', and the effective, if limited, veto power of the GDR workforce, have often been remarked upon.[6] Following the uprising of June 1953, the regime never again dared to risk quite such unpopularity on the economic front. Frequent unofficial work stoppages – small acts of sabotage, protest or mini-strikes and walk-outs – were constant reminders of the importance of keeping the workers at least satisfied, if not happy; sops to consumerism were repeated ploys to keep levels of unrest from rising. The SED also made strenuous efforts to gauge, influence and respond to the popular mood, not only through Stasi reports and surveillance, but also – perhaps more importantly – through mountains of regular reports from functionaries (such as the reports from local functionaries of the SED and FDGB on popular 'mood and opinion'), and through opinion poll surveys carried out by social research institutes, such as the SED's own research institute, the Institut für Meinungsforschung beim ZK der SED, and the sociological institute for youth research based in Leipzig, the Zentralinstitut für Jugendforschung (ZIJ). Citizens' letters ('petitions', complaints or *Eingaben*) and controlled public 'discussions' of policies were also the SED's variation on the Western practices of controlled leaks, the publication of White Papers, or the use of 'focus groups' and opinion polling. No modern government can seriously risk ignoring the views of the population – least of all a government that wants at least some basis for the claim that it is supported by 99 per cent of the population.

There were, too, subterranean socio-cultural currents transmitted over generations within the private sphere. Traditional conceptions of gender roles, with a tenaciously persistent division of labour in the privacy of the home, and often unconsciously biased expectations in the workplace or public life, proved remarkably resilient. Similarly, to take a quite different example, certain religious traditions survived and developed, leading to what some have termed the 'Protestant Revolution' of 1989, symbolised by the prevalence of pastors, prayers and candles. Tales told in the privacy of the home – about what grandpa actually did in the war, or why Great-aunt Amalie was a committed member of the Nazi women's organisation – also undercut simplistic historical lessons of heroes and villains presented in school. Despite the high prevalence of single-parent families and predominance of collective socialisation outside the home, the influence of the family retained considerable significance.

As important as changes in class structure and official ideology were changes in patterns of social and political organisation, and in the ways in which East Germans were not merely coerced, but also in many cases actively and voluntarily participated in the manifold organisations and institutions of the state. An emphasis on the collective rather than the individual was a fundamental element in the GDR. It was a key feature in all areas of life, from collective potty training in state-run crèches and nurseries, through conformity in youth organisations, schools and military service, to the participation in the work brigades, the frequent campaigns and regular public rallies, and the mass organisations and bloc parties of adult life. None of these organisations was ever completely successful in encompassing all of the target audience. The state youth organisation, the FDJ, for example, was constantly competing for the attention of young people with Western popular culture – from blue jeans, Elvis Presley and rock 'n' roll in the 1950s, through beat music and jazz in the 1960s, to rock concerts in the 1970s and '80s – or with the alternative culture and discussion groups held under the ambiguously protective umbrella of the Churches. But it has also to be recognised that many of these state-controlled mass organisations not only sought political control and influence, but also offered some genuine pleasures and benefits to members. Many were upheld not only by paid employees of the state and the SED, but also by the active participation of honorary functionaries, who sustained their activities and who both represented and supported grass-roots activities in all manner of ways. The picture is thus far from being simply one of repression and containment; there was not only much mutual support within these organisations, but also, interestingly, a degree of genuine representation and the possibility of the facilitation of individual interests. Such activities and channels for the pursuit of individual pastimes came to be seen as ever more 'normal', particularly by those younger generations born into the GDR. At the same time, wider patterns such as the growth of consumer culture and the 'privatisation' of aspects of life and leisure, as well as the individualised channels of complaints and grumbling – all fostered and sustained by official policies – ironically led to or reinforced the growth of individualism in this would-be collectivised society.

The GDR lasted, it should be remembered, for forty years – long enough for new generations to be socialised, to grow to maturity and to experience their everyday life as 'perfectly normal'. Younger generations, born into the GDR, differed in crucial respects from the older generations of those born before the Second and First World Wars respectively (often termed the 'Hitler Youth generation' and the 'Front generation'). The extraordinarily slippery concept of 'normalisation', with its linguistic variations of 'norm' and 'normal', can refer to the internalisation of culturally and historically specific norms; it may refer also to the ways in which people are able to predict the parameters of their situation and be prepared to behave 'as if' they accepted the dominant norms in order to achieve certain goals, and to the routinisation of structures and institutions – to the stability and predictability of the social world. Arguably, in all these ways the GDR enjoyed (if that is the right word for this very modest 'achievement') a period of 'normalisation' in its middle decades.[7]

It is important also to remember that the SED did not simply seek to exercise and retain power for power's sake. The SED actually wanted to do something with their power: to transform society into what they thought would be a better, more egalitarian, more just society. In pursuit of these ends they deployed means that from a democratic perspective can never be justified – the Wall stands as a symbol for the SED's attempts to control by force what could not be achieved by consent – but at the same time there was a great deal more willing (or unthinking) participation, even goodwill, in politically less contentious areas. Analysis of topics such as healthcare, demography, gender, leisure, housing and work reveals a world that is not often represented in traditional political histories of the GDR, a world in which, of course, the big questions – questions of human rights, freedom of speech, association and movement – could not be discussed, but in which there was far more openness and genuine debate about how to improve the basic conditions of everyday life than might be thought.

To say all this – to point to the existence of a dialogue of sorts, and within limits – is not to deny the dark side of the regime. The sinister Stasi, with its long shadow of unofficial informers (IMs), was everywhere, and observed and reported on everything. For those among the very small minority of active, principled dissenters (or to use the words deriving from Rosa Luxemburg, 'those who thought differently'), including committed Christians and human rights activists, life in the GDR was far from 'ordinary'. Prevented from progression through higher education in any subject except theology, or from any professional career except in the environs of the Church, many principled dissenters were constantly aware of the boundaries set by the regime. Anyone found to have transgressed permissible limits, in whatever way, could be subjected to brutal measures of repression, arrest and incarceration, as well as physical and mental maltreatment; some were forcibly exiled against their will, while others had their lives within the GDR subjected to sometimes unintelligible distortions and miseries in both professional and private lives. Any freedom to choose subjects of study, place of occupation or residence, was severely curtailed. Even for those who did not step quite far enough over the boundaries of acceptable behaviour to attract adverse attention from the authorities, the effects of living in a dictatorship were often evident. There is no denying the constraining effects of pressures for conformity in the education system, the frustrations borne of lack of freedom to choose holiday destinations, or the extraordinarily difficult personal choices faced if developing an intimate relationship with someone who was not a GDR citizen. And, at the very end, the frustrations were massively exacerbated by the ever more visible, tangible collapse of the East German economy. Once it was clear that the political deprivations would not even be to some degree compensated by social security and a modest degree of material well-being, for huge numbers of East Germans there could be no justification whatsoever for the continued existence of SED rule. Thus for very many people the limits were very obvious, and affected their behaviour in myriad ways, to which the rich repertoire of GDR jokes bears ample witness.

Once one breaks loose from a focus solely on the formal structures of social and political institutions to explore the wider dynamics of GDR social history, it becomes clear why a framework emphasising power, repression and fear does not do justice to the very different memories of many of those who lived and worked under this regime. Both among grass-roots functionaries who did their best to improve living and working conditions in their local areas, and among large numbers of essentially apolitical people who at least thought that they were able to live 'perfectly ordinary lives', there were many East Germans of goodwill and good faith. To categorise them as immoral collaborators and accomplices in an evil regime, or simpleton dupes of ideology, or even heroes of opposition and victims of repression, is fundamentally to misrepresent the ways in which East German society, for the most part, functioned. And while it is vital to understand patterns of political repression and dissent in a dictatorship, it is important also to reinsert back into the wider historical picture the vast areas of life that cannot be adequately encompassed by such a focus. There was, in curious and multiple ways, also a 'normality' about the history of the GDR that needs to be recaptured.

Rethinking approaches to GDR history

The old dictum that 'social history is history with the politics left out', if indeed it is ever true, could not be less apposite with respect to the GDR. The social history of the GDR was fundamentally affected by politics; it cannot be understood without analysis of political structures and processes. Accounts of politically determined social policies are not only integral to any social history, but blindingly obvious in a highly interventionist state such as the GDR, in which a fundamental and explicit political aim to transform society was evident from the outset. Yet, for a variety of reasons, the social history of the GDR is neither exhausted nor comprehensively explained by an analysis of the effects of – or resistances to – top–down policies alone.[8] Of course it was a dictatorship. But it was not only a dictatorship.[9]

All modern societies are in large measure intrinsically constituted and affected by political regimes that claim responsibility for a wide range of matters from birth, through socialisation, education and employment, to retirement and death; from collective welfare to warfare. There is no modern society in which people's individual lives – in aspects ranging from birth weight, through acquisition of social or regional accent, probabilities of educational success, patterns of social mobility, consumption and life chances, to even the causes, timing and manner of death – are not in some way affected by the political system in which they live. Nor is there any modern state that has succeeded in shaping its social policies to achieve exactly the effects intended: there is always more to societal and cultural change than what any given government of the day seeks to achieve. Yet, while no Western historian would seek to write the social history of a Western society solely in terms of regime policies and popular resistance, this is very much how the social history of the GDR has been conceived, particularly when added in to general historical overviews of political developments.

These considerations suggest we need to rethink approaches to GDR history. First, GDR history needs to be considered not merely from the perspective of 'dictatorship', or 'communist state', but also from that of 'modern industrial society'.[10] Changes in society were not merely driven by the political agendas of the ruling elite. There was of course clearly an interaction between the ever-changing international context and the articulation and execution of SED goals and policies. This was most notable in the manner of the GDR's birth and eventual demise in relation to the Soviet Union: the GDR was a product of the Cold War, and its end came with the end of the Soviet empire and the bipolar system. But the social history of the GDR was implicated in and affected by far wider trends that were not merely political in the narrow sense of the word. Despite the marked differences in organisational framework, not to mention official ideology, there were interactions and similarities between trends in East German society and those of Western industrial states from the 1950s to the 1980s. This does not mean rejecting the narrative of politically driven social change, but rather both augmenting it and recasting it within a wider framework of changes occurring across many industrial societies in the later twentieth century.

The GDR, however politically isolated by the Iron Curtain between East and West, was not insulated from broader socio-economic and cultural changes in the latter half of the twentieth century. East German society was no less affected than other modern industrial states – though in different ways, through a different institutional system, and at a different pace – by the implications of industrial production and technological revolution, internal migration and the growth of urban areas and new towns, and the internationalisation of communications and the spread of youth culture in an increasingly global system. Collective mentalities and subcultures were affected by changing styles in, for example, youth culture and popular music, exposure to Western television, and the increasing porosity of the inner-German border. Patterns of consumerism, materialism and increasing individualisation were noticeable in East Germany, if in different ways from those of the West. Both the wider population, and those responsible for taking key economic decisions, were affected by these trends. The utopian hopes and aspirations of the 'age of ideology' gave way in the GDR, as in different ways in so many Western states, to a form of everyday 'consumer socialism', in which the individual pursuit of the fulfilment of everyday hopes and needs took precedence over collective projects and idealistic plans for the future.

Secondly, it is necessary to rethink the social character of political processes in the GDR, with respect to the means, the structures and the goals of politics. In this book, I develop the notion of a 'participatory dictatorship'. This somewhat oxymoronic expression is intended to emphasise the extent to which 'democratic centralism', as practised in the GDR, did actually involve very widespread participation of large numbers of people, for a wide variety of reasons: not always or necessarily out of genuine commitment to Marxist-Leninist ideals; nor always or necessarily as a result of being simply coerced or cowed into compliance; nor merely in a sometimes defiant representation of one's 'own interests', as suggested by the notion of *Eigen-Sinn* (hard to translate – literally, 'own meanings' or 'own sense', but generally used to focus on the active defence and pursuit of personal interests).[11] The notion of a participatory dictatorship is intended to underline the ways in which the people themselves were at one and the same time both constrained and affected by, and yet also actively and often voluntarily carried, the ever changing social and political system of the GDR.

The exercise of power was in many areas both far more multifaceted and complex, and also less sinister and repressive, than totalitarian theorists would have us believe. The 'state' or the 'regime' was not a unitary actor, which simply did (mostly nasty) things to the ill-defined, undifferentiated mass of 'the people'. There were clearly hugely repressive and utterly reprehensible aspects of the SED regime; but there were also areas in which thousands of citizens cooperated and felt they were able to pursue common goals and ideals.[12] The notion of what constituted the East German state thus needs in some way to be extended to take into account its less sinister, less oppressive aspects. We have to recognise that political goals were not always or only to do with the maintenance and retention of power; there were many common humanitarian goals, as in areas of health policy, housing and gender equality, that were not achieved in practice largely because of economic constraints, but which were not always or intrinsically manipulative, coercive or repressive. A very small ruling elite, with a linked apparatus of repression and injustice, was supported and sustained by a very much larger number of people who played key roles in trying, under exceedingly difficult circumstances, to build a better society, or at least to make the best of the present through engaging in such communal activities as attempting to 'beautify' their village, construct a new swimming pool, or organise a youth sports festival. At the same time, 'society' was far more diverse, and characterised by complex varieties of subcultures and milieus, than an undifferentiated notion of 'the people' – let alone of a society that was allegedly 'frozen' under the dead hand of the regime – might suggest.

This analysis, particularly with respect to state policies but also in relation to popular participation and patterns of conformity, inevitably entails moral evaluations of the spectrum of what is more or less 'reprehensible'. The point here, however, is not so much what historians as outside observers think about these issues (although clearly some historians see it as a central task to engage in either denunciation or apologetics); rather, it is to highlight the fact that people living in the GDR were active participants in a more complex maze of practices, and inhabited a more complex moral and political universe, than has frequently been posited. There was at least limited space for more dialogues and 'conversations' in the East German SED state than is allowed for in many approaches. These were, of course, asymmetrical conversations; but there was a great deal more input from a variety of quarters, at least within a narrow range of policy areas, than is generally recognised.[13] Over time – and particularly with détente and international recognition of the GDR – citizens were not only enabled, but actively encouraged, to voice their opinions in a variety of (well-controlled) ways. The treatment of issues arising from 'discussions' and letters of complaint, as well as related reports by trade-union officials, parliamentary committees and investigative commissions and inquiries, provide evidence of very real concern about, and strenuous efforts to deal with, questions relating to housing, transport, childcare, shopping, the demands of shift work and so on. The widespread, if not universal, desire to find a resolution of these everyday issues, with their immense impact both on the economic productivity of the system as a whole and on any sense of individual satisfaction or well-being, was common both to those complaining and those charged with providing responses to complaints. Moreover, many of the conflicts that existed in the GDR were not between 'state' and 'society' or 'Party' and 'people', but rather within and cross-cutting different levels of political and social hierarchies. On some issues, and at some times more than others, policymakers made efforts to listen and respond to the voiced needs and frustrations of certain groups of people, particularly the economically productive – so long, of course, as they stayed within the closely defined limits of permissible debate and did not touch on the fundamental parameters of the GDR's very existence.

Paradoxically, this very sensitivity to popular opinion on domestic social-policy issues contributed both to the short-term stabilisation and the ultimate downfall of the GDR. Honecker's policies of the 1970s were designed to improve material conditions and heighten popular support as well as raise productivity. At the same time, there was an institutionalisation and routinisation of a 'grumbling culture' that led people not only to expect, but even to demand, delivery from the state. Just as – in very different ways – heightened expectations of the state in the post-war society of the Weimar Republic produced systemic frustration in the 1920s such that particular problems became conflated with critiques of 'the system' as a whole, so too in the GDR the regime's unrealisable claims to be the provider and organiser of all finally contributed to its undoing.

By phrasing it thus – participatory dictatorship – we can wilfully emphasise both the relatively broad popular participation, and the undoubted differences between this form of dictatorial political system and the representative democracies of the capitalist West (which, it should not be forgotten, have their own priorities with respect to which voices can be heard and what issues are on the practical agenda, as well as their own shortcomings with respect to resultant inequalities in practice). And we can seek to do justice to the realities of life as actually experienced by the vast majority of GDR citizens, while not overlooking the constraints and injustices of the political system within which they lived their lives.

Rejecting a totalitarian interpretation does not entail sticking one's head into the sand and denying the brute facts of force and repression in communist society, nor overlooking the utopian moments – the visions which, for the committed, provided the justification for highly proactive interventions in social policy – as well as manipulative and repressive means for clinging onto power. Without understanding these broad (and by now relatively familiar) parameters, both in terms of the changing overall shape of society and in terms of changing domestic and international politics, one cannot fully comprehend changes within any specific area of inquiry.[14]

To paraphrase Karl Marx, East Germans sought to make their own history, although in conditions not of their own choosing. Some were indeed victims of oppression or heroes of resistance, although such roles would have been merely elements in more complex biographies; others sought to lead lives that cannot be reduced merely to compromise, acquiescence, retreat into private niches and public conformity. This vocabulary of life in a dictatorship is applicable only to a proportion of the population at particular times and moments in their lives; it by no means captures comprehensively the ways in which the vast majority of East Germans lived multifaceted lives, made careers, cared for family and friends, and sought to improve their conditions and to make sense of their modes of being in the world in a great variety of circumstances.

Viewed from the perspectives just outlined, distinctive patterns can be discerned. Although emerging somewhat differently in different areas, two simultaneous, and perhaps in part mutually contradictory, developments begin to become evident over the course of GDR history.

On the one hand, the character of the new institutional landscape and its constitutive collective entities – state institutions, social organisations, economic enterprises, bloc parties and so on – changed over time such that what was initially forcibly imposed from above eventually became routinised, accepted or 'carried' by very large numbers of people in ways that are not adequately exhausted by notions of dictatorial imposition by a repressive Party-state. There was an enormous penumbra of overlap between what from one perspective can be seen as 'state', and from another as 'society', indicating the difficulties with this old dichotomy as a tool of analysis.

Yet at the same time, the desired 'socialist personalities', the individuals whose lives were supposed to be devoted to the collective enterprise of building socialism, did not emerge. Quite the opposite in fact. Over time, one can observe a complex set of processes that may roughly be subsumed under the concept of emergent individualism, or an enhanced focus on the fulfilment of individual goals, which were increasingly frustrated by the constraints of a failing economy. These mutual trends can be observed, in one way or another, in virtually every area of society.

In the process of exploring East German social history, it becomes ever more clear that 'society' was neither 'frozen' – 'laid to rest', as some interpretations have it – nor merely some faceless mass that was the passive recipient (or victim) of decisions made on high. Rather, East German society included a wide diversity of people, a range of social groups and subcultures, who actively participated in all sorts of ways in making their own history and thus the history of the GDR. In this way, it becomes possible to understand the paradox of history and memory with respect to the GDR.

Finally, it is worth pointing out that this paradox is not merely a parochial question about what some would dismiss as a 'footnote' in German history. GDR history, as much as the history of the western Federal Republic of Germany, represents one version of the possibilities that were immanent in the Third Reich. It illustrates the lack of closure in history – the multiple possibilities and routes out of any given constellation of forces. Moreover, the formation of a distinctive East German society is central to the understanding of united Germany after 1990. It is as much a part of the complex and divided history of the German present as is the history of West Germany.

But GDR history is also of more far-reaching significance. It is rooted in a wider set of questions that have exercised political and social thinkers for centuries: how is it possible to bring about a fairer, more equal, more just society? How is it possible to bring about a secular paradise, a utopia not merely of the imagination or of the heavenly afterlife, but rather in this world, which can be reached through realistic mechanisms of change? The answer, according to the prophet of secular paradise in communist colours, Karl Marx, entailed a revolutionary transition, with violent struggle against the privileged and powerful and consolidation under initially dictatorial rule before pure communism could be achieved. In its Leninist and Stalinist variants, this transitional phase saw its bleakest realisation. In the GDR – and indeed in all 'actually existing' communist regimes of the twentieth century – the need for dictatorial control was never transcended: earthly paradise was never attained. While committed communists felt that the ends justified the means, those not committed to the Party vision argued that the use of repressive, manipulative and brutal means nullified any chance whatsoever of achieving the visionary humanistic goals embedded in Marx's ultimately utopian vision. People simply did not change in the ways they were meant to: repression continued to be necessary.

So this book is about the experiences of the people in this wider and ultimately doomed search to achieve paradise on earth; and the ways in which their experiences, perceptions and actions contributed to the complex social and political history of their country, which was not purely made by the ruling Party's policies and practices. It is about the ways in which East German society changed, such that – for all the undisputed political constraints and repression – many East Germans came to feel that they were able to lead 'perfectly ordinary lives' within the GDR. It is about the intersections and disjunctures between dictatorial structures and the experienced normalities of everyday life. This book explores the ways in which the ruling Party's attempts to realise a communist utopia on earth brought about instead the picture revealed when the Wall fell: the built legacies of decades of good intentions, with soulless new towns and decrepit housing estates; the giant factory complexes – 'people's own enterprises' – or rusting dinosaurs of industry, belching lurid fumes and choking dust; the drab shops and the dearth of decent consumer goods; the symbol of aspiration, endearment and ridicule, the 'Trabi' car; as well as a measure of gender equality, a widespread sense of community and collective responsibility, and the civil courage of those who came out on to the streets in the 'gentle revolution' of 1989. And it asks how different East German society had become from that of those 'fellow Germans' in the West, who shared a common language and history, but had very different experiences during the extraordinary decades of separation following the collapse of the Third Reich. Social history, on this conception, is not history with the politics left out; rather, it is history with the people put back in.

The organisation of the argument

The book is organised in three major parts, although the themes within each overlap and run, in different ways, throughout the book.

From its inception, the GDR was characterised by a combination of repression and vision. Following a brief overview of the changing shape of East German society as a whole, Part One focuses more closely on some of the pragmatic and everyday consequences of visions for a better society. Succeeding chapters explore such seemingly mundane topics as housing, leisure and health, and examine the ways in which social identities rooted in the supposedly 'biological' categories of age and gender changed over nearly half a century. All these areas of life – some of which one might think were hardly 'political' at all, others of which are more obviously of direct relevance – have major implications for the ways in which we conceive GDR history. Whichever area one looks at, distinctions between 'state' and 'society' appear ever more difficult to sustain. Even conceptions of 'ruling through' society, or society being 'drenched with authority' do not fully allow us to think of the ways in which the characters of people's behaviour, attitudes and physical lives were constructed and affected by the period and place in which they were living. Yet to say this is not as yet to say very much.

Artificial distinctions are often drawn between the 'public sphere' and the 'private sphere'; it is also frequently alleged that East Germans could 'withdraw' into private 'niches', escaping the pressures of the intrusive state. It is of course true that in all societies people can at times withdraw from the stresses, tensions, challenges, rewards and opportunities of one area of their endeavours into the different combinations of such forces and experiences in another sphere; and that, for many but by no means all people, for much but by no means all of the time, the experiences of home, family and leisure activities may seem more relaxing and pleasurable, more under personal control, than those of work or politics, where centres of power are more distant and daily activities less under individual control. But this does not mean that possibilities and constraints of the supposedly 'private' spheres of home and leisure are any less shaped by the wider social and political environment. Similarly, people's experiences of health and illness, family size and life expectancy, may well be interpreted by themselves as the results of fate, genetics or personal lifestyle choices. But as physical animals, from birth to death human beings are also shaped (even literally) by the times and places into which they are born, and the character of the states within which they live. These points are true, in principle, of all societies, though there are very wide differences in practice in the ways in which the character of a state affects the life-experiences of its population. Analysis of the ways in which the areas of housing, leisure, health and lifestyle developed and were experienced in the GDR yields some surprising findings.

One of the most notable is the sheer extent of broad agreement between sections of the SED leadership and significant groups among the wider population over general aims and goals, even if for often different reasons. Within the undesired but unchallengeable confines of a walled-in state, it was in most people's interests to be able to lead as comfortable, enjoyable and healthy lives as possible. Frictions and disputes were generally rooted in disappointed expectations and common frustrations about the ways in which widely shared ideals could not be realised in practice. During the earlier part of the GDR's existence, experienced shortcomings were seen by many people, in so far as they considered the matter in any depth, as rooted in the legacy of the wartime past; in insufficiencies that might in principle eventually be overcome through increased productivity and economic development; or which might be dealt with successfully on an individual level, through active pursuit of 'connections' and the like. But the balance of both popular perceptions and the economically practicable changed over time. A scheduled improvement in the GDR's economy remained on the official historical agenda for a very long time after it was no longer seriously plausible, but it became increasingly apparent to increasing numbers of people – SED functionaries as well as 'ordinary' citizens – that inadequate facilities, crumbling housing and environmental pollution were endemic to a collapsing economy.

Part Two addresses the complex issues of structural and societal change, of social revolution and patterns of stratification and social inequality in 'actually existing socialism'. In theory, pure communism should have produced a class-less society in which the imposed division of labour was overcome and all humans were free to follow their own interests and develop their own aptitudes. In practice, the GDR never officially reached this stage: even the 'actually existing socialism' of the Honecker era remained riddled with social inequalities that, while evident to GDR sociologists, were resistant to easy conceptualisation; historians and social scientists since 1990 have not had much easier a job of making sense of the cross-cutting patterns of stratification. The situation is riddled with ambiguities. Power and social stratification interacted in ways that do not neatly overlap; the GDR as communist state and the GDR as modern industrial state often faced conflicting demands and challenges, with intrinsic tensions and inherent contradictions. There were, in effect, multiple systems of stratification: older notions of status and prestige were increasingly challenged and displaced by new hierarchies of power; there was an inversion of the inherited class–prestige hierarchy; and there were new inequalities of lifestyle and consumption. The duality noted in the rhetoric, if not the reality, of the Third Reich, was put into practice with the East German social revolution. Political power displaced economic capital as the key to elite status and control over resources.[15] Given the curious combination of high official prestige and often appalling working conditions for the manual working class, 'class' in the sense of occupation in the sphere of production remained highly significant; but it was overlain and cross-cut by issues to do with prestige and consumption. And curiously, the tendency of this most collectivist society was towards a pattern of increasing individualism under consumer socialism.

Part Three looks at ways in which not only the political elites and the cultural intelligentsia interacted and debated (or sought to channel and contain attempts to debate) but also at the ways in which ordinary people were intrinsically and intimately involved in the 'enactment' of the state in everyday life. The extent to which large numbers of East Germans actively participated in social and cultural institutions, contributed to collective 'discussions', or used individual channels of complaint, is very striking, particularly from the point of view of received theories of 'totalitarian dictatorships'. This was not 'democracy' in the Western, liberal sense: no whiff of freedom of association, let alone of freedom of movement if this meant what was designated as the crime of *Republikflucht* – escape from the Republic. But there was far more space both for active participation, sustaining the institutions and practices of East German society, and also for what might be called 'constructive griping' over shared aims with respect to domestic issues, than totalitarian theory allows space for. Very large numbers of East Germans made a significant contribution, under very difficult circumstances, in contested attempts to realise conflicting visions of a better society in the here and now for those who had to live in it. To more of a degree than is generally recognised, East Germans were indeed able to have some input into 'making their own lives', and particularly so in areas of widely shared goals and values.

The state was involved in all areas of life. But the experience of this state involvement ranged from the oppressive and unpleasant, to the facilitative and supportive. For many people it is also arguable that, in terms of everyday life, it was possible both to expect much of the state – for example in terms of housing – and yet at the same time almost to ignore its demands and expectations if one had few ambitions within the system. The main problem for a state party that claimed to be doing 'everything for the well-being of the people!' ('Alles zum Wohle des Volkes!') was, however, that it also had to take all the blame. Since the East German economy not only never reached a level of performance that could compete with that of West Germany, but actually entered a process of ever more visible decline, East Germans in the later 1980s had ever more to complain about. It was not merely 'ordinary' East Germans, nor only those involved in the running of economic enterprises, but also the many functionaries of the mass organisations, and those involved in town planning, housing construction, or in running a variety of leisure facilities, who were concerned about growing inadequacies and shortcomings. Complaints were thus not so much, or not only, about the impositions of or constraints imposed by the state – which could by many people be relatively easily navigated, exploited, or even to a large extent ignored – but rather, or also, about the ways in which the state failed to live up to expectations and fell short of achieving its own proclaimed goals. Actively sustaining the state, feeling one could live a 'perfectly normal life' within the GDR, and ultimately critiquing it and contributing to its downfall, were thus not mutually incompatible.

The issues discussed in each section are overlapping, the themes dealt with in each part being relevant across the whole book, and are merely separated out in this way for a degree of convenience; but the hardest part of writing a social history is the recognition that all the parts are interrelated in innumerable ways. Analysis is not mimesis.

Part I

Visions of the good society
(and how they were not realised
in practice)

Chapter Two

The East German social revolution:
Violence, utopia and consumer socialism

Violence and the memory of violence were integral to the social history of the GDR. Without understanding the conditions of its birth, and the mentalities of those who had struggled against the evils of Nazism, it is impossible to understand the peculiar mixture of utopian dreams and repressive means that marked its history. Yet in the course of this history, from the bombed-out ruins of the defeated Third Reich to the crumbling rubble of an ailing communism, the utopian dreams faded into the normalities of everyday life, while the repressive means became ever more subtle and invisible, though no less insidious.

A real 'social revolution' did take place in East Germany, but it was not a matter of a popular rising from below, as envisaged in the Marxist theory of revolutions. Rather, it was in large measure an imposition from above by a relatively small Communist Party, massively facilitated by the brute facts of Soviet military occupation and by the total defeat and utter moral disrepute of Nazi Germany. The political and economic elites of Nazi Germany were rapidly and thoroughly displaced; for over forty years thereafter, a society allegedly on the road to a 'classless' utopia was dominated by a small political elite, continually struggling to remould society into a communist image. This was sought in a context of relatively slow industrialisation, constantly hampered by the GDR's political location as part of a divided nation in a wider, Cold War context. In these circumstances, 'democracy' was simply not on the immediate historical agenda. Rather than the ends justifying the means, the means continually subverted and ultimately destroyed the ends; and, particularly in the early Stalinist period, the means were often visibly violent and brutal. Visions of utopia could only be pursued against the will of the majority of the people.

War's end: Myths of an innocent birth

Ordinary East Germans, often lumped together as the innocent 'people' on whom a communist dictatorship backed by Soviet military power was imposed, had experienced the preceding Nazi Third Reich in very different ways. Many had been so-called *Mitläufer*, or fellow-travellers, in Nazi Germany: these were the people who experienced the 1930s as 'normal times', even as the 'good years', after the miseries of national degradation, political instability and violence, inflation and later rising unemployment in the course of the 1920s and early '30s. Some Germans were convinced and ardent supporters of Hitler and the Nazi project; many more were willing to cheer Hitler's foreign-policy triumphs and the expansion of German power, and were prepared to go along with, or at least turn a blind eye to, multiple acts of anti-Semitism, of petty brutality, and of the exploitation and humiliation of those considered to be 'inferior' human beings. By contrast, for communists, socialists and other political opponents of Nazism, for Jews and others deemed to be 'racially inferior' or 'hereditarily diseased', and for those with religious and moral qualms about what was clearly a brutal, murderous regime beyond any sense of law and justice, the experience of the Nazi *Volksgemeinschaft* ('people's community') had, right from the beginning, been very different. Political opponents were among the first targets of the Nazi regime in the initial weeks after Hitler was constitutionally appointed chancellor at the end of January 1933, and within a couple of months the German-Jewish community, too, had a frightening foretaste of the characteristic combination of pseudo-legalism and naked hatred that was to characterise the subsequent 'twisted road' leading ultimately, for so many of the Jewish communities across Europe, to the gas chambers of Auschwitz.[1] The promises of a bright new future in the 'Thousand Year Reich' were promises only to those included in the *Volksgemeinschaft*, and the fulfilment of these promises was predicated on the exclusion, degradation and, eventually, annihilation of the outcasts.

In the event, there was no 'Nazi social revolution' in the sense suggested by Nazi propaganda: far from producing the rural idyll of blond peasants on fertile pastures depicted in Nazi 'blood and soil' ideology, Hitler's policy priorities for Nazi Germany had been geared to war. Right from the start, and most particularly from 1936 with the 'guns and butter' policies of the Four Year Plan under the direction of Hermann Göring, Nazi Germany was preparing for an aggressive, expansionist war of exploitation and conquest. And preparation for war had meant the continuation, even exacerbation, of previous trends in a modern industrial society: the continued concentration of capital, and the growth of big business, alongside continued migration from the countryside to ever-growing urban areas. In so far as there was any kind of 'social revolution' in Nazi Germany, it was not in respect of the broad outlines of the socio-economic structure. The realities were in part more brutal, and in part more complex, than a focus on the economic system and class structure alone would suggest.[2]

Of all Nazi policies, war and racism had the most profound impact, not merely on German society but across Central Europe and indeed the wider world. Millions were killed, whether as a result of Nazi incarceration, torture and mass murder on 'racial' and political grounds, or as a result of the war. Millions were physically and psychologically maimed. Millions were displaced from their homelands, uprooted and disorientated, from a very wide range of different groups: potential victims of Nazi persecution who fled the Third Reich in good time and managed to emigrate; allegedly 'inferior' foreign labourers who were forced into the service of the Third Reich; 'ethnic Germans' who fled from the advancing Red Army in the winter of 1944–5 or who were forcibly expelled in the redrawing of territorial boundaries after the end of the war. Even if perceptions of class and the possibility of social mobility were not fundamentally altered by Nazi policies, the character of collective life was altered, with implications for younger generations in particular; and the military defeat of the Third Reich irreversibly broke the power and prestige of old elites who had held sway for generations. Less easily definable, and in some respects more subtle, were the wide-ranging effects of the experience of Nazism, and more particularly of war, on attitudes and collective mentalities.

How the war, and particularly its closing stages, was experienced depended massively on questions of age, gender and class, as well as political, religious or 'racial' categorisation. Victor Klemperer, a German-Jewish academic who had survived thus far by virtue of the semi-protection of a 'mixed marriage' was in early February 1945 within days of deportation and certain death. For Klemperer, the controversial bombing of Dresden on the night of 13/14 February 1945, in which perhaps a hundred thousand civilians died, came as unexpected salvation. Amidst the raging fire storms, the chaos of collapsing buildings, the dust and ruins, the decomposing bodies of often dismembered corpses and the meanderings of disoriented survivors, Victor Klemperer and his wife Eva were able to escape from the custody of the 'Jews' house' in which they had been held and make their way to a somewhat fearful freedom in Bavaria, where they managed to survive incognito until the war came to a spluttering end, at first registered only through rumour, a few weeks later.[3] For Filip Müller, who had been deported from Slovakia to Auschwitz as early as April 1942, and who, amazingly, survived to tell the tale, the war's end was, as he puts it, 'incredibly, a complete anti-climax'.[4] Lying apathetically on a rafter in the barracks in which their death-march had halted, covered in lice and drowsing in and out of consciousness, barely noticing the 'moaning and groaning' of the still-dying among the already dead on the ground below him, Müller was scarcely in a physical or mental condition to take in the moment of liberation by American tanks.

The predominant experience of the vast majority of 'ordinary Germans' with the collapse of Nazi rule was of course very different: and it was in the main one characterised by misery and self-pity, with no obvious sense of responsibility or guilt. The notion of 'Germans as victims' has recently again become a key theme, with the belated re-assertion of a 'right to mourn' for suffering under bombing raids and living among ruins – a right that in some curious way is completely dissociated from recognition of the ways in which 'German suffering' was a direct consequence of prior German aggression, exploitation and violence.[5] The 'loss of history', and the death of any faith in Nazism, began right from the moment of defeat. As the ever-perceptive Victor Klemperer noted in his diary already on Friday 11 May 1945, still marooned where he had been hiding in a small Bavarian village and until now cut off from news from the outside world:

> The people are absolutely without history, in every respect. In the evening a young woman came … young, not unintelligent. She seemed to be originally from Munich, and had been by bicycle to Munich for a day … I asked the woman if she had heard anything of Hitler and the other big names of the NSDAP: *no*, she had not had time to ask about that, in other words: this did not interest her any more. The Third Reich is already as good as forgotten, everyone had been opposed to it, had 'always' been opposed.[6]

For the vast majority of ordinary Germans, the immediate post-war priorities were sheer survival and rebuilding their own personal lives out of the ruins. Their myth of an innocent birth entailed tales of individual heroism and survival.

Civilians crawling out of cellars and air-raid shelters were aghast to walk through the ruins of bombed-out cities. One anonymous diarist described her impressions of conditions in Berlin on Thursday 10 May 1945:

> The Kleistpark is a desert. Underneath the arcades there are encampments of rags, mattresses and ripped-out car seats. Everywhere piles of excrement, with flies buzzing around … Everything belongs to everyone. The widow and I whispered involuntarily to one another, our throats were dry, the dead city took away our breath. The air in the Park was full of dust, all the trees powdered over white, shot through with holes and badly damaged. A German shadow hurried past, trailing

bedding. At the exit a Russian grave, surrounded by wire ... [I]n between, a flat granite slab, on which it says, painted in chalk, that heroes rest here, fallen for the Fatherland.[7]

For German women in Berlin and elsewhere in what became the Soviet Zone of Occupation, the war-time experience of living in cellars and air-raid shelters gave way to the daily fear and the frequent experience of rape at the hands of Russian soldiers.[8]

For hundreds of thousands of men, the war did not even really come to an end in 1945: many remained interned as prisoners of war, often for very lengthy periods and under conditions from which many never recovered; the last survivors to be released from imprisonment in Soviet camps only returned to Germany a full ten years after the end of the war. Men returning from internment were often barely recognisable, even by their own families. As the East German novelist Brigitte Reimann, at the time a child of twelve, put it in a letter to a friend then living in western Germany:

> You simply can't believe how miserable Daddy looked! He had disgusting old rags and a rough Russian coat on and a dirty Russian cap ... Add to this the skeletal face, the shorn-off hair and – the voice! ... [T]he voice repelled me so much, that I simply couldn't say 'Daddy' to him. I can hardly describe to you how it was! So nervous, so ill and – and I don't know, just so terribly strange! ... Naturally he is totally undernourished, had a double lung inflammation, and barely escaped death ... He is terribly nervous. But we thank God that He sent Daddy back to us at home at all![9]

A similar description of German prisoners of war returning from Soviet captivity is given in a letter of 1949 from 'Hellmut' in Chemnitz (later renamed Karl-Marx-Stadt) to an English person who had befriended him while he was a prisoner of war in England: 'They looked terribly ragged, just sacks bound around their feet, hair shorn off bald, facial expressions pitiable, no expression of any joy in life ... [T]he East has shown us just as clearly its inhumanity, depravity, and contempt of human rights.'[10] As in so many other contemporary accounts, this writer appears to have no awareness of the prior Nazi contempt of human rights that had brought Germans into this state.

For millions of civilians on the move in 'treks' – at first refugees in the winter of 1944–5 and later expellees from lost eastern territories – the war's end was equally prolonged. Over three and a half million refugees were present in the Soviet zone in 1946, ranging from those who had been well-to-do landowners or members of the bourgeoisie in the areas now taken over by the Soviet Union and Poland (which had been effectively shifted westwards) to the very poor. The treks were characterised by undoubted personal misery, with homes and possessions abandoned, and the elderly and very young often dying of disease, starvation or hypothermia along the way; those who survived were often deeply traumatised by rapes, robbery and the death of their loved ones. Acute self-pity – well-founded as far as personal tragedies were concerned – was again very often totally dissociated from any conception of German responsibility for having unleashed the war ultimately giving rise to these conditions. Heroic tales of flight often unthinkingly reproduce Nazi prejudices, as in 'Ina's' letter to her sister (who was at the time interned as a former leader of the Reich Labour Service for young women): 'We often tried to continue our journey by train or truck, but everywhere there were Jews and they wanted a lot of money or material, and I had already lost everything to the Poles. We had no luck.'[11]

These experiences were followed by lengthy periods of resettlement, often in appallingly overcrowded temporary conditions, before further moves. Many did not immediately give up hope of returning at some point to their former homelands. Billeted with families already living in overcrowded conditions, often in ruins (particularly in cities badly affected by bombing), competing for scarce food and resources, they did not immediately integrate well with a native population that often had quite different cultural, religious and linguistic characteristics, and many of whom were equally under terrible personal and psychological stress. Many ultimately landed in the Western zones of occupation that became the Federal Republic of Germany: over twelve million residents of West Germany, or around one fifth of its population in the early 1960s, was a refugee or expellee; of these, over nine million were present already in 1950, and a further three million or so fled from the newly created GDR prior to the building of the Berlin Wall in 1961.

While those who had suffered terribly at the hands of the Nazis were now finally able to begin a slow and difficult recovery – psychologically and physically so scarred and so traumatised by unspeakable experiences and irretrievable losses that to speak of 'recovery' is almost absurd – many Germans were now full of complaints about the new conditions in the Soviet zone. The anti-communism of the Nazi era continued almost seamlessly into the new era of occupation, richly nourished by the anti-democratic activities of the Soviet occupying power and its puppet party, the SED. Recreated and newly founded political parties and social organisations were rapidly constrained by communist control, and massive reparations and economic restructuring exacerbated an already difficult material situation. The economic situation was 'catastrophic', illness and hunger widespread, constraints on freedom only too visible: as one contemporary put it, 'It is sad but true, here there is no freedom, only repression and enslavement as well as exploitation and the extermination of all good human values, it is a real life in hell in which evil rules under

Russian leadership.'[12] Later, many East Germans would appeal to the ways in which they helped to 'build up' the new state, clearing the rubble in bombed-out cities, working in arduous conditions in the uranium mines of Wismut, or clearing the pine forests and founding the iron and steel communities of 'socialist new towns' such as Eisenhüttenstadt (for a while named Stalinstadt). At the time, a number of people certainly did feel they were being granted new opportunities; but the large majority simply made the best of a bad job, grumbling and complaining and hoping somehow simply to be able to survive, with little thought for either past or future. Not utopian hopes, then, but rather everyday fears and struggles for physical and psychological survival predominated.

Building a better Germany?

For the tiny minority of active communists, however, the priorities were rather different. The small groups of German communists who had survived Stalin's purges and who flew in from Moscow to the Soviet Zone of Occupation were entrusted with the task of taking over the reins of power on the ground, seeking out like-minded comrades and building a new and 'better Germany'.[13] With Soviet backing, they formed the core of the new political elite: those who were to shape the future of the German Democratic Republic, founded in October 1949 in the context of rising tension between the former wartime Allies in the emergent Cold War. And the founding myth of this new state was that of 'anti-fascism': the myth of German 'liberation', of innocent workers and peasants formerly oppressed by the yoke of Nazism, from which they were eventually released by the glorious Red Army. It was a myth that was indeed true for some, but by no means for the majority of the East German population, among whom essentially racist and anti-communist attitudes took far longer to die than did the more transient, and effectively already dead, faith in Hitler as Führer.[14]

The founding myth of 'liberation' rather than defeat, and the related myth of the 'anti-fascist state', are complex issues.[15] Clearly, much was simply a matter of claims by a small political elite that barely correlated with the experiences of the vast majority of East Germans. But the founding myth was a flexible one, which could be adapted in many ways, even for those who were not part of the (all-too-limited) genuine resistance to Hitler. Moreover, war was an experience that massively shaped even the perceptions of those who were children at the time. Thus variations on the founding myth could readily be established, particularly for those from humble social backgrounds and professing the appropriate political sympathies.

Manfred Uschner, later a functionary in the office of Hermann Axen, the Politburo member responsible for foreign affairs, writes for example of the nightmarish scene of the 'flaming inferno' as his home town of Magdeburg was bombed on the night of 16 January 1945. At the time a seven-year-old boy, Uschner was awakened by his grandparents and pulled, along with his then four-year-old sister, from the collapsing walls of their house. As they rushed through the back courtyard to escape, his grandmother was hit by an incendiary bomb. Manfred Uschner and his little sister turned and watched in horror as their grandmother burnt to death before their eyes, her 'loyal' sheepdog 'jumping helplessly' around her. The following day they picked their way through the still-burning streets of Magdeburg over 'mountains of burnt corpses'. In Uschner's summary,

> This terrifying experience branded us for ever. I have never been able to get over it. And it was the key to the fact that I became political, asked political questions, acted politically. It moved me to become a member of the children's branch of the FDJ already in 1947, and to become a Young Pioneer in 1948. As a child, at anti-fascist gatherings on the Magdeburg Cathedral Square and in the 'Crystal Palace', I called out with tremulous voice that adults should ensure that a new war and new catastrophes would never happen.[16]

Clearly, such an account of a 'key experience' ('Schlüsselerlebnis'), written half a century later, was to some extent stylised, itself a part of an inherited political rhetoric and self-defining narrative convention. But even this fact is important. Among those with left-leaning backgrounds and inclinations, early post-war hopes for a better future under 'anti-fascist' auspices were not merely entirely understandable, they were also the fundamental legitimation of all that was to follow.

What is curious about Uschner's account here is that it was, presumably, Allied bombing that was responsible for his terrifying childhood experience; the victims were not 'anti-fascist resistance fighters' but rather ordinary Germans, residents of Magdeburg: grandparents, children and family pets – the German home front. More usual in GDR official rhetoric was reference to terror directly inflicted by Nazis themselves, and subsequently, by implication, their alleged 'successors', the 'imperialist-fascists' in the West and the 'class enemies' at home, against whom vigilance must always be maintained. Yet the experience of terror and the elision of different sources of suffering in one great conflagration, as in Uschner's representation, in some inchoate way managed to combine these elements, without directly inquiring into the primary causes of the Allied bombing of Magdeburg, in order to unite both the suffering of 'ordinary Germans' and the fight against any future wars under the political banner of anti-fascism in communist colours. If this could be accomplished, then much by way of communist-inspired violence and terror could be portrayed as legitimate measures against some vague but terrifying notion of potentially far-greater dangers.

Fear and hatred of Nazism itself were, of course, more direct influences on the 'founding fathers' of the GDR, those who were to become the new ruling elite following the defeat of Hitler's Reich. Those individuals who formed the core of the Communist Party that was to become, in the hybrid shape of the SED (formed out of the merger between the KPD and SPD in April 1946), the ruling party of the GDR for forty years, were deeply affected by years of persecution – in some cases imprisonment within the Reich, in many other cases exile in the Soviet Union or the West. Those who emerged from hiding or returned from abroad, having lost years of their lives in an often terrified and violent struggle against Hitler, had good cause to have little trust in the political judgement of the millions of their German compatriots: the millions who had either actively supported Hitler or had passively acquiesced in his rule. For those who had survived the concentration camps of the Third Reich, who had suffered brutality and torture at the hands of the Gestapo or SS, or who had been forced to flee for fear of their lives and who had borne the news of the murders of friends, comrades and family, any notion of 'democracy' in the Western sense was almost meaningless.

Although there can be no justification for the oppression and injustices in the following years, there can also be no understanding of these developments without bearing in mind this horrendous background. The title of a well-known early post-war film, *Die Mörder sind unter uns* ('The Murderers Are Among Us'), was not merely factually apposite, but also representative of complex post-war mentalities involving mutual suspicions, volatile emotions, psychological scars and also – in many quarters – attempts at camouflaging a compromised past. The paranoia that afflicted the East German political leadership may have been exacerbated by later Cold War developments – and the insistence on the 'anti-fascist fight' may have ultimately become more a matter of rhetoric than real feeling; but these were originally rooted in only-too-real experiences of Nazi aggression and terror. The 'latent civil war' that has been identified between repressive communist regime and innocent East German people, and which in fact never existed in quite this pure form, had its origins and background in the horrific divisions of the Third Reich.

For a while, the notion of building for a better future really meant something – at least among a minority of committed socialists. The notion of

Aufbau ('building up', not merely 'constructing' or 'reconstructing') informed – even inspired – a range of creative projects, from architectural plans for new 'socialist' towns, through production of films and writing of novels that engaged critically with the difficult processes of social transformation in an imperfect present, to the devotion of practical energies to overwhelming everyday tasks. In the struggles of the 1950s, the attempts at reform of the early to mid-'60s, and even the bombastic proclamations and new self-confidence of the early '70s, there are repeated signs of hopes that a genuinely better society could be developed from these unpromising beginnings. But the paranoia and growing apparatus of repression in this Cold War period constantly undercut the utopian visions of a communist paradise. The increasing control of the East German state by the SED, under the watchful and controlling tutelage of the Soviet Union, and accompanied by an ever-expanding apparatus of state security and repression, is by now very well known.[17]

There were, of course, key moments of challenge, followed by increased repression and further disillusionment. The suppression of the June Uprising of 1953, itself a complex phenomenon open to political appropriations of a variety of colours; the suppression, again, of splutterings of revolt in the GDR and of more serious challenges to communism in Poland and Hungary in 1956; the muted indications of de-Stalinisation under Khrushchev, which however made hardly a dent in the system of communist repression under Walter Ulbricht; the erection of the Berlin Wall in 1961; the forcible suppression of the Czechoslovak Prague Spring in 1968; these were among the most notable and visible moments in which brute power overrode utopian vision. Yet despite such blows to any prospects for democratic socialism in the Soviet bloc, many on the left clung to the hope that a better society could yet be achieved, provided the conditions were right and the appropriate strategies and tactics were pursued. And such hopes, too, were embedded in the official propaganda, still bearing the marks of the early aspirations. It is remarkable just how often the words 'not yet' ('noch nicht') or 'still' ('noch, immer noch') crop up in the documents: functionaries from the highest to the lowest levels seemed to have internalised the conception of a progressive development, in the course of which people who were 'not yet' won around to the cause, who were 'still' indecisive or 'wavering' ('schwankend'), could eventually be brought into the fold of the converted. This linguistic pattern in the official documents continued right into the 1980s, although towards the end there is a sense of empty ritual and decreasing meaning.

Utopian hopes nevertheless faded, alongside memories of war. East German history can be seen as a process in which members of an older generation – including, among the founding fathers, those who had bitter memories of the privations of the First World War and the inflation and unemployment of the Weimar years – sought in some respects to set right the wrongs of their own childhoods, combating unemployment and the lack of adequate food and housing as the greatest evils. But in the meantime, new generations came to maturity, those more interested in comparisons with the prosperity and mass culture of the post-war West, not merely taking for granted but actively critiquing the modest achievements of the repressive if paternalistic state. Utopian dreams thus faded into pragmatism, and pragmatism in turn gave way to coping with, and eventually merely trying to cover up, the ever more evident inadequacies of daily life, as the old guard sought hopelessly to cling to power.

Social revolution from above

The social revolution that took place in the GDR was a multifaceted process in which two major waves can be discerned. During the first two decades or so of the GDR's history, massive interventions in the character of economic owner-ship and the fostering of the previously disadvantaged classes at the expense of the capitalist elites took place, serving radically to alter the whole social structure. In the latter two decades, more gradual economic changes combined with specific social policies to effect a slower reproduction of the new class structure and more gradual transformation of a new type of society, not the desired communism, but rather what was dubbed the transitional but long-lasting stage of 'actually existing socialism'.

Poor transport and communications, a totally inadequate food supply and real threat of famine, the prevalence of a wide range of virulent diseases complicated by malnutrition, and an acute shortage of habitable housing combined to make post-war German society hardly the starting point for a successful social revolution. In the West, the British and Americans soon decided that rapid economic recovery assisted by Marshall Aid was the solu-tion, in the context of remarkable continuity in social and economic structure; in the Soviet zone, the Russians – initially keeping their options open with respect to the future – adopted a strategy of early asset stripping and taking reparations in kind, alongside rapid transformation of the socio-economic structure under the partial guise of denazification. Within little over a year after the end of the war, the ownership of land, industry and finance in the Soviet zone had been revolutionised. Farms over a certain size, or belonging to former Nazis, were expropriated without compensation and land was redis-tributed: the old Prussian Junker class was thus ousted from its landed estates, and many former aristocrats, seeking to salvage what they could, fled to the

West. Large areas of industrial production and finance were either nation-alised, or taken directly into Soviet control. The only social institutions not affected by radical socio-economic change were the Churches; yet they, too, experienced increasing control and constraint over their manifold activities, including the squeezing out of religious education in schools. The whole system of local government, justice, education and welfare in their turn expe-rienced major transformations. Whatever Stalin's initial intentions with respect to the Soviet Zone of Occupation, by the time of the foundation of a separate state in 1949, this zone was already economically and socially very different from the still-capitalist Western zones of occupation that became the Federal Republic of Germany. In the following two decades, more permanent structural changes gathered speed.

The forcible imposition of massive social changes against the will of those adversely affected by them was continued, for the most part with little or no regard for popular support. The 'Building of Socialism', suddenly announced in 1952, entailed the speeding up of industrialisation, with a concentration on heavy industry at the expense of consumer goods, alongside the enforced merging of small peasant farms into larger agricultural collectives. Associated political unrest, flights from the land and disruption of food supplies to the towns were exacerbated by the physical strengthening of the inner-German border and the forcible relocation of those living within a five-kilometre distance who were not considered politically reliable. Growing popular unrest was evidenced in part by increased numbers fleeing the GDR for the West in 1952–3; and it exploded into the more visible uprising of 17 June 1953, with widespread popular demonstrations ironically precipitated by a sudden reversal of many of these policies with the announcement, under Soviet pres-sure, of a 'New Course'.[18] This demonstration of widespread unrest, eventually quelled by Soviet tanks, put a temporary end to the rapid construction of socialism that had been announced the previous year, and it imbued the polit-ical culture of the ruling elite with a somewhat paradoxical combination of paranoia and paternalism, contributing to the simultaneous growth of the repressive forces and consumerist policies, a pattern that proved to be charac-teristic of the rest of the GDR's history.

The transformation of what Marx would have called the 'social relations of production' – that is, the ownership or non-ownership of the major means of industrial production – nevertheless continued in less dramatic ways. Despite initial concessions to consumerism in the wake of the June Uprising, the major focus of the centralised planning system of the 1950s was on the expansion of state-owned heavy industry, with a combination of pressures exerted on small tradesmen and craftsmen, serving to squeeze out remaining private industrial concerns. Already by 1953, well over one half (58.2 per cent) of the workforce was employed either in factories that were at least formally owned 'by the people' (VEBs, or 'volkseigene Betriebe'), or in collectivised farms; by 1960 this had risen to 81.4 per cent, and, at the start of the Honecker period, to 92.4 per cent in 1972.[19] The state appropriation of industrial production was more or less complete by 1972, with a last push to take over remaining small private firms into state ownership; by 1989, no less than 94.7 per cent of the workforce were employed in state-owned factories or collectivised farms. Thus, throughout the 1970s and '80s, only a tiny fraction of the employed population remained outside the socialist structures of production.

If 'social relations of production' changed rapidly, changes in the technical 'means of production' were rather slower. Overall, however, the development of the East German economy reflected, if tardily, general patterns of industrialisation in later twentieth-century Europe: the growth of the service and white-collar sectors, a shrinkage in numbers of those employed in agriculture and forestry, and a shift from the land to the towns. Again, the major shifts took place in the first twenty years or so, with only modest change thereafter. In 1949, the percentage of the population working in industry was a little over a quarter (27.2 per cent); this had risen to over one third (36.8 per cent) by 1970, and then remained more or less steady. It reached a peak of 38.2 per cent in 1975 and declined again slightly to 37.3 per cent by 1989. The percentages working in agriculture and forestry showed similar rapid changes in the first two decades, followed by relative stability: while nearly one third (30.7 per cent) of the population worked in these areas in 1950, only 12.8 per cent did so in 1970, declining very slightly to 10.8 per cent by 1989. And, as we shall see in the following chapters, the educational qualifications, experiences and attitudes of people working in these areas changed considerably over this period, as peasants effectively became agricultural specialists. The 'non-productive areas' of the economy (including not only those tertiary sector occupations common to Western industrial states, but also a growing hidden army of state employees, including those working for the highly secretive Stasi) showed a steadier pattern of growth: from 12.4 per cent in 1950 to 17.5 per cent in 1970 and by nearly as much again to 21.6 per cent in 1989.[20]

The very rapid and forcibly imposed changes with respect to the ownership of the means of production in the first two post-war decades were accompanied by equally forceful social policies designed to foster the upward mobility of those members of previously disadvantaged classes – workers and peasants – who were willing to make the necessary compromises and commitments.[21] So-called 'Workers' and Peasants' Faculties' ('Arbeiter- und Bauernfakultäten') were set up to provide people from disadvantaged backgrounds with the chance of entering further and higher education. Immense efforts were devoted to encouraging women to consider obtaining higher qualifications and entering or remaining in the labour force. Preferential treatment with respect to education and training opportunities for at least the politically correct among the labouring masses was accompanied by varying degrees of discrimination against the ideological and social 'class enemies' of the regime: Christians, members of the bourgeoisie, political opponents. Bitter battles were fought over, for example, the witch-hunt against members of the Christian youth groups (the 'junge Gemeinde'), and the introduction in 1954 of the state rite of passage, the 'dedication of youth' or *Jugendweihe*, replacing confirmation in church. Young people from Christian and bourgeois backgrounds were discriminated against in school, and prevented from completing their secondary education and progressing to university; many children of pastors, doctors, or parents from well-to-do professional backgrounds, chose to leave and study in the West while the opportunity was still open. Young adults, too, with professional prospects in mind left for the West in disproportionate numbers. In the turmoil of the 1950s, while the border through to West Berlin was still passable and the future looked uncertain, over three million predominantly young, skilled and professional East Germans took the opportunity to flee to the West. In all, a total of around one in six of the East German population registered their dislike of, and lack of confidence in, the GDR, a dislike that was sufficient for them to sever ties with their homes and families, and to uproot and seek to start a new life elsewhere.

For those who remained and who for whatever reasons were willing to contribute positively to the GDR's future, this massive exodus further assisted unprecedented patterns of rapid upward social mobility, already fostered by the huge demographic losses of the war. In the 1960s, with Ulbricht's faith in scientific and technological progress, there were not only major new opportunities for attaining qualifications and pursuing a career for people from backgrounds where such aspirations would formerly never have been dreamt of, but also unprecedented numbers of vacancies.[22] The situation in which there was a constant haemorrhage of skilled labour soon came to an end, however, and by the mid-1970s it was clear that far more people with high qualifications and skills were coming out of the education system than there were appropriate openings available. Moreover, the fact that so many young people in their early twenties had in the late 1940s and '50s taken on positions of political and economic significance meant that the GDR was dominated by the generation of those socialised in the Third Reich, who effectively blocked the chances for upward mobility of those born into the GDR. In the 1970s and '80s, the new social structure began to reproduce itself.

The changing shape of East German society was integrally related to wider changes in the international context. In the 1950s, massive social upheavals were accompanied by huge uncertainty about the future of the GDR. Long after what seems to historians in retrospect to have been the very last, and indeed extremely slim, chance for German unification with the 'Stalin notes' of 1952, many Germans themselves continued to believe in the possibility of some form of resolution of the German question through reunification – as Austria had indeed managed in 1955. At the same time, there was widespread fear of war in Europe. But matters changed greatly in the 1960s. While the erection of the Wall and the subsequent introduction of military conscription symbolised in the most brutal terms the repressive character of the regime, they also signalled the end of the 'hot' period of Cold War, at least as far as Central Europe was concerned. After the Cuban Missile Crisis of 1962, the US turned its attention to south-east Asia, becoming embroiled in its own conflicts in Vietnam and choosing effectively to ignore the Central European upheavals of 1968; thus even before the détente with West Germany and the 'normalisation' of German–German relations in *Ostpolitik*, superpower tensions in Central Europe had somewhat subsided. Tensions only rose again in the later 1970s and '80s, with the stationing on European soil of Western Cruise and Pershing missiles and Soviet SS20s, the Soviet invasion of Afghanistan in 1979, and the raising of military expenditure and the stakes in the arms race with US President Ronald Reagan's 'Star Wars' programme of the 1980s. In this wider international context, the middle two decades of the GDR witnessed a degree of apparent internal stabilisation, albeit a stabilisation built on fragile and ultimately unsustainable foundations.

SED First Secretary Walter Ulbricht, who had in the 1950s earned a reputation as a ruthless Stalinist hard-liner resistant to any kind of 'Third Way' communism or acknowledgement of de-Stalinisation on Soviet leader Khrushchev's lines, now began to emerge, on some accounts, as a closet reformer – or at least as an intelligent thinker searching for new ways to grapple with well-nigh intractable problems under changed circumstances.[23] With the building of the Berlin Wall in 1961 and consequent assurance of a secure labour supply, the economic situation began to stabilise. Economic reforms that had been held to be out of the question in the 1950s were officially embraced in the early '60s; considerable faith was placed in the powers of scientific and technical experts to set the GDR on a course of modernisation.

The New Economic System, inaugurated in 1963, appeared to provide ways of introducing a new flexibility into economic planning and management.

At the same time, a raft of reforms and initiatives with respect to culture, education, women and young people were introduced with widespread publicity and well-controlled debate, apparently signalling some hope for the construction of a more equal and fair society for those who remained behind the Wall. The difficulties and internal contradictions in the socio-economic policies of the 1960s were at the time only partially apparent, and there was, at least in some quarters, an atmosphere of informed debate among experts who held that teething troubles could in principle be overcome given time, even if constantly overshadowed by political considerations.[24] Modest economic growth rates in the 1960s heralded increased leisure time with the introduction of the five-day working week, and there were small rises in wages (although offset by rises in prices and massively overshadowed by comparisons with West Germany's 'economic miracle'). Although the New Economic System came under increasing attack from 1965 and was quietly terminated by the end of the decade, a focus on consumerism and the improvement of material conditions continued unabated. Other reversals too were double-edged: the suppression of the Prague Spring in 1968 was for many East Germans a massive political disappointment, but hopes for a better future were rekindled in the early '70s with international recognition of the GDR following *Ostpolitik* and the acknowledgement of human rights in the Helsinki agreement of 1975.

The social revolution from above thus radically altered the economic structure and the character of social groups in the first two decades or so after the war. The ownership of the most important means of production was taken out of private hands: the state, 'on behalf of the people', ran a centrally planned economy in which the industrial working class officially enjoyed an exalted social status. Large landowners were dispossessed, agriculture was collectivised and peasants were gradually turned into agricultural specialists. And the old professional and propertied middle classes were transformed into a new socialist intelligentsia. Massive social mobility was both facilitated by the demographic upheavals of a post-war society, with migration westwards, and also deliberately fostered by social policies designed to facilitate the education and careers of previously disadvantaged groups. Power and political commitment replaced property ownership as the key determinants of position in the new system of social stratification. While West German society from 1945 to the mid-1960s was marked by continuities in both structure and personnel, East German society was radically transformed. By the 1970s, this was no longer a society marked by the legacies of Nazism and post-war upheaval: it was a more stable and very different kind of society, officially labelled as 'actually existing socialism', and thought by many to be there to stay.

Built on shifting sands: Stabilisation, stagnation and decline

Yet, with the benefit of hindsight, the seeds of eventual decline can readily be traced to the end of the period of Ulbricht's reforms in the mid-1960s and the transition to Honecker's policies, however little the implications of these shifts may have been apparent to contemporaries or to outside analysts at the time.

Erich Honecker has much to answer for here: in the beginnings of a protracted power struggle that culminated in his own rise to the position of SED General Secretary in 1971, Honecker played a key role in the notorious Eleventh Party Plenum of December 1965, which not only signalled the slow demise of the New Economic System (and, during the period of its preparation, precipitated the violent death of one of its chief architects and defenders, Erich Apel) but also put a sudden and dramatic end to policies of cultural liberalisation and flexibility towards young people.[25] Less immediately apparent than Honecker's ill-tempered tirade against 'western decadence' (the climax of a wide-ranging speech lasting two hours) but of arguably greater long-term importance were the accompanying and subsequent shifts in socio-economic policy. Ulbricht's short-lived experiments with economic reforms might have been riddled with inconsistencies that the reformers were never granted the time to try to work through, but the renewed centralisation of the economy under Honecker was based on quite disastrous premises that proved the key long-term underlying cause of the GDR's decline. The costs of social policy continually rose, and the disparity between increased costs and what the economy could sustain continually widened. And while Ulbricht was prepared to engage in debates and sought the views of experts, Honecker neither liked real discussion nor did he seem prepared even to acknowledge, let alone seriously grapple with, increasingly uncomfortable economic facts.[26]

Following the dramatic social revolution of the Ulbricht period, with the almost total transformation of the class structure and an unprecedented facilitation of social mobility, the Honecker period was characterised by a day-today determination to improve living conditions in the present for the citizens of a now apparently securely established 'actually existing socialism'. In the process, the socialist project was radically transformed. Utopian goals were effectively abandoned in favour of seeking to satisfy the material needs of the population, with little regard to the longer-term costs. Nor was there a real strategic overview or control of the different elements of the strategy. Quite apart from the purely formal role taken by the GDR Volkskammer (parliament) with respect to strategic decisions on the direction of policy, not even the Council of Ministers or the SED's Central Committee (ZK) played an active role. Decision-making appears to have been extremely fragmented, with no real overview or control by a wider body; each appears to have defended his own policies against the interests of others, rather than taking a jointly agreed approach in the light of more widely shared common goals. Individuals such as Günter Mittag, an effective economic tsar commanding a wide range of areas, possessed enormous power; others operated in more circumscribed spheres. The real decisions were taken among a very small closed circle of Politburo members, sometimes after discussion with one or another internal departmental expert, and effectively rubber-stamped once presented to the Politburo as a whole.[27]

But some issues seem to have been virtually non-negotiable. One such issue was that of price subsidies, which were generally criticised among the small circle of decision-makers, but without any visible impact on Honecker's views.[28] A fear of popular unrest (the ever-present ghost of 17 June 1953), a perhaps genuine concern for the 'well-being of the people' anachronistically understood in the light of his own generation's experiences of deprivation in the First World War and the Weimar years, and a desire to seek popularity among the working masses, seem to have combined to stiffen Honecker's resolve here.

Thus the great proclamations accompanying Honecker's coming to power, which appeared to usher in a new era of hope for a better future under a dynamic young leader promoting an image of reform, in reality contained the seeds of later troubles. Honecker, having air-brushed Walter Ulbricht almost entirely out of the historical record – removing references and photographs, down-playing the ceremonies over his death, which was conveniently displaced by the international youth festival going on in Berlin in August 1973, even having his Berlin house demolished so there should be no shrine for former adherents of any muted personality cult – then sought to adopt the mantle of charismatic moderniser himself. Honecker's rather surprising declaration in 1972 with respect to culture that there should be 'no taboos' as long as cultural production proceeded from a 'firm basis of socialism' – even more surprising given Honecker's own vituperative explosion against liberal cultural currents at the Eleventh Plenum – proved in the event to be not only severely circumscribed but also extremely short-lived. It came to an abrupt and traumatic end with the forcible exclusion of the singer and guitarist Wolf Biermann while on a concert tour in the West in 1976, provoking a wave of protest on the part of prominent intellectuals and previously critically supportive members of the GDR cultural intelligentsia. Honecker's proclaimed 'Unity of Economic and Social Policy', by contrast, was sustained to the bitter end. It may have brought some genuine short-term improvements in social conditions and morale among those groups that benefited, but in the longer term the effective lack of any genuine 'unity' between Honecker's social and economic policies (and indeed the incapacity of the latter to provide any kind of foundation for the former) was ultimately highly counterproductive, and arguably one of the most important factors in the GDR's ultimate demise.

Honecker effectively reversed Ulbricht's maxim that 'the way we work today determines the way we will live tomorrow'; instead, he held the view that subsidised consumption would precede and improve productivity. His determination to present the GDR as a modern and efficient industrial welfare state required reliance on imports and constant borrowing from the very beginning, since it could not be financed out of current economic production. Already in 1972 Gerhard Schürer, Chair of the State Planning Commission from Apel's death in 1965 to the very end of the GDR in 1989, had warned the Politburo that Honecker's proposed social policy programme would not be economically sustainable; he was given very short shrift by Honecker, who accused the State Planning Commission of sabotaging the decisions of the Party Conference. Schürer was rebuffed again in 1977. A similarly curt response was given to Siegfried Wenzel, a colleague in the State Planning Commission who claimed that he could see from 1980 onwards that the economy was heading for the abyss, but that anyone who brought this to the attention of senior SED figures was dismissed as a 'calculating machine' ('Rechner') and threatened with disciplinary measures for not carrying out the Party line.[29] A whole range of aspects of social policy – state subventions for cheap transport, housing, basic foodstuffs, children's clothing, and an extensive system of maternity benefits, health care, pre-school care and after-school care – continued to function as sacred cows that could not be slaughtered even in the more difficult years of the 1980s, when it was becoming increasingly evident even to those without access to the real statistics that the GDR economy was in deep decline. The oil crisis of 1979 and the Soviet Union's decision in 1980 to cut its oil supplies to the GDR by two million tons meant a shift to the exploitation of the massively polluting lignite (brown coal) reserves in the 1980s; and increasing pollution, in a situation of palpable economic decline, played a major role in rising popular frustration and growing dissatisfaction, even among political and economic functionaries, in the 1980s. The statistics for poor air quality, poisoned water supplies, dying trees, levels of dust, smog, and other forms of pollution, the disintegration of old buildings, the rising rates of respiratory infections and other pollution-related illnesses, were all kept secret; but even this secrecy was counterproductive. The consequences were experienced daily in many major industrial centres, even to the extent that doctors were 'prescribing' a move to a less polluted area for some of their patients as the only hope for amelioration of their symptoms.[30] Meanwhile, increased borrowing from abroad only exacerbated the GDR's levels of indebtedness and incapacity to service its debts.

The development of consumer socialism

While East Germans could never be unaware of the quality of their environment, they were also constantly engaged in the project of improving their material circumstances, and this in a manner that combined individualism and a high level of dependence on the state. The GDR was, curiously, from its inception a modern consumer society, yet one characterised by an ultimately fateful combination of constant shortages on the one hand, and state responsibility for just about everything on the other. Developments in the sphere of consumption thus further complicate the history of East German society.

Rationing was not merely a feature of the war-time and very early post-war years (as in Britain) but remained in place until well over a decade after the end of the war, in 1958 (and was briefly reintroduced for some goods a couple of years later).[31] The June Uprising of 1953 gave the SED a rude awakening, after which consumer needs were never again ignored; the supply of a sufficient and appropriate range of clothing, household goods and the 'thousand small items of daily need' was eventually a top political priority, and one that was never entirely or satisfactorily resolved.[32] Food was, and remained throughout the GDR's history, a direct responsibility of the state. There were continuing periodic and longer-term difficulties: a shortage of potatoes in the exceptionally hard winter of 1970–1, coffee in the later 1970s and early '80s, and a continual shortage of exotic fruit (including bananas, which became for West Germans a symbol of the East Germans' former deprivations and most urgent desires on crossing to the West in 1989–90). The state's responsibility for the quality of food even extended to cooked meals. In 1978 between one half and one third of people ate their main weekday meal in a school or works canteen. The state provided seven million dinners daily.[33] These were not universally well received. A study by the Leipzig Central Institute of Youth Research (Zentralinstitut für Jugendforschung, or ZIJ) found in 1984 that dislike for school meals (as probably universally across schools in Western Europe) increased with age. While just under one in five pupils (19 per cent) in Class 7 disliked school meals, this more than doubled to 41 per cent by Class 10.[34]

But the hard statistics do tell a story of a continually rising, if limited, standard of living, however much frustration was associated with variable supplies of foodstuffs, as well as delays and difficulties in the acquisition and repair of hard goods. Numbers of television sets, fridges and other consumer durables rose, if far more slowly than in the West. Everyday pleasures were catered for in one way or another; consumption of alcohol, for example, played an increasingly important role in the lives of many East Germans (although, as we shall see below, the consequences were not always unproblematic). The numbers of cars owned by East Germans rose from 17 per hundred households in 1971 to 57 per hundred households in 1989.[35] The state even tried to help those who could not gain access to washing machines (or spare parts when their machine broke down): easing the burdens of everyday life would also help productivity. Thus, for example, Klaus Lohse, the Deputy Minister for Bezirksgeleitete Industrie (regional industry) and Lebensmittelindustrie (the food industry) became very excited about the possibility of 'Kontaktlose Wäscheannahme', a 'contact-free' washing service that was a cross between a Western-style do-it-yourself launderette and an over-the-counter laundry service.[36]

Thus it was a key aim of the SED – prioritised more at certain times than others – to ensure that consumer demands were met, first of all through the state-owned HO (Handelsorganisation) shops, which supplied basic goods, and also – remarkably – through mail-order systems, not merely to cater to those in outlying villages and towns who could not readily access larger stores, but also to help to even out the patchy distribution of scarce but desired goods across the GDR.[37]

Alongside all this, however, a 'second economy' began to emerge for the provision of luxuries and higher quality goods to those who had the requisite forms of privileged access. The first step towards the introduction of more desirable goods for these few took place with the opening of the first Intershop in Rostock in 1955. Expanded further to the neighbouring Baltic ports of Wismar and Stralsund, and then in 1962 to the international crossing point at Friedrichstrasse in Berlin and the international trade fair city of Leipzig, these Intershops were designed initially to cater for international visitors and not the indigenous East German population. But their number was greatly expanded under the Honecker regime, and with the decriminalisation of the possession of Western currency in 1974, they were also officially open to East Germans with the requisite bank notes and coins. By 1976 – perhaps the 'high point' of the GDR's history – as much as 85 per cent of the revenue of Intershops came from East Germans. The related chain of Interhotels, primarily designed to cater for foreign visitors, also by this time found that four fifths of their customers were actually GDR citizens. Alongside the Intershops came two further outlets for desirable goods and consumables, at a price: the Exquisit shops, first opened in 1962, and the Delikat shops, opened in 1967. The numbers of these shops also increased greatly in the later 1970s, such that quality produce could be bought by those with spare spending power.

This expansion of shopping took place in a changing social context that was comparable in some respects to that of Western societies in the 1960s and '70s. The introduction of the five-day working week (totalling 43.75 hours) in 1967 gave people more leisure time. Growing access to Western radio channels, to which the vast majority of households listened in the 1960s, and increasingly also to Western television stations with the rapid growth of television owner-ship and the official tolerance of Western viewing in the 1970s, meant that East Germans participated in wider trends in leisure and culture. The development of a youth music and fashion market, and the expansion in private means of transport – motorbikes and private car ownership – in the 1970s meant that leisure time for those with means could be spent in ways not easily controlled by the East German state. As with so many other aspects of policy in the Honecker period, the official solution was one of partial acceptance and appropriation for reproduction in communist colours. Thus blue jeans or Levis, once desperately desired by dissident youth as symbols of the West, were mass produced for the home market; rock and beat music, at first officially frowned upon and partially rejected, partially tolerated, was to a degree even-tually incorporated and reproduced in a form of attempted inoculation against the more deadly strain of the capitalist virus.

The development of a specifically GDR form of a state-sponsored consumer culture was not without its contradictions.[38] It meant different things to different generations: those who had suffered the privations of the war and early post-war years had a very different approach to the modest improve-ments of living standards in the GDR than did members of a younger genera-tion. The officially sanctioned emphasis on consumer satisfaction imported standards from the West in a competition against the Federal Republic that the GDR could never hope to win. The scarcity of certain goods rendered their value, when acquired through personal efforts in an advanced form of 'hunter-gathering', even higher. But one of the ultimate contradictions was in the implications of GDR consumerism for class.

East German social structure under 'actually existing socialism'

Unaware of shifting economic foundations, not to mention the extraordinary developments on the international front and the utterly surprising political end that was to come in 1989–90, people sought as best they could to make their own lives and improve their circumstances, and within these wider parameters a new form of society developed in what Honecker liked to term the no-longer-transitional phase of an 'actually existing socialism', a form of society that he thought was there to stay.

In the 1970s and '80s, the new system of stratification in the GDR became more stable and began to reproduce itself, even, arguably, to stagnate. Differentiated social policies and wider trends began to produce new forms of inequality. Selective support of the politically important, the productive and the reproductive members of society – the Party faithful, workers and mothers – was accompanied by relative disregard for the unproductive and the outcasts – pensioners, 'a-socials', the politically suspect. With a relative levelling of the incomes of those who were employed and an increasing prevalence of two-income households, the major problem for most people became one of a lack of sufficient quantities of desirable consumer goods on which to spend their money. Those with access to Western currency or special 'connections' then entered a separate class of their own, cross-cutting the hierarchies determined by power and occupation. And wider trends of consumerism, materialism and globalisation of culture – even across the Wall – began to erode traditional class milieus and to produce patterns of individualisation comparable to, if developing somewhat later than, those also evident in the West.

By the 1980s, East German society was very different from that of West Germany. Living conditions, social institutions, widespread expectations and experiences had all been dramatically transformed by the forty-year experiment in attempting to construct a socialist society as understood by the SED. The one thing this new society was not was a classless society, at least in the sense of a society without inequalities and clear system of stratification. Whatever the official position with respect to elites and class, an acute consciousness of the persistence of social differences is registered repeatedly in the documents of the GDR, from GDR political and sociological analyses, through works of creative literature, to other contemporary records. However, the stratification system was a complex one, in which issues to do with prestige and status, power and privilege, life-style and income, nature of work and wider milieu, cut across each other in patterns quite different from those characteristic of Western capitalist societies in the later twentieth century.

Social inequalities in the GDR were rooted in a complex combination of factors other than private ownership of the means of production. The most significant bases of inequality were: power, and the wider implications of a particular position in the power hierarchy; status in political ideology; informal hierarchies of prestige; the nature of the work done, including conditions of work and degrees of autonomy, specialisation, pressures and constraints; and command of crucial resources, which included access to Western currency, appropriate 'connections' and informal suppliers of 'under-the-counter' goods and 'out-of-hours' services. Added to some of the 'regular' dissonances in individual status, such as the combination of high official prestige, modest incomes and poor working conditions of most of the manual working class, were almost fortuitous variations, such as whether or not one happened to have a Western relative providing easy access to Western goods and currency. East German social structure cannot therefore be readily summarised in terms of single aspects, such as the relatively small spectrum of differences in income, or simple phrases such as the 'levelled-off society' ('nivellierte Gesellschaft') or 'the state of little people' ('Staat der kleinen Leute'). Nor, as we shall see in all the chapters that follow, was it a society that was in any way 'frozen' or 'laid to rest'.[39]

Participation in the changing enterprise that was the GDR thus took on many colours over time, and the groups who constituted the key protagonists changed accordingly. The old regime was overthrown and the old ruling elites and dominant classes ousted in the quest to create a new classless society. But for the 'transitional' period to the new communist society – which was never achieved – the 'dictatorship of the proletariat' effectively meant the dictatorship of the Marxist-Leninist party, the SED, and, more particularly, the dictatorship of the SED leadership. Power and political conformity replaced ownership or non-ownership of the means of production as key determinants of the stratification system of the new East German society. Yet one of the curious characteristics of power in the SED state was the way in which it was diffused, spreading like a stain through all areas and ranks of society. Political functionaries and informal collaborators at all levels from the centre to the grass roots, scientific and technical experts, and cultural producers of meaning, were all involved, in different ways, in the complex enterprise of trying to create (continually contested versions of) the socialist future.

There is, however, more to the question of relations between power and social stratification than a focus on the GDR primarily as communist dictatorship reveals. East Germany was also a modern industrial state. It has often been remarked that 'knowledge is power', and this is particularly the case in advanced industrial societies, whether capitalist or communist. The East German stratification system was thus further complicated by the presence of educated and professional classes who enjoyed (if that is not a wholly inappropriate word in this context) a markedly ambivalent relationship with the political elites. The old propertied bourgeoisie ('Besitzbürgertum') was a vestige of the old capitalist order, doomed to 'wither away', in Marxist terminology, with a little rather unwelcome help from the SED. But the power of the 'educated bourgeoisie' ('Bildungsbürgertum'), based on education and technical expertise, was clearly vital to the efficient functioning of a modern industrial state. Nevertheless, the roles, political outlooks and prestige of the 'educated bourgeoisie', or new 'socialist intelligentsia', were constantly the subject of some uncertainty in the self-designated 'workers' and peasants' state'. Similar ambivalences and tensions existed in relation to those possessing 'cultural power', or the capacity to endow life with meaning. Independence of thought, while crucial to the development of a viable society capable of commitment, self-reflection and reform in pursuit of a better future, could also open up dangerous whirls of dissent, potentially providing channels for the invasion of the 'class enemy' (*Klassenfeind*). Although rather differently related to the socialist enterprise, with religion theoretically doomed to 'wither away' along with the state and classes, the 'spiritual power' and related social contributions of ministers of religion and committed Christians working in a variety of social welfare and health institutions were also not so readily dispatched to the allotted historical dustbin. Thus a combination of constraints and privileges marked out members of different professional groups, whose status in 'actually existing socialism' was never completely clarified in either theory or practice.

Finally, the sphere of consumption was as important as the sphere of production in analysing social inequalities in the GDR. Differential access to desired goods, combined with increasing leisure time, might mitigate inequalities rooted in power and work. The SED's own policies – particularly in the Honecker era – reinforced a fixation on Western goods and conceptions of consumer society. While SED social policies sought to ensure a minimum standard of living for all in terms of food, transport and housing, the official determination to prove superiority over the West, on the West's own materialistic terms, simultaneously served to undermine the egalitarian ideals of socialism. But the sphere of consumption introduced new aspirations and inequalities that complicated East German social structure further and produced currents of individualism to challenge notions of socialist collectives and collective goals.

In the 1980s, there was little still evident of the utopian hopes of the early post-war period. Even among the grass roots of the SED, and much more so among the wider population, there was rising criticism of Honecker's rule, further exacerbated when the younger, more dynamic and reforming leader Mikhail Gorbachev came to power in the Soviet Union in 1985. But if utopia had been displaced by normality, there was also little of the real distress of the early post-war years; death and hunger among ruins had been replaced by the more comfortable or at least predictable miseries of everyday life in 'actually existing socialism'.

Ultimately, expensive social policies and state subventions simply could not be sustained in a period of growing debts and economic crisis. The SED leadership was increasingly incapable of rising to the challenges of a global economy, and failed almost entirely even to acknowledge, let alone adequately respond to, a rising mountain of domestic problems in its descent into environmental disaster and economic bankruptcy in the 1980s.[40] The emergent political challenges of the 1980s were met by enhanced political surveillance and repression – which proved inadequate once the Soviet Union signalled its unwillingness to intervene in 1989.

This plunge into political crisis was, however, not merely an effect of changed Soviet policies under Gorbachev. Nor was it simply a result of a long-standing dislike of the system in principle that could precipitate political action once conditions were right. Rather, in part it resulted, ironically, from the combination of enhanced popular participation in political processes and heightened expectations of the improvements of which the GDR might have been capable under Honecker. But the state claimed to deliver more than it was capable of; and people's goals – which, under consumer socialism, in many material respects overlapped with those of the regime – were increasingly frustrated. The response of the ruling gerontocracy in the 1980s was an attempt to deny that problems even existed. The response of many of the people, in so far as this was an option, was – as before 1961 – to want out. Attempts to square an impossible circle of economic decline led, not only towards the mass stampede to the West once conditions changed in 1989, but also to the recognition on the part of many state functionaries as well as grass-roots members of the SED that reforms of some sort were essential; hence the 'gentle revolution', which ultimately culminated in the totally unexpected and rapid collapse of the GDR and absorption into the Federal Republic in 1990.

In the end, in the context of a collapsing economy that precipitated the end of the Cold War, the individual search for material well-being and personal freedom won over the utopian dreams born in the violence of the Second World War.

Chapter Three

Citizens at home

The SED had high ideals for the everyday life of its citizens. Visions of the good society included:

> good housing conditions, childcare and shopping facilities, clean streets and pathways, well-maintained gardens, playgrounds and sports facilities, quality restaurants, the care of citizens of advanced age, the shaping of an interesting cultural life, including youth dances, discotheques and harvest festivals, the cultivation of village traditions and the furthering of a sense of *Heimat* [attachment to homeland] . . . civil defence, disposal of rubbish and sewage, ensuring the winter road service and other communal political tasks essential to life.[1]

Associated with the fulfilment of these needs was 'raising the authority of local mayors as representatives of state power and persons in whom citizens could have trust'. As ever in the GDR, nothing could be apolitical, not even sewage or rubbish removal, sandwiched as they were between civil defence on the one hand and maintenance of safe conditions on winter roads on the other.

Belief in the ideals of a decent life, in a basic minimum of fulfilment of everyday needs, was genuine. These aspirations were not just about maintaining the trust and confidence of duped citizens, but were rooted in a real desire to better the lot of ordinary people – however compromised this desire was in practice by corruption, political instrumentalisation and the sheer incapacity of the centralised economy to deliver the kind of material growth that would make the realisation of such visions practicable in reality. Nevertheless, failure to deliver the material goods cannot be compensated forever by good intentions. And the situation becomes worse when problems are not admitted to and addressed, but rather attempts are made to deny them through slogans and propaganda. When citizens are acutely aware – as they were in the GDR – of the fact that material conditions could be very much better under a different system, they will not continue to swallow promises of a better future if an alternative present becomes more readily available. The gap between the ideals and the realities – the sort of gap that gave rise to slogans such as 'make ruins without weapons' (nicely rhyming in the original German: 'Ruinen schaffen ohne Waffen', a play on the peace movement slogan of 'make peace without weapons') on decrepit, crumbling buildings – was a significant factor in the continued orientation towards the more affluent West of the vast majority of East Germans through to the final collapse and reunification. Yet at the same time, to say all this is not to give any kind of adequate or comprehensive picture of life in the GDR.

Underlying the developments considered here there is a far wider point of fundamental importance. Having a roof over one's head, a decent place to live, is fundamental in any society. What was distinctive about the GDR, in contrast to most contemporary Western societies, was the sheer extent to which the state took responsibility for housing. If, in the West, one could blame rapacious private landlords, banks and building societies, or the vicissitudes of the impersonal market for one's housing problems, in the GDR it was increasingly the state that stood to take the blame. And the state simply could not, for a variety of reasons, satisfy everyone's needs. While post-war West Germany had money and know-how pumped into the economy through the Marshall Plan and managed within a couple of decades to rebuild and renovate the housing stock, East Germany – whose major urban centres had been hit far harder by bomb damage, most notably of course in the case of Dresden – found its economic recovery hampered by Soviet policy's focus on reparations rather than investment. In subsequent decades, the weakness of the centrally planned economy was exacerbated by the GDR's involvement in Comecon, tying it to the fates of far less industrialised and less productive regions of Eastern Europe. This was in contrast to the Federal Republic's very much more benign experience of an 'economic miracle', and closer economic cooperation with other capitalist states in the context of the European Economic Community founded in 1957.

General economic weakness thus rendered attempts to solve the GDR's housing problems almost doomed to long-drawn out struggles, with much frustration along the way. And these frustrations would inevitably be vented against the well-meaning, paternalistic state. In the area of housing, as in so many areas of life in the GDR, there could be no truly 'private sphere', in some sense utterly unrelated to the wider political context. Housing was truly a political matter.

Home, sweet home?

Housing was, and remained, a central problem of the SED regime, and one of the chief causes of popular dissatisfaction: by far the largest category of complaints in individual citizens' petitions, or *Eingaben*, were complaints about inadequate housing.[2] There were two key challenges: repair and rebuilding of housing stock in areas that had suffered heavily from bomb damage or sheer ageing and neglect; and the provision of large quantities of new housing in areas of new industrial concentration, such as oil and petrochemical works. As always, the outcomes represented an unsatisfactory compromise between high ideals and utopian visions (particularly with respect to 'socialist new towns') and severe economic constraints.

The housing stock in many urban areas of eastern Germany after the war was in an abysmal condition. Around two thirds of the housing stock in large cities had been destroyed. Major cities such as Berlin and Dresden had been bombed out of all recognition; simply clearing the rubble, restoring sanitation and ensuring roofs and walls were leak-proof were the major priorities of the early post-war years. But much of the older housing stock remained barely fit for human habitation, and its condition, even after basic initial restoration, continued to deteriorate with time. In 1989, the crumbling plaster and still-visible battle pock-marks from the Second World War came as a dramatic shock to previously ignorant Western visitors to East Germany. Although attempts began to be made, particularly in the 'history-and-tradition-boom' years of the 1980s, to restore older housing in town centres – or at least to prevent total decay and possibly dangerous physical collapse of older buildings – renovation of older housing stock was not always as simple or cost-effective as building anew. Thus the major focus was on constructing new and relatively cheap, purpose-built apartment blocks in towns, or constructing entirely new out-of-town residential areas that, like Halle-Neustadt, were essentially satellite towns for large industrial centres.

Renovation was most extensive in the Ulbricht period, and declined steadily from the later 1970s, while from the early 1970s Honecker had given top priority to the construction of new housing. Ulbricht himself was personally very interested, not only in the construction of new industrial satellite towns, but also in architectural schemes for town centres, including Berlin, Dresden, Halle and the major district towns. He was deeply interested in the details of architecture and design, and was even perceived as such by ordinary people. He allegedly exclaimed, on seeing in 1952 the monotonous blocks rapidly constructed for workers in the new town of what was then Stalinstadt, later Eisenhüttenstadt, 'those are barracks, those are not houses [fit] for workers!'[3] Honecker, by contrast, was more interested in the visible expression of the 'unity of economic and social policy': he wanted to be seen personally handing over the one-millionth new home in Berlin–Marzahn to an ordinary working-class family, and took pride in the sheer numbers of new flats that were being constructed.[4] Statistics for the numbers of new homes built annually were only kept from 1958; from then until the end of the Ulbricht period in 1971, an average of 60,000 to 70,000 new homes were built each year (with a high of 85,580 in 1961). When Honecker came into office, there was a vigorous drive to push up these figures, with around 100,000 new homes (sometimes over 110,000) being built every year from the mid-1970s to the mid-'80s. This figure dropped to a low of 83,361 in 1989.[5]

There were a few well-known architectural prestige projects, such as East Berlin's Stalinallee (renamed Karl Marx Allee), notorious as the place where the workers first downed tools and set off to protest on 16 June 1953, inaugurating the popular uprising of the following day. But GDR housing construction was not merely a matter of individual prestige projects or unrealisable visions. Architects who had cut their teeth on the socialist ideals of the 1920s, or been influenced by the Bauhaus school of modern design for the masses (based in Dessau), as well as a few who had absorbed or participated in Nazi ideals of construction for the 'folk community', strove to produce new housing that was functional, liveable and 'modern', as well as capable of being individualised according to personal tastes.[6] In the 1960s, the vision was one in which every household, of whatever size, should have adequate space in which to deploy functional furniture – built-in cupboards, flexible sets of do-it-yourself shelving, tables and chairs – in a variety of ways to create unique and homely living spaces. But this vision had to be realised in terms of available machinery and materials: 16-metre cranes that would produce four-storey buildings of five sections, or three-storey buildings of six to seven sections; pre-formed slabs for the walls of what were called *Plattenbauten,* or prefabricated high-rise blocks; cheap asbestos cement rather than traditional tiles for the roof. With the crane producing a radius around which the buildings could be located, apartment blocks were arranged around what eventually became somewhat dismal open spaces.

In the event, the shortcomings of the economy, as always, frustrated the full realisation of utopian visions, both in the new towns and with respect to the renovation or construction of new housing in old towns. One of Honecker's few genuinely popular pronouncements was his promise to increase the housing stock as rapidly as possible; yet utopian visions, as so often in the GDR, turned increasingly into miserable realities. Vast numbers of East Germans in the 1970s and '80s remained dissatisfied with their housing conditions. In 1974, over one third of young couples were 'extremely dissatisfied' with their housing conditions, and as many as one in five (20 per cent) of young couples who had been married for less than two years were unable to live together because they could not obtain housing and an additional partner could not be accommodated in either of the parental homes.[7] As late as 1986, as many as one in fourteen families (7 per cent) with two or more children still did not have their own home.[8] And those that did were not all entirely happy with what they had. In Dresden in 1980, only one third (35 per cent) of young residents of older housing were satisfied with their accommodation, compared to over three quarters (76 per cent) of those living in newer flats. This was scarcely surprising, given that less than half (44 per cent) of the older flats and houses had hot water, only 60 per cent had a bath or shower, and 65 per cent an indoor toilet, compared to figures of 89 per cent, 100 per cent and 100 per cent respectively for newer residences.[9] Getting oneself a decent home was indeed the highest 'life goal' of young people in a survey carried out in Leipzig in October 1984: over half of those surveyed (53 per cent) put 'settling in a modern flat' as their most important goal in life. This figure compared with just under a half (48 per cent) seeking an 'occupation in which they could be totally fulfilled'; and, at a mere 27 per cent, a 'full and total commitment to socialism' barely topped the more materialistic 'pursuit of all possibilities for earning money', named as a major life goal by precisely one quarter of young people.[10]

It has sometimes been suggested that housing in the GDR was not as strongly associated with social class as it is in, for example, Britain or the US, where the contrasts between luxurious private housing and rented accommodation in slums or public estates (council housing in the UK, the 'projects' in the US) were and remain extremely marked. In the GDR, by contrast, only a small fraction of new building was in the form of private ownership: there were on average around 11,000 to 12,000 new private homes a year in the 1980s, a mere one-tenth of the amount of public housing being built at the time.[11] Thus the private/public divide, so marked in Western capitalist societies, arguably became ever less salient in the GDR. Members of the bourgeoisie – or socialist intelligentsia – nevertheless still lived in large villas amidst trees or at the lakesides on the outskirts of Berlin, or in the spacious *Gründerzeit* flats around courtyards in the centres of the cities that had grown so rapidly in the late nineteenth and early twentieth centuries, while the old working-class slums of the cities remained as depressed as ever. But in new housing estates, members of the working class and professionals would, so at least it was claimed, live side by side in identical apartment blocks, and make use of the same shops and transport services.

Like so much else, this claim is not entirely borne out by the facts. Social class and other social inequalities still played a role in the unequal access, for whatever reasons, to newer rather than older housing stock. Older and weaker members of society tended disproportionately to live in older houses and tenement blocks of flats. The least educated members of society also lived in the worst housing conditions.[12] Highly qualified and politically privileged workers were prioritised over others in the allocation of scarce new housing stock. The contrast between older and newer housing stock was, as indicated, very stark: as late as 1984, around one in six older flats and houses in Leipzig still had *none* of the sanitary amenities (hot water, indoor toilet and shower or bath) that most Westerners took for granted in the latter half of the twentieth century. In certain areas, it is notable that while nearly two thirds (64 per cent) of young professionals ('Intelligenz') lived in accommodation with all modern sanitary facilities, less than a half (49 per cent) of young working-class people enjoyed such amenities.[13]

To Western eyes, the new housing estates might appear bleak and soulless. Even contemporaries made jokes about these estates – in which some eight-storey blocks had no lifts – as 'stone deserts' ('Steinwüsten'), 'silos for living in' ('Wohnsilos'), 'lockers to keep workers in' ('Arbeiterschliessfächer'), 'comfort cells' ('Komfortzellen') and 'housing ghettos' ('Wohnghettos'). And the crime statistics speak for themselves: apart from East Berlin, crime rates were highest in the new town areas of Eisenhüttenstadt and Schwedt in the Frankfurt/Oder region, and around the Buna and Leuna works and in Halle Neustadt (known popularly as 'Hanoi', with a 20 per cent higher crime rate than the neighbouring old town of Halle) in the Halle region. The distinction is borne out too on a micro level, with higher crime rates in the *Plattenbau* areas of the town of Schwerin than in older urban areas or the surrounding countryside. The old city of Dresden had the lowest rates of criminality (as well as of divorce).[14]

Perhaps one of the greatest sources of frustration with respect to housing was the widespread dependence on the state, and the significant lack of personal control over the quality and state of repair of one's living conditions or the chance of moving. The sheer difficulty of being able to achieve any improvement – from simple housing repairs to a complete change of location – is evident in vast numbers of citizens' letters to official authorities over the whole period of the GDR.

In 1962, for example, the 51-year-old Frau P., who was severely disabled, was desperate to move out of her decrepit flat in the back courtyard of an apartment block: she had no running water, no toilet, and the roof and walls appear to have been falling in. When the resident of a flat in the front of the block suddenly died, Frau P. hoped to be able to effect a rapid move; but the owner of the block refused, saying that she needed the newly vacant flat as an 'exchange object' to get her own son a larger flat, 'although the son of the home-owner already had a flat large enough for himself and his family'.[15] Frau P. was then given extremely short shrift by the relevant local council official when she uttered the sentiment that, had she known how little help she would get with re-housing, she would have gone to her relatives in the West when her husband died.

Despite massive efforts in the meantime to improve the housing stock, letters written two decades or so later read in a remarkably similar vein, though with fewer mentions of the West. In 1980, Frau Lotte A., resident in Borna, a small town in a poor brown-coal mining area, describes her horrendous housing situation, with rain coming in, windows falling out, the area all around the house being cordoned off (presumably because of safety issues) and the cellar in such a state that 'the potatoes all go bad on us'.[16] This poorly written letter was by a woman who had to revert to being a housewife following a stroke, with a husband who, despite being severely disabled, had a job as a shift worker in the brown-coal industry, and a son who was also disabled and confined to a wheelchair; only the other son, also working in the brown-coal mine, appeared to be in reasonable health. Frau A.'s letter reeks of desperation – that the family simply could not continue to live in such appalling conditions.

Similarly, a letter from Frau Gabriele S. in 1988 depicts her difficulties with a husband who turned violent and started beating her and the four children, including his own baby and the three children she had from a previous marriage; Frau S. had to flee with her four children and live for some considerable time cramped up in a one-and-a-half room flat with her 71-year-old grandmother before the authorities managed to organise her a new flat in Schwedt.[17] This move was achieved on the basis that she was not merely in desperate need, but also deemed not to be 'an asocial problem case', with a good work record on a collective farm and a willingness to take up any sort of work, anywhere in the GDR. The official dealing with the case noted that he was currently juggling annual figures of around 700 applications for housing and more than 550 'socially urgent cases' against a total maximum number of around 70 to 80 flats becoming vacant each year.[18] Frau B., who in 1978 lost not merely her flat but also her son when her marriage ran into difficulties and her husband insisted on divorce, found that her problems with alcoholism and depression played a major role in the authorities' responses to her case; the amount of care and time lavished by the authorities on what was in effect a form of personal counselling is quite remarkable, given that some of the immediate practical problems were so hard to solve.[19] Other cases were treated as less deserving and received somewhat more peremptory responses. The 51-year-old Frau Helga S., for example, in 1988 found it difficult to make the 30 kilometre journey between her home in Braunsbedra and that of her 82-year-old mother in Querfurt, for whom she wanted to provide personal care in her own home, given the lack of adequate facilities for care of the elderly and her mother's preference for care by a member of the family; but the Querfurt authorities, noting that the granddaughter had already achieved a flat exchange from Merseburg to Querfurt for this reason, advised Frau S. that her mother was therefore not to be considered as in need of care and that she would have to try to organise a swap privately.[20]

Even for those lucky enough to be rehoused, new problems might merely be created. An extraordinarily wide-ranging letter from Frau Ingeborg R., speaking for a large number of women with whom she had informally talked, and covering the whole gamut of frustrations from the non-availability of children's clothing in certain sizes, through the total absence from the shops of grapes, peppers and peaches, to the inadequacies of the health service in her area, included also perceptive comments on the difficulties for many women associated with moving house. That small minority who managed successfully to move house then found knock-on effects with difficulties in childcare arrangements, which were often located very far from either place of work or residence, and sometimes necessitated a change of occupation or a switch to shift work and further frustrations.[21] The close links between workplace, childcare, housing and the state could, when untangled, lead to a vicious circle in which no single aspect could easily be unpicked without upsetting all the others.

Common to very large numbers of East German citizens, then, was a sense of near total dependence on the state for the most basic need for shelter, for habitable accommodation. State authorities appear to have expended considerable time and effort trying very earnestly to treat each case on its merits, and devising refined strategies for trying to identify and deal with what were seen to be the most socially urgent, vulnerable and needy cases first, so long as they also came into the rather inchoate category of 'deserving' with respect to commitment to the GDR, lack of 'asocial' behaviour or character and so on. The dependence on the state of more robust citizens could in part be alleviated by the private organisation of apartment exchanges and the private organisation of house improvements and repairs through do-it-yourself activities. This in turn often required the 'liberating' of appropriate materials from the workplace and the fostering of a range of acquaintances with appropriate skills. Illegal purloining of materials from the workplace accounted for very significant sums: in 1984, for example, the FDGB estimated that materials valued at somewhere in the region of 778,000 Marks were taken from the workplace, accounting for the vast bulk of the 'special incidents' of that year.[22] It was indicative that losses were greatest in the areas of building materials – wood and metal; they were minimal in the areas of science (actually nil in 1984), art and education.[23]

If finding acceptable basic accommodation was a very widespread problem, then a common compensation for a fortunate and sizeable minority was a weekend escape to a 'second home' of sorts. Arguably the most agreeable abodes – if one is more interested in atmosphere than size or the boasting of all 'mod cons' – were the innumerable weekend cottages, often little more than garden sheds, dotted around on the allotments or small plots of land (*Schrebergärten*), that served a double purpose as private fruit and vegetable patch and weekend retreat. Untrammelled by official flags and slogans, and lovingly painted and renovated with copious use of materials from the black market, these served a number of vital functions in the lives of many East Germans. The ways in which these retreats were constructed and renovated with materials and labour obtained through contacts, friends, barter and exchange is yet another illustration of levels of popular initiative and energy in making one's life. And for those lucky enough to own such a retreat, the possibility of sitting with family and friends and drinking generous quantities of beer and spirits under the apple trees on a warm (if mosquito-infested) summer night could arguably more than compensate for lack of indoor sanitary facilities. Here a little decorated rustic wooden sign with the time-worn slogan beloved of many Germans over the previous century or more could be proudly displayed: 'Klein, aber mein' – 'small, but mine'.

Visions of a new society

In part, the attempt was made not merely to provide people with decent housing, but to create a wholly new form of society, bringing workers and gigantic new industrial enterprises together in entirely new communities. Founded in the 1950s and '60s, 'socialist new towns' were designed not merely to house the working masses required for major new industrial plants; they were based in a far more ambitious vision and designed to produce built environments in which a new socialist lifestyle could be realised and socialist communities flourish. 'Flourish' may perhaps be overstating the case; but distinctive community patterns did develop in these areas. Of particular importance, again, is the question of relations between the state and any 'private sphere'. In major new towns, the complex of industrial enterprises (or 'combines'), housing, healthcare, childcare, social and sporting facilities were so very closely intertwined that the people who lived in them were essentially living through and within a network of GDR social institutions, in which no area of life was not in some way coloured and informed by state policy. While this could be disagreeable, many people – particularly those coming from a harsh background of poverty, war and uprootedness – genuinely had positive experiences to report.

The first of the 'socialist new towns', founded in 1950, was based at the old town of Fürstenberg on the redrawn border with Poland on the Oder river. Fürstenberg itself, despite its long history of mining, shipping and glass-blowing, was nearly a ghost town at the end of the war, with so many of its inhabitants fleeing from the advancing Red Army that there were a mere twenty-eight residents still in place when the Red Army entered in April 1945. By 1948, one third of the residents were not people who had returned to their homes, but refugees from lost German territories east of the Oder river.[24] For a variety of reasons, Fürstenberg was well situated to become a centre of the major heavy industrial production foreseen in the GDR's five-year plan of the early 1950s, and construction of the Eisenhüttenstadt works and the barracks for workers took off at a tremendously fast pace. Following Stalin's death in March 1953, the new town was in May given the name of Stalinstadt, with a ceremonial event graced by the presence of Walter Ulbricht at the podium, although apparently with little input or agreement from residents, many of whom felt uneasy about such a name a mere decade after Stalingrad. It was subsequently renamed Eisenhüttenstadt in 1961, after Stalin's fall from the pantheon of communist heroes five years earlier and the consequent embarrassment of the name was rather belatedly officially registered in the GDR.

Vast numbers of people – often refugees from lost eastern territories, orphans, single mothers, young men with no strong roots or prospects anywhere else – were attracted to work in the near wilderness conditions of 'sand and pine trees' by the chance of secure employment, better provision with foodstuffs and the offer of a flat, at least in the near future: the population grew from 15,000 in 1953 to nearly 45,000 in 1969 and then more slowly to over 53,000 in 1988.[25] It was repeatedly emphasised to workers that this was a special place: the GDR's 'first socialist town', where no church towers would be built, but where there would be all the cultural amenities, schools, hospitals and shops – none private – required to construct the perfect new community. The architect of the early residential areas stressed the importance of light, sunshine and air, and of cultural and social amenities close to hand. This was to be a liveable community, not merely barracks for workers, even if it would take time to complete. For those who could not entirely stand conditions in the as-yet-unfinished utopia, there was always the possibility of a quick shopping trip to the private bakers' shops in the old town of Fürstenberg on the other side of the railway line, or drowning one's sorrows in beer with the workers' collective at the end of the shift.

From the accounts of people interviewed in 1989, before the end of the GDR, and also of individuals interviewed in 2004, fifteen years after the collapse of the SED regime, experiences in the early years were characterised by a combination of considerable hardship and yet high hopes.[26] Despite horrendous working conditions with exhausting labour amid hot furnaces and exceedingly primitive living conditions, with even those lucky enough to obtain a flat of their own still lacking the most basic furniture, there nevertheless appears in the 1950s and early '60s to have been – at least in memory – a sense of building up something new (*Aufbau*), being part of a collective spirit, making a contribution to a better life in the future. The willingness to work regardless of reward, to step in when needed for emergencies or overtime, the sense of 'ownership' of the enterprise and the related cultural and social facilities were, according to some participants' memories, displaced in the course of the 1960s and '70s by a retreat into individualistic concerns, with a growing focus on home, family and private gain.[27] According to others, the positive sides of the new community continued to outweigh negative aspects: older residents interviewed in 2004 recalled what they saw as excellent childcare and educational provision, social and cultural facilities that were genuinely for the 'people' (*Volk*), and a real sense of community spirit, with people willing to help each other when in personal difficulties, or to put time and energy into communal building schemes.[28] For these residents, the sense of community more than made up for what they saw as far less significant disadvantages of pre-1989 life: the paucity of 'southern fruits', the relative lack of telephones, the long wait for a car. In place of these purely material possessions, they prized more highly aspects such as enhanced 'law and order', with police ready to discipline rowdy or work-shy youngsters; the ways in which the work collective would help out when a *Sorgenkind* (a young person giving cause for concern) failed to turn up for work, or when a colleague's marriage was in trouble; and the cheap and enjoyable holidays in the FDGB-owned holiday facilities on the Baltic island of Rügen, or the trips to destinations in Eastern Europe, most often to Czechoslovakia or Hungary. Not everything was entirely rosy, however. A major battle of these later decades appears to have been finding a way around the SED-sponsored technical interference in what could have been perfectly good Western television reception by 'organising' the installation of special antennae and convertors to gain access to the blocked Western channels; this was a battle in which the SED only finally capitulated in 1979.[29]

Eisenhüttenstadt was in some respects unique: renowned as the 'first socialist town', relatively well provided for, and with a genuinely pleasing architectural design, at least in the areas constructed before the new concrete-slab building techniques of the 1960s were introduced. It was soon followed by other new town developments: the decision was taken in 1955 to build a new satellite town at Hoyerswerda, in the south-eastern part of the GDR for the growing workforce of the energy production enterprise, the Schwarze Pumpe; in the 1960s further developments at Leuna II (oil refinery) and Halle-Neustadt expanded the chemical complex around Halle and Leipzig; and a number of developments in Schwedt (paper and packaging works, oil refinery and petro-chemicals combine) followed Eisenhüttenstadt as part of the expansion of new industries in the previously relatively thinly populated border area to the north and south of the major centre of Frankfurt-an-der-Oder.

Hoyerswerda was the pilot project for the industrialisation of building techniques, boasting the first use of the concrete slab or *Plattenbau* techniques: the first such mass-produced large block of the GDR was opened in Groß-Zeisig near Hoyerswerda in 1957.[30] But Hoyerswerda was important for more than merely building techniques. The intense architectural competition for control of this project, in which the renowned architect Richard Paulick (1903–79) was ultimately successful, was in part rooted in much grander visions than merely producing a cost-effective dormitory town for workers. Paulick, who had during the Weimar Republic worked with the Bauhaus Director Walter Gropius in Dessau, was associated both with attempts to restore and develop a traditional architectural heritage (Schinkel's legacy in Berlin) and with prestige projects to represent the new (including part of the Stalin-Allee development).[31] Located in the Sorbian Lausitz area, Hoyerswerda was intended in part to be a centre of Sorbian culture, with prestige buildings to house the Sorbian 'parliament' or representative council (Domowina) and a Sorbian national museum, as well as a Sorbian theatre, cinema and restaurant. But by the early 1960s, the Hoyerswerda project was plagued by uncertainties about the speed and cost of construction, and dramatically increased estimates of the numbers of people who would need housing (at least 90,000 new residents, against the figure of 54,000 for which the plans had originally been designed). The plans to link the new town with the old town centre and to provide appropriate leisure facilities were first postponed, and then shelved; Paulick left to take on other commitments (Schwedt from 1962–4, and Halle-Neustadt from

1963–8); and when the Cottbus District took over control of the project, the central authorities lost interest. In 1968, over a decade after the first housing block had been opened, the first department store was finally opened in the central square, and in 1975, a full two decades after the foundation stone had been laid, general facilities for the new town area were finally constructed. The original idea of an extensive 'culture park' linking the old and new towns, however, was dropped in the later 1970s in favour of memorials to the 'Red Army fallen' and the 'Victims of Fascism', alongside new housing estates, a school and some shops. Finally, some three decades late, a glass structure with seating for 820 people was opened as a 'House of Culture'.

The utopian visions for new towns – which, it may be noted, were not unique to the GDR but shared by many capitalist states at this time (the early example of Welwyn Garden City in Britain, for example, followed by Basildon and Milton Keynes) – were thus not entirely realised. But the socialist new towns of the GDR did differ in significant respects from the old, and from their counterparts in the capitalist West. For one thing, the construction of new Christian churches was not part of the socialist design, assisting processes of secularisation by omission. For another, new towns in the GDR were generally remarkably homogeneous in terms of the occupations of inhabitants and their close relation with their places of work, which in turn very strongly affected the character of urban social life. So, for example, the location of new industries in the area around Frankfurt-an-der-Oder in Schwedt, Eisenhüttenstadt and Guben led to a large influx of workers from other areas (including migrant Polish workers from across the river).[32] Between 75 per cent and 83 per cent of the workers in these three towns worked in the massive, interrelated chemical combines of the area (the Chemiefaserkombinat in Guben, the EKO or Eisenhüttenkombinat Ost in Eisenhüttenstadt, and the PCK or Petrolchemisches Kombinat in Schwedt). With a high proportion of female workers, many of whom were 'commuters' (*Pendler*) working in a different location from their partners, particular attention was paid to the provision of adequate childcare facilities, good transport links, shops and health care facilities. The massive semi-conductor plant (Halbleiterpflaume) in Frankfurt-an-der-Oder dominated the social, organisational and political life of the area: it had close connections with local schools and cultural centres (partnership and twinning arrangements); it organised sports teams and competitions; and its workers were nominated to the local town council, played a significant role in local parties and mass organisations and served as chairs of residents' committees. Similarly, the EKO dominated the whole cultural and social life of its town. There is no doubt that a new form of society rooted in both the demands and the support provisions of the workplace developed in these socialist new towns; and although it was not always entirely the form of socialist society originally envisaged, there is much evidence to suggest that perhaps a majority of residents in particularly those areas far from Western borders developed ways of living that were both meaningful and satisfying to them without closing their eyes entirely to the associated disadvantages of GDR conditions.

Meanwhile, in certain areas of older city centres, other sorts of very localised community were developing that were not entirely of the sort officially envisioned or desired. In Berlin's Prenzlauer Berg, for example, a form of retreatist, semi drop-out subculture of dissident artists and poets developed; similar though internationally less renowned subcultural currents were evident in other cities in the later 1970s and '80s, including Leipzig and Dresden. In part, disaffected individuals were seeking a degree of self-expression and self-fulfilment in alternative lifestyles; in part, new forms of communal living were merely an attempt to make the best of the often appalling housing conditions.

Finally, it is worth raising to attention the likely regional distribution of political discontent in 1989 and the related roots in social history. The weekly Monday demonstrations in Leipzig and comparable, if at the time less renowned demonstrations in Dresden, Schwerin and elsewhere, have rightly been the subject of major historical attention. What has received very much less attention is the relative lack of political activity in the autumn of 1989 in other areas, such as Cottbus and Eisenhüttenstadt. Residents of these areas – at least those that chose to remain once the opportunity to leave for the West had been available for more than a decade – spoke of the ways in which they and their friends, relatives and colleagues almost 'slept through' the revolutionary autumn.[33] The differential regional distribution of 'social peace' and discontent would be well worthy of further investigation.

Regional disparities in a centralised state

During the lifetime of the GDR, the percentage of the population living in cities with over 100,000 inhabitants barely rose, from one fifth to just over a quarter (20.7 per cent in 1950, rising to 25.9 per cent in 1985 and 27.1 per cent in 1989).[34] Extraordinarily by Western European standards, in the 1980s a similar figure of just under a quarter of the total East German population – a little over 23 per cent – still lived in tiny hamlets and scattered rural communities with less than 2,000 inhabitants, where the physical appearance changed very little from the 1920s right through to the '80s, giving much of rural East Germany an extraordinarily old-fashioned air as far as Westerners were concerned. Like a film set viewed from afar, in many areas one could for decades pretend that one was looking at Germany in the 1920s.

But appearances are deceptive. These general continuities in terms of statistics disguised massive changes in the structure of industry and agriculture, significant movements of population within the GDR, and even more significant differences in the social composition and atmosphere of different areas.

Towards and just after the end of the war, millions of people were on the move: evacuees returning to search for their former homes in the ruins of bombed-out cities; prisoners of war returning from incarceration; and refugees fleeing from the advance of the Red Army in the eastern territories, or 'expellees' forced out by the resettlement and redrawing of post-war borders. Estimates suggest that a total of somewhere between 11 and 18 million people left their former homelands in Eastern Europe in this massive migration westwards.[35] While many treated the Soviet zone as merely a staging post on their way further west to the areas that became the Federal Republic, millions remained in what was to become the GDR. In some areas, such as the previously relatively sparsely populated rural expanses of the northern province of Mecklenberg, the social landscape was permanently altered by this influx.

The expropriation of industry and agricultural estates, and the subsequent central planning of economic development had a major impact on the social geography of the GDR. In 1952, with the abolition of the *Länder* (federal states) a totally new administrative structure introduced new regional disparities.[36] Fifteen new *Bezirke* (regions or 'counties') were created, which were in turn made up of smaller *Kreise* ('districts') and *Gemeinden* (local communities or – to use anachronistic religious language – 'parishes'). The capital, East Berlin, was always advantaged over other areas of the GDR, as were cities such as Leipzig, host to international trade fairs. Towns that were key administrative or industrial centres were advantaged in terms of investment in housing and infrastructure, as well as supplies of food and consumer goods, over other towns and villages. New towns were constructed, producing concentrations of population in areas of new industry in previously sparsely populated rural areas. There was a relatively high proportion of 'mono-structural regions' concentrating on one form of production to the virtual exclusion of other types of economic activity.[37] Thus there could be extraordinarily rapid growth and investment in some areas because of administrative or industrial importance while other areas – particularly city centres and tenement buildings in residential districts of older towns – suffered from massive neglect.

Regional disparities in the GDR, while never entirely disappearing, thus changed markedly in character over the course of four decades. This is all the more surprising given a lengthy historical background of strong regional identities – rooted in centuries of decentralised patterns of political authority and cultural attachment – within the German lands.[38] Disparities between sparsely populated rural areas and the older areas of traditional handicrafts and industry were augmented and in part overlain by new disparities between the areas of massive expansion – with the growth of new urban centres and commuter towns – and areas of relative neglect. New industrial towns with a predominantly blue-collar manual working-class population, or a high proportion of 'peasant-worker' migrants, were very different socially from areas with a more settled population, and those with a more highly educated workforce and institutions of further and higher education. Changes in the organisation and methods of agricultural production led to new relationships between people and the land that they farmed, with the dissolution of the close ties between 'blood and soil' that Hitler had sought to foster, and the emergence of a new breed of educated agricultural specialists. Extensive brown-coal mining in lignite-rich areas, particularly in the 1980s after the USSR withdrew significant volumes of oil supplies to the GDR, led to the literal undermining and effective destruction of large numbers of villages in affected areas. Intensive development of certain areas of industry, associated with massive under-investment in health and safety measures, exacerbated inequalities in environmental pollution, with the worst affected areas concentrated in the Halle, Leipzig and Cottbus regions.

Regional disparities in access to scarce goods were to some extent overcome by travel – for example, regular forays across country in pursuit of spare parts or desired consumer items, or shopping trips to Berlin. But travel by highly subsidised public transport, despite being remarkably cheap, was time-consuming and arduous. Private car ownership only expanded in the course of the 1970s and '80s, which clearly made a difference to those households fortunate enough to be in possession of a fully functioning car (not always the case); but, with the exception of the transit autobahns in part maintained by Western money, and the autobahns of strategic (and potential military) importance to the regime, the state of the roads, generally pock-marked by potholes and often still cobbled, rendered car journeys a rather slow and inconvenient means of travel. Lack of telephones – the largest saturation was to be found in East Berlin – meant that many friendships were local or maintained by letter-writing and periodic face-to-face contacts.

Overall, it is true, a degree of homogenisation can be discerned, formed partly out of increased labour migration, but even more through negotiation of common institutional structures and economic constraints within very limited political boundaries. Within this common wider framework, there nevertheless remained striking regional and cultural variations. Thus, while much of the landscape may have looked to the casual visitor – and particularly to the tourist strenuously evading the polluted air and dispirited atmosphere of major industrial centres – little changed from the 1920s and '30s, the character and experience of the lived environment changed considerably with the development of the new East German society. This was even more true, eventually, of the less easily visible, but equally important, social and institutional environment: the network of institutions and practices within and through which East Germans came to lead their lives.

Chapter Four

Citizens at play: Leisure

To read '1989' backwards into the whole of the previous forty years, or focus concentration primarily on official aims and institutions, is to paint only a partial, and hence a distorted, picture. In part, the story is clearly one of good intentions subverted by economic shortcomings: thus the housing problem was never satisfactorily resolved, and indeed, despite numerical successes on paper, over time the physical realities appeared ever more dilapidated. But at the same time, life in the GDR was about far more than decrepit physical circumstances or a constraining political framework. It is extraordinary just how much of East Germans' lives were lived outside of formal political institutions or official organisations. The greater part of the leisure time of most people was spent not in political gatherings or at organised meetings, but with friends and family. 'Recreation' meant not only participation in the offerings of the mass organisations, but also talking, walking, playing games, swimming, playing or listening to music, drinking beer or watching television. Leisure in the GDR for the vast majority of the population was far more 'normal' than studies of official organisations on the one hand, or oppositional subcultures on the other, would suggest when taken without this wider context .

Of course life was lived within a context of social, political and economic pressures and constraints. But where is it not? The conditions, constraints and points of tension and conflict in the GDR were of a different order and character from those in capitalist democracies; but a concentration on official pressures and the institutional framework alone does not give a complete picture of how life was lived and experienced for most of the people, most of the time. For many East Germans, *Freizeitgestaltung* meant precisely that: an active shaping of one's free time. And ironically, the development of consumer socialism served to sustain and enhance the tendencies towards the ever more individualistic pursuit of personal goals for 'private happiness': a narrowing down of focus onto home and garden, car ownership and television, rather than the grand task of 'building socialism'.

In short: leisure activities could readily be politicised, and the voluntary use of leisure time could on occasion hit politically neuralgic points, but there was also a great deal going on between these two poles.

'Free time'

The SED was of course concerned to organise leisure time and harness the spare energies of people to fruitful pursuits. The official conception of leisure time was that it played a different role in capitalism and communism. In capitalist countries, leisure supposedly fulfilled the function of therapy from the exhaustion of work; but in socialism, leisure should, on the official view, serve the development of talents, capacities, creativity, health and physical well-being.[1] Operating, too, on the communist version of the Calvinist principle that 'Satan finds work for idle hands to do', certain sections of the leadership of the SED were somewhat fearful of the potential threat of the 'class enemy' in the form of subversive Western influences, particularly in the area of youth culture, if leisure time was not strictly controlled. Thus, in addition to making available a wide range of state-sponsored activities, a close eye was kept on what people actually did in their remaining free time – from the time of its foundation in 1966, the Leipzig Central Institute for Youth Research (Zentralinstitut für Jugendforschung, or ZIJ) was particularly active in this connection. Nevertheless, despite political interest in leisure activities, ZIJ publications by the 1980s provide a remarkably relaxed approach to the character of leisure and the importance of voluntary activities and personal enjoyment of leisure time.[2] Articles on television, discos, fashion, lifestyle issues and personal relationships jostle for space alongside entries on art, sport, learning and the organised activities available in state youth clubs; much of the advice from ZIJ experts (for example, on healthy eating and the dangers of smoking) could as easily have been given in any equivalent Western publication of the 1980s. It is, of course, difficult for the historian to tap into activities that do not show up either in the success stories of political, state and mass organisations or in the records of authorities concerned with dissident, 'criminal' or politically undesirable behaviour. But there is nevertheless a substantial amount of evidence, from both the ZIJ research and a range of other sources, for the relative 'normality' of everyday life and leisure in East Germany for most people most of the time.

The unconstrained experience of childhood free time was relatively untouched by the heavy hand of the state, except in so far as that impinged on the availability and energy levels of parents. Young people engaged in all manner of initiatives and pursued cultural, musical and other interests often almost regardless of the state youth organisations' official offerings and interventions. Adults socialised and drank with family, friends and neighbours, although often also in the context of factory-based gatherings and outings. Over time, even with the growth and stabilisation of state-run organisations, there was arguably an increasing 'individualisation' in the sphere of leisure, with ever-larger numbers of people having access to private motorised transport (motorbikes, cars) and individual sources of entertainment (radios, television). Leisure was of course flavoured by GDR circumstances: but it was not all a matter of either official indoctrination and control, or subcultural subversion and dissent.

A wonderful insight into children's experiences of family life and leisure in the early 1960s is, for example, given in a collection of children's essays from 1964.[3] Apart from the essays written under the title 'How would I like my parents to be?', 81 copies of which were collected and retained, there is a further analysis of the original total of 576 essays, including those written in response to the questions 'How I spent last weekend' (referring to the weekends of 29 February–1 March 1964, and 7–8 March 1964) and 'How I would like to spend the weekend'. The ages of the essay writers ranged from 10 eight year olds at one end to one seventeen year old at the other; about two thirds (381) were aged between ten and twelve. Nearly 90 per cent of the 292 boys and 284 girls spent the weekend 'alone, with brothers and sisters, or with friends'. Rather more than half of them (301) watched television, 95 visited a cinema, 75 of them read, and 58 went for a walk; 108 played in their own room, and 176 played outdoors. Only a small minority listened to radio (27), played sport (23), watched a sporting event (29), or went roller-skating (25) or cycling (7). There were seven who confessed to playing with dolls, and four who went to church. A mere two went to an organised event at a Jugendklubhaus (youth club centre). This startling figure – less than 0.5 per cent – should perhaps help to put the state organisation of leisure activities, at least in the early 1960s, into some perspective.

The 81 essays about the ideal parents reveal for the most part a very similar picture, in somewhat more detail.[4] Many children mention that they have to spend a lot of time looking after their young siblings and that their parents do not have the time or energy to do much by way of recreational activity with them. The pressure on most of the parents, and their sheer exhaustion at the end of the day, comes through in many of the essays. So too, however, does a conception of 'normal' leisure activities, which must have formed at least a part of the children's real experience, if not in their view a sufficient part, for them to write about with such enthusiasm. There is much mention of the small pleasures and pains of life: being allowed to buy sweets on a shopping trip to the nearest town, wanting to have more pocket money, to be sworn at less, to have *Bratwurst* and *Kartoffelsalat* (sausages and potato salad) for dinner. Most of the children write that they would like to spend more time with their parents: just talking, going swimming in summer, playing badminton and table-tennis, going for walks or to 'take photographs' in the woods on Sunday afternoons (photography receives a remarkable number of mentions), playing popular card and board games (Rommi, Skat, 'Mensch, ärgere Dich nicht', Mühle and Dame are all favourites) or watching television together. Some yearn for family outings to the Baltic Sea, or the possibility of going to a holiday camp for a week. Although the strains on the parents of long working hours and having to attend evening meetings are repeatedly palpable in these essays, the overwhelming sense is that the conception of leisure time is not so very different from that of many youngsters in Western Europe in the early 1960s, or indeed in the early twenty-first century, although the technology and material conditions forty years later (computer games, CDs, DVDs, fast foods and steamy leisure pools) are very different from the board games, potato salad and lake swimming of the early 1960s.

Available leisure time increased in the later 1960s, in part due to the introduction of a shorter working week in 1967, and, for agricultural workers, to the re-organisation of agricultural work in collective farms such that farming was no longer a seven-days-a-week year-round occupation. There was at the same time a growth in ownership of radios and television sets in the 1960s, allowing increasing numbers of East Germans the chance of greater access to Western news channels and the Western popular culture of the 1960s (on which more in a moment). The potential dangers of these developments prompted greater official interest in the character and implications of leisure time.

Surveys by the ZIJ from the later 1960s onwards confirm the picture of the ways in which most people's free time continued to be spent outside of official activities and organised channels. A confidential report in 1968 by the ZIJ on free time and youth, based on an intensive survey of 350 young people in the small town of Grimma (population 17,000), used a combination of time-budget diaries, interviews and questionnaires. The researchers found that far and away the largest proportion of leisure time was spent on 'socialising' (*Geselligkeit*), housework or gardening, and watching television. Only minimal time was devoted to 'community work' or activities within an institutional framework.[5] Friendship groups were extremely important for these young people, and the report noted that the FDJ had 'up till now barely any influence on these groups'.[6] Most young people spent the bulk of their free time 'often or very often' with close friends, or with their parents; only 6 per cent of those questioned spent their time 'often' with their FDJ group, and a miserable 1 per cent spent their time 'very often' with their FDJ group (presumably this 1 per cent included all the functionaries).[7] Yet 84 per cent of those questioned claimed to be members of the FDJ.[8] In 1971, the ZIJ once again found that 'informal leisure groups ... [are] a very typical and normal form of communication among young people ... that possess great significance for personality development'.[9] Between 90 per cent and 100 per cent of young people by this time had access to radio and/or television, and only 7 per cent of fourteen- to nineteen-year-olds did not watch or listen to Western media.[10] A study in November 1979 confirmed once again that the top leisure pursuit, at 92 per cent, was 'spending time with friends, acquaintances, partners'; a somewhat unspecified 'recreation and relaxation' came a close second at 81 per cent, followed by 'travel and tourism' at 70 per cent and 'fashion' at 65 per cent.

Even these apparently informal and innocuous leisure pursuits could of course have political implications. From fears of the subversive influence of Levis blue jeans, symbol of the US, to apocalyptic reactions to long hairstyles for boys, fashions in appearance were inevitably at certain times highly controversial political issues. It might in passing be noted that this in itself is nothing new in human societies: styles in self-presentation are always key aspects of cultural and political stratification, identity claims and role-playing. But perhaps few governments have taken the outward appearance, particularly of youth, quite so seriously as did that of the GDR.

In the course of the 1960s, male hair length and androgynous or provocative clothing styles among females aroused fears among certain SED functionaries and older members of the wider East German population about the collapse of morality and the end of civilisation as they knew it, in a manner not dissimilar from generational responses to youth styles in Western societies at the time. Ulbricht had already given the moral lead from the top with his 'Ten Commandments for the New Socialist Person' of 10 July 1958, including in ninth place the commandment to live 'in a clean and decent manner and respect your family'; his moral concerns were repeated frequently in the 1960s, as for example in an impromptu interjection in a Central Committee discussion of the draft Youth Law in 1963, when Ulbricht threw in a critical comment about 'female teachers who go into schools wearing make-up and short skirts etc., giving the children this example' (one wonders what lay behind the 'etc.').[11] Briefly, from 1963 to 1965, there was a moment of greater apparent toleration.[12] But in the later 1960s, in a new phase of repression of popular youth culture, extraordinary measures were taken not merely to criticise the 'layabout' or 'drop-out' hairstyle (*Gammler-Haarschnitt*) of boys and the 'dirty and disorderly clothing styles' common to both boys and girls (allegedly providing clear evidence of the 'influence of the capitalist way of life'), but even on occasion actively to arrest young people on the streets and take them for a compulsory haircut.[13]

Fashion only ceased to be a major arena of generational and political conflict in the course of the 1970s. As a report of the ZIJ put it in 1979, by which time blue jeans were no longer the mark of the Western devil but had indeed been domesticated and produced in socialist colours (at least metaphorically, for they were still made of blue denim): 'It took the authority of the Party and its General Secretary to make it clear that the length of hair and the tightness of trousers are not sufficient indicators of political attitude and societal involvement.'[14]

More importantly in the present context, it is worth underlining the fact that the vast majority of young people, aged between their mid-teens and mid-twenties, were barely involved in activities arousing significant political attention, let alone oppositional or confrontational behaviour. And by the later 1970s a significant minority were also participants in activities central to the functioning of the regime (or knew where their future prospects lay): 34 per cent were engaged in some form of further political education, a quarter (24 per cent) were by now actively involved in the FDJ, and one in ten (11 per cent) in some form of societal activity in their residential area or in the National Front.[15] Percentages are not very different among the 1,800 young adults (mostly at work, but including 330 apprentices) surveyed by the ZIJ in a study of October 1984. Just over one third (35 per cent) participated in some kind of further political education, and around a quarter (26 per cent and 24 per cent respectively) participated in organised and non-organised sporting activities. Only 7 per cent participated in some form of organised 'cultural-artistic' activity (singing groups or bands, theatre, film or photography).[16] At the other end of the spectrum, it is worth remembering that an arguably even smaller minority were involved in what were seen as potentially subversive youth subcultures, from the 'young hooligans' (*Halbstarken*) and rock 'n' roll fans of the 1950s to the punks of the '80s, attracting a great deal of attention from the authorities at the time (as well as later academics), as we shall see in a moment.

As in any Western state, unofficial leisure activities varied according to the size and character of the local community, with notable differences between urban and rural areas. Although in the 1960s village life had been viewed as a merely 'transitional' phenomenon (an *Übergangserscheinung*), by the mid-1980s the policy was to stabilise life within villages and seek to prevent further rural–urban migration. An important element in this strategy was to ensure that those living in small communities were able to enjoy their leisure time. A report by Kurt Krambach and colleagues is remarkably straightforward in its commentary on this question.[17] According to Krambach and his 'authors' collective', those engaged in manual labour in agriculture have distinctive leisure needs, including a lot of rest and relaxation, reliance on consumer goods and sources of entertainment within the home (radio, television, newspapers and books), and the facilities for socialising. Although the possibility of membership of the various mass organisations receives a mention, the far lengthier discussion of the need for simple 'time out' with family, house, garden and pets, for occasional replenishment of social as well as physical needs in *Gasthäuser* (local pubs, restaurants and hostelries), and the desirability of making communal facilities available for young people to hold dances, are rightly recognised as being higher up most people's agendas for spending what leisure hours remained after the rhythms and demands of rural life have been met.

The official view in this report by Krambach and his colleagues is remarkably factual and informative. Nevertheless, it does tend to paint a somewhat idealistic picture of how life in small communities ought to be. Other sources suggest that life was not always experienced in quite this essentially picture-book manner of a harmonious community or *Gemeinschaft*. Both lack of adequate facilities for different activities and conflicts of interest between different age groups and subcultures played a part. A study by the ZIJ in 1979 found that while young people in rural areas had more than two hours a day leisure time, few were satisfied with their leisure opportunities. Their favourite pastimes were watching television, listening to music and going to discotheques and dances; very few were in any way active in cultural or artistic pursuits, and young women appeared to spend much of their 'free time' on housework duties.[18] A 1980 study of commuters from small communities in rural areas into larger towns during the 1970s found that such *Pendler* had very little leisure time in any event, particularly young women with children. Over 75 per cent of small communities had nearly a third of their residents commuting out elsewhere to work, and in 15 per cent of communities as many as three quarters of the residents actually had to travel a significant distance to work in a larger town, so this was no negligible proportion of the overall population of the GDR that found there was indeed precious little leisure time left after the work shift, travel and essential household duties had all been accomplished. Nor were there many leisure facilities available in the small communities in which they were resident once they had returned.[19] Leisure activities in the so-called *Randdörfer* – the villages and small towns on the outskirts of larger urban areas – also appear by all accounts to have been increasingly dismal. As one letter of complaint put it in 1982:

> Since the restaurants and pubs are nearly all closed down, or as holiday facilities of factories elsewhere are only occasionally open to us, we hardly see each other any more. If on occasion somebody dies, then the survivors all come together again [for the funeral]. The cultural facilities of the villages for our young people are the bus stops. This is where private discos and other events take place ... Our grocery shops of the 1950s and 1960s have become alcohol sales outlets, which are not there to satisfy the needs of the population. If you want to buy daily necessities, you have to go to the local or district town.[20]

Many people thus had to make their own informal leisure activities inside the home or with circles of friends almost by default.

It has also to be remembered that patterns of what one wanted or expected from leisure time varied dramatically across different social groups. Reading some of the diaries, letters and fictional and autobiographical writings of the East German intelligentsia such as Christoph Hein, Günter de Bruyn, Christa Wolf, Brigitte Reimann or Maxie Wander, one gains a very different sense of the character of life and leisure in small communities in the GDR.[21] Much informal circulation of books, often hard to get hold of, and attendance at literary and cultural gatherings, seems to have lent interest to the leisure time of the intelligentsia and even among wider members of the community. Brigitte Reimann, for example, writes in a letter of March 1969 to Christa Wolf about readings she has given in small country villages:

> A lot of fun [*lustig*], above all out there, in villages off the beaten track, where the people are very nice, uninhibited, decent, read an amazing amount – in some communities of about 700 souls more than 350 people are regular readers in the library – tell stories, stuff a person who is too thin for this spot of land with huge quantities of cake, and where there are teachers who remind one of women in Russian films ... Then driving at night between fields which also, in the moonlight, have something Russian about them, wide open spaces ... instinctively you listen out for a wolf howling somewhere.[22]

Clearly a one-off visit for a reading by a Brigitte Reimann would be something rather out of the ordinary for these villagers. And not all rural and small-town East Germans were as interested in reading as those who turned out for a meeting with Reimann. Christa Wolf, in a letter of February 1969 to Reimann, commented rather more critically on the less intellectually inclined people she had met on her winter holiday: 'there are no happier people in the GDR than the semi-state manufacturers and their sons and daughters . . . Well-fed, contented people do not write or read.'[23] But the attempt to 'bring culture to the masses' through lending libraries and cultural activities was widespread and, in many respects, increasingly routine – not necessarily a heavily politicised activity, but increasingly just a part of 'normal' leisure, often organised by functionaries with no party affiliation.[24]

Life in certain urban areas could be just as dispiriting as that described for the deserted 'satellite villages' or *Randdörfer*. A revealing collection of photographs of the Grünau new-town area of Leipzig was taken by Harald Kirschner and students from the Hochschule für Graphik und Buchkunst Leipzig to accompany a report on the ways in which young people in a 'large socialist city' spend their free time.[25] These photographs depict dispirited-looking groups of young people standing around in the communal waste lands between the large housing blocks of a no longer quite so new-looking estate, with rubbish bins, washing lines, bicycles, Trabi cars, prams and a 'Waffle Shop' as the somewhat dismal background. It would take only a few changes of the accompanying material props (make of car, style of pram) to transpose these scenes to estates built in the 1960s and '70s in the more economically deprived areas of virtually any Western European city. Groups of friends could usually find somewhere to meet (though not in the generally small apartments), with variations depending on area. Older city centres were often totally dark and deserted at night, while there might be a youth club, discotheque, ice-cream parlour or even fair ground operating in one of the new town suburbs.

But in urban areas the range of possible cultural attractions was nevertheless greater than in the small towns and villages of the GDR. In 1983, the GDR had approximately half as many theatres as the Federal Republic (178 compared to 346), despite having well under a third of the population; production of highly subsidised German classic plays remained a priority in the land of Goethe and Schiller's Weimar, although more recent theatrical works were subject to the inevitable political considerations, as was the politically acutely relevant production of cabaret performances.[26] Theatre visits per thousand of the population in the 1950s ranged from 761 in 1950 to 986 in 1958.[27] Going to the cinema was an even more popular pastime: in the 1950s, visits to the cinema per thousand of the population ranged from 10,251 in 1950 to a high of 15,744 in 1958, declining again slightly to 12,823 in 1961.[28] It was estimated that as many as 26,000 East Germans crossed the inner-Berlin sector border every day in 1956–7 to see films in West Berlin's 'border theatres', where East Germans allegedly made up 90–100 per cent of the cinema audience on occasion.[29] This opportunity was, of course, no longer available after 1961; but cinema-going remained highly popular, particularly among young adults. In the early 1980s, young people made up on average 70 per cent of audiences, and the average age of film-goers was twenty-four years.[30] Individual films from the 'non-socialist foreign territories' were by far the most popular, with 'Flaming Inferno' topping the list as the favourite film of 17 per cent of 'normal' film-goers surveyed. The rather distinctive audiences for the film *Märkische Forschungen*, based on a novel by GDR author Günter de Bruyn, were somewhat older than the average cinema-going public, and nearly half belonged to the intelligentsia; the film topping this audience's list of favourites was the rather more highbrow *Mephisto*, and they also commented favourably on other 'artistic films' such as *One Flew over the Cuckoo's Nest*.[31] The GDR's own DEFA studios in Babelsberg, Potsdam, produced not only obvious propaganda pieces and light entertainment but also films of some considerable quality and often continuing interest, although under conditions of considerable political constraint and at times severe censorship, most notoriously, of course, the films banned in the Eleventh Plenum of 1965.[32]

More important on a day-to-day level for most people, particularly from the later 1960s onwards, were the offerings of television, including both GDR and Western channels (with the exception of people living in those areas, such as the far south-east of the country, known as the 'valley of the clueless', which was unable to receive Western broadcasts); and despite the clear politicisation, particularly of news channels, there were some genuinely popular East German television programmes, including the consumer-oriented programme 'PRISMA', and often good coverage of sport.[33] Other programmes, almost universally hated, nevertheless made their unintentional contribution to a GDR sense of collective identity and humour: the long-term television broadcaster and moderator of the programme *Der schwarze Kanal*, Karl-Eduard von Schnitzler, for example, was widely known only as 'Karl-Eduard von Schn ...' because it took precisely until this point in his name, announced at the start of his programme, to get up and turn the television off.

Not all magazines were as evidently and narrowly political as the daily SED newspaper, *Neues Deutschland*, although all were necessarily produced under licence and clearly subject to political conditions. But there was nevertheless more space for politically non-contentious light reading than one might think. Readers of the monthly periodical *Das Magazin* (licensed by the Ministry of Culture) in the 1960s and '70s, for example, were treated to translated extracts and short stories by international authors including Aldous Huxley, Ernest Hemingway and others; articles on topics ranging from the death of Marilyn Monroe, an illustrated travel guide to Sri Lanka and the shock occasioned when filmstars Gina Lollobrigida and Elizabeth Taylor turned up to the same film festival wearing an identical dress, to a discussion of the interpretation of dreams; guidance on what to do to stay young, how to look chic in knitwear ('chic mit Strick') and other helpful fashion advice, and whether single women for whom the biological clock is ticking should launch a 'mini-family' without a stable partner; as well as recipes, cartoons (even reprints from the *New Yorker*), brain-twisters and crossword puzzles, lonely-hearts-club listings, readers' letters, tips on Christmas preparations, periodic pictures of naked women and advertisements that look remarkably Western.[34] Younger readers might enjoy losing themselves in the comic *Mosaik*, produced monthly by the Verlag Neue Welt, under the auspices of the FDJ. This exciting series of adventures of the 'Abrafaxe', three plucky youngsters romping through societies around the world and civilisations over time, is perhaps best described as something of a cross between Asterix and Hergé's adventures of Tin-Tin.

Getting away from it all?

Leisure time most of the time was not about film or theatre visits, attending concerts or exhibitions, or getting involved in organised activities. But official policies and organisations were nevertheless for the vast majority of people an essential ingredient in leisure pursuits. Dependence on the state was particularly evident in relation to holidays.

Holidays, even when taken with the family, were not for most people the privately organised affairs characteristic of Western capitalist societies. Dependence on state institutions for holidays started very early on. In the early 1960s, at a time when the increasingly affluent West Germans were beginning to organise their individual dashes for the Mediterranean beaches in cars faster than the British could produce or afford, and mass travel agencies in Britain were springing up organising cheap flights and package holidays in the sun, East Germans were increasingly reliant on holidays and camps organised by state institutions. In 1961, for example, a total of 80,000 children were able to take holidays in camps for Young Pioneers; 750,000 people had holidays organised by their workplace; and nearly 1,500,000 young people, from children through to apprentices, participated in local holiday activities including swimming, walking and youth camps. At a more specialised level, the paramilitary Gesellschaft für Sport und Technik (Society for Sport and Technology, or GST) organised camps for 'Young Patriots'.[35] In total, 70 per cent of all schoolchildren and apprentices participated in some form of organised holiday provision.

Large though these numbers may sound, and however much the system was expanded and developed over the subsequent decades, there were never enough holiday places for those who wanted them, at the times that they wanted, or of a quality with which they were satisfied. Even by the Honecker period, with its greater emphasis on consumer satisfaction and looking after the well-being of workers, the files are full of related appeals and complaints: as many as 47 of the 177 *Eingaben* of 1974 to Fritz Rösel's office in the National Executive Committee of the FDGB related to problems about holidays, and this proportion was not untypical through the 1970s and early '80s.[36] Some concerns were simply about the sheer lack of availability of places.[37] Frau Luzie R., of Karl-Marx-Stadt, writing in 1986, was concerned that since her small enterprise with 60 employees had been submerged into a large enterprise with 3,200 workers, they had lost control of their own funds and holiday places, which had now gone into the general pot with only 72 beds in holiday homes available, on a fortnightly cycle, for the entire workforce; Frau R. bitterly pointed out that it took little mathematical ability to work out just how infrequently any given worker, along with their family dependants, would actually be able to come up with a holiday on this basis, particularly for those families with children of school age.[38] Although the claim was made that families with two or more children would be given priority, it was even officially conceded that there were too many such families for all of them to be able to take a holiday in the summer months.[39] There were also particular difficulties for other groups, such as holidays even out of season for pensioners who had not belonged to the FDGB.[40] There were problems of holiday places for diabetics needing a special diet and appropriate care facilities: as one letter put it, 'more should and must be done ... for putting into practice the policy de-cisions of our organisation and our state' with respect to the special needs of diabetics.[41]

Those lucky enough to gain a holiday at the right time and in the right place could still be critical, as in the case of the comprehensive critique of the state of the holiday home 'Fritz Weineck' in the otherwise idyllic mountain resort of Oberhof, on behalf of workers from four major industrial enterprises (the VEB Leuna-Werke 'Walter Ulbricht', the VEB Chemische Werke Buna, the CKB and the VEB Filmfabrik Wolfen). Very long waits and high prices for meals, a three-day menu leaving little choice for those with dietary restrictions, no places available for the special New Year's Eve celebrations, difficulties with obtaining tickets for other events despite long queuing, suspicions of 'under the counter' privileging of non-guests, all allegedly required investigation and rectification 'in the interests of our workers in the industrial zone of the Halle District, who daily, under difficult conditions, devote their energies to the fulfilment of our Plans and accomplish high achievements for the strengthening of our Republic'.[42] Frau Renate S., after working for her enterprise for VEB Herrenmode for sixteen years, was finally fortunate enough to be allotted what she thought would be the holiday of her dreams only to find that the expected 'bungalows' turned out to be camping with sanitary facilities that she deemed entirely inappropriate for a family with young twins: thus, 'on the basis of the most utterly primitive preconditions', the family felt obliged to abort their planned thirteen-day holiday and return home after only one night.[43] Others who did get a holiday in buildings of a more permanent character were critical of aspects such as the rain coming in, the heating not working, the poor food, the lack of a colour television, and the expensive wine that was the only one on offer, as in the case of Herr S., who had been used to better things: 'Since I was employed in the military organs of the state apparatus and in other societal organisations, I often took my holidays abroad or in homes belonging to the enterprises themselves'; this time, he had been to a general FDGB home in the Harz Mountains, and been far from impressed.[44]

This last case illustrates a more general point. People were to varying degrees dependent on the state, and received differential treatment and rewards according to their place and type of occupation and their perceived degree of need. Holidays also more broadly reflected and reinforced class distinctions, more so in the 1960s than in later years given the shifts in the character of class and occupation over this period. In 1966, a survey of 21,000 people living in 6,400 households representative of 90 per cent of the population (excluding only pensioners) found that, while three quarters (74 per cent) of the intelligentsia and two thirds (67 per cent) of the self-employed had taken a holiday that year, only just over half (54 per cent) of workers and employees and fewer than a quarter (24 per cent) of agricultural workers had been able to enjoy a holiday.[45] The vast majority (85 per cent) of these holidays were taken within the GDR, and only 15 per cent abroad. By the 1980s, as many as four fifths of the population (80 per cent) were able to go on at least some form of holiday, including by now many more agricultural workers, but still only one fifth (20 per cent) of holidays were taken outside the GDR, generally in the closely neighbouring Eastern Bloc countries.[46] Around 90 per cent of all holidays in the 1980s were organised by the trade union organisation (FDGB) and the state travel agency.[47] The state travel agency for foreign travel was used primarily by the intelligentsia and the few self-employed people, while young people were occasionally able to organise independent travel on very limited resources.[48] Attempts to make other informal arrangements, such as swapping of country retreats, could be subjected to administrative hassles such as difficulties in obtaining permission to put an advertisement in a local newspaper.[49]

While people were able to arrange unofficial visits to friends and relatives, state-subsidised organised holidays were very keenly sought after. The length of holidays in factory- and state-owned holiday centres was a maximum of thirteen days, and the accommodation was, as indicated, apparently not always of the highest quality. But while the tents, wood cabins and 'immobile homes' in campsite locations were not exactly the air-conditioned, five-star international hotels in exotic locations advertised in Western glossy brochures, they did afford large numbers of ordinary working people a real break in often pleasant surroundings with relatively fresh air and a variety of leisure facilities. Despite the criticisms splattered across the archival legacies of the GDR, it is highly likely that the vast majority of people who did not write in with complaints actually enjoyed the cheap, affordable facilities offered by the state. Certainly in the nostalgic views of many East Germans after unification, affordable holidays within the GDR or neighbouring socialist countries were remembered with pleasure, in contrast to the situation, at a time of high unemployment, when in principle they were free to travel anywhere in the world, but in practice did not have the money to leave their own home town.

Organised leisure

Similarly important for large numbers of people was state support of regular sporting and other recreational activities.

Sport was – like so much else – very much a two-edged sword in the GDR. On the one hand was a conception of sporting facilities for the wider population; on the other was the massive state support, particularly in the Honecker period, of elite sport as a means of gaining the GDR international recognition and fostering a sense of GDR pride as a result of Olympic sporting successes. The latter were considerably assisted, as it later turned out, not merely by the abuse of punishing training schedules and practices but also by extensive use of illegal drugs, which took away or put in doubt the significance of any successes in international competition. And the total lack of trainers' respect for honesty, legality and the rights of an individual over his or her own body led for many top sports-people who were the victims of the regime to very serious physical and mental consequences, including the effects of hormone treatment on the sexuality of high-performance athletes dependent on physical strength and muscularity, and early disability and invalid status in the case of some former gymnasts and dancers.[50]

The two aims – sport for the masses and international excellence – were, given the economic constraints, not entirely compatible. The early identification and fostering of sporting talent in order to produce the national sporting elite was a key goal for the regime, and resources were devoted accordingly. In 1989, the GDR boasted a total of 25 special schools for sport, which encompassed 989 classes, with an average of 10.2 pupils per class and a total student population of 10,053. This was far and away the largest sort of special school in the GDR (the next largest was for foreign languages, with 6,496 pupils, followed by special schools for those with scientific and technical ability at 2,790 pupils, and music at 1,683 pupils).[51] The figures on popular sporting facilities, however, indicate a much lower level of investment. In 1983, there were 886 swimming pools (compared to 3,400 in the Federal Republic) and 3,324,291 people belonged to a sports club (compared to 18,375,270 in the Federal Republic).[52] Even given the disparity in population sizes, with roughly three times as many residents in the West than in the East, the contrast is evident. The problem with raw data such as these is that they give no indication of the quality of the facilities, or indeed whether or not they were even open (many East German swimming pools were repeatedly closed 'for repairs'); and those that were open were often reserved for competitive training or special events.

But at a local level, active participation in, or enthusiastic support for, parochial sporting events was genuine and widespread. Organised sport was the province of the Deutscher Turn- und Sport-Verein (DTSB). Founded in 1957, this brought together 35 different sporting associations, with, by the later 1970s, close to 2,800,000 members, of whom over 2,000,000 were male. Football, fishing and gymnastics were the most popular associations. Although the DTSB was organised, like all mass organisations in the GDR, on the principle of 'democratic centralism', there is evidence to suggest that, by the later 1970s and '80s, the grass-roots functionaries of this organisation were genuinely representing the interests of local communities in attempts to improve facilities and supplies of equipment under worsening economic circumstances.[53] But participation in sporting activities was strongly encouraged by the regime and extended well beyond the membership of the DTSB. Children and young people were encouraged to participate in the periodic *Spartakiaden*, collective sporting contests named after the Roman gladiator Spartacus and designed to get young people involved in competitive sports. Joint campaigns of the DTSB, the FDGB and the FDJ also encouraged adults to engage in sport: thus, in 1980, it was estimated that nearly 5,000,000 East Germans participated in 28,500 sports festivals in factories, residential areas and villages.[54] Even allowing for a little light exaggeration, it is clear that many forms of recreational sport were genuinely popular. Over a third of a million people (340,000) seem to have taken part in the 'Table Tennis Tournament of the Thousands' (Tischtennistournier der Tausende), over 107,000 were involved in volleyball tournaments, and 1,800,000 young people took part in the heats and finals of the various sports included in the National Youth Festival of 1980.[55] Walking and rambling remained highly popular pastimes (as indeed they had been for a century or more), and the German Association for Rambling, Climbing and Orienteering of the GDR (the DWBO), one of the constituent groups of the DTSB, assisted with the production of paths and organised walks. The 'Join in, stay fit!' ('Mach mit – Bleib Fit!') campaign also seems to have attracted high participation rates, as did badminton, bowling and less energetic 'sports' such as chess. Encouragement to take up jogging was fostered under the motto 'Eile mit Meile' (very roughly, 'Make haste with mileage'), while encouragement for children to participate in sport came under the slightly less snappy title: 'For health, recreation, and the joy of life, for capacity to achieve and desire to achieve, for peace and socialism! Everyone do sport!' Organised sport appears not merely to have spawned a veritable avalanche of the classic GDR rhyming slogans, but also even to have permitted an unexpected and slightly inaccurate anglicism, more characteristic of West German language use: one document asserted that 'in some forms of sport more attention needs to be paid to Fairplay [sic]' ('In einigen Sportarten muß stärker auf das Fairplay geachtet werden').[56]

Widespread active participation in sport was increasingly fostered through the holiday and leisure facilities of the FDGB and through the workplace. Whole factories could, from 1980, be honoured with an award for 'exceptional achievements in leisure and recreational sport'; and the FDGB started a brigade competition 'Who can run the most miles?' ('Wer läuft die meisten Meilen?'). In 1982, as many as 3,300,000 East Germans were members of a sports club. Factories supported their own football teams, and heroes in other sporting endeavours appear to have been genuinely popular in their local neighbourhoods. The one team about which there seems to have been considerable ambivalence was the FC Dynamo, Erich Mielke's Stasi team (criticised even for having bought up in advance all the best seats for a particularly important football game).

The not-very-hidden agenda behind the policy of encouraging physical fitness – suggesting a degree of continuity with Nazi emphases – was betrayed in the slogan of the Sports' Awards Programme, 'Be prepared for work and for the defence of the homeland' ('Bereit zur Arbeit und zur Verteidigung der Heimat'). In some areas the paramilitary agenda was even more explicit in practical terms, with training in shooting and related activities. This was very explicitly the case with respect to the GST, with its superior facilities and programme of activities for young people. Acquiring a driving licence, sailing, gaining experience of flying or learning how to be an amateur radio ham were possible alongside learning how to shoot a moving target from a distance. More than four fifths of members of the GST in the mid-1980s, according to one survey, participated in paramilitary sports 'because it's fun' ('weil es mir

Spaß macht'); a mere 14 per cent gave the officially appropriate answer, 'because I would like to prepare myself for military service'.[57] It was notable that this survey was carried out in 'particularly strong GST branches'; and even in these nearly a quarter of the young people surveyed (and fully one third of the female members) confessed to being either religious or agnostic, with only 77 per cent giving the desired answer of being a committed atheist. GST members apparently also watched and listened to Western television and radio as much as to the GDR media.[58] Whatever the intended function, clearly the members were gaining some personal enjoyment from the facilities without completely buying into the associated worldview.

The larger significance of sport as a spectacle for the masses and a means of building collective pride in the achievements of the GDR was no more lost on the authorities in the GDR than it was in other later twentieth-century states. The significance of preparation for the Olympics was underlined already in a document presented to the Central Committee of the SED on 28 November 1962, in the run-up to the 1964 Summer Olympics: 'The political-ideological education of professional sportspeople and their successors is to be oriented towards the stronger development of a sense of socialist patriotism, a clear relationship with and open commitment to our workers' and peasants' state, and a firm link with the party of the working class among all sportspeople.'[59] These attempts were met with at least partial success. It is difficult to gauge accurately what the real responses of the citizens of the GDR were to sporting successes of their team representatives on the international sporting stage. The documents are so frequently full of apparently spurious positive comments that one probably has to discount at least some of the tidal wave of enthusiasm gushing from the pages of the reports on popular opinion (*Stimmungen und Meinungen*) with respect to national sporting successes. However, the reactions are so overwhelmingly positive, and there is a degree of naivety in the reporting that suggests perhaps a firmer bedrock of positive opinion lurking within the reports than is perhaps sometimes the case. Thus, for example, the report of 31 August 1972 (following the success of *Ostpolitik* and the international recognition of the GDR) claims that 'many citizens are filled with great joy, pride and satisfaction that for the first time a completely sovereign and independent GDR team, with full rights, is participating in the Summer Olympics'.[60] A week or so later, the report is if anything even more enthusiastic in tone:

> Among the overwhelming majority of our citizens there is enormous enthusiasm, recognition and high regard for the achievements to date of our sovereign Olympic team. Reports in the press, radio and television repeatedly unleash new joy and

satisfaction. Many citizens are extremely enthusiastic about the competitive spirit [*Kampfgeist*] of the sportspeople of our Republic.[61]

Perhaps the only slightly critical note sounded in these reports had to do with repeated questions about the limitations on travel permits and the restricted numbers who could actually attend as spectators. The enthusiasm about sporting successes does nevertheless seem to have been genuine; the contrast with the tone of the reports on the new border regulations of 1 September 1972, which did not appear to arouse any comparable positive reactions, is quite striking in the corresponding reports in this file. There were, however, some intimations that the enthusiasm for German sporting successes was not strictly limited to socialist compatriots, but had wider national resonance, as revealed for example in the following rather typical remark: 'Whether GDR or FRG, we keep our fingers crossed for all Germans, and we will be happy about all their victories.'

For those with more cerebral inclinations, there was a variety of avenues for the exploration and expression of cultural interests – all similarly geared to the ultimate purposes of the socialist state, but to varying degrees dependent on area. The Deutsch-sowjetische Freundschaftsgesellschaft (German-Soviet Friendship Society) was, with 5,500,000 members, the second largest mass organisation after the FDGB. This was perhaps the classic fig-leaf organisation. Its primary task was to bring a love of Soviet culture to the Germans, through films, cultural activities and learning the Russian language. It appears to have barely impinged on the lives of many members, who might have done little more than go to an occasional film viewing. It probably did, however, have some impact on East German cultural trends at the level of 'high culture'.[62]

A far broader remit was held by the Kulturbund (KB), or League of Culture, which was primarily targeted at intellectuals with 'discussion circles' and 'philosophical circles', through such organisations as Klubs der Intelligenz; but it also encompassed an extraordinary range of special-interest groups of less obviously intellectual character. These covered leisure pursuits across an amazing spectrum, from sailing, allotment gardening and small-animal breeding, to caving, bird-watching, the cultivation of roses and orchids, cacti and other succulents, 'aquarium friends', and those interested in esperanto or astronomy.[63] Some of these were almost entirely apolitical, serving their members' interests in terms of, for example, the production of specialist publications of little wider fascination, and on occasion assisting in sorting out neighbourhood disputes (as in the case of over-loud music or boisterous social events in allotment gardens, a favourite weekend excursion goal for hundreds of thousands of East Germans). In the later 1980s, a majority of GDR house-holds had an allotment or garden plot of some sort (producing no less than 98.9 per cent of the GDR's honey supplies, and 42,400,000 eggs each year); around 3,500,000 GDR citizens were in some way connected with the Verband der Kleingärtner, Siedler und Kleintierzüchter (Association of Small Gardeners, Settlers and Small Animal Breeders) and nearly 1,500,000 were full members of this in 1988.[64] Others were designed with more obviously political goals in mind. The Gesellschaft für Natur- und Umweltschutz (Society for the Protection of Nature and the Environment, or GNU), one of the small special interest groups under the wing of the Kulturbund, provides a perfect example of the flexibility of the East German system for incorporating and channelling the potentially more political activities and interests of its citizens. Once environmental pollution had become a serious concern in the 1980s, and unofficial movements in the penumbra of the Protestant Churches appeared to be linking this issue with those of peace and human rights, the SED saw the need to channel and contain environmentalist energies.[65]

The women's organisation, the DFD (Democratic German Women's League), combined both overtly political goals and the kinds of general activities found in Western voluntary women's organisations of the later twentieth century. It included in its membership an extraordinarily high percentage of women who did not belong to any political party. Here, arguably, the SED was at its least manipulative. The aims of the DFD were of course – as with all mass organisations and bloc parties – to 'reach the parts the party cannot reach'; and women were notoriously apolitical and hard to contain in any of the traditional communist organisations, appealing as these did primarily to the organised industrial male working class. The DFD therefore of course had as a primary function the task of trying to reach out to women and translate the SED's message into terms that would be more easily accessible on otherwise unreceptive ground. However, at the same time a reading of DFD documents suggests on the part of many DFD activists a genuinely emancipatory vision – and this in a curiously individualistic and humanistic sense. Efforts to get girls to think beyond 'work for a couple of years before getting a husband and a home and children' were not just parts of an attempt to tap a labour reserve at a time of scarcity of labour. There were repeated efforts to get young women to set their sights higher, to consider not only further training and the acquisition of qualifications, but also to work towards taking up positions of leadership and authority. Much of this appears to have been a genuine attempt to persuade women to realise their full human potential rather than internalising and reproducing received traditional roles.[66] Yet at the same time the reports are full of activities that would be familiar to anyone looking at Western women's organisations at much the same time: evenings spent in activities and discussions of matters of traditional interest to women whose primary focus remained that of the domestic sphere, such as cooking, needlework, fashion and issues to do with pregnancy and childcare.

A snapshot of the DFD compiled in April 1962, for example, reveals that of the 1,312,980 members by far the largest single occupational group (454,620) was that of housewives. They were followed by 'workers' (366,044) and 'employees' (*Angestellten*, 276,516).[67] Women working in collective farms made up 98,922 of the members and there were a further 17,895 agricultural workers not in LPGs (agricultural production co-operatives). Those working in educational positions numbered 45,211, and women employed in the health services totalled 26,893. A mere 6,962 women were classified as members of the 'intelligentsia'. How many of this cross-section of the East German population were really active members of the DFD is less easy to quantify. The report notes that older women preferred to attend meetings of the Volkssolidarität, and professional women preferred to attend meetings of the National Front because they could go along with their husbands; in addition to other drawbacks, housewives were apparently unwilling to attend 'because they are afraid that they would immediately have to take on a functionary role'.[68] But while DFD meetings at this time rarely attracted a turnout of more than 20 per cent of the membership (actually remarkably high in comparison with, say, Labour Party ward meetings in central London), there appear to have been higher turnouts in rural areas, particularly when little else was going on. If, however, there was competition from a village club or other meeting, even peasant women would shun the DFD for fear of being pressured into taking on a function.[69] A report of late 1962 reveals that women only selectively attended when the meeting might be on a topic of particular interest:

> Women and DFD groups were often initiators in forming choirs, amateur dramatics and Agit-prop-groups as well as other circles of artistic and cultural grass-roots activity. It turns out that a large proportion of women – above all also younger women – who do not otherwise participate in political events in their residential area can be brought to take an interest particularly in cultural events, cultural and sports circles, in practical courses for women and in interesting lectures of all kinds. The largest attendance figures are for those events that deal with literature, with readings from books or poetry, or which deal with problems of education, health, travel reports, household tips, cosmetics and fashion.[70]

In 1961, no fewer than 1,200,000 East German women appear to have attended events of this nature – as many as a fifth of the adult female population.

Similar selective enjoyment of at least a sampling of what state facilities and organisations had to offer – attending the intrinsically interesting, avoiding the overtly political, evading the risk of having to take on a functionary role – is evident across a very wide range of sources. It is particularly apparent in relation to youth activities, where the FDJ had a very clear political role, but where state facilities such as youth clubs were readily used by young people to their own ends and were not always under the control of the FDJ.[71]

Rethinking leisure in the GDR

Throughout the GDR's existence there was thus a constant interplay between a surprisingly wide range of grass-roots activities and initiatives, and state efforts to channel, harness, foster and control popular interests, always with an eye to the wider international context and the potential political implications of the seemingly apolitical.

As far as organised leisure was concerned, state organisations sought to offer a range of well-controlled activities to cater for different interests as well as providing channels for political influence and 'selection' of promising cadres. Beyond the age of about six, the coverage of the East German population by one or another mass organisation was more or less total. One would have to be an exceedingly rare individual never to have belonged to a single one of these organisations (arguably only an unusually religiously committed, unemployed person of extraordinary willpower, lack of leisure interests or ambitions, and remarkable capacity for survival as a loner in this most collectivised society). The importance of the system of mass organisations in the shaping and experience of East Germans' lives cannot be overestimated. But the nature of this influence is harder to define clearly.

The mass organisations of the GDR are generally represented as 'transmission belts' through which the SED's powers of control, surveillance and indoctrination could be exercised.[72] The mass organisations were, of course, in essence creatures of the SED; they were also intended to organise and influence people. It is often suggested that people joined these organisations because they could not withstand the 'pressure for conformity' or because certain social privileges and professional career chances were attached to such membership, as well as opportunities for leisure activities and travel. On some accounts, only a minority of members swallowed the 'political-ideological slogans' of the respective organisations at face value.[73] Such an interpretation makes it look as if there was simply a form of malevolent control, surveillance and indoctrination at work at one end of the equation; and a degree of largely enforced, unwilling conformity under pressure, or opportunistic pragmatism, at the other end combined with a possibly cynical enjoyment of the marginal pleasures that could be had while ignoring the ideological wrappings.

However, true as all this may be, there was a great deal more to it than that: the picture is a great deal more complex. For one thing, depending on the organisation, the character of those who constituted the 'representatives of the state' in the shape of functionaries in the mass organisations needs closer inspection. There was very often a genuine community of interests between the functionaries or power-holders in the organisation, particularly at the grass roots, and those ordinary members whose views they sought to represent. On some recent interpretations, there was not so much a process of the 'state drenching society' but rather one of 'society affecting the state' or 'societalisation of the state' (*Vergesellschaftung*; characteristically, this play with labels works better in German than English).[74] By the 1980s, functionaries were often becoming increasingly frustrated with central authorities at the failure to provide the means or material resources for members to pursue their interests as well as they would wish.

In addition, there were also often what may be termed 'cultural affinities' between what the state had to offer and what many ordinary members wanted; indeed, considerable efforts were expended in the attempt to ascertain and cater to widespread interests. There were serious attempts to attract people to attend particular organisations by putting on varied and supposedly attractive programmes of events, without which no wider influence could possibly be exerted. Good recreational, sporting and holiday facilities were genuinely in the interests not merely of those enjoying the immediate pleasures of leisure time and vacations, but also of an industrial state needing a fit and healthy workforce. And many of the ways in which people chose to spend their free time were in any event politically more or less irrelevant, or only relevant in a trivial sense.

The essential point here is to note that the mass organisations were therefore not simply or always experienced as (merely) coercive, but were for many people at one time or another enabling, and experienced as a provider of entertainment and facilitator of holidays, hobbies and interest groups. In some respects, the extraordinarily high degree of organisational channelling of social activities has a long history in Germany (one need only think of the plethora of such social organisations in Wilhelmine or Weimar Germany). The difference in the GDR was, of course, the fact that all were SED monopolies, without the richness of choice of pre-1933 Germany (Catholic, Protestant, SPD and other rambling, cycling, musical or reading associations, for example); and the SED had a strong political agenda, although with greater consequences in some contexts than others. But within this state-controlled organisational framework, large numbers of people were genuinely able to pursue certain leisure activities and follow their own interests, from fishing, singing and bee-keeping to cacti collection, pottery and cooking, particularly when these were not obviously of immediate political relevance. The concept of 'niche society' is therefore hardly apposite in this context.[75]

Finally, the vast majority of most people's free time was spent in ways that were neither actively fostered nor actively hindered by the state – except of course in so far as the faltering economy proved a brake on the development of many leisure possibilities for many people, not to mention the blindingly obvious fact of the Wall providing a rather serious visible obstacle to foreign travel (and rather more evident to the naked eye than the fact of limited financial means restricting the capacity for foreign travel of the poor in capitalist societies). The history of specific clashes, conflicts and confrontations between state repressive organs and certain social subgroups has been better served than the history of the 'silent majority' who had little interest in what were quite widely seen as the subversive activities and 'scenes' of various minority subcultures, and this not merely on the part of SED apparatchiks and hardliners. It is, of course, crucial to write the histories of those groups whose interests were suppressed, silenced, distorted, by SED and Stasi repression; but it is important also, in the interests of a more comprehensive understanding of the complexities of East German society, to recognise that arguably the majority of the population were not participants in these subcultural currents. For many, the sense that they had been able to lead 'perfectly ordinary lives' was grounded in part in experiences of pleasure in leisure, aided by an often supportive environment at least at local level, if not at all times, by an inefficient regime that could not always deliver the goods in this area as in so many others.

Chapter Five

Matters of life and death

The situation with respect to health and illness immediately after the war was dire. Those who had survived the war within Germany were shattered physically and mentally by their experiences of shortages, bombing raids, injuries and illnesses, as well as of living among ruins and daily confronting death. Massive numbers of adult males had been killed in the Second World War, and many others returned from the front or from internment suffering from severe war wounds and near-starvation. 'Dealing with the past' was for many Germans at this time not so much a matter of confronting the crimes committed by the Nazis, as one of sheer physical survival.

Famine was a serious problem. The post-war rationing system provided, as many bitterly complained, too little to survive, too much to die: in the winter of 1945, the basic rations amounted to around 750 to 1,200 calories on average per day, about half of what an average adult person needs.[1] Brigitte Reimann, in a letter of August 1947 to a schoolfriend in the West, describes graphically how hungry and thin everyone was, so much so that, when her brother fell badly and grazed his abdomen, each sticking-out rib had a separate graze.[2] People who had work often complained, even as late as 1949, that what they were given to eat even on relatively privileged ration cards was insufficient and that having to work prevented them from going on 'hamstering' expeditions for food in the countryside.[3] Much energy was devoted to considerations of how to increase the food to which one was entitled, leading, for example, to unseemly squabbles about who qualified for what sort of 'victim of Nazi persecution' status, if this was to bring additional rations.[4]

Hunger had an impact on lowered resistance and heightened susceptibility to disease. In 1945–6 there were 129,000 cases of typhus, from which 16,830 died; 56,780 cases of infectious tuberculosis, from which 23,600 people died; 149,580 cases of diptheria, as well as thousands of cases of other serious infectious diseases.[5] Sexually transmitted diseases were also rife. About one in three Berlin women appears to have been raped by Soviet troops in 1945.[6] There were very high rates of illegitimate births: in the years 1935 to 1939, the rate of illegitimate babies per hundred live births had hovered fairly steadily around 7.7 or 7.8; immediately after the war the number of illegitimate births doubled, with a rate of 19.4 per hundred live births in 1945 and 15.3 per hundred in 1947.[7] This led to a relaxation of the anti-abortion laws in many areas, allowing a 'social indication', in addition to the medical and 'eugenic' reasons, as a legitimate ground for abortion.[8] At the same time, only about one quarter (8,500) of the pre-war total of 33,000 hospital beds in Berlin were still available for use after the war; and only 2,400 doctors were still active out of the 6,500 formerly in practice.[9] In this situation, public health was a major priority. Apart from ensuring that there were as many functioning doctors as possible – with only very light denazification of the highly nazified medical profession – there was a radical overhaul of the structure, philosophy and character of the health service.[10]

Over the following forty years, the GDR did indeed make many strides, particularly in amending the structure of provision; yet, like so much else that was dismantled after the collapse of the GDR, its health service – and the health of the people that it was supposed to have served – has been the subject of considerable criticism and controversy. Arguably, the shortcomings lay less in the system in principle than in the wider economic and social context that so fundamentally affected the lives and deaths of people in the GDR. The health care of the citizens of the GDR was characterised by a curious combination of economically constrained compassion on the one hand, and callous disregard for some of the human consequences of economic policies on the other. The physical lives of East Germans were similarly affected by circumstances and work pressures that were outside of the control of most citizens, as well as a variety of more or less voluntary habits, customs and lifestyles relevant to health. Here, as everywhere, the very physical existence of people – their births, the pattern of their illnesses, the manner and timing of their deaths – cannot be disentangled from the circumstances in which they lived.

Philosophy and institutional structure

For all the political specificities of a communist state, health care in the GDR built on long-standing German traditions of connecting the health of the individual with the health of the 'people' or wider community (*Volksgesundheit*).[11] The notion of the collective health and welfare of the community was one that had deep roots in Germany, and which had been given an added racial twist under Nazism, with its conceptions of the 'healthy folk community' (*Volksgemeinschaft*). Thus, the collective emphases of health care in the communist successor state, the GDR, almost paradoxically resonated with previous traditions of a very different ideological colour. Collective elements (for example, in relation to vaccination of the population) prioritised the health of the whole community over the principle of individual choice with which Western liberal traditions were more concerned. These general emphases were, however, combined with specifically communist features and traditions.

Overlying the older German notions of the healthy folk community was the newer Soviet ideal of health as a prerequisite for enhanced productivity, or *Leistungsfähigkeit* (actually not so very different from the Nazi programme of 'Strength through Joy', or *Kraft durch Freude*, connecting physical fitness with work productivity, although excluding members of 'inferior races' or forced labourers). This was evidenced in the GDR, for example, in the propaganda for the Hennecke Bewegung ('Hennecke movement', emulating the heroic worker Adolf Hennecke, who had performed mighty feats over-producing and breaking all previously existing work records and who in one day allegedly produced 387 per cent of expected output). This movement extolled the virtues of the activists who could produce more per shift, work longer and harder than ordinary mortals, and whom good GDR citizens were urged to emulate. Furthermore, the health of a population is commonly taken to be an indicator of quality of life. The United Nations, for example, uses life-expectancy figures as a good proxy for standard of living, perhaps a better indicator of overall quality of life (including psychological well-being) than statistics such as average per capita income. The GDR was concerned to show that its statistics bore comparison with, or even excelled, those of Western capitalist states. Thus, for example, the SED was particularly proud of statistics showing markedly declining infant mortality rates in the 1970s and '80s.

This complex of traditions led to a peculiar mixture in the GDR. There was a genuine desire, for pragmatic reasons to do with economic productivity and international prestige as well as more humanitarian compassion, to provide an excellent health system; at the same time, there were serious constraints on the realisation of this objective, as in all health systems in the later twentieth century, arising from a wide range of factors, including an ageing population, ever more expensive new technology, heightened expectations, and coping with the effects of environmentally polluting economic exploitation carried out without adequate regard for the human costs. The GDR documents on health are thus replete with both genuine humanitarian concern, and the frustration borne of a realisation that goals can never be fully achieved (and in some cases, barely even pursued); they betray, too, an awareness that patterns of ill-health are closely related to social conditions, and that in a context of continuing economic constraints and political stresses, the health of different sections of the population may often be compromised.

The institutional network of health provision to cure or care for those with temporary or permanent illnesses and physical and mental disabilities was a comprehensive one, but one that suffered increasingly from totally inadequately resourcing.

There were major changes made to the financing and institutional system of health care. The old private practices belonging to individual doctors were largely phased out and replaced by a 'collectivised' health-care system.[12] This included specialist and general hospitals serving the region (*Bezirk*) or the district (*Kreis*), 'polyclinics' or large multi-purpose health-care centres in the *Kreis*, outpatient departments (*Ambulatorien*), and work-based health centres with varying degrees of provision from fully staffed polyclinic to small health clinic, sometimes with specialist facilities for particular types of work. Polyclinics had teams of doctors and nurses and were able to provide a variety of quite specialist diagnostic and outpatient services; typically, they would consist of a minimum of five doctors' surgeries, one dental surgery, one chemist and one physiotherapy clinic. They in turn were linked in with the local general hospital and the more specialised hospitals at *Kreis* and *Bezirk* levels. In theory, while the notion of free choice of a personal doctor or family GP was abolished in the 1950s, it was envisaged that one doctor within any given practice would be able to oversee his or her patients right through any course of treatment, from polyclinic through to general or specialist hospital. In practice, the system did not work entirely as desired, and in 1971 the concept of free choice of doctor was again recognised.

In the course of the 1970s and '80s, the numbers of doctors and dentists steadily rose. In 1970, there were 27,255 doctors, just under 160 per hundred thousand inhabitants; by 1989 the number had risen to 40,143 doctors, or nearly 242 per hundred thousand inhabitants. The figures for dentists were 7,349 or 43 per hundred thousand inhabitants in 1970, and 12,011 or just over 72 per hundred thousand inhabitants in 1989.[13] The underlying idea was, however, effective prevention and treatment of disease with a minimum of hospitalisation required. Thus, while numbers of doctors were increased, the numbers of hospitals and available beds were reduced. The total number of hospitals was cut from 626 in 1970 to 539 in 1989, including a reduction of 61 state hospitals (from 523 to 462), the closure of 7 hospitals run by religious bodies (from 82 to 75) and 19 run by other bodies (from 21 to 2). However, since the latter were on the whole extremely small, the loss of beds was a tiny percentage of the total number (accounting for a mere 2.5 per cent or only 689 of the 26,720 beds lost in the wider drop from 190,025 to 163,305).[14] A snapshot picture in the Honecker period reveals that in 1977 there was a total of 571 hospitals with around 180,000 beds, averaging out at 107.5 beds per hundred thousand inhabitants (compared to 111.8 beds per hundred thousand inhabitants of West Germany at the time).[15] Just over 10 per cent of beds were in clinics attached to universities or other research institutes.

Outside the state system, there was an extensive supplementary system of care homes for children, orphans, those with physical or mental special needs and the elderly run by charitable bodies. The Churches in particular had a long tradition of caring for the weak, the sick and the terminally ill, and were proud of their unstinting service (putting the needs of patients above clock-watching for the end of a shift, for example). Their institutions had the further advantage, very often, of receiving financial support, equipment and assistance with spare parts and maintenance from West German Churches. In 1950, there were as many as 299 hospitals in private hands, with a total of 19,429 beds. By 1977, the number of such hospitals had fallen to a mere 89; yet those hospitals that still remained in the hands of religious communities or 'other private owners' managed to offer 12,997 beds, indicating that it was the smallest 210, together accounting for only 6,432 beds, that had closed. The privately run institutions also included eight of the GDR's 44 psychiatric institutions. Despite the decline in overall numbers of such institutions, they played a significant role in the GDR's health-care system.

In terms simply of quantity, therefore, the GDR health-care system was by any standards comprehensive. The same could not necessarily be said of quality. The propaganda for the GDR sought to represent conditions in their institutions in rather rosy terms.[16] After the collapse of the GDR, the former Deputy Director of the Health Department of the ZK of the SED, Dr Christian Münter, admitted as much.[17] His spirited defence of the GDR health system and structure in principle is followed by a detailed and increasingly gloomy list of the shortcomings in practice. These included: apart from heart pacemakers, most modern medical equipment (such as ultrasound and computerised diagnostic machines) had to be imported, which was economically impossible in the quantities required; only around 30 per cent of the equipment needed for heart surgery and transplantations were available in 1988; in the 1980s, the full range of drugs and medicines was never available, with around ten to thirty medicaments always lacking (with striking regional variations); and the 'liquidation' of the last small- and medium-sized production units in the early 1970s had proved 'catastrophic' for the production of medical disposables such as rubber gloves, syringes and scalpels.

The problems did not stop at the state of the buildings and medical supplies. In April 1974, for example, the district hospital in Pasewalk (where, incidentally, Hitler had recovered from the temporary blindness caused by a mustard-gas attack in the trenches in 1918, and where he first received news of the Armistice and Germany's defeat in the First World War), was complaining of too much bureaucracy and paperwork, insufficient personnel, and shortages of essential supplies in just about everything. The exasperated report writer complained of the overload of reports that had to be written for the district leadership (*Kreisleitung*), the Party leadership (*Parteileitung*), the trade union leadership (*Gewerkschaftsleitung*), the district medical director (*Kreisarzt*); the impossibility of carrying out appropriate FDJ work in the children's section of the hospital because of a basic shortage of doctors and nurses; and the total inadequacy of supplies in everything from medicine to gloves, thermometers, food trolleys, lead aprons and even toilet paper, which seems to be the final straw for the despairing report writer at the end of a long list of concerns: 'So for example, through the lack of toilet paper, the following situation has developed: the toilet paper which was borrowed from a shop [in private hands] cannot be given back, because we have still not had a delivery. But those who have lent us the toilet paper are now getting impatient and demanding its return.'[18] This is a 'situation' that does not bear too literal an imagination.

It has been rightly pointed out that after 1990 criticisms of the East German health system confused questions of structure with questions of the technical and material level of the facilities.[19] It can be argued that the factory- and locality-based system of all-purpose polyclinics and health centres, with their wide preventive and social as well as diagnostic and curative remits, was in principle a potentially very effective system. It has even been suggested that, up to the mid-1970s, the GDR health system performed at levels comparable with Western health systems, looking very roughly at 'value for money' in terms of improvements in indices such as life expectancy and perinatal mortality rates.[20] Its performance worsened in the 1980s, when there were growing discrepancies in performance between the health systems of Western societies and the GDR. These discrepancies were in part due to the declining performance of the East German economy, and political decisions on prioritisation of investment, starving the health system of the funding it needed for up-to-date technical equipment, refurbishment of buildings and adequate supplies of medication. Thus it was not so much the health system as such, but rather the inadequate funding and the wider economic problems of the GDR that led to the dismal condition of East German health facilities and health care by the end of the 1980s.

In a condition of shortages and patchy provision, principles of rationing – determining, often rather brutally, who can be cured or adequately cared for based on some notion of whose lives are 'worth more' than others – become ever more significant. In many capitalist societies principles of collective provision (such as the British National Health Service) or a variety of private insurance schemes seek to even out the horrendous inequalities of purely individualistic health chances based on personal ability to pay. In the GDR, the vision of equality for all was rudely tempered by prioritisation of politically committed and productive citizens.

Health rationing by power, privilege and (re)productivity

Most resources were devoted to those who held positions of power, and those whose economic or biological productivity (that is, their work, or their capacity for reproduction) was of crucial importance to the economy. It helped, too, that the category of 'reproduction' did not need much by way of resources. Other groups – the mentally and physically disabled, the elderly – found themselves in a far worse position with respect to allocation of scarce resources.

With the exceptions of a few large new regional hospitals, and the renovation of the famous Berlin Charité Hospital, the general state of hospital buildings was bad. Only in the special hospital in Berlin-Buch for members of the political elite, a few university clinics, and sometimes in specialised hospitals like the one designated for uranium workers in Wismut, were the conditions anywhere near approaching desirable.[21] The priorities were the medical care of political and military cadres, and – to a somewhat lesser extent – other privileged groups, such as veterans of the 'anti-fascist struggle'. According to a 1979 report the justification for this was, despite continuing 'political-ideological and other problems', becoming clearer to health workers: 'It is ever better understood that the medical and social care of comrades who were persecuted by the Nazis is in part aimed at the preservation and transmission of the rich experiences which they gained in the class struggle, which proves its worth in all sorts of ways in our socialist everyday life, above all in the communist education of young people.'[22]

Those who were part of the wider socialist elite, including members of the cultural intelligentsia, often also had the requisite renown or personal connections that could help them achieve a move to a hospital offering better care and facilities; but the tensions with those less well placed to achieve better health care were evident. Thus Maxie Wander, following her (as it turned out, very botched) mastectomy in September 1976, and unhappy with her treatment even in the relatively good facilities of the Charité Hospital in Berlin, commented in her diary entry of 28 September: 'I risk talking of the possibility of having my further treatment in Buch. The women [other patients in her ward] say to me, that would be a breach of trust, you can't do that! But I can't hold out here any longer, without a doctor that one can relate to. Everything is anonymous here, the patients and the doctor. An atmosphere in which I can't get well!'[23] Brigitte Reimann, also suffering from breast cancer, managed, with considerable support from her friend Christa Wolf, to receive favourable treatment in Buch, and even a single room in which she was able to do some writing.[24] In following the personal accounts by these two writers of their experiences of diagnosis, treatment and the eventual realisation that cancer had progressed to a stage where it was incurable, it becomes clear just how tardily and inadequately they were dealt with, and how little the medical personnel saw fit to tell them about their diagnoses, even when under the very best medical care the GDR had to offer. Brigitte Reimann only discovered quite by accident that her condition was malignant, when her husband and close friends had known this for months. But in this context it is worth remembering that diagnostic techniques, programmes of treatment, standards of care and practices relating to patients' rights to information have developed greatly over recent decades, and the experience in many Western societies might in some respects not have been greatly dissimilar in the 1960s and early '70s.

There were questions not merely of differential treatment for different groups, but also of conflicting priorities with respect to different areas of health. Regional and district hospitals may have been somewhat lacking in advanced technical equipment as well as the more minor supplies mentioned above, but they concentrated a great deal of effort on effective low-technology care. Massive concern with the health of pregnant women and investment in maternity facilities in fact led to considerable improvements in the sphere of maternity care. A major priority in a state that was constantly in danger of a declining population – whether in flight to the West before 1961, or non-reproduction of indigenous families in the 1960s and '70s – was that of perinatal and infant mortality. Effective prenatal and antenatal care resulted in a lowering of infant mortality rates and of maternal deaths in childbirth, statistics of which the GDR was proud. In 1950, as many as 20.62 mothers died per ten thousand live births in West Germany, and 20.57 in the GDR; in 1959 the figures had dropped to 10.83 in the West, and 9.86 in the East.[25] This was a notable success story for the GDR at a time of considerable official optimism about 'overtaking the West', and continued improvements in this area could be notched up as further success stories over subsequent decades. Perinatal mortality figures showed that 13.1 infants per thousand live births died in

1978, declining steadily to 11.4 infants per thousand live births in 1982.[26] Enormous efforts were also devoted to encouraging women to have more children, and with some success.[27] By 1985, the East German birth rate was 13.7 per thousand, compared to 9.6 per thousand in West Germany.[28] This was, given the political sensitivity and high visibility of the birth rate, perhaps a peculiarly well-bestowed area. It was easy to represent the increased birth rate as a measure not merely of health but also of a sense of security in the present and faith in a rosy future, in which women had the institutional support to combine motherhood and a career.

But economic constraints and staffing difficulties radically reduced the quality of state-run institutions for less obviously productive members of society: the young, the permanently disabled and the elderly.

A report written in the early 1980s on the problems of childcare and children's homes, for example, lists a veritable litany of problems, including the relatively high illness rates among young children; the lack of adequately motivated and qualified staff; the relatively high turnover of staff; the lack of adequate medical care (with the exception of immunisation visits); poor facilities, including simple lack of sufficient beds for children to sleep on; and lack of adequate outdoor play space.[29]

If the care of the young and the temporarily sick left much to be desired in some areas, then the care of the permanently physically or mentally disabled was arguably even more deficient. Again, it has to be stressed that the principles were highly laudable, in total contrast to the Nazi policies of 'euthanasia' (actually murder) for the 'unproductive' or those who were allegedly 'burdens on the state'. The GDR was committed to high ideals in this area.[30] There was additional support for families with disabled children up to the age of eighteen, and mothers of the most severely affected children were entitled to shorter working weeks without loss of income and higher holiday entitlements. There was what seemed on paper to be a fairly extensive network of provision (7,600 pre-school places, 470 special schools for those of school age, 16 for the deaf and partially deaf, eight for the blind and partially visually impaired, 29 for physically disabled and those with psychiatric and neurological problems), alongside additional programmes in day-care centres or hospitals for those not capable of schooling.[31] But the economic shortcomings meant, here as so often in the GDR, dilapidated buildings, inadequate facilities and equipment, great regional variations in provision (particularly poor in rural areas), and a shortage in numbers of care places. Given the high proportion of families in which both parents worked and neither could allot much time to the care of a disabled child, if more appropriate places were not available, children with physical or learning difficulties were frequently put into homes for the elderly and left to vegetate in bed without appropriate therapeutic treatment or medical care.[32] Children with learning difficulties had no right to an education appropriate to their abilities and needs if they were not able to attend a normal school or undertake a normal apprenticeship; yet their placement in special schools kept them isolated from the wider community and the 'lowest common denominator' form of 'education' offered in these institutions often was not appropriate to the wide range of needs of particular individuals. Often children who were simply somewhat slow and possibly disruptive were pulled out of normal schools, classified under an all-purpose heading as 'debilitated' (*debil*) and sent to special schools where the label would soon become a self-fulfilling prophecy.[33]

The conditions of psychiatric institutions were terrible: most of these were over a hundred years old, and had not been properly maintained since 1933. Psychiatric problems tended in any event to be a taboo topic, along with alcoholism, suicide, child abuse and work-related ill-health. Nor were there even sufficient numbers of places in such institutions. The lack of care facilities for young adults with psychiatric problems often meant that they too were placed in care homes for the elderly, where the staff were not trained to deal with the kinds of challenges posed by these patients. A 1985 study of 575 psychiatric cases in 14 homes for the elderly in one *Bezirk* revealed that only three homes had trained medical supervision; yet 80 per cent of patients received regular psychopharmacological medication, although only 43 per cent had been examined by appropriately trained staff prior to admission and prescription. Indeed, 10 per cent showed such severe disturbances that they should in no way have been in residential homes for the elderly.[34] Although standards varied enormously across institutions, and individual examples of dedicated personal care could always be found, the general picture is one of a simply overstretched system with inadequate resources. The result was that the mentally and physically disabled, of all ages, were effectively marginalised, removed from visibility and, while cared for in sheer physical terms, both categorised and treated in very much less than optimal ways.

As in other industrial societies with rising life expectancy, there was a growing problem of care for the elderly, with too few institutional care places for the increasing proportions of the surviving elderly in the GDR (and with some of these places taken up, as indicated, by younger citizens with a range of other problems). For all the public propaganda about 'senior citizens', there were disturbing reports about the real state of care for the elderly. Again, high ideals could not always be realised in practice because of the failure of an ailing economy to meet the needs of elderly people, who constituted a steadily growing proportion of the total population.[35] The renovation or construction of sheltered accommodation for the elderly was as problematic as the housing situation more generally; dedicated homes were often too few in number, and far from acceptable in their physical condition. Even in 1971 the Parliamentary Committee for Citizens' Petitions recognised the question of institutional care for the elderly as an issue increasingly present in *Eingaben*: women (note the assumption that it would be females who took primary responsibility for care of elderly relatives) could no longer devote the time, if they also had paid employment outside the home; and housing was a growing problem, with new flats too small for extended families.[36]

A related question was that of how to deal with issues surrounding dying and death in a secular, indeed militantly atheist, society. The Hygiene Director of the Bezirk Neubrandenburg wrote an exceedingly thoughtful report in 1982 on the ways in which both birth and death were being increasingly removed from people's direct experience, affecting the ways in which they experienced the passage of generations and the meaning of life.[37] Death in the state-run hospitals and old people's homes was an ever more lonely and meaningless event. Dying people were given little beyond the most basic care: there was a lack of clarity about what should be done to prepare them for death, and despite good intentions it was more or less impossible to accommodate visits of relatives, many of whom did not even wish to think about the impending death. Relatives were neither given the facilities to stay with the dying person, to give them company in their final days and hours; nor were they encouraged to pay their last respects to the body after death. As the Director of Hygiene put it:

> Repression of this duty of care, like repression of any thought of the experience of dying, is becoming ever more common among all social strata, and is quite evidently becoming more apparent among the rising generation . . . It is the exception that close relatives stand by to give psychological strength, relief and companionship on the last and hardest part of the way. It is the horrifying rule that in old people's homes the dying are left alone.[38]

Corpses were kept in almost 'indescribably' dreadful conditions: the situation was not such that bodies could remain in a fit state to be viewed for more than a few hours after death, and the mortuary rooms were simply 'shattering' (*niederschmetternd*) in atmosphere. The reporter feared an 'impoverishment in the sense of an ever more superficial attitude to life'. And even this state official could not help making a comparison with religious institutions that put the latter in a more favourable light:

In the reports from those districts in our *Bezirk* in which the continued existence of confessional institutions allows a comparison to be made, it is quite clear that in state institutions generally there is nothing in quality equivalent to, let alone better than, what remains of the religious care of souls as a humanitarian, active approach to the consciously dying, as well as the guidance of relatives and the preservation of the dignity of the dead.[39]

It is worth underlining the fact, however, that humanitarian concerns appear to have been widely prevalent among practitioners in the East German health service, irrespective of the difficult conditions in which many of them struggled.

Lifestyle patterns, ill-health and consumer socialism

Prevention is always better than cure. The GDR shared with many Western capitalist states a growing concern with individual responsibility for the maintenance and building of health. Lifestyle 'choices' were thus a matter of increasing concern, although some aspects of lifestyle can hardly be seen as a matter of individual choice and others were strongly influenced by prevalent social and cultural expectations and widespread ingrained habits. Roughly speaking, one can say that the patterns of ill-health in the GDR that were related to consumption issues developed from those of shortages to those of over-consumption, though filtered through the particular circumstances of the GDR, and this even in a society that is not normally considered under the conceptual heading of consumer excesses. Smoking and excessive consumption of alcohol eventually took the place of the hunger and epidemic diseases prevalent in the immediate post-war period.

In the course of the 1950s, the major existential crises of the early post-war period were overcome. From the 1960s onwards, despite periodic acute seasonal shortages and lack of wide choice (with notable shortages, such as potatoes in 1970–1, coffee in the late 1970s and early '80s, and exotic fruits at all times) East Germans had plenty to eat in terms of quantity, with incomes more than adequate to purchase any amount of the subsidised foodstuffs. By the 1980s, as surveys carried out by the ZIJ reveal, a younger generation with no memory of the post-war hunger was more concerned with cultural trends and peer-group pressures to conform to the thin body images currently fashionable across advanced industrial societies (not merely, it seems, in the decadent capitalist West). Breakfast was irregular, with many pupils skipping it (perhaps scarcely surprising, given the early start to the school day and the standard break for a 'second breakfast'), and many girls claimed that they were trying to lose weight even when, as the report pointed out, they had no need to.[40] In a context of widespread fulfilment of basic needs, consumption of less healthy 'luxury items' such as cigarettes and alcohol – particularly the combination of beer and spirits – continually rose.

Cigarette smoking rose dramatically in the GDR in the first decade or so after the war. From being a highly desired luxury and an unofficial unit of currency in the black market of the immediate post-war years, the cigarette was soon transformed into the familiar symbol of glamour, elegance, adulthood and sexuality popularised in innumerable films in America and Europe in the 1950s and '60s. As part of wider efforts to present the regime as catering for the needs of the people and enhancing individual consumer choice, cigarette vending machines were soon widely installed across the GDR in the 1950s. Consumption rose rapidly, with 70 per cent of men and 20 per cent of women being regular smokers by the early 1960s. At the same time, deaths from lung cancer rose by a staggering 300 per cent: from 1,761 in 1947 to 5,225 in 1961.[41] The link between nicotine and cancer, or between smoking and ill-health more generally, became a matter of considerable public debate in the GDR in the 1960s, with women in particular – who were predominantly non-smokers – vociferously objecting to exposure to passive smoking in the workplace.[42] The failure to resolve essentially irresolvable issues – the question of how to balance the conflicting priorities of public health, individual freedom of choice and toleration of differences when the behaviour of some impacted on the well-being of others – resulted, however, more in rhetorical fudges rather than in any effective means of dealing with ever-increasing cigarette consumption.

In many respects, the history of debates on smoking in the GDR parallels that in other Western societies, with a shifting focus of discussion away from chronic diseases to an emphasis on individual responsibility for lifestyle choices. But there were interesting differences. In the UK, smoking was transformed from a cross-class activity in the 1960s to a highly class-specific addiction by the 1990s.[43] While 51 per cent of men and 41 per cent of women smoked in 1974 – spread relatively evenly across all levels of society – the percentages had fallen by 1998 to 28 per cent of men and 26 per cent of women, with the greatest reductions in the higher social groups. By the end of the twentieth century, unskilled male manual workers in the UK were three times as likely to smoke as their professional male counterparts; and only 13 per cent of women in higher social classes smoked, compared to 35 per cent in lower social groups, while a remarkably high and sustained figure of 60 per cent of single mothers continued to smoke. Smoking in the UK was thus closely related to social deprivation and stressful family circumstances. In the

GDR, smoking appears to have remained an accepted way of life across a far wider spectrum of society, although still clearly related to lower social class and single-parent families. Nevertheless, smoking was virtually endemic among the political classes and functionaries as well as ordinary workers in the GDR.

Perhaps oddly, given the different political systems, public discussion of the effects of passive smoking appears to have developed later in the West (on the public agenda in the US in the 1970s, and the UK in the 1980s) than in the GDR, where this was already a focus of concern in the 1960s. A cynic might suggest that perhaps the interests of tobacco manufacturers in profits, and governments in tax revenues, played a greater role in capitalist societies in seeking to downplay for as long as possible the hard facts – known in principle, if not in detail, from the path-breaking study of Austin Bradford Hill and Richard Doll published in 1950 – of the link between smoking and cancer, and that one in every two regular smokers dies prematurely from a smoking-related disease; and that the extra short-term burdens on national health services might well be cancelled out by the occupational and state pensions that need not be paid out and the care places for the elderly that would not be taken up by the prematurely deceased. Yet for all the public discussion of smoking in the GDR from as early as the 1960s, it remained endemic across large proportions of the population.

The ZIJ found that in the 1980s habits of smoking increased steadily with age: while under a quarter of children (23 per cent) in Class 7 smoked, nearly two thirds (59 per cent) did so by Class 10.[44] Smoking correlated directly with poor grades in school: while none of those whose grade average was 'very good' in Class 9 were daily smokers, just over a third (34 per cent) of those whose grade averages were 'unsatisfactory' smoked regularly. Smoking also correlated with social class: the proportion of regular smokers among children of fathers with further or higher education was less than half that among children whose fathers were unskilled or manual labourers. According to another study, while younger children found it difficult to obtain cigarettes and often had to bribe older friends or siblings to buy them for them, ease of purchase for those over the age of sixteen rapidly increased consumption levels. By the age of sixteen 94.3 per cent of boys and 75.3 per cent of girls had tried at least one cigarette.[45] While in Class 8 the smoking of specific brands was linked to status and prestige in the peer group, by Classes 9 and 10 for many children it had simply become a habit to smoke; and two thirds of children came from homes where other family members were regular smokers. Non-smoking children were more likely to come from two-parent families.[46] Thus, by the time they were adults, the majority of East Germans viewed smoking as a perfectly normal part of daily life. The GDR collapsed too early for it to participate in the momentum towards banning smoking in public places that increasingly swept across Western societies from the 1980s onwards.

The growing problem of alcoholism in the GDR was by contrast politically more contentious, and was only subjected to any degree of even muted public debate in the later 1970s and '80s. Alcohol was an integral part of virtually any East German social gathering or indeed domestic table. Even in the tiny flats inhabited by many East Germans, a nicely arranged sitting corner with an eating table, complete with white lace-fringed table cloth and vase of flowers, would be reserved for family meals and wider social gatherings; on many occasions, including most evenings after work, this would soon be liberally decorated further by a growing cluster of beer bottles and an ashtray brimming with stubs. Beer-drinking in quantity was for most people simply a normal part of life. But, over time, there were more serious consequences for an increasing proportion of the population. Alcoholism among adults was a rising problem in the GDR, with repercussions not only – eventually – for the overburdened health service, but also for economic productivity and for rates of criminality. Yet officially it was impossible to concede that rising rates of alcoholism could in any way be related to social conditions in the GDR. By the 1980s it was eventually viewed, first, as a form of criminal behaviour producing actions that required punishment, and then, increasingly, as a form of individual mental illness that could only be tackled by effective incarceration of the affected individual in a psychiatric institution. Thus recognition of a growing problem was accompanied by resistance to more searching exploration of wider social causes beyond the individual's own 'culpability' or 'disease'.

In 1960, East Germans consumed, on average, 3.2 litres of still and sparkling wine, 79.5 litres of beer, and 3.5 litres of spirits per person. These levels of consumption rose steadily in the following two decades. In 1982 the corresponding averages were 9.7 litres of wine (thus consumption had tripled), 147 litres of beer (nearly double previous levels), and 12.7 litres of high-alcohol spirits (of which consumption had thus nearly quadrupled). Considering that these figures were averaged out over the population as a whole, the real levels of consumption among those adults who actually consumed the alcohol were clearly very much higher. While West Germans consumed more than twice as much wine per head as East Germans, and about the same quantities of beer, their consumption of spirits was only half that of the East Germans.[47]

A 31-page report from 1967 documented in tones of what can only be described as rising hysteria the growing problem of alcoholism in the GDR, which was held to be closely related to criminality.[48] According to this report, between 1960 and 1966 the proportion of crimes committed under the influence of alcohol had risen from under a quarter (22.8 per cent) to nearly one third (31.8 per cent). For robbery, the proportion was over one half; for damage to persons and property, around two thirds; but far and away the highest percentages of crimes committed under the influence of drink were against the state, with 78 per cent for the (highly regime-specific) offence of 'slandering the state' ('Staatsverleumdungen') and 85 per cent for the (similarly regime-specific) offence of 'resisting state force' ('Widerstand gegen die Staatsgewalt').[49] There was allegedly a strong correlation between excessive consumption of alcohol and failure to complete school education, failure to embark on or complete some form of occupational training, and to become 'work-shy' ('Arbeitsbummelenten'), characterised by being 'unstable, morally weak, Rowdys or attention-seeking' ('labil, moralisch haltlos, Rowdys oder geltungssüchtig') with family relationships that were 'disturbed or broken' ('gestört oder zerrüttet').[50] The percentage of divorces that were held to be related to alcohol abuse rose from 13 per cent in 1964 to 20 per cent in 1965.[51] Among other supposed causes, excessive drinking was allegedly related to the 'ideological diversionary influences of the Class Enemy and Western decadence' as well as 'inadequate social order, discipline and control'.[52] Yet despite this moral outrage, alcohol consumption continued to rise in the GDR.

Sauferei, or constant drinking, was endemic even during working hours, and posed a serious problem for morale and work productivity in some areas. The particularly inebriating combination of beer and cheap spirits (*Schnaps*) was integral to the lifestyle and macho image of the East German adult male working class. Drinking was not a matter merely for after-hours relaxation or special occasions, but a regular part of daily working life and sign of masculinity. As such, on-the-job drinking inevitably had side effects. Any cursory reading of the 'special incident' reports ('besondere Vorkommnisse') of the trade union organisation, the FDGB, will immediately confirm the impression that alcohol was a constant concomitant of factory disputes and unofficial strikes.[53] Such drunkenness very often also affected the trade union officials themselves.[54] The quality or quantity of beer at work could even itself be the cause of an unofficial strike.[55]

Landolf Scherzer describes graphically the conditions in the VEB Kettenfabrik in Barchfeld, Kreis Bad Salzungen. It was only when a decision was taken to cut the premiums of those *Meister* who allowed workers in their departments to consume excessive alcohol during working hours that any serious effort was made to get men out of the pubs and back to work.[56] In general, it appears that levels of drinking that were perceived as 'normal' and even to some extent fostered in male workplace culture tipped over into being seen as 'excessive' if the consumption of alcohol by one member of the work brigade adversely affected productivity (and related awards and bonuses) of the whole work collective. Once drinking had crossed a certain threshold and the individual affected was almost totally incapable of a 'normal life', the person might become classified as an *Assi* or 'asocial': a 'work-shy', poorly dressed, poorly fed and permanently inebriated non-productive member of society. In this extreme case, the individual was likely to be stigmatised by the majority of 'normal' members of society, among whom there was a definite conception of when the boundaries of the acceptable had been transgressed. Public opinion was therefore very often in support of the efforts of the state authorities, in the form of the police, in trying to 'deal with' such asocials: common practices of stigmatisation and exclusion were shared across surprisingly large numbers of the population, showing certain lines of continuity with perceptions of alcoholism and 'asocial behaviour' during the Third Reich.

In the 1980s, the files of the Ministry of Health reveal that the rising proportion of alcoholics among psychiatric patients, and the rising numbers in ordinary hospitals with alcohol-related physical problems such as liver disease, constituted a cause for mounting official concern, as was the medical cost of caring for patients after accidents in which alcohol was a major factor. Given that alcohol is in effect a socially permissible drug, the question of what constituted excessive alcohol consumption and alcohol abuse was something of a problem for the authorities. Yet one authority raised the question of whether the 'enjoyment of four beers within four hours' was really excessive.[57] Such sentiments were widely echoed among the general population: as one letter from the DFD Leipzig District Executive Committee put it, reporting on a discussion with a distressed woman with an alcohol problem whose husband had insisted on divorce, the woman claimed that 'she just drank like anyone else' ('getrunken hat sie wie jeder andere Mensch auch').[58] And the percentage of alcoholics among psychiatric patients was in itself at least in part a consequence of the way in which alcoholism was conceptualised and dealt with in the GDR.

In 1987, it was estimated that the rather staggering proportion of 12 per cent – roughly one in eight – of the population suffered from some form of alcoholism.[59] However, this was still a relatively taboo topic, and alcoholism was seen primarily as a problem of individual punishable behaviour rather than as an illness. If alcohol abuse was related to 'criminal asociability' it tended to be the punishable offences related to alcohol consumption, rather than the alcoholism as such, that were addressed. In the 1980s, alcoholism came increasingly to be seen as a form of illness, but as one which – in the GDR, the best of all possible worlds – could not possibly have social roots and was therefore, in the nature of an individual mental illness, to be treated by a period in a psychiatric institution. In both cases, the effects were much the same: a period of total abstinence while in institutional care would be followed by a return to the outside world where abstinence was seen as totally abnormal, and former drinking habits would be rapidly resumed. Very few dared explicitly to raise the question of why so many East Germans felt the need to 'anaesthetise the strain', or queried whether the policy of subsidies embodied in the 'Unity of Economic and Social Policy' should really embrace alcohol as well as essential foodstuffs, rents, transport and children's clothing. Yet the increasing consumption of alcohol was ultimately an imperfect barometer or proxy indicator of mounting problems in an economy of excess of income over available consumer goods, in a context of constant frustration and increasingly visible strains.

Alcohol consumption among schoolchildren also increased and became more routine with age: a 1984 survey found that, while 71 per cent of pupils in Class 7 never drank alcoholic drinks, the proportion had shrunk to little over a quarter (26 per cent) by Class 10.[60] Those who did drink alcohol fell into three groups of roughly equal size: those who drank once or twice a month, those who drank once a week, and those who drank several times a week. There were, by the early 1980s, far higher frequencies of drinking among pupils than there had been in a comparable survey undertaken ten years earlier, and the report-writers indicated concern about rising alcohol consumption and alcohol abuse among youngsters.[61] A report produced later in the same year repeated the concerns about alcoholism, food intake and smoking, but interestingly neither here nor elsewhere was there mention of any drug abuse, a rising problem among Western teenagers at the time.[62] One former member of the East German 'alternative' music scene of the 1960s, such as it was (or was able to be, given the circumstances), mentions using sleeping pills instead of soft or hard drugs to achieve a 'drug effect'.

Suicide, although it claimed far smaller numbers, was even more problematic. Taking the decision that killing oneself is the only 'way out' is clearly not only a private affair, although there is of course a bedrock of individual cases arising from acute personal stress, illness or mental instability: it is also, beyond this, a very sensitive barometer of social conditions and unbearable pressures. As Émile Durkheim argued long ago, this apparently deeply personal, individual act is strongly influenced by the conditions in which people live: the suicide rate as a whole is a social rather than purely individual phenomenon, and it has social as well as psychological causes.[63] Only with a most macabre style could one describe the decision to put an end to one's own life as a 'lifestyle' choice, but suicide rates are very closely related to the circumstances that an individual finds intolerable and, as such, suicide rates were for a long time a taboo topic in the GDR.[64] To kill oneself could – as in the renowned case of Pastor Oskar Brüsewitz who in August 1976 set fire to himself in protest against the treatment of Christians and the Churches' stance in the GDR – be an extremely public political act. The rather numerous cases of suicide among prominent politicians, such as Erich Apel in 1965, were also potentially highly politically sensitive. In such cases, great efforts would have to be made to redefine the state of mind of the suicidal individual, to attempt to suggest mental instability or physical illness. Thus although suicide statistics were published for a few years in the later 1950s, from the early 1960s onwards the topic was seen as one of potential serious embarrassment to the regime, and statistics were again kept secret. A study on the topic of suicide for the ZIJ was suppressed. The authors of an authoritative West German study published in 1987 were unable to find any statistics on suicide, and had to make guesses based on numbers of deaths whose causes were not identified in the official GDR figures.[65] Since unification, however, the picture has become much clearer, with details now available from a range of sources.[66]

Following the high rates of suicide at the end of the war, suicide rates settled back into a pattern that did not depart significantly from the average suicide rates (always somewhat higher for men than women) of the previous century. Suicide rates in the 1950s were slightly lower than in the following two decades; there was a peak in 1966, and again in the mid 1970s (the year of the highest figures being 1974), declining again thereafter with a significant and sustained drop in suicide rates throughout the 1980s.

It has now become evident that suicide was a particularly significant cause of death among young people aged fifteen to twenty-five.[67] Young men tended to commit suicide (or more accurately, to have their deaths recorded as suicide) more frequently than young women. And suicide rates very clearly correlated with political events. The worst year for male suicides was 1962 – the year in which military conscription was introduced, following the erection of the Berlin Wall the previous year – when as many as 406 young men aged fifteen to twenty-five took their own lives. More usually the figure for young males was between 200 and 300. The two lowest figures for young male suicides are found in 1969 (oddly, just after the upheavals of 1968) and 1989 (with prospects for radical change on the horizon), with 197 and 186 deaths respectively. Female suicides were usually in the region of over 100 per year; the highest figure recorded is 185 in 1963, it being the highest single cause of death and accounting for over a quarter (26.5 per cent) of all deaths of young women in that year. Like young males, young women appear to have been less depressed, or more hopeful about the future, in the later 1980s: the lowest figure is 57 in 1989, following a steady decline from 104 in 1985 (79 in 1986, 78 in 1987, and 63 in 1988); clearly the Gorbachev era was associated with expectations of improvements. As for young males, suicides of young females show a high in the early 1960s and a low in the later 1960s: 155 in 1961, 166 in 1962, 185 in 1963; there were only 99 and 72 in 1968 and 1969 respectively – again an odd dip that is not easy to explain.

Not all suicide statistics are politically relevant, but some clearly are, however small a minority this may be. For an individual to choose to remove him- or herself from the 'collective' enterprise that was the GDR was the ultimate in the strategy of 'exit': unlike 'flight from the Republic', which could to some extent be dealt with by erecting – or eventually tearing down – an ever-more impenetrable Wall, flight from life itself could not be redeemed from beyond the grave.

The economy and health: An irresolvable problem?

Some theoretically preventable ill-health was totally out of the control of the people affected. The deteriorating character of working and living conditions, and particularly the growing problems of outdated equipment and highly polluting chemical industries and brown-coal energy supplies, meant that there were increasing problems of industrially related accidents and ill-health.

In August 1968, for example, an explosion in the PVC factory in Bitterfeld left 32 dead and 238 injured inside the factory, of whom a further eight died subsequently, and two killed and 20 injured outside the factory, as well as long-term consequences for heart and circulation problems from the gas emitted.[68] The report indicated, among other criticisms, that workers were not wearing the appropriate safety clothing, and that the Production Director emphasised higher productivity at the expense of work safety. The trade union files are full of similar accident reports, though generally not quite on this scale. Industrial diseases, chronic bronchitis and accidents at work through the use of outdated machinery and unsafe equipment were all integral parts of a failing economy in the later 1970s and '80s. In this area, the circle could never be squared: without a healthier economy, investment in health and safety at work could not be achieved; but without such investment, ill-health would continue to burden the health service and hence the economy. While the degree of decay of East German industry was no secret, particularly when the sheer extent of it became only too apparent after the fall of the Wall, the humanitarian concerns of those charged with the health of the people were a better-kept aspect of the GDR's hidden history.

In the battle between health and the economy, the latter always won at the expense of the former; or, to put it in more personal terms, the Minister for Health during the entire Honecker period, Ludwig Mecklinger, never seems to have been able to prevail over the economic tsar Günter Mittag, let alone over Honecker with his sacred cows of social policy and consumer subsidies. There was a constant tension between the growing needs of health care and the ever-more apparent shortcomings of the economy. Within the Politburo, health issues were constantly subordinated to other economic needs, powerfully controlled by Günter Mittag. Although there appear to have been no open conflicts within Politburo meetings, unwillingness to face up to politically sensitive issues with respect both to taboo health topics and economic decline seems to have kept health off the political agenda at the top.[69]

Those responsible for health were well aware of the difficulties, but unable to do much to improve the conditions that lay at the root of much ill-health. Mecklinger in particular comes across – at least in the records of his ministry's files – as having been a thoroughly conscientious and concerned (as well as politically committed) individual. Although aware of the difficulties and sensitivities involved in making available the relevant information on associated problems, Mecklinger took great pains to make the strongest possible case where matters of health were concerned.

Thus in 1984, for example, he wrote a letter to Kurt Hager as Secretary of the ZK of the SED and Politburo member, drawing attention to the 'massive danger to health' posed by conditions in 31 factories in which there were serious infringements of pollution levels and other major health and safety issues.[70] The numbers exposed to poisonous substances and dangerous incidents in these factories ranged from 15 affected by asbestos in the VEB Bauchemie Leipzig to the 2,010 people exposed to excessive levels of lead in the VEB Mansfeldkombinat, where symptoms of 'lead poisoning [and] pathological laboratory results' had also been found in local residents, particularly children. In the VEB Chemiekombinat Bitterfeld, Aluminium-Werk, there had already been two deaths from mercury poisoning, and there were other serious problems with dangerous substances in a wide range of factories listed by name. In addition, there were far wider problems of noise, heat and vibration, which tended to be largely overlooked in light of the more immediately obvious effects of poisonous substances. Many factories were only continuing to operate under 'exceptional permits' ('Ausnahmeregelungen') pending changes. While they were doing their best to prevent further individual cases of ill-health, this could not replace a fundamental overhaul. However, as far as the required investment was concerned, there was little help from above: 'In the discussions which have already taken place, my approach did, it is true, find some resonance; but, referring to the implications for investment of such a far-reaching cleansing of working conditions, those responsible see at the moment the possibility of a thorough alteration of the situation only in a few individual cases.'[71] Mecklinger was made only too well aware that any attempt to deal with these issues would essentially be at the (metaphorical) level of sticking plaster, rather than root and branch; to do the latter would have major implications for industrial investment and the priorities of the next five-year plan. He also turned personally to the Minister for Chemical Industry, and, in July 1985, to Dr Möbis, Secretary of State and Director of the Working Group for Organisation and Inspection of the Council of Ministers of the GDR. In this letter, Mecklinger requested, if possible, a personal discussion about 'particular aspects of the economy which, for a not inconsiderable number of working people, inevitably entail immediate, serious damage to their health'.[72]

Similarly, Helga Spädtke, Director of the Chief Inspection Office of the Ministry of Health, spoke confidentially of the problem: she prefaced her remarks on the numbers of people who were at risk of ill-health ('gesund-heitsgefährdet') and had to be constantly monitored as the 'reservoir of those who would later be those with occupational illnesses' with the phrase 'but I beg you not to make [any public] use of these figures'. This fear of undue publicity was scarcely surprising in view of the fact that in 1977 in Bezirk Leipzig alone, no fewer than 41,000 people were under constant treatment for conditions that would later lead to the label of occupational illnesses; and this was esti-mated as no more than 90 per cent of the true figure.[73] Of the 1,137 workers in Leipzig who had already been recognised as suffering from occupational ill-health, nearly two thirds – 62.5 per cent – had impaired hearing due to exces-sive noise at their place of work. One authority estimates that, at the end of 1980s, approximately 20–40 per cent of all illness was 'determined by work'.[74]

General environmental pollution was also an increasing cause for concern among those at the top of the Ministry for Health, and not merely among the growing body of environmentalist activists generally counted as being the 'opposition' in the GDR.[75] A report dated January 1982, for example, included detailed statistics of excess sulphur dioxide emissions and associated health problems in a variety of areas, particularly Halle, Karl-Marx-Stadt (now Chemnitz), Leipzig and Berlin; very widespread exposure to a range of other poisonous substances, including asbestos, lead and cadmium; and the fact that around 13 per cent of people were drinking water with dangerously high levels of nitrates. Even cyanide appeared to have posed a significant problem: in 1980, no fewer than 260 of 463 industrial enterprises had exceeded permitted levels of cyanide, posing an 'acute endangering of supplies of drinking water'.[76] Other public health hazards commented on in tones of great concern in

Ministry of Health reports included outbreaks of salmonella in children's holiday camps, an epidemic of rabies among hamsters in April 1983, and an incident in which a poisonous insecticide was dropped on people from a plane flying over Holdenstedt on 14 July 1983.[77] Unsurprisingly, given the general state of the GDR economy in the 1980s, little could be done; and, while Mecklinger's concern is undoubted, it seems that Mittag and Honecker preferred to pretend that such problems simply did not exist. What was blindingly obvious to the vast majority of workers and residents in the GDR could only be swept under the table as a confidential matter by politicians.

A plague on both their houses?

We tend to notice, to be particularly interested in, what is different: in the (unique or almost unique) fact that the GDR was part of a divided country, its population walled in and held under extraordinary conditions of surveillance and the threat or reality of repression. Those aspects which we abhor, we measure against the standards of our own societies, perceived (rightly or wrongly) as 'free', 'open' and characterised by the right to self-determination. We tend not to be (terribly) interested in the things we barely notice, because they seem to be 'the same', or at least only slightly different – and, if different, then at best slightly inferior: the functions and essentials of everyday life (and death); illness, health care, death, food, friendship and relationships.

We call the glow surrounding good influences the 'halo effect'. In the case of analyses of the GDR, it is rather the opposite: what one might call the 'contamination effect'. Because we know of the very different, very bad things – the Wall, the Stasi, to mention but two – we assume all else to be affected by their shadow. This leads to what one might call the 'yes, but' syndrome in readings. From a democratic and human rights perspective, whatever appears at first blush to be 'good' immediately suffers the contamination effect – the 'yes, but . . . it was only ideology, propaganda, for ulterior motives, not to be trusted, cynical, authoritarian, condescending, essentially manipulative', and so on. This is because our perspectival starting point is that of the critique of what is startlingly different: in other words, the anti-democratic aspects. The situation is rather more complicated when we focus on somewhat more neutral terrain.

But if we start from a quite different perspective, that of a common issue in advanced industrial societies, the picture begins to look rather different. In the case of health care, in a situation in which medical advances and demographic trends have produced populations with ever-growing proportions of older people and heightened expectations of success in treating diseases and disabilities, we find quite other constellations of similarity/difference: similarities between the humanitarian aims of, for example, the National Health Service of Britain and the health service of the GDR; and striking differences between the latter and that of the Third Reich, with its murderous approach even to the weaker members of its own racially defined *Volksgemeinschaft*, as evidenced in the grotesquely misnamed 'euthanasia' programme. Comparisons between 'dictatorships' seem to evince fewer similarities here than do comparisons between 'advanced industrial states'. Given the focus of some historians of Nazi Germany on the supposed 'modernity' of some of its eugenic ideas and practices, it is worth highlighting the enormity of the difference between murderous racism and more humanitarian world views. The fact of state attempts to manipulate population size (not in itself particularly 'modern', actually) should not allow notions of 'modernity' to obscure the fundamental impact of dramatically different political ideologies.

What prevented the humanitarian goals of the GDR health service from being fully realised were the same in principle – though not in degree and character – as those in any Western welfare state: insufficient financial means in a situation of rising costs, demands and expectations; the need to institute systems of rationing and to set priorities; staffing difficulties; and conflicts over the division of resources with other areas of policy. None of this would be news to any Western politician or civil servant in charge of a complex health service. Similarly, although there were differences in the character of the various failures to live up to desired or perfect standards in health care, the sheer fact of inequalities – differential privileges and systems of exclusion, of health divides reflecting other patterns of social inequality – is common to both democracies and dictatorships. What was different had to do with the relative balance between individual choices and collective goals, and the social, political, cultural and economic factors affecting patterns of lifestyle, disease and death.

One does not have – in the case of this area – to share any sympathy for general political objectives. We have here potentially the largest spectrum of agreement with the view that the fostering of good health and the alleviation of physical suffering is A Good Thing. So we can start with a large degree of empathy, and look more dispassionately at the obstacles encountered, the choices made, the conflicts over priorities and strategies, the outcomes for the quality of life, and patterns of illness, morbidity and mortality, without being narrowly 'political' (as, for example, in the totalitarian approach).

Nevertheless, there are political elements in this particular example, and the 'contamination effect' will no doubt seep through the relevant cracks and channels. To take two obvious ones: the rationing system, or setting of priorities; and the broader context of capacity (or otherwise) to achieve medical or humanitarian goals.

Rationing or priority setting can never be avoided in any health-care system; there are simply different – overt and covert – principles and means by which rationing is achieved. In many capitalist welfare states, the system of rationing is largely or partly determined by the (not-so-hidden hand of) the economy: private health-care systems, and private and professional insurance schemes, supplement and in some states totally overshadow any basic state provision of health care. Even where there is a very extensive state health-care system (whether based on insurance schemes or taxation) rationing of some sort takes effect: decisions of local and area health authorities, for example, can make a big difference as to what treatments are available on the NHS in different areas in the UK.

In the GDR, the rationing system was essentially political. This is, of course, substantively different from the combination of NHS and private health care system in the UK (where those who can pay can jump the queue for non-urgent medical treatment), or the American insurance-based system (where family members may begin to despair if an ailing relative lasts beyond what the insurance will cover), but it is a moot point whether it is more or less unfair in principle. Neither type of system can boast total equality, total and free avail-ability of treatment at the time of need (as in Bevan's vision for the the NHS). Neither type of system actually wanted or wants to deny treatment to those in need, and neither successfully devised a means of fully realising the vision, so different – economic (capitalist) or political (communist) – principles were adduced to determine how rationing was to be effected in practice. From the point of view of those excluded from privileged treatment – in either system – neither can be regarded as 'worse'.

Much more broadly, we can also say that the general failures of the East German planned economy had to be at the root of the lack of adequate resources for a more successful health-care system – and hence, of course, ulti-mately there are 'political' reasons for failure to realise the vision of the good society as far as fundamental matters of life and death were concerned. The second example of political contamination would thus be that of priority setting in different areas of the overall economy, the place of the health service in relation to other priorities, and of the wider economic and political context within which the health service has to operate. Health needs had to be balanced against the competing demands of – to take a particularly striking example – the chemical industries, in the knowledge that lives would be adversely affected and premature deaths would be caused if the needs of chemical production were allowed to take priority over investment in health and safety measures.

Contamination effect? Let he who is without sin cast the first stone. For years, Western tobacco manufacturers and asbestos companies knew about the links between smoking and death from lung cancer and heart disease, and between exposure to asbestos and death from asbestosis and mesothelioma; but they continued to promote smoking, to expose workers to asbestos and other dangerous substances, and to advertise their products. Even government attempts at deterrence (health warnings on cigarette packets and advertisements) have been hampered by economic interests in tax revenues and donations. If mass public health was the agreed humanitarian goal in both capitalist and communist systems of the later twentieth century, perhaps it is again – at least from the point of view of the vulnerable and the victims of any system – a case of 'a plague on both their houses'.

Chapter Six

Youth

Creating a new kind of society required the creation of a new kind of human being, ideally not the competitive individualists of rampant capitalism, encouraged by the system to pursue personal goals of 'self-fulfilment' even at the expense of others, but rather human beings who would put themselves out for the wider community, who would subordinate individual wishes to the collective good. To do this, it was not sufficient merely to transform the relations of production; it was necessary also to instil in young people from their earliest years the sense of belonging to a larger community, having wider responsibilities for a collective future.

The 'socialist personality' was the key link between the 'individual' and the community. In its mid-1970s model, the 'socialist personality' was officially defined as:

> an all-round, well-developed personality, who has a comprehensive command of political, specialist and general knowledge, possesses a firm class outlook rooted in the Marxist-Leninist world view, is notable for excellent mental, physical and moral qualities, is thoroughly imbued with collective thoughts and deeds, and actively, consciously and creatively contributes to the shaping of socialism.[1]

Far from being the 'uniform' robots caricatured by Western 'imperialist ideologues' for the purpose of 'discrediting' socialism, such personalities would be characterised by 'creative autonomy' and initiative, facing the future with openness and optimism.[2] Only in socialism were the preconditions allegedly present for the development of this paragon of virtue, who would make a full and active personal contribution to the construction of socialism and the cause of world peace.

Notions of active citizenship and community spirit are, of course, not unique to communist states; capitalist states also on occasion force citizens to prioritise the 'national interest' over individual concerns in times of warfare, and encourage a concern for collective welfare in regular community service activities or charity donations. But the GDR took this to particular extremes: mobilisation against the 'class enemy' was more or a less a constant feature of life, and, with variations in degree at different times, the weapons of the class enemy could be seen in the most absurdly trivial aspects of dress and behaviour; in addition the SED had a near monopoly of community activities and institutions, challenged only in part by the Churches. The GDR was thus not merely a state in which collective goals took priority over individual wishes, it was one in which at times even the most apparently personal and private questions of morality and lifestyle, fashions and hair length, were seen not merely as ethical questions but also as political matters to be dealt with at the highest levels.

Historians have tended to focus on educational and social institutions and official policies towards young people, and have highlighted the ways in which that minority of 'deviants' whose behaviour earned them a place in the archives were categorised and maltreated.[3] But histories of official youth policies tend to shed less light on the activities and interests of young people who neither participated actively nor rebelled vociferously. It is often only possible to trace official conceptions and initiatives, and explicit battles over the souls of the rising generation, while gaining only more fleeting impressions of the attitudes and experiences of successive cohorts of conformist young people within the GDR. Even so, some generalisations are possible.

As with so much else in the GDR, different official aims and challenges proved difficult to reconcile with each other; and changing SED policies were in any event but one element in a far wider set of social and cultural trends affecting the patterns of attitudes and behaviour among East German citizens over the forty years of the GDR's existence. Ultimately, patterns of individualism (ironically in part fostered by the SED's own policies) and participation in international cultural trends proved more powerful than the attempted collective production of 'socialist personalities' who were one hundred per cent committed to the construction of 'our GDR'. Even the deeply moralising tone on the part of the SED power elite in the early years gave way to greater moral relativism and even a partial if suspicious toleration, within controlled limits, of an increasingly pluralistic youth culture by the later 1980s.

The young people of one decade were the Party functionaries, factory workers, miners, engineers, doctors, dissidents, teachers, collective farm chairmen and, indeed, parents of the next. The 'youth' of the 1950s were the adults of the 1970s; and the influences of school and socialisation are inextricably intertwined with the wider historical context and formative experiences of the period, as becomes evident when looking more broadly at different generations in the GDR. Furthermore, 'youth' is not merely an age category imposed by an outside observer, but is also a social construct at a specific historical time and place. If the notion of 'teenagerhood' was something of a historical invention of later twentieth-century affluent consumer societies, particularly in the 1960s with the growth of mass markets for teenage fashions and pop music, then the SED's concept of 'youth' to cover those aged between fourteen and twenty-five (and sometimes well beyond, in the case of functionaries) was even more extended, but for rather different reasons. Here, however, 'youth' is interpreted in the broadest sense, to cover the whole period of socialisation from birth to young adulthood.

The 'smallest cell': The family

Both changing family forms and expectations of intimate relationships were profoundly affected by GDR social policies and economic conditions. Like so much else, it is simply ahistorical to talk of the family as a 'niche', as though it were some unchanging little cell to which one could escape from the big bad world of politics.[4] Family size and form, the duration of family bonds, the character of inter-personal relationships, were all as profoundly affected by the changing socio-economic and political environment in the GDR as they have been in capitalist societies. And the family remained of great importance for young people growing up in the GDR, though not necessarily always in the ways officially intended.

The family in the GDR was officially seen as the smallest unit or 'cell' of the collective socialist whole, rather than (as in prevalent Western ideals of the late twentieth century, if not always in practice) merely a 'private sphere' of mutual love, protection and retreat from the pressures of outside life, an arena for 'authentic' relationships and the transmission of independent moral traditions. In this, there are remarkable formal similarities between SED views of the family and official conceptions of the role of the family under National Socialism, though of course under very different ideological colours. The family was held to be the primary instance of socialisation of the 'socialist personality', for the formation of which 'education in the family, in the state educational institutions, in the FDJ and its Pioneer organisation "Ernst Thälmann" are of the utmost importance'.[5]

The role of the family was enshrined even in the Law on the Unified Socialist Education System of 1965, in which parents and the family were singled out as being given 'a new moral and educational role'.[6] As Alexander Abusch, Deputy Prime Minister and Chair of the State Commission for

Formation of a Unified Socialist Education System, put it in his introductory remarks on the new law:

> Here [bei uns], the interests of the family and of society are not in contradiction to one another ... Our socialist society, surely like every good family, wants to bring up and educate young people as well as possible for a secure, peaceful and happy future. The higher ethical-moral significance of the family as the smallest cell of our new society results from the fact that it has been liberated from the destructive influences of capitalism.[7]

Yet the family, thus 'liberated', developed in rather different ways than those Abusch had anticipated.

Divorce rates were relatively high in the early post-war years and on into the early 1950s. Many couples, on being reunited after separation during or after the war, found that periods of military service, incarceration as prisoners of war and the heightened stresses of living in ruins and trying to rebuild shattered lives had wrought far-reaching changes in their expectations and behaviour patterns; for many, attempts to readjust in this period of upheaval proved too great a strain on their marriage. During the course of the later 1950s and '60s, the divorce rate steadily declined; but with changes in the position of women – notably their increased legal and economic independence – and with the social policies of the Honecker period, more and more people came to view marriage as a temporary arrangement between consenting adults, rather than a partnership for a lifetime. The overall rise in the divorce rate is in part related to the fact that there was simultaneously a significant rise in the proportion of divorces instigated by women: by 1989 more than two thirds (69 per cent) of divorce proceedings were initiated by the female partner. The divorce rate rose from 14 divorces per one hundred new marriages in the early 1960s, to 38 in 1989; the greatest rise was in the Honecker period when, in a context of rising female employment and enhanced state-run childcare facilities, divorce rates effectively doubled.[8] And, alongside the inhabitants of East Berlin, 'capital of the GDR', it was ironically the residents of the socialist new towns – which had been precisely designed to facilitate the development of the new 'socialist personality' – who displayed the highest rates of marriage breakdown. There were similar differences between older residential areas and new housing estates; thus in the later 1980s people living in the vast new housing estates, such as Marzahn and Hellersdorf, were around twice as likely to sue for divorce than were residents of older areas such as Köpenick and Lichtenberg.[9]

Alongside rising divorce rates there were nevertheless high rates of remarriage: East Germans clearly expected the relationship of marriage to be one of a life partnership, and were prepared to re-embark on such an enterprise even after previous attempts had failed. But the relationship between adults did not necessarily have to be tied to parenting: there was an ever-growing tolerance of giving birth outside the relationship of marriage – frequently having the first pregnancy and child before marriage – and of single parenting even when cohabiting with a new partner. Thus the traditional family bonds – while still, it should be remembered, of a conventional character among perhaps half the population – were dissolving among the remainder of the population. The stigma previously attached to statuses such as 'divorcee' or 'illegitimate' ('bastard') collapsed along with the changing patterns and habits of increasing numbers of East Germans.

Given that children were no longer seen by many East Germans as a reason to try to keep a failing marital relationship at least formally together, more and more children were affected by parental divorce. With the expansion of crèche and kindergarten provision, more and more children were also socialised within a wider context than that of the conventional 'housewife at home' model. The effects on personality have been much disputed: psychotherapists have arguably grotesquely exaggerated the consequences of such a socialisation context for the vast majority of those well-balanced and functioning East Germans who did not make their way into a psychoanalytic surgery. While for some commentators 'deformations' within the socialisation process 'repro-duced in the family situation the pathology that would later be required for the integration and maintenance of an abnormal social situation', other scholars have suggested that the family remained a 'private niche' within which East Germans could escape for love, comfort and authenticity.[10] Neither pole of these polarised views quite encapsulates the situation adequately.

The family was not an 'escape'; it was where one started from. Family back-ground had, in the GDR as in contemporary Western societies, an enormous influence on young people's attitudes, behaviour, ways of speaking and thinking, aspirations and chances in life. At the same time it is clear that, whether East Germans were aware of it themselves or not, the character and structure of the family unit changed in significant ways, and these changes were arguably more the result of East Germans' own choices about the struc-ture of their lives and relationships in a changing employment and social policy context than they were of the official conceptions of the role of the family as the 'smallest cell' of socialist society. But such changes did not neces-sarily entail the denial of love and care to offspring, whether born within or (increasingly) outside the institution of marriage, born to older or (increas-ingly) younger parents, or raised by a cohabiting couple or (increasingly) a single parent. And the insecurities of upbringing in the 1970s and '80s may have been different from, but were arguably no more disturbing than, the very different insecurities of birth and socialisation within the devastated family conditions of the Second World War and shortly thereafter. There is considerable evidence to suggest that, despite – or even perhaps because of – the deprivations of the wartime and post-war period, children in the 1950s and '60s had good relationships and a great deal of empathy with their (remaining) parents. Generational conflicts in the later 1960s were not carried out within families, whether as 'teenage rebellion' in the cultural sense, or political critique of parental pasts and politics, but rather in the wider sphere of the workplace or politics. Often there was, in contrast to the Western generational conflicts of the time, considerable solidarity within individual GDR families in respect of difficulties faced by their members in the outside world.[11]

Education and training

On the appropriate education and training of young people rests the future of any modern state; all advanced industrial states rely on the fostering and development of relevant technical expertise and an enhanced capacity for flexibility and innovation. As a modern industrial society, the GDR needed a degree of individual initiative and enterprise, for scientific and technological innovation, for finding new solutions to problems, for economic efficiency and organisation, and for cultural creativity and inspiration. But there were, too, far wider political aims with respect to youth. Young people were particularly crucial to the communist project, as the SED sought to capture the hearts and minds of a new generation untainted by the compromised Nazi past, to protect them from the allegedly adverse moral and political influences of the 'class enemy' in the West, and to select and train a new cadre of potential leaders of the future. The core problem, through every area, was that of the balancing and the fostering of individual initiative with conformity and commitment to officially prescribed goals – a problem that never was, and arguably in principle never could be, resolved. Youth policy in the GDR was thus repeatedly characterised by tensions between attempts at control from above, and a degree of insight into and recognition of the fact that young people could never mature into the desired 'socialist personalities', or independent and creative adults capable of constructing socialism, if they were not given a degree of freedom and initiative.

The education system was geared to the transformation of both individual personality and the structure of the wider society. The old German system, in which the children of the upper classes and professionals would go to the so-called 'Gymnasium' – a form of grammar school – marking them out for university study and the reproduction of privileged status, was replaced by a system intended to give more advantages to children from all backgrounds, and particularly to those from peasant and working class families. There was a series of major reforms of the education system in the period of real social revolution in the first two decades after the war, starting already in the occupation period. The 1946 Law for the Democratisation of German Schools was the first step in a process of removing the influence of both religion and of inherited wealth and privilege from schools. This was followed by a series of reorganisations of the education system in the 1950s, providing a comprehensive education system for the vast majority of East German children; in addition, a small minority were selected for specialised or elite schools designed to foster and indeed force particular talents, particularly in the area of sports, but also in science, maths and languages. Finally, the Law on the Unified Socialist Education System of 1965 provided a unified structure and philosophy of education running more or less from infancy to senility. The education system under the long-serving Education Minister Margot Honecker (Deputy Minister from 1958, then Minister for the People's Education from 1963 to 1989) was fundamentally related both to the perceived 'needs of society' and to an individual's political conformity.

With the introduction of a fully comprehensive school system, the majority of children went through a 'polytechnic' school (Polytechnische Oberschule, or POS) after their primary schooling together until, in the final two years, vocational and academic paths began to diverge. The more academically inclined would go on to an 'extended upper school' (Erweiterte Oberschule, or EOS) in which they could take the final academic school leaving exams, the *Abitur*, which was the academic prerequisite for university study. It was also possible to arrive at this point by other routes, such that further educational development was never closed off for those with the appropriate motivation and intelligence. But academic success alone was not enough. Political conformity, the appropriate family background, lack of religious commitment, willingness to play a full role in the life of the FDJ, and similar considerations were equally important to ensure the opportunity for future study. Although having come through this system university students had at least learnt to appear conformist, it remained important at this level to ensure that a watchful eye was kept on potentially independent-minded young people: the system of Stasi informants was thus relatively thick on the ground, particularly in highly sensitive areas of university study, but also even among school-children.[12]

Education was, of course, not merely about instilling political conformity, but also about producing a highly skilled workforce for a modernising industrial society. Ever closer links were to be developed with the world of work and industry through 'twinning' agreements between schools and industrial enterprises (*Patenschaften*), and through the annual Messe der Meister von Morgen ('Fair of Tomorrow's Masters'), the first of which took place in Leipzig in 1958, and which continued to play a major role right through to the 1980s.[13] While this latter seems to have encouraged many young people into careers as engineers, technical experts or 'inventors' in the widest sense, the twinning arrangements seem to have been somewhat more mixed in their consequences. Children were taken to their partner economic enterprises not merely to gain exposure to the atmosphere of adult life and to encourage a sense of positive identification with the heroised industrial worker, but also to give real assistance in reaching production targets. Recent research suggests that while on the one hand teachers were often happy to gain additional materials (and even food) from the enterprises with which their classes were twinned, reactions among schoolchildren on occasion consisted of boredom, disillusionment and a degree of shocked surprise at the dirty conditions and prevalent drunkenness that were characteristic of some East German workplaces.[14] Yet the rather dirigiste attitude to encouraging children into certain future career paths (*Berufslenkung*), with guaranteed apprenticeships and workplaces, was seen in a rather more positive light.

Huge emphasis was placed on the possibility of continuous education and training, and the acquisition of further qualifications throughout life, with evening courses and periodic Party schools. The latter in particular were often experienced as both demanding and dull, a strain, and a large demand on 'private' time, putting many people off the idea of 'promotion' or taking a position of further responsibility. Furthermore, by the 1970s the system of further and higher education had expanded so much that more qualified graduates were being produced than there were appropriate workplaces for such a skilled labour force. Many over-qualified people thus felt they were working below the level for which they had been prepared. Political commitment was hence the price to be paid for further promotion in this situation.

In principle many of the goals and the underlying philosophy sounded not only idealistic, but even highly laudable from any political perspective: removing barriers to educational opportunity rooted in inherited wealth and privilege, providing opportunities for further and higher education at any age to anyone capable of benefiting. But there were two major problems in practice: first, the massive gap between ideals and realities rooted in problems of inadequate material and human resources; and secondly, the huge ideological pressure for political conformity, with an enormous price to be paid by those 'who thought differently' (to use a phrase from the Rosa Luxemburg quotation about freedom that so irritated the authorities when displayed on a banner by dissidents in January 1988). Many accounts see the GDR education system almost entirely in terms of 'breaking one's backbone', or as an 'educational dictatorship'. Others are more nuanced, and many East Germans remember with some fondness the lenience of individual teachers. Furthermore, for those who wanted to train to be a specialist in pig farming or to be a tractor mechanic, or had no real idea of what they wanted to do, there were enormous opportunities: no young person need fear lack of a place to gain further qualifications, or an appropriate apprenticeship and eventual job. This aspect was remembered particularly fondly by East Germans after unification, when their own sons and daughters had immense opportunities and individual choice, but in a situation of strong competition and high unemployment. But for those who wanted to go on to higher studies, particularly in politically somewhat sensitive areas, the position was a great deal more problematic in terms of the pressure for expressing an ideologically appropriate worldview.

Battles for the soul: Religion and militarisation

Inevitably, the focus not merely on training but also on claiming the souls of youth meant clashes of values between those of the state and those of some families, particularly where the private values in question were strongly held religious beliefs.

The widespread strength of religious belief and practice in the early 1950s may be hard to gauge in retrospect, but in some areas it was clearly very great. One report from Kreis Salzwedel estimated that over 50 per cent of children in the Jahn-Oberschule, and over 60 per cent in the Heinrich-Heine Schule were active participants in the church youth group.[15] One major campaign seeking to deal with the continuing power of religion was the introduction – or rather resuscitation – of an older secular ceremony for youth, the *Jugendweihe*, in 1954. This caused major confrontations through the 1950s between the churches and individual religious families on the one hand, and the state authorities on the other. It only began to die down as an issue at the grass roots in the course of the 1960s, when more and more families began to interpret the avowedly atheist *Jugendweihe* as not inherently incompatible with religious belief and practice, and when in any event the numbers of committed and practising Christians began to decline.

For those who accepted the *Jugendweihe* as a normal part of life, it functioned as a fairly routine version of what in Western capitalist societies goes by a variety of names, such as the sessions in 'personal, health and social education' (PHSE) in the United Kingdom in the late twentieth century. By the end of the 1960s, most East German children participated in the *Jugendweihe*, with only one or two exceptions in any given class. High points of the programme generally included a visit to a former Nazi concentration camp (possibly Sachsenhausen, in addition to the effective 'national shrine' of the GDR, Buchenwald), as well as cultural visits (the German classics, with Goethe and Schiller in Weimar, perhaps a theatre production and discussion with an actor), and links with local industry involving visits to and twinning with specific factories. Files on the preparation for the final celebrations at various schools in the early 1970s illustrate the way in which a standard speech, which varied little from year to year, could be adapted for particular anniversaries – whether the 25th year since the 'day of liberation', or the 25th anniversary of the GDR, or something vaguely to do with Lenin's birthday when all else failed – and into which the changing names of pupils deserving special mention could be inserted by their class teacher. The speech was wilfully religious in phraseology and referencing (though it is hard to translate the resonance of phrases, which almost leap straight from Biblical originals): 'In a short time you will belong to those people from whom much will be demanded by Society, for much has been given to you by Society . . . Dear young friends, your whole life shall be a confession of faith [*Bekenntnis*] in socialism. Give to this life your reason and your strength, give the power of your hearts . . . In this spirit let us take the oath.'[16] A more naked demonstration of the Durkheimian interpretation of religion as commitment to society could hardly be imagined. And it has to be emphasised that the vast majority of young East Germans went through this aspect of their socialisation in the GDR almost unthinkingly.

For those dwindling numbers who still saw the *Jugendweihe* as being in contradiction with their own religious beliefs and practices, however, it continued to pose a major problem, as was the case for the pastor in Schlöben, Bezirk Gera, who complained in early 1962 that undue moral pressure was being exerted on parents and children. In Rostock, it was claimed in the early 1960s that religious observance was actually rising, and that pastors were refusing to give religious burials to anyone who had taken the *Jugendweihe*.[17] And although the *Jugendweihe* as such began to wane as an issue, religiously rooted dissent in schools did not. In 1980, for example, eleven students at the Forstborn-Oberschule in Leipzig, who were members of a church youth group (the *Junge Gemeinde*), were – apparently influenced by their pastor – able to organise a successful 'boycott' of a citizenship lesson by persuading the class to engage in total silence from a specific moment on in the lesson.[18] This minor incident was but part of a far wider pattern of developments characteristic of the in part religiously influenced growth of grass-roots political activism in the 1980s.[19]

Moral issues proved to be of far wider resonance among East Germans, beyond the circles of conventional church-goers. A particular problem was that of the continuing, and growing, militarisation, about which relatively large numbers of East Germans felt strongly. Young men who, following the introduction of conscription in 1962, chose to take advantage of the introduction two years later of alternative military service as 'construction soldiers' (*Bausoldaten*), not bearing weapons, drew attention to themselves as political nonconformists with serious consequences for their future education and careers. Many found they could only pursue a livelihood in the environs of the church. And while individual Christians continued to be discriminated against, the issue of the militarisation of education and mentalities more generally was a far wider pressure. Large numbers of East Germans were so incapable of understanding why they should view friends and relatives in West Germany as their enemies that this issue repeatedly crops up in just about every kind of archival record, from parents' meetings at schools in the early 1960s, through the orchestrated 'discussions' of the National Document of 1962 or the new constitution of 1968, to the more informal discussions of a whole range of policy issues in the 1970s. In Erfurt in late January 1962, young people were claiming that conscription was merely a means of saving money; parents who walked out of school meetings as a protest or made 'pacifist' comments along the lines of 'we will not shoot on our brothers' were greeted with much applause.[20] Interestingly, in a series of school-based discussions of the National Document in May 1962 – less than a year following the erection of the Berlin Wall – it was only in a boarding school, the Erweiterte Oberschule in Ludwigsfelde, where the supervision and influence of teachers were far greater than in normal day schools, that politically 'correct' answers were given.[21] For those young people exposed to a wider range of influences, including those of family, friends and neighbours, 'lack of clarity' and 'false opinions' remained 'still' rife; report writers were at least linguistically extremely optimistic, copiously qualifying the less-than-satisfactory news with the word 'still' (*noch*), as though the passage of time and further 'discussions' would eventually rectify the situation.

This hoped for rectification did not, however, materialise according to plan. It is true that some young people did come to take military service for granted. But a wide-ranging report on developments in the 'consciousness' and behaviour of youth in the later 1970s, based largely on surveys carried out in 1976 and 1977, found evidence of an 'underestimation or an as yet [*noch*] insufficient recognition of the essence of Imperialism', with too positive an image of West Germany and the US. There was a danger of a 'depoliticised' or 'deideologised' attitude to life; and, quite apart from those sections of youth that remained religious, a further significant number had 'consciously or unconsciously religious or irrational conceptions . . . (for example, around one quarter of them more or less believe in life after death)'. While they understood that the GDR offered 'social care and security' ('soziale Gerborgenheit und Sicherheit'), they 'still' had 'many illusions' about the Federal Republic of Germany.[22] Such 'uncertainty' was demonstrated by the inadequate numbers of recruits for the armed forces. The introduction of Military Education (*Wehrerziehung*) as a separate subject in schools in 1978 failed to produce an increase in numbers of willing and committed recruits.[23] Rather, it prompted a further wave of unrest and protest, and played an important role in the development of wider sensitivities and fears about threats to peace in the 1980s.

A study of 1,600 young people aged between sixteen and nineteen in 1986 revealed a wide range of negative expectations and fears about military service. Comments of young people covered the full gamut of aspects of life in the Army: they were worried about 'physical exertion, tricks being played on you, being subjected, being ordered around, stinking toilets, no money, being humiliated ... no alcohol'; distance from friends and family, worries that relationships with steady girlfriends would not last the separation; 'fear of accidents and death in exercises and manoeuvres, fear of having to shoot at a person, if it came to the real thing, fear that during the period of service a war could break out'; 'fear of having to serve on the border, because I am afraid of dying'; and 'it's all pointless anyway, when the atom bombs go off it's all over'.[24] Those demonstrating more positive attitudes were generally those in the academic upper schools (EOS) who were hoping to get a place to study the subject of their choice; even some of these had doubts about losing 'the best three years' of their life, but nevertheless felt the chance of studying was worth volunteering for the extended three-year service.[25] A few produced precisely the sort of ideological statements about defence of the fatherland that would be expected of them; presumably they had been well trained in the art of conformity. Religious people were least likely to have a positive view, though one, who had opted for alternative service, had a surprisingly measured approach:

> I am going to be a *Bausoldat*, and I am sure I will feel good there. First, because of my faith. And secondly, because I have got to know people who became *Bausoldaten*, whose behaviour and character I really liked. I feel better around people who are honest, who have understanding, and who don't make themselves out to be more than they are or throw their weight around. I often experienced this when I worked in a barracks. And this is why I have no fears about being a *Bausoldat*, no worries and problems.[26]

For many others, negative comments were based on the reports of elder brothers and friends who had already done military service, rather than on any published material, which all painted the army experience in a far rosier light.

The vast majority of young East German males did in the end perform their military service, with effects on their attitudes and behaviour as adults that warrant further investigation. Many simply conformed and then got on with 'normal' civilian life; some joined the paramilitary 'combat groups' (*Kampfgruppen*) of their workplace; and a minority even opted to make a career in the National People's Army. These latter groups have until recently received remarkably little attention from historians more interested in dissent and opposition.[27] But the issue of militarisation remained high on the conscious agenda of many others. By the later 1980s, fears about peace were highest on the agenda of young people's concerns. As Walter Friedrich, Director of the ZIJ, reminded a meeting of the Scientific Council for Youth Research in October 1987, fifteen to twenty year olds of 'today' were born just before or after the Eighth Party Conference, and thus were well and truly products of the GDR. Yet the research showed that young people constantly registered discrepancies between 'textbook truths [*Schulbuchweisheiten*] and everyday experiences'. The very top issue for young people was the 'acute intensification of the threat to peace, real danger of self-destruction'; second on the list came 'global environmental problems'.[28]

Socialisation and leisure: Organised youth

There were constant efforts to control and direct the energies of young people through state-organised leisure activities. Among the most important of the mass organisations were the groups catering for this group: the Ernst Thälmann Young Pioneers (ages six to ten) and the Ernst Thälmann Pioneers (ages ten to fourteen), and the FDJ for those aged from fourteen to twenty-five. These were systematically designed to socialise, co-opt and channel youth in certain politically specified directions.

The FDJ was there not only to socialise and educate the rising generation, but also to provide a training ground and selection stadium for future leadership positions (the cadre reserve); its importance was further underlined by the fact that two of the three SED General Secretaries, Erich Honecker and Egon Krenz, cut their political teeth as head of the FDJ. Founded in March 1946, the FDJ was the only permitted youth group in the Soviet zone.[29] Initially characterised by a relatively high degree of grass-roots democracy, from 1947 onwards it was steadily 'co-ordinated' such that from the early 1950s onwards it was firmly under the control of the SED leadership. Participation and membership figures for the FDJ have to be treated with a little caution, and indeed, not all functionaries agreed in any event whether the aim was to capture (a totally unrealistic) 100 per cent of young people in the age range, or merely to encompass and harness the most willing. In the event, the best estimates of membership figures can show tendencies, if not exact and totally accurate numbers.[30] These figures, when treated with all due caution, suggest that over two thirds of the age group were 'organised' in the FDJ by the winter of 1952, but that this fell sharply to little over 40 per cent in the upheavals of the following summer of 1953. Membership continued to be bumpy at best during the 1950s, with particular troughs in 1959 and 1962 (the year when compulsory conscription was introduced), but then climbed steadily thereafter. From the later 1960s through to the later 1980s, membership appears to have been continually slightly rising, until a decline set in again from late 1987, interestingly mirroring the increased political unrest and growing repression characteristic of the last two years of GDR history before the fall of the Wall.

For most of the Honecker period, at least formal (if not active) membership encompassed between two thirds and four fifths of the age group. Although membership was not compulsory, the penalties for conspicuous nonconformity were a consideration for those with serious career aspirations. Membership was highest among schoolchildren for whom the organisation was school-based, since groups were often run by class teachers, and meetings seemed simply a routine part of the weekly timetable; it remained relatively high among university students with politically relevant career aspirations, but fell off among apprentices and young workers who were often, in any event, by this time in the FDGB and other organisations of adult life; and membership was lowest among young people working on the land.

The FDJ was designed not merely to socialise young people, but to train them and harness their energies into projects of strategic importance to the GDR. From 1952, learning to shoot was part of the increasingly militarised programme of the FDJ, despite some unwillingness on the part of young people. In the same year, the misleadingly entitled Society for Sport and Technology (GST) was founded as an essentially paramilitary organisation and pre-military training ground; in addition to paramilitary education, this offered unique opportunities for specialist activities such as sailing, gliding, amateur radio and obtaining a driving licence, thus making membership particularly attractive.[31] From the late 1950s, some FDJ members assisted the state police and security services in maintaining domestic security and social disciplining through membership of the 'FDJ disciplinary squads' (FDJ-Ordnungsgruppen), which dealt with a range of moral transgressions from 'Rowdytum' or listening to Western media channels, through being work-shy or under the 'influence of the class enemy', to engaging in shady dealings and criminal activities. Members of these groups were, for example, instrumental in the 'Ox Head' (*Ochsenkopf*) campaign of September 1961, swivelling the antennae of television aerials away from receipt of Western television channels.

Young people's labour power was also harnessed to more obviously useful economic tasks. For a few months from the summer of 1952 until February 1953, the so-called 'Service for Germany' (Dienst für Deutschland) sought with little success to harness the labour power of young people to the mammoth task of sudden rearmament. In the later 1950s, other campaigns took over, including the 'Activists' Movement' (Aktivistenbewegung) and the 'Fair for Tomorrow's Masters'. Young people were also entrusted with particular 'youth projects' (*Jugendobjekte*), such as the construction of the oil pipeline and oil processing works in Schwedt, and construction works on the East Berlin Schönefeld airport. Youth projects were officially defined as 'precisely measurable and time-limited tasks for the completion of which a Youth Collective is given responsibility ... [An] effective means for the socialist education of the young generation, and the development of their socialist consciousness.'[32] In 1959, young people were employed on around 700 such projects, a figure that had risen to no fewer than 68,370 projects, involving 854,912 young people, by 1974. The largest of these was work on the 550-kilometre-long natural gas pipeline between the Soviet Union and the GDR, a project decided on by the Politburo in 1974. Thus those young people who were willing – and there were hundreds of thousands of them – were repeatedly absorbed into and affected by the activities of the official state youth organisation.

Many young people simply accepted the routine activities of the youth organisations, most of which took place on school premises as a regular part of the school calendar, without much thought. Memories consist of being lined up in the playground for a flag ceremony, of excited anticipation of reaching the age to be awarded the scarf of the next age group up the youth-organisation ladder, of having fun – or getting bored – listening to stories or singing songs together at a regular meeting on school premises, taking the roll-calls (*Appelle*) with a pinch of salt, and not thinking much about the words to the songs they sang. If there were organised activities away from home, many enjoyed going to camps, learning how to shoot, having camp fires, and generally having time off with friends in often-pleasant surroundings in the countryside. Many former *FDJler* speak of how they remember such times as 'fun', although the compulsory May Day parades were more a matter of boredom and going through the essential motions. More politically aware East Germans, particularly those coming from a religious or other dissident background, were more conscious of the differences between the youth organisation's aims and their own values; yet even so, the Young Pioneers and the FDJ were often seen as simply 'normal', routine aspects of everyday life, just like going to school.[33] On the other hand, it is also clear that the FDJ was totally incapable of dominating the lives of most young people, most of the time.

Support and subversion: Youth subcultures

The conflicts between the more stridently educational and political purposes of organisations targeted at the rising generation of 'socialist personalities' and the ways in which East Germans reacted to, participated in and used (or ignored) these initiatives become clear even through only a cursory sampling of the records. The picture is, however, more complex than the story that is most easily recounted: that of straight battles between (a frequently heroised) dissident youth culture and a (readily demonised) repressive state that conceived of youth as the 'enemy within'.[34] This was of course the case at certain times and with respect to specific incidents, such as the notorious clash between young people and the authorities in Leipzig in late October 1965, providing a foretaste of the crackdown in the Eleventh Plenum a few weeks later. But the wide diversity and range of youth subcultures across the forty years cannot be simply summarised in the terms appropriate to this particular, politically significant confrontation.

The Leipzig incident has aroused considerable interest among historians, not least because it symbolised a key moment in the transformation of state policies towards young people, bringing to an end an extraordinary and controversial brief period of partial liberalisation and reform.[35] Somewhat critical of the shortcomings of the FDJ, in 1963 Ulbricht, along with his newly appointed and relatively liberal Chair of the Youth Commission, Kurt Turba, sought ways of gaining a greater involvement and genuine enthusiasm on the part of young people in the GDR. In the wider context of the economic modernisation drive of the New Economic System (NÖS) and the focus on science, technology and creativity, the new youth policies unleashed a climate of debate and widespread discussion of reforms. The Youth Communiqué of 1963 promised in its very title to 'give youth trust and responsibility' ('Der Jugend Vertrauen und Verantwortung'). A high point was reached with the third 'Germany Meeting' (Deutschlandtreffen) of 1964, a gigantic international youth festival in Berlin, with a full programme of not merely dull political speeches but also genuinely popular events, music, dances and films – essentially an enormous street festival involving over half a million young people. A new radio station, DT64, was set up to relay popular music (subject in due course to a 60:40 ratio of indigenous to Western tunes), and in the following months young peoples' music-making was encouraged through the 'guitar movement' and a 'guitar competition' initiated by the FDJ. This liberalisation had, however, always had its enemies: Erich Honecker, in particular, was strongly opposed to this Western 'decadence of the worst sort' and 'the introduction of the American way of life', which he perceived as entering the GDR in this way. In the summer and autumn of 1965, Honecker took the initiative to change course; massaging and greatly exaggerating youth criminality figures, he began to portray matters in a very different light. On 11 October, at an extraordinary meeting of the Secretariat of the Central Committee, in the absence of Walter Ulbricht, Honecker succeeded effectively in reversing the whole thrust of youth policy, terminating the guitar movement, and withdrawing licences to play.[36]

It was in this context that the demonstration of 30–31 October in Leipzig against the 'Beat-Ban' (Beatverbot) took place. With the change of policy, no fewer than 44 of the 49 bands active in the Leipzig area had been forbidden to play, shattering the whole Leipzig youth scene. Around 2,500 young people came together in the town centre to demonstrate against the ban; police intervened brutally, equipped with tanks, water hoses, truncheons and bloodhounds; 267 young people were peremptorily arrested, and many sent to work camps for punitive correction sentences. Local newspapers seriously distorted the event in 'reporting' it, contributing further to the generational conflicts that the Honecker faction wished to unleash. It has been suggested that even this event – which supposedly 'proved' youth criminality – was not simply a matter of spontaneous demonstrations of protest on the part of young Beat fans. It was indicative that perhaps only somewhere between one fifth and one third (500–800) of the demonstrators were genuine supporters of Beat groups; the majority of 'demonstrators' were apparently members of the SED, the FDJ and the Stasi, determined to provoke an incident that could then be used to justify the policy changes that had already been decided on.[37] In any event, it inaugurated the new phase of cultural crackdown that was to characterise the period from the Eleventh Plenum of December 1965 through to the Honecker era and the surprising announcement of renewed liberalisation in the early 1970s with the policy of 'no taboos'.

The Leipzig incident is clearly of major symbolic and political importance. But it should not serve entirely to obscure the more complex picture of less clear-cut realities for most people most of the time. For long periods, for very many young people – arguably a majority, given the tiny numbers of active dissidents and of those who for various reasons became embroiled in serious trouble with the Stasi and police – the interactions were far more fuzzy, with grass-roots initiatives at times flourishing irrespective of, at times with the support of, state authorities. And far larger numbers than those involved in by-now-notorious protest incidents were involved in the more mundane activities of youth clubs, which were neither entirely under the control of the FDJ, nor fountainheads of teenage rebellion and protest.

The leisure activities of young people frequently took place in the context of clubs that were both supported by, and yet simultaneously appeared often to be somewhat out of the control of, the SED and the FDJ. A glance at myriad semi-organised leisure activities at the grass roots reveals a characteristic mixture of the well-meaning and the boring, the inspirational and the disruptive, the facilitative and the repressive. Although the political context and ideology were very different, some of this complexity – not easily plotted into a coherent story – is very reminiscent of contemporaneous developments in Western European societies.

On the one hand, grass-roots clubs and organisations could certainly be used for a range of activities, some more and some less political, initiated by well-meaning adults. Thus a programme targeted at girls in 1956, for example, included sessions on supposedly traditional 'female' interests such as cooking, sewing, cosmetics and fashion, as well as 'Sexual problems of newly-weds', 'Abortion and its consequences' and 'Does having a child mean you have a duty to get married?', alongside 'Summer Night Ball with a Fashion Show from the Baltic Lands'.[38] In 1963 a new youth group was set up associated with the Rostock Folk Theatre (Volkstheater), which attracted a membership of 231 young people, mostly aged fourteen to eighteen (64 boys and 157 girls). The success of this group contrasted rather sharply with that of the one associated with the Rostock Music Conservatory, where 12 Dozenten (junior teachers) turned up to find an audience consisting of only two children – both private pupils of one of the Dozenten – present and demonstrating any interest in what they had to offer.[39] Meanwhile, the youth club attached to the Dessau Theatre found that the 'Twist' and the music of Gershwin brought large audiences. The conclusion drawn by the SED was, at this time, that one had to start from the interests of the young people themselves, in order to 'lead them forwards'.

A report of December 1963 on the activities of young people in Potsdam, however, gives a rather different view of activities in the 19 youth clubs of this area.[40] The average number of young people attending those clubs where relatively little was going on was around 30; the Schopenhauer Straße Youth Club attracted around 80 young people with its variety of events including dances, sport, lectures and debates, while the highest attendance figure, of around 500, was scored by the students' club at the Pädagogische Hochschule for a lecture by Prof. Dr Neubert of Jena on matters to do with sex. Lectures held by functionaries on less obviously riveting topics such as 'The Development of the Workers' Movement in Potsdam', 'The Balance of Powers and Western Military Strategy', or 'What has Dance Music got to do with Politics?', all billed on the programme for November 1963, appear to have been considerably less successful than sex in drawing the crowds.

SED dissatisfaction was evident in another more general report on the development of cultural life in Potsdam the same year.[41] While the work of many of the youth clubs was held to be good, prevailing interests in many clubs were not in line with the 'cultural-political demands' of the SED. Some clubs were refusing offers of a cultural programme (presumably featuring talks along the lines detailed above), because they wanted to develop their own initiatives. Meanwhile, there existed a quite startling richness and variety of cultural activities involving people across the whole age range and life spectrum, strongly reminiscent of the organisation of cultural life in Wilhelmine and Weimar Germany, with around 110 groups including choirs, instrumental music, ensembles, dance, writing, entertainment, cabaret, amateur dramatics and amateur film groups. Much of this grass-roots cultural activity was strongly fostered by SED support. Some of it was equally clearly resistant to SED control (although it was noted that even some of the choirs with more elderly members were being persuaded to learn a few socialist songs), while the attempted development of 'workers who do creative writing' in factories and residential areas was 'totally unsatisfactory'. Youth subcultures need to be set in this wider context of grass-roots leisure pursuits.

The record of youth clubs in 1965 in Berlin's Prenzlauer Berg district – an area that became well known in the 1980s as the centre of an 'alternative scene' and dissident poetry – was, according to the SED, even worse. Young people attending the seven clubs in this district appeared to be interested only in dancing and getting drunk, televisions and radios were tuned into Western stations, and there was no attendance at all at political lectures.[42] Whether this total absence of an audience was preferable to the experience of a speaker at the Jugendclub 'Friedrich Ebert', Berlin, on 29 November 1964, whose attempt at giving a lecture on 'July 1944 and the NKFD' was systematically disrupted by a youthful heckler, is another matter. The heckler appears to have prepared a rather more interesting speech than the official lecturer (who was, interestingly, a former German Wehrmacht General): the youthful protestor delivered a well-prepared critique of the GDR, the SED, Walter Ulbricht, the crimes of Stalin, the departure of Khruschchev, and the question of why the East

German population was never honestly informed on anything.[43] Meanwhile, there were complaints about the youth club in Berlin-Grünau where the FDJ had 'as good as no influence', and where there were 'hot' discussions about the issue of long hair. Political views among the young people here appear by contrast to have verged on the nationalist. While they were able to repeat accurately the arguments they had been taught at school, if talking about the Second World War, they appeared far more likely to show the influence of older work colleagues, were much influenced by nationalist arguments, and felt their national pride was 'wounded' by presentations of German soldiers in films and books.[44]

In Rathenow, a little over 50 kilometres west of Berlin, the so-called 'Club 64' was founded on 27 December 1964 as the 'Club of Modern Art', intended to be 'a communal association for the meaningful use of free time and the education of its members'.[45] It appeared to cater largely for the young intelligentsia of the area and included among its activities a variety of amateur guitar groups. The FDJ struggled in vain to control and coordinate its activities, and to throw out those who were considered to be 'trouble-makers'. But the troubles in Rathenow appear to have extended far beyond the walls of this club. In 1965 the singer Heinz Quermann fell out with a Rathenow amateur guitar group, 'The Fellows', during a test for a television recording; local schoolchildren intervened with a petition and signatories. The affair blew up and rumbled through the local newspaper, the *Märkische Volksstimme*, from August through October, and by November even Ulbricht, Honecker, Hager and Norden had to be informed.[46]

Conflicts often involved young people not only from the local community, but also those travelling from wider areas. In 1967, for example – in the period after the 1965 Plenum, when attitudes towards youthful self-expression and musical exuberance were far less sympathetic than they had been in the brief period of 'liberalisation' from 1963–5 – a 'Beat-Kapelle Wettstreit' (competition between Beat bands) was organised by the Dorfklub Waßmanndorf, Kreis Königswusterhausen, in conjunction with the Seebad-Casino of Rangsdorf, Kreis Zossen, south-east of Berlin.[47] Despite being forbidden by the Cultural Department of Kreis Zossen, the organisers continued to make their arrangements, and to publicise the event, including displaying posters in Berlin. As well as three Beat groups, one of which had been expressly forbidden to perform in Berlin, around 500 young people had already turned up by the scheduled opening time of 19:30, of whom 60 per cent were estimated to have travelled out from Berlin. With news that more were travelling out on the S-Bahn, around 60 'active comrades of the Rangsdorf local party organisation' had to be mobilised to go in and attempt to swamp the audience. Their appearance among the long-haired 'dirty and poorly clad' youngsters, whose appearance 'clearly showed the influence of capitalist lifestyles' must have been somewhat disconcerting, but it was apparently not sufficient to suppress the event entirely, although only one Beat group was allowed to perform.

The hardline policies announced from on high in 1965 were never completely translated into consistent practice on the ground, and by the later 1960s a relaxation in practice was already widely evident. In the 1970s and '80s, the official policy became one of attempted cooption of a somewhat more pluralist scene, although it is notable that differences between hardliners and pragmatists continued both in the higher ranks of the SED and among local functionaries.[48] Watching Western television, strictly forbidden in the 1960s, was finally permitted in 1972. Listening to Western music, ambivalently permitted in the 60:40 ratio to the benefit of home-grown communist music, was never fully under state control and even this ratio was often not adhered to even by the official radio stations. Guitar movements that had been briefly supported by the state were briefly clamped down on and displaced in 1966 by the 'singing movement' (*Singebewegung*) and singing competitions in the later 1960s; but by the later 1960s and '70s, a shift in atmosphere fostered a GDR-version of home-grown Beat. A Central Studio for Entertainment Art was opened in 1968 and transformed into a 'Committee for Entertainment Art' in 1973, providing something of a springboard for artists who later became inter-nationally quite well known, such as Nina Hagen. Popular music-making was sufficiently fostered in the 1970s and '80s to produce some East German bands of genuine talent, originality and popularity, most notably perhaps the Puhdys, who provided music for the highly popular 1973 film *Die Legende von Paul und Paula*. The development of a distinctive style of GDR Rock in the 1970s was not merely officially tolerated, but actively supported at organised events such as the FDJ 'Workshop Week' on 'Youth dance music' in 1972, and on a far larger – indeed massive – scale in the tenth 'World Festival' (Weltfestspiele) of the summer of 1973 in Berlin. An annual rock festival under the title 'Rock for Peace' ('Rock für den Frieden') was organised by the FDJ from 1982 to 1987 in the Palace of the Republic in order, as Kurt Hager put it, to develop 'our' rock music 'as a constituent part of socialist national culture'.[49]

At the same time, a wary eye was kept on subcultural tendencies that appeared politically subversive. The emergent punk scene of the 1980s was treated with hostility and open repression, as well as considerable infiltration by Stasi informers. The tensions between neo-Nazi skinheads and punks were exploited, with skinheads being given free rein by the GDR security forces to

beat up punks emerging from a dissident musical event at East Berlin's
Zionskirche in October 1987.[50] Uncertain how to deal with the proliferation of
minority youth subcultures, including 'grufties' and heavy metal fans alongside peace activists, environmentalists and people simply wanting to engage in
GDR variations on the theme of 'dropping out', the Politburo in the later 1980s
sought unsuccessfully to persuade the FDJ to take firmer control of the youth
'scene'.

The wider international cultural context was also omnipresent, with its
political implications for an increasingly beleaguered GDR regime. By the
1980s, watching Western television and listening to Western music in the
privacy of one's own home was no longer controlled, but attempts to listen to
Western rock concerts, with famous bands playing in the open air next to the
Reichstag in West Berlin on the occasion of Berlin's 750th anniversary celebrations in 1987, were quite another matter. This required major efforts on the
part of FDJ functionaries and security forces to try to prevent young people
from gathering in East Berlin's central avenue, Unter den Linden, and congre-
gating right up against the Wall in the vicinity of the Brandenburg Gate to
listen to the sounds of the decadent West. Eberhard Aurich, First Secretary of
the FDJ Central Council, wrote to Egon Krenz, then in charge of security
matters, proposing that 1,000 members of FDJ 'disciplinary squads'
(Ordnungsgruppen) and 1,000 FDJ functionaries and students should be sent
to infiltrate the crowds as 'agitators', and a further 1,000 should be sent to the
concert itself. The Brandenburg Gate area should be physically sealed off, 'on
the pretext of a planned provocation on the state borders'; Aurich requested
Krenz's blessing on this plan so that he could proceed with the necessary
preparations.[51] The SED authorities nevertheless also went to the Western
concerts to learn; planning their own mass open-air events in some competition, they took close notes of key technical details (including the average queue
length and waiting time for temporary toilet cabins), and went on to facilitate
the open-air performances of politically acceptable Western stars such as Bob
Dylan (who was allegedly disappointed by the slow sale of tickets for his
planned concert in the West) and Bruce Springsteen in the late 1980s.[52]

It is arguable that even these notable events still only affected a minority of
East German youth. The number of youth clubs fluctuated as clubs were
opened and closed according to political evaluations of their reliability or
potentially subversive nature, most evidently in the 1960s, as we have seen. But
their activities appear both to have expanded and to have become somewhat
more routine in the course of the 1970s and '80s. Growing largely as an initiative of the early 1960s in the larger towns and cities, by 1963 there were over
800 youth clubs.[53] The figures for May and December 1972 were 1,025 and

2,378 respectively; in December 1972, there were allegedly 60,973 participants in these youth clubs.[54] By the late 1970s, uncertainty remained over the exact number of youth clubs, though one study guessed that there were by this time somewhere between 5,000 and 6,200 clubs, with between 500,000 and 750,000 young people attending on a more or less regular basis, and around 70,000 young people genuinely active in the committees steering the activities.[55] In 1979, it was estimated that there were just over 3,000,000 East Germans aged between fourteen and twenty-five; thus perhaps around a quarter of the population in the relevant age group attended a youth club fairly regularly in the later 1970s.[56] In the mid-1980s, 85 per cent of young people surveyed in a cross section of communities of different sizes lived in a place where there was a youth club; while 46 per cent claimed they 'seldom or never' went to it, this nevertheless meant that by the mid-1980s, perhaps around half the population of young people did attend such clubs, and more than one in ten were very active members performing one or another function in the activities and programme of the club.[57] While 83 per cent in the mid-1980s thought discos should 'definitely' be on the programme, only 22 per cent were as enthusiastic about 'political discussions and lectures'.[58] Higher numbers were almost always involved on occasions such as dances and concerts, when conflicts within communities and between subsections of the community and the authorities were most likely to occur. To write the history of the mundane activities and experiences of young people in these clubs is more difficult than to focus on the moments of conflict and protest. But it is worth gaining at least a sense of the extent of the less eventful hinterland beyond the clashes that have so far hit the historical headlines.

'Socialist personalities' and East German individualism

A vision of individuals as constituted by, participating in and contributing to wider collective entities and forces permeated the whole of the official Marxist-Leninist world view in the GDR. It was a key strand running through the published sociological literature discussing questions of social structure, productivity, scientific and technological progress, and the continued road to a better society. It pervaded politically driven historical writing (and Marxist historiography more generally), in which the key actors were not individuals, with their unique quirks and motives, but rather collective class actors – the 'imperialist capitalist bourgeoisie', the oppressive landowning classes, the proletariat and so on – who were occasionally given a political twist when, clouded by 'false consciousness', they failed to act appropriately and required a little help from the 'vanguard party' of the working class. It pervaded the teleological view of history as all driving towards one Goal, the ultimate (and effectively predetermined) ends justifying the use of forceful and repressive means, which would dispose of awkward individuals who stood in the way of Progress. It informed much of policy making, which was targeted at groups rather than individuals; social policy was oriented towards collective security and an almost religious sense of safety, being looked after and cared for in a paternalistic state, encapsulated in the notion of *Geborgenheit*, rather than fostering a Western-style enterprise culture of individualism. And it made life extremely uncomfortable for any individual who went beyond the category of being 'still hovering' or plagued by 'uncertainties' ('*noch schwankend*', '*Unsicherheiten*') to being under the influence of the 'class enemy', that mysterious and unseen force who more or less enjoyed the status of Devil in certain official GDR discourses. The question of whether the individual pursuit of happiness as conceived by Western liberals (from J. S. Mill to American mainstream popular culture) was intrinsically in conflict with, and should be subordinated to, notions of the collective good, was one that, if at all, could be discussed only obliquely in the realms of creative literature and film.

Yet it rapidly became clear that the mere formal transformation of the social relations of production would not be sufficient to transform people's personalities over night. Thus the system of education, youth organisations, and facilities for organised leisure, were all subjected to intense political scrutiny and control. But all the effort and thought put into the design of policies and institutions aimed at the achievement of 'socialist personalities' was ultimately undercut by far wider trends, not merely common across the Western industrialised world of the later twentieth century, but also to a degree facilitated by the SED regime itself.

There is of course a dramatic difference in the ways in which citizens were involved in social, cultural and political processes in the Western democracies and the communist states of the later twentieth century. But every society has a framework of institutions and social processes in the context of which people make their lives. Different societies simply have different criteria for the kinds of behaviour they reward and suppress, encourage and constrain. Even the notion of the free-standing 'individual' outside of 'society' is very much a product of a particular type of Western philosophy in a capitalist society – and a historically erroneous notion at that. 'Individualism' as expressed in variations on current fashions in capitalist consumerism is as much influenced – if less consciously so – by prevailing cultural, economic and political circumstances as were the notions of collective in the GDR, and as accompanied by conflicts and contested identities, though played out in terms of very different rules and with very different kinds (and degrees) of penalty attached.

Tendencies towards 'individualisation' among young people in the 1980s, despite all the best efforts of the SED over nearly four decades, were registered by researchers at the ZIJ. A summary given by Guenther Lange in April 1988 claimed that, in comparison to previous years, studies revealed

> an increasing tendency to emphasise autonomy, personal independence, individuality and a high degree of self-confidence among young people. At the same time there is a weakening of societal engagement, of identification with the goals of socialism, with our state and also with the Soviet Union. Today's young people are genuinely interested in matters political ... On the other hand, many young people express dissatisfaction about the manner and level of political information and discussion in daily life.[59]

A lecture by Lange's ZIJ colleague Peter Förster reported that fully half (50 per cent) of those who were not members of the FDJ claimed that it did not represent their interests at all; more shattering news for his FDJ Central Council audience were the accompanying findings that nearly a third (31 per cent) of members of the FDJ were of the same opinion, as were a staggering 16 per cent even of FDJ functionaries. A mere quarter (25 per cent) of FDJ functionaries professed to be in full agreement with the statement that the FDJ did represent their interests.[60] Most of the employed young people among those questioned also felt they did not have much of a say in the affairs of their factory. These were hardly, then, the model citizens or 'socialist personalities' of the future.

Ultimately, the SED failed in its attempt to create 'socialist personalities' committed to building socialism. Consumerism, global culture and tendencies within East German society itself contributed to an individualism that was also characteristic of Western societies in the 1980s. A sense of individual competition in the economic sphere might have gone, in contrast to the capitalist West, but there was still the emergence – or continuation – of trends towards individualisation rooted in private leisure patterns and consumerism. In conditions in which there genuinely appeared to be greater political choice or the possibility for change, this individualism could have political implications. Yet this was not necessarily always in opposition to the state or its representatives in terms of functionaries on the ground. It is crucial to remember when trying to understand the notion of 'ordinary lives' in a highly intrusive state, that most East Germans managed to do two things that are usually missed from 'top-down accounts' couched in terms of SED policy and effects: they lived vast areas of their lives outside of formal Party and state organisations and they were able to take initiatives that were at times fostered by, at times coincided with, and only sometimes clashed with, top-down initiatives. At the same time, many individuals in the GDR developed a high sense of moral responsibility – for peace, for the environment, for the nature of their own society and its future. If not quite the 'socialist personality' of official propaganda, there were nevertheless distinct traces of socialist idealism as well as Western consumerism to be found among East German citizens.

Chapter Seven

Gender

Official conceptions of masculinity changed very little during the forty years of the GDR. The rather muscular ideal of the 'traditional' working-class male, characterised by physical strength and stamina, and widely prevalent in the official imagery of the 'workers' and peasants' state', was not greatly affected by the long-term shift towards more white-collar and professional jobs: the symbols of suit, tie and briefcase that proliferated in West German marketing imagery did not manage to displace the blue overalls and hard hats of East German propaganda. Those East German men who found themselves challenged to rethink their domestic roles or develop notions of the 'new man' did so largely out of necessity: the growing participation of women in the paid labour force, and in particular the demands of shift work, led many men to take on greater responsibilities for childcare and household duties. If East Germany was a more 'working class' society in its official imagery and rhetoric than West Germany, then it was also in many respects more 'male' in a very traditional construction of masculinity.

But the gendering of propaganda images did change in one crucial respect. Women were pictured, too, in overalls and hard hats, driving trucks, cranes and operating heavy machinery. This signified one crucial area of change in gender constructions in 'actually existing socialism'. At the same time it became ever more clear that gender roles cannot be transformed by focusing on one side of the relationship alone. The alleged 'emancipation of women' in the GDR was for all sorts of reasons at best lopsided and partial. There were very radical changes in the public roles and professional aspirations of women, and only minimal changes in assumptions about what was 'normal' for men. Policies were often out of line with practices, professed ideals out of line with ingrained attitudes. In any event, the notion of 'emancipation' would require far wider rethinking to encompass questions of freedom of choice and equality of opportunity for all – a discussion going way beyond the question merely of the respective roles of men and women and changing constructions of gender. Yet if one remains with a more limited focus, the transformation in the roles of women is one of the areas of greatest social change in the GDR.

In 1950, many women in East Germany thought that it was only 'normal' for young girls to aspire to get married and have children rather than careers, and for married women to stay at home and to look after their families – however much the post-war realities departed from this ideal. By 1990, the majority of East German women thought that it was only 'normal' to go out to work – whether or not they were married, whether or not they had children. Around half the East German labour force in the 1980s was female; after unification, women were laid off disproportionately and affordable childcare facilities slashed, hitting East German women particularly hard. Such was the transformation, over forty years, in what was perceived to be 'perfectly ordinary' with respect to women's lives in the GDR.

The roles of women in the GDR have been generally considered in terms of a problematic pair of concepts, usually held to be polar opposites: 'emancipation' or 'double burden' (*Doppelbelastung*). Closer inspection suggests that there is far more at stake here than simply a pair of alternatives. The notion of 'double burden' instantly reveals one aspect of the problem: that the roles of only half the population, namely females, were subject to close scrutiny, and that, for women, traditionally male tasks were simply added on to traditionally female roles. Male roles were not subjected to the same scrutiny, and there was no comparable degree of rethinking the division of labour in the domestic sphere. Most men – including the men at the top, the policy-makers in the Politburo – still assumed that primary responsibilities for housework and childcare lay with women, even beyond the first few months of a baby's life, when breastfeeding was perhaps the only service that fathers genuinely could not perform. The focus in the GDR was thus essentially on women, rather than on gender roles as such; with the exception of the ideas of a handful of feminist intellectuals, there is little evidence of any concomitant rethinking of the roles of men.

The notion of 'emancipation' opens up a far wider set of philosophical and political issues. The question may obviously be asked about the extent to which either men or women were, or could be, genuinely 'emancipated' in a paternalistic dictatorship in which, despite claims that everything was 'for the good of the people' ('Alles zum Wohle des Volkes'), there were vast areas of life over which 'the people' had little power or control. Yet this question is not one simply of comparison between dictatorships and democracies; the formal freedoms of capitalism may not actually feel much like 'emancipation' for most people either (least of all those at the bottom of the social heap), when the iniquitous hidden (and not-so-hidden) forces of the market, the class system, the biases of privilege and the injustices of unfair education systems, mean that structurally shaped inequalities and major constraints on freedom of choice can be camouflaged by the language of meritocracy and individual 'success' or 'failure'.

What would constitute 'emancipation' is in any event a far wider issue than that of the simple notion of (at least apparent) freedom of choice for individuals, however fundamental a human right this may be held to be. The complexities are rooted partly in the fact that individuals live in social communities where – as it is often rather concisely formulated – 'your freedom ends where my nose begins', a point noted both in the liberal tradition of J. S. Mill, in which freedom should not extend to areas where one person's actions might cause harm to others, and in the Marxist notion that true 'emancipation' is only possible in a fundamentally equal society in which the 'condition for the free development of each is the condition for the free development of all'. It is rooted also in the paradox, noted more by Marxists than by liberals, that even though we may think we are free to do what we want, we are not necessarily free to want what we want – that is, individual aspirations are themselves very much a product of the social and historical environment in which they are formed.

So the question of women's roles is in fact intrinsically and inescapably about a larger set of issues concerning the social construction of gender more broadly, including men's roles; issues of power and conceptions of freedom; and the social shaping of individual aspirations and choices. Within this wider set of considerations, analysis of the dramatic changes in East German women's roles and aspirations over forty years provides a fascinating demonstration of the interplay of regime-specific social policies, domestic political forces, changing socio-economic conditions, and wider social and cultural developments.

Kinder, Küche, Kirche? The pre-1949 background

For centuries, women have of course worked. What changed with industrialisation was the growing prevalence of women in paid employment with fixed hours of work outside the home, farm or domestic environment. Increasing participation of women in the paid labour force, particularly in the growing white-collar and service sectors of the economy, had already been a feature of the early twentieth century in Germany. This trend was massively assisted by the absence of men at the front during the First World War, and the influx of women into factories, as well as clerical jobs in offices and the traditional domestic-service roles. The emergent political emancipation of women was a notable feature of the Weimar Republic, with women having the vote for the first time in the constitution of 1919, and women being elected to the National Assembly in Weimar, which had the highest number of female parliamentary representatives in any Western state at the time. Nevertheless, female 'emancipation' remained a highly contentious issue, ranging from disapproval of *Doppelverdiener* (dual-income families, where married women were also in paid employment) to conflicts over women's control over their own fertility through the use of contraception or the practice of abortion. Nor were the political parties that particularly supported female emancipation necessarily the parties most women favoured with their newly found voting power; women tended to vote disproportionately for conservative and religious parties (such as the Catholic Centre Party) while the SPD and KPD, with their pro-feminist policies, failed to make much of an inroad into the female vote.

During the Third Reich, a number of mutually contradictory developments took place simultaneously, although interpretations of these developments remain contentious.[1] On the one hand, explicit Nazi ideology with respect to women was exceedingly traditional, stressing the return of women to the domestic and nurturing spheres of 'children, kitchen, church' ('Kinder, Küche, Kirche') – although actually, in Hitler's ideology, the 'church' part was more notable by its absence. Nazi ideology was one of 'biological essentialism', with fundamentally different roles for men and women. This was, however, no injunction for women to retreat into a 'private sphere' of family life, for Nazi racial ideology was deeply intrusive.

Racial and political prejudices cross-cut and took priority over essentialist views on gender.[2] It was the perpetuation of the Nazi racial community and its wider interests that was at the centre of Nazi views on gender: hence 'women' were not a homogeneous group in the Third Reich, but were rather divided on racial and related criteria into those who were to be primarily producers (such as those designated for forced labour) and those who were to be the physical reproducers of the 'national community'; in other words, the biologically defined category of women was further subdivided according to which subgroups were considered to be most useful to the various purposes and goals of the 'master race'. Women deemed to be of healthy, 'Aryan' descent were to be the 'breeding stock' of the future *Volksgemeinschaft*: pro-natalist policies such as tax incentives, subsidies, housing loans and 'Mother's crosses' combined with a prohibition on the use of contraception and the rigorous enforcement of Paragraph 218 of the Civil Code outlawing abortion, were designed to encourage the production of as many 'racially desirable' children as possible.[3] Women who, for one reason or another, were by contrast deemed to be 'inferior' or 'undesirable' as breeders were subjected to compulsory sterilisation: around 400,000 compulsory sterilisations (on both men and women) were carried out in Nazi Germany.[4] And, at the end of the spectrum, 'racially inferior' women (such as Jews and gypsies) and others who were designated outcasts or active opponents of Nazism (Jehovah's Witnesses, lesbians, socialists and others) faced forced labour or murder in the death camps. So even when talking about the Nazis' 'traditional conception' of women's roles, it is important to remember that this role was one that was not private and individual, but rather seen as the way of women making a personal contribution to the collective goals of the wider *Volksgemeinschaft*, as epitomised in the slogan 'every woman, every year, [should produce] a child for the Führer'.

Furthermore, there were marked dissonances between Nazi ideology and policies on the one hand, and what actually happened with respect to the roles of women during the Third Reich on the other.[5] Despite the fact that women were excluded from the higher echelons of Party and state, increasing numbers of women acquired leadership skills through participation in the Nazi girls' and women's groups (the League of German Maidens, and the National Socialist and German Women's organisations) – admittedly of no real political influence and importance in the wider scheme of the Nazi state, but arguably important experience for the women themselves. Despite Nazi pro-natalist policies, and despite an increasing number of marriages in the 1930s, the twentieth-century trend towards the small nuclear family continued. The rise in births, from a low of 14.7 per thousand in 1933 to a high of 20.3 per thousand in 1939, could be explained as much by increasing confidence in conditions of economic recovery from the depths of the Depression as by Nazi pro-natalist policies; nor did it fully recover to pre-Depression levels. The early twentieth-century trend towards increasing employment of women also continued: despite Hitler's opposition to women in politics and the law, and his ambivalence to their participation in professional occupations (with the exception of such 'caring' professions as medicine), the squeeze on women's professional employment was never complete. In 1933, 34.4 per cent of women worked, yet by 1939 this had risen to 36.7 per cent. The proportion of women employed in traditional roles in domestic service declined, compared to the proportions employed in the more visible areas of industry, trade and government; and two million more married women were in employment.[6] During the war, with men away at the front, Nazi policy-makers argued over whether women should be enticed in even greater numbers into the labour force in order to fill the gaps, or should still be encouraged to remain at home (leaving aside for the moment women's own preferences for avoiding hard and exhausting factory labour). And, with increasing responsibility for the running of small family businesses and farms, women began to acquire more managerial, organisational and financial experience. Similarly, while there was an enforced drop in the number of female university students in the peacetime years, many women were able to take up university places when men were away at the front in the war.

In short, the balance sheet of Nazi policies towards women is at best ambiguous; and the Nazi rhetoric of 'children, kitchen, church' was far from realised in practice. Whatever one makes of the polarised and often over-simplistic arguments over whether women should be seen as 'victims' or 'perpetrators', it is quite clear that the record of women's experience in the Third Reich was exceedingly variable according to class, politics and 'racial' categorisation.[7] As with so many areas of the social history of the Third Reich, racial policy and foreign policy had the greatest impact, and the experience of war left the largest mark on the roles and experiences of women, who took over major responsibility for the sheer physical survival, as well as the psychological well-being and socialisation, of their families. After the war, the image of female strength was perpetuated in the concept of the so-called *Trümmerfrauen* or 'women of the ruins', in what became known as the 'hour of the women'.[8] Although this image is clearly overstated – many women fell prey to exhaustion, hunger, illness and rape – the experience of war had a far deeper impact on women's roles than any Nazi ideology or policies.

War had also, in a far more brutal and direct way, altered the character of the labour supply: the number of men of working age had been decimated by Hitler's suicidal policies on behalf of his *Volk*. In the closing months of the war, ever more and younger men and boys had been thrown into the war effort, in a vain attempt to halt the onward march of Allied tanks by conscripting bunches of half-grown, half-trained sixteen year olds. The post-war demographic tree was, as a result, extremely lopsided, with a heavy preponderance of females over males. In 1946 there were 7,800,000 males and 10,560,000 females in the Soviet Zone of Occupation. In 1950, just after the foundation of the GDR, there were 8,160,000 males and 10,230,000 million females, and in 1955, 7,970,000 males and 9,860,000 females.[9] Given the disproportionate losses among the adult male population that had been thrown into battle by Hitler regardless of heavy losses of life, the preponderance of females over males in this age group was even greater (see Figures 1 and 2 below). Gender roles were also affected by the very poor physical state in which many men found themselves after the war, with war wounds often compounded by the effects of lengthy periods of internment as prisoners of war.

1 'German–Soviet friendship' (1): Just a few years after they were engaged in bitter military conflict, Germans and Russians were supposed to forge close links of authentic friendship. Here, former opponents engage in a chess championship in the 'Maxim-Gorki House of German–Soviet Friendship' in Schwerin, November 1953.

2 'German–Soviet friendship' (2): A Russian soldier ostentatiously demonstrates 'friendship' with a very small GDR citizen in the symbolic surroundings of the grandiose Soviet War Memorial in Treptow Park, surrounded by monuments adorned with copious quotations from Stalin, May 1952.

3 Capturing the hearts and minds of the future (1): A massive poster, claiming that 'young activists work for peace and for a better life', advertises the 'Second Congress of Young Activists' in Erfurt, April 1949.

4 Capturing the hearts and minds of the future (2): Young Pioneers and their leaders on a 'tourism' training camp, August 1955.

5 Changing the face of German industrial production (1): The entrance to the 'Eisenhüttenkombinat' works in the first socialist new town, given the name 'Stalinstadt' (and later renamed Eisenhüttenstadt), May 1953.

6 Changing the face of German industrial production (2): The renowned Krupp works in Magdeburg, formerly owned by the Krupp armaments family and after 1945 taken into the 'ownership of the people', was in May 1951 renamed the 'Ernst-Thälmann-Works' in honour of the communist leader martyred by the Nazis in Buchenwald concentration camp. The building is further festooned with a slogan praising the Soviet Union, beneath a picture of Stalin.

7 The collectivisation of the peasantry (1): A 'Machine and Tractor Station' for lending heavy machinery to peasants. This one, photographed in March 1960 and half obscured by a placard proclaiming the victory of socialism, soon had to change its name when the Chinese communist leader Mao Tse Tung fell out of favour with the Soviet leadership.

8 The collectivisation of the peasantry (2): The compulsory collectivisation of remaining independent peasants, forced into 'LPGs' or agricultural cooperatives. This board triumphantly celebrates the achievement within 48 hours in the spring of 1960 of 100 per cent of LPG membership in the village of Marxwalde (originally Neuhardenberg but renamed after Karl Marx on 8 May 1949 to mark the anniversary of the end of the war).

9 Political propaganda for the 'participatory dictatorship': An election slogan for the single list of the 'National Front' in the parliamentary elections of November 1958, in which voters had no genuine choice between parties, exhorts citizens to 'plan together, work together, govern together'.

10 Political propaganda for 'consumer socialism': A poster celebrating '15 years of the SED' since its foundation in April 1946, and an iconic photo of the SED leader Walter Ulbricht, amongst a typical display of jars, tins and boxes in a Leipzig shop window, April 1961.

11 Before the Wall: A perfectly ordinary street-corner scene in Bernauerstraße, at the end of the French sector in Berlin.

12 The Wall goes up: The East is effectively cut off from the West in Bernauerstraße, 13 August 1961.

13 Three young women from Berlin receive paramilitary training in the euphemistically entitled 'Society for Sport and Technology', August 1967.

14 Notwithstanding their sulky body language and sullen facial expressions, these members of a 'youth brigade' are being congratulated by the Works Director on their outstanding contribution to the fulfilment of the production targets of the Kombinat, August 1970.

15 The changing face of the East German peasantry: Female operators of massive combine harvesters at shift change, July 1975.

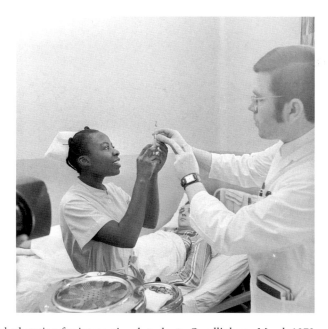

16 Medical education for international students, Quedlinburg, March 1973.

17 Housing (1): An elderly couple are presented with two new armchairs as a gift from the Berlin city council on the occasion of the festive handover of their newly renovated flat, supposedly the 5,000th flat to have been renovated in the context of 'participatory competitions' ('Mach-Mit-Wettbewerbe'), October 1974.

18 Housing (2): Dresdeners move into a new apartment block in November 1975.

19 A somewhat sexist sign indicates the 'Best quality worker [in the masculine gender] in the socialist competition' among this all-female labour force of a textile factory in the 1970s.

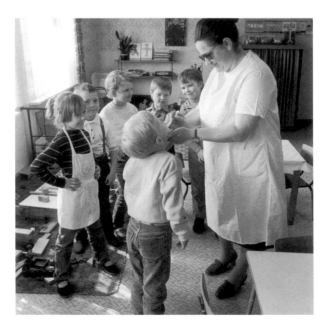

20 This district nurse, here examining the health of kindergarten children in a rural area of Bezirk Schwerin in 1986, also served as a CDU representative on the Schwerin Bezirk Council for over ten years, nominated and supported by her collective.

21 A classic scene of a work brigade of young building labourers helping to construct a new housing estate, 1986.

22 A socialist youth delegation from Korea lays a wreath in honour of the former communist leader Ernst Thälmann at the monument in the Ernst-Thälmann Park, Berlin, September 1987.

23 Residents of the Berlin suburb of Hellersdorf involved in the weekend cooperative ('Mach mit!') improvement works for the children's facilities in their housing estate, 1988.

24 Citizens of the future: Children playing in one of the many childcare facilities in a new town area of Cottbus in mid-July 1989, just a few months before the fall of the Wall and little over a year before the end of the GDR.

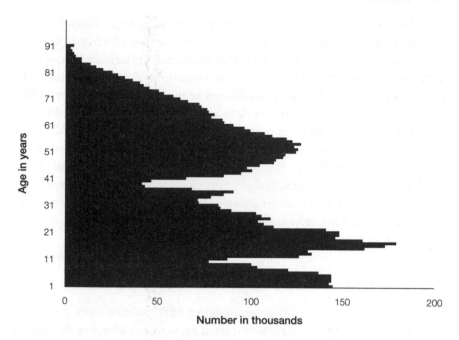

Figure 1: *Demographic tree for 1955: males*

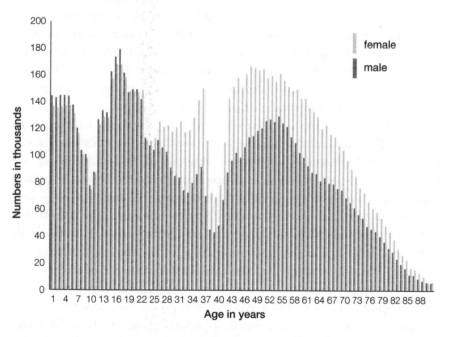

Figure 2: *Comparison of male and female age profiles in 1955*[10]

While the post-war need of the West German labour market for an increased supply of adult males was soon met by the flow of refugees from the lost German territories of the east – 3,500,000 from East Germany alone, many millions more from further east, with the proportion of refugees constituting as much as one fifth of the total population of the Federal Republic by 1960 – the GDR was not so fortunate. The demographic imbalance produced by war was further exacerbated by the disproportionate loss of male skilled labour across the 'Iron Curtain' in the 1950s. So, while West German women in the 1950s were lulled back into the domestic sphere, with a resurrection of the ideology of 'children, kitchen, church', East German women were desperately needed for the economic reconstruction of the GDR. The 'hour of the women' – with all its attendant ambiguities and burdens – was not to be so short-lived on the eastern side of the inner-German border.

The institutional and legal framework of gender in the GDR

There were two main priorities underlying SED policies with respect to women: first, the undoubted economic need for women's labour in the light of the circumstances just outlined, and therefore the need to ensure that the demands of production and reproduction were not mutually incompatible; and secondly, a principled belief in the need for the 'emancipation' of women arising from the Marxist philosophical tradition. While the first priority was largely met in the GDR, the second – at least if one does not share the SED's views – was not. Women were increasingly provided with the conditions necessary for full participation in the labour market, but neither men nor women were entirely emancipated from traditional gender stereotypes, let alone from more fundamental restrictions on human rights.

An underlying theme is the tension, here as elsewhere, between high-minded, vague-but-laudable negative goals (abolition of exploitation and such like) that can be broadly shared across different political and philosophical perspectives, and the rather specific conceptions that the SED sought to put in their place. Thus the emancipation of women did not mean quite the same thing for the SED as it does for Western liberals or feminists. The latter usually adopt a rather individualistic conception of 'emancipation' in terms of the rights of and possibilities for individuals to exercise freedom of choice with respect to virtually every area of life, from career goals and leisure pursuits, through material possessions and economic independence, to physical appearance, relationships, timing and pattern of reproduction, and so on. Such freedom of choice of course entails rejection of old material and legal constraints and of the internalised psychological repression of a 'patriarchal' society, a programme of opposition to old forms of oppression wholeheartedly endorsed by the SED. But the SED generally sought to replace oppressive patriarchal structures and mentalities not with liberal notions of individual freedom of choice, but rather with new forms of collectivism as defined by the leading Party. So with 'emancipatory' moves often came the specification of new duties and responsibilities revolving around the fulfilment of collective goals. The future of society as a whole, and women's contributions to that future, were as much at stake as the future of women as individuals. Nevertheless, it is important not to reify the 'SED' as a unitary actor or sole initiator of policy with respect to women; it rapidly becomes clear that a variety of processes were at work, with different social and political factors shaping the pattern and character of policies affecting gender roles in the GDR.

It has sometimes been argued that GDR policies with respect to women fall readily into two major phases: an early, 'genuinely' progressive and idealistic phase in the 1950s and '60s, concerned with the 'emancipation' of women from patriarchal constraints, and the realisation of full equality with men; and a later, more 'pragmatic' phase in the 1970s and '80s, in which women's policies were designed primarily to ensure that they would both produce more children and contribute effectively in the workforce. As with many other attempts to draw sharp distinctions between the Ulbricht and Honecker periods on these lines, this periodisation tends to oversimplify the position. For one thing, pragmatic and idealistic considerations were present throughout, though differently weighted in different quarters; there was no single monolithic 'SED view'. For another, the presumed 'needs of society', or at least a conception of the system as a whole, informed policy changes throughout, and women were continually seen not as isolated individuals but as integral parts of a family that itself was a key element in the construction of socialist society.[11] To make a sharp break with Honecker's accession to power is both to overlook significant continuities and more subtle long-term changes.

Key measures challenging traditional notions of women's roles were instituted already in the occupation period. The SMAD Order 253 of 17 August 1946, issued by the Soviet Military Administration, enshrined the principle of equal pay for equal work. In the course of the occupation period, with the very large number of rapes of German women and girls by Red Army soldiers, and numerous consequent unwanted pregnancies in the extremely difficult conditions of widespread disease, inadequate or ruined accommodation, and often near-starvation rations, a number of *Länder* introduced a relaxation of

Paragraph 218 prohibiting abortion. With the formal foundation of the GDR, matters were very quickly regularised on a new basis.

The equal status of men and women was firmly embedded in the 1949 Constitution, which asserted that men and women had equal rights, including the right to work, equal wages for equal work, and particular protection for women, marriage and the family. In September 1950, the Law for the Protection of Mother and Children and the Rights of Women (Gesetz über den Mutter- und Kinderschutz und die Rechte der Frau) was designed to ensure that women not only enjoyed equal rights in theory, but that also the 'still persisting inequalities in practice' could be dealt with.[12] A wide-ranging series of important practical measures was introduced, including financial support, improved hospital and medical care, the provision of crèches and other childcare facilities, as well as rights at work (such as consideration for mothers of small children when arranging overnight shift work) and even – especially important at a time of continuing widespread hunger – the doubling of the mother's entitlement to food rations from the sixth month of pregnancy to the end of breast-feeding or the completion of the baby's first year of life. The one element in this document that caused concern to many women was §11, reinstating the effective prohibition of abortion by removing the so-called 'social indication' and allowing abortion only when a continuation of pregnancy would risk the life or health of the pregnant woman, or when one parent was a carrier of a serious hereditary disease (the so-called 'medical' and 'eugenic' indications). Yet this was in line with the general ideological tenor of policies towards women, given the integrated focus on women, children and the family as crucial elements of the future of the community as a whole: 'Children are the future of the nation, and therefore one of the primary tasks of our democratic state is the concern for children, for the strengthening of the family, and for encouragement of large families.'[13] Or, as §12 put it: 'A healthy family is one of the fundamental pillars of a democratic society. Strengthening the family is one of the most important tasks of the government of the German Democratic Republic.'[14] Thus the duty of women to produce the socialist citizens of the future was held to override their individual freedom of choice to terminate an unwanted pregnancy.

There was a more or less constant stream of practical measures in the 1950s and '60s that sought to affect the roles and aspirations of women, including measures for the introduction of equality in schools (co-educational comprehensive schools, abolition of separate sport and leisure activities, and separate academic or vocational curricula for boys and girls); the extension of maternity leave and support provisions; the introduction of a paid 'day of housework' for married women and also single mothers under specified conditions; the extension of provisions for child care, including workplace crèches in enterprises with large proportions of women workers; special provisions for single mothers; and the introduction of child-benefit payments with the abolition of rationing.

The variety of obstacles to women's full participation in the economic as well as the domestic sphere included not only practical but also psychological barriers to equality of opportunity. In the early 1960s, a great deal of energy was devoted to attempts to identify and remove these obstacles. A key statement was the Politburo communiqué of December 1961, 'Die Frauen – Der Frieden und der Sozialismus' ('Women – Peace and Socialism').[15] The ideal was depicted in unmistakable terms: 'With self-confidence, intelligence and prudence, women accomplish outstanding achievements in their careers, in bringing up their children, and in the direction and leadership of our state'.[16] The document was designed to exhort people in institutions at all levels to discuss how best to further women's positions and interests, and to alleviate the difficulties of everyday life. It recognised the weight of inherited prejudices – although ironically also reproducing them, in so far as 'women's duties' in the home appear to be simply reaffirmed – and summarised very aptly the difficulties faced on the ground by women:

> Often women who already have leadership functions are over-burdened by excessive work without consideration of their duties as a mother and housewife. More is often demanded of them than of a man in the same position. Many [male] colleagues in positions of leadership are, without explicitly saying so, of the opinion that women have to 'prove' themselves through exceptional achievements. Instead of helping women and girls to deal with their greater burdens, they invent arguments that are supposed to prove that putting women into middle-level and higher functions is not possible. In particular it is asserted that the employment of a woman with a household and children to look after is economically not 'viable'; that men are more reliable and would not be absent as often; yes, there is also the 'argument' that women have less understanding for technical-organisational problems than men.[17]

After praising the achievements of women in all manner of fields, the complaint was made that these achievements had not been adequately acknowledged, either to assist women's own development, or for the purposes of social progress. As if the point had not already been made clearly enough, the document continued by identifying the major problem:

> The main cause of this is the still-prevalent underestimation of the role of women in socialist society, particularly on the part of men, including functionaries in leading roles in the Party, state and economy and trade unions.[18]

The solution proposed in this communiqué was that of open public discussion. Such discussion should take place as widely as possible: not only in the parties, the mass organisations, the National Front, the state and trade union organisations, but also

> In factories and residential areas, in the club houses of towns and villages, in newspapers and magazines, on radio and television, with the help of writers and artists and above all through the active participation of women themselves, everywhere the great debate about *Die Frauen – der Frieden und der Sozialismus* should take place. In the process, all questions and doubts should be expressed frankly, and the critical comments of women should be analysed and evaluated.[19]

In the event, there were indeed widespread discussions of women's issues at all levels in the GDR in the 1960s.

In March 1960, a Women's Commission (Frauenkommission) was founded under Edith Baumann, responsible to the Secretariat of the SED Central Committee. In February 1962 this was made responsible to the Politburo, under the leadership of Inge Lange, who was also leader of the women's department (Abteilung Frauen) of the Central Committee.[20] The FDGB met with representatives of workplace women's committees at a women's conference in May 1960. A decision of the Council of Ministers in 1962 laid down a number of principles for the furtherance of women in a wide variety of areas, ranging from education, training and the mundane issues of the workplace, to women's participation in politics, the creative arts and literature. The Family Law of 1965 (the Familiengesetzbuch), which came into effect in 1966, gave both parents equal responsibility for parenting (*Erziehungsverantwortung*). Divorce was also made much easier, such that, alongside the increasing financial independence of women through paid employment, the functions of marriage changed rather dramatically. Meanwhile, and without any publicity (indeed, under conditions of confidentiality), the 'medical indicators' for abortion were relaxed in 1965, such that the woman's 'health' was now interpreted more broadly to include not only physical health but also social and psychological well-being, thus greatly enlarging the proportion of pregnant women seeking termination who could be considered eligible for legal abortions. Women's roles were reconsidered in the wider context of the role of the family, and of young people as the embodiment of the future, with the Politburo Youth Communiqué of 21 September 1963, 'Giving Trust and Responsibility to Youth' ('Der Jugend Vertrauen und Verantwortung'), followed by the Youth Law (Jugendgesetz) of 4 May 1964 and the integrated Education Law of 1965 (Gesetz über das einheitliche sozialistische Bildungssystem). The focus of social policy in these areas reinforced the point that women were viewed not as isolated individuals, but rather more broadly as part of 'socialist society' in which 'socialist marriage and the family' were seen as the building blocks of the socialist future.[21]

Given the general emphasis on increasing the birth rate, the Abortion Law of 1972 appears at first glance to run in quite the reverse direction, giving women the option of terminating a pregnancy on demand within the first twelve weeks. Although its precise timing was influenced by the possibility of visa-free travel to Poland (with the consequent possibility of obtaining abortions across the border), this law – passed within less than a year of Honecker's accession to power – was, more importantly, the culmination of a longer period of debate and the shifting climate of opinion in the 1960s.[22] A younger, more female medical profession agreed with many women that individual freedom of choice was important, and the high disease and mortality rates associated with illegal abortions were now taken as arguments in support of legalisation, rather than used as evidence against abortion altogether. In the event, following a brief but dramatic rise in numbers of abortions to 113,232 in 1973 – along with the simultaneous introduction of free contraception to prevent unwanted pregnancies and a range of measures to encourage wanted pregnancies – abortion rates steadied to rates generally between 80,000–95,000 per year, alongside rising birth rates, in the course of the 1970s.[23]

The major emphasis of policies towards women in the Honecker era was primarily targeted to extending women's dual role in production and reproduction; the needs of 'non-productive' and 'non-reproductive' women (such as old age pensioners, the vast majority of whom were female) tended to be somewhat neglected in comparison. A declining birth rate in the 1960s compounded the problems brought about by the earlier loss of young adults in the years before 1961. Financial inducements for having children were repeatedly extended. Child benefits were constantly increased, with higher benefits for second and third children. Maternity leave provisions were expanded, with ever more extended periods of leave possible after the birth of first and subsequent children (by 1986, a full year on pay following the birth of a first child, eighteen months for a third child, two or three years in the case of multiple births). A comprehensive system of baby and childcare facilities was built up, such that from a very early age children could be looked after by a state institution: crèche, Kindergarten, or after-school care, depending on the age of the child. Thus there was not the economic disincentive – or sheer practical impossibility – faced by Western parents who had the 'luxury of choice' between working and not working, but who found that in practice there were no affordable child-care facilities to allow any real choice. A further practical measure designed to assist East German parents was that of the concentration of functions such as shopping, laundry facilities and health-care centre attached to the workplace and well within easy reach. The quality of many of these institutions was, however, often quite another matter. The pro-natalist measures nevertheless appear in many respects to have been successful: the number of live births went up by as much as a quarter, from 180,336 in 1973 to a peak of 245,132 in 1980.[24] However, a number of factors played a role in women's choices, including not only financial inducements and childcare facilities but also the availability of counselling for teenagers, periodic scare stories about the effects of the pill, and views about future prospects in changing circumstances. And there continued to be measures to ensure that women were fully involved in employment and education, and were encouraged to achieve further qualifications whether as school leavers or as mature students, often through evening courses or retraining schemes.

Most policies were, as before, designed primarily to achieve the compatibility of motherhood, employment and contribution to the construction of socialism, rather than being informed by Western liberal notions of the 'emancipation' of women in the sense of individuals seeking 'self-fulfilment'. Nor did they entail much, if any, rethinking of traditional male and female gender roles, despite the fact that both GDR sociologists – such as some of those working at the ZIJ and at the women's research group at the Humboldt University – and prominent women writers such as Christa Wolf, Irmtraud Morgner, Maxie Wander and others, were increasingly discussing these issues at this time. Yet the changed institutional and legal framework, for all the necessary caveats, did nevertheless help to unleash or support changes in attitudes in the GDR that had far wider implications. This is evident in the ways in which gender was constructed and enacted in the various spheres of the workplace, organised politics and informal political activism, and in the domestic sphere and everyday life.

Gender assumptions and the division of labour

Far more problematic than changing the legal, institutional and social policy framework was the question of changing attitudes about the gendered division of labour among ordinary members of the population – both male and female.

The long prehistory of women's roles was still deeply ingrained in the consciousness, aspirations and activities of young women in the early years of the GDR. An immediately recognisable picture is presented, for example, in a report of September 1955 on young women in the district of Greiz, where, despite a predominance of females in the local textile industry (approximately

80 per cent of the workforce in textile factories), very few women held qualifications or leading positions. While the men claimed that women were
physically too weak to become *Meister*, the report writer identified low aspirations on the part of young women:

> Numerous girls do not yet adequately recognise the role of women in our state.
> They often only intend to work just until they get married, in order to obtain the
> basic essentials for the marriage. These intentions are generally supported and
> furthered by the parents. It is the case that those girls who are prepared to go on to
> study and who set this goal themselves are for the most part from a petty bourgeois
> background, while working-class children are only after a longer and persistent
> process of persuasion willing to work for qualifications.[25]

The sights of most young women were predominantly set on the traditional
targets of marriage and motherhood:

> The majority of girls aged over eighteen, in so far as they have not yet got married,
> demonstrate the natural [!] desire to prepare themselves for marriage. This is often
> accompanied by a tendency to pursue individual interests more strongly and to play
> less of a part in societal work ...
>
> However, to this must be added the fact that the attitude of girls towards the [Free
> German Youth] organisation and towards societal work in general is often heavily
> dependent on the influence of the boyfriend or fiancé, since most girls just agree
> with their opinions. Girls from the age of eighteen to twenty-five are interested
> above all in learning how to cook, bake, sew, look after babies and bring up children,
> and in women's illnesses, the new Family Law, furnishing a flat, questions of fashion
> and make-up, etc.[26]

In so far as young women engaged in such elevated pursuits as reading, they
appeared to choose predominantly light literature such as adventure stories,
travel stories and love stories (some of which unfortunately appeared to have
come from West Germany, and hence had unwanted political implications).
And in so far as they had any career aspirations alongside the desire for
marriage and family, it was with a view to traditionally 'female' jobs and
nurturing roles:

> As far as choice of career is concerned, it has to be said that, alongside the opportu-
> nities presented by the textile industry, girls who are leaving school have a prefer-
> ence above all for careers such as seamstress, retail positions, baby care and
> nursing.[27]

Such a picture, with local variations with respect to prevailing local employment patterns, could be repeated from virtually anywhere in the GDR in the
1950s.

In the early years, traditional attitudes towards 'children, kitchen, church' were prevalent: perhaps a majority of East German women and men did not think that women, if they could afford the luxury of choice, should be involved in politics or paid employment once they had a family. Views such as 'Politics is a matter for men, it's not appropriate for girls' or 'A good marriage is only possible if the woman devotes herself exclusively to household and family' were widespread.[28] But official images and propaganda worked hard to counteract such views. The early heroisation of the *Trümmerfrauen* was soon replaced by the new idols of the *Aufbaugeneration*, the builders of the new society. Illustrations on posters and in the state-controlled media (magazines, newspaper articles) sought to portray women in occupations that were traditionally seen as 'male', such as tractor-drivers or 'firemen' (now even in the anglophone world known under the more politically correct term, 'fire-fighters'); beautiful blondes in hard hats on construction sites, or in surgical uniforms bending over patients in hospital beds, stared out of the pages of glossy magazines in an effort to revise traditional stereotypes. Broader changes in the structure of the economy assisted this process of reconceptualising the roles of men and women at work. The ideal of muscular masculinity, evident in the paintings and statues of socialist realism, was highly emphasised in the early years. Thus, for example, the posters exhorting people to work harder, in the 'Activists of the First Hour' movement and the state-sponsored idolisation of the worker Adolf Hennecke, stressed the importance of physical strength. The emphasis on sheer physical might was toned down as faith in the possibilities opened up by technical-scientific progress took over in the 1960s. Brain-power became more important than physical power as the preferred solution to the GDR economy's ills. Skills and training became the watchwords of the 1960s, areas in which (unlike sheer physical force) women could be seen to be potentially as proficient as men. Organisations such as the FDJ and the DFD devoted immense amounts of time and energy to trying to raise the educational aspirations and career goals of young women with the general focus on the need for a more highly skilled workforce in the 1960s.

As a report from the FDJ from the late 1950s (probably 1957) noted: 'Every day one meets girls and women who have not yet grasped what it means to be a fellow creator of our new society with equal rights ['gleichberechtigter Mitgestalter unserer neuen Gesellschaft']. They still voluntarily subject themselves to their husbands and sacrifice the possibility of further career development to household duties.'[29] The FDJ saw it as its own particular duty 'to participate actively in the creation and development of a new socialist women's generation, a women's generation that has freed itself from the chains of the past that condemned women to exploitation and repression.'[30] To some extent this aim was achieved, though arguably with little credit due to the activities of the FDJ in the process: over time, women's aspirations did change, although more as a result of changing opportunities and experiences than of FDJ exhortations; and women were not always overly keen to swap the discredited 'chains of the past', the exploitation and repression of capitalist patriarchy, for the new chains of political subservience and control in the communist version.

There were indeed crucial shifts in attitudes as younger women, socialised within the GDR, grew to maturity and entered the workforce. These shifts were evident already by the start of the 1960s. A particularly wide-ranging and insightful report of May 1961 on women in the textiles industry argues that, despite continued use of very antiquated machinery (usually forty to fifty years old, but in one location still the original eighteenth-century machinery!), young women were becoming increasingly productive. Moreover, they were increasingly committed to their work in principle:

> For many young female workers their work has already developed into a need, and the desire to work permanently is increasingly growing. In the 'Nortex-Girls' brigade there was a serious dispute because the District Secretary of the FDJ said in his speech to the District Delegates' Conference that, while women admittedly achieved good results by way of productivity, they still suffered from great ideological confusion. This was evident in the fact that some of them would not want to continue working after marriage. The young female workers decisively challenged this, and expressed the view that, while they may still have thought this way eighteen months earlier, today it was clear to them that they would go on working constantly.[31]

Often differences in opinion between younger and older women led to conflicts within the workplace. This was particularly the case when new methods were introduced, which were adopted more easily by younger women, who were both more flexible and often also better educated: 'In the process, the authority of young women workers with the economic functionaries grows, in opposition to the older women workers.'[32] Such conflicts were not always easily resolved: 'Often the younger ones have reservations about introducing new methods or improving the organisation of work, because they then get characterised as "bringing wages down" [*Lohndrücker*] by the older women workers.'[33]

Many of the older generation in the workplace did not trust their younger colleagues; but at the same time, they appear to have poured out their own life experiences – which were often, in the case of this war-time generation, quite traumatic – and sought to counsel younger women and give them the advice of the worldly wise. As the report writer complains:

> Not to be underestimated is also the influence of a series of older women workers, who, on the basis of their own experiences from capitalist times give the young women workers bad advice . . .
>
> Precisely in the textile industry there is a strong concentration of such women, whose own happiness in life was destroyed by the World War. On the basis of this bitterness their relationships with the younger women workers are often formed in a very ugly, jealous and immoral manner. Such pieces of 'advice' are expressed in comments such as: 'Don't be so dumb, girl, get yourself a man who earns well, don't go running to work all your life. I would be happy if I didn't have to.'[34]

Whether or not such report-writing was in part informed by wishful thinking, there is a wide range of evidence to suggest that attitudes towards women and work began to change with the shift in generations in the 1970s and '80s. In 1970, 37 per cent of men still felt that the employment of married women with children would have adverse effects on family life; by 1982, only 5.9 per cent of men and 9.7 per cent of women continued to think that women should resign from employment when they had children.[35]

Attitudes to the domestic division of labour, by contrast, proved remarkably resistant to change, although there is evidence again of at least incipient generational shifts. In 1968, for example, a report-writer complained that:

> The awareness of many citizens concerning the necessary division of labour between husband and wife with respect to childcare and household duties is still nowhere near the level that the Family Law is striving towards . . . In addition many women, through lack of self-confidence, are evidently inclined to use their household and childcare duties as a reason for not using more fully the possibilities for the development and application of their own faculties.[36]

The commentators suggested that:

> Political-ideological work needs to be more strenuously developed on the basis of the Family Law. With the help of press, television and radio, and perhaps also through popular scientific films, examples should be used to show how husband and wife can together share responsibility for family and household duties. Strengthening the self-confidence of women also remains now, as previously, an important task.[37]

A study of 1970 found that fewer than one in five men and women were unreservedly in favour of women working, while around half (52.9 per cent of men and 45.8 per cent of women) favoured only part-time employment for women. Interestingly, while only a quarter (26.4 per cent) of women thought both partners in marriage shared their household duties in common, as many as 43.2 per cent (!) of men seemed to think they contributed equally.[38] Meanwhile, another study in the same year found that maintenance of the household took up as many additional hours a week as the normal paid working week; and, what is more, the women did the lion's share of this additional unpaid labour. Of the average 47.1 hours a week spent on housework per household, women did 37.1 hours, men did 6.1 hours and 'others' did 3.9 hours.[39]

In the mid-1970s, simple financial necessity was still given as the main reason why women should work, rather than the pursuit of a career for its own sake. Nevertheless, by now two thirds of women (64.6 per cent) were also of the opinion 'that they could no longer imagine a life without professional employment'. However, old attitudes towards the domestic sphere died hard: twice the proportion of men (37.5 per cent) as women (17.9 per cent) were of the view that 'The employment [of the woman] has an unfavourable effect on the upbringing of the children.'[40] Even in the 1980s, when women's paid employment was more or less taken for granted, women still took primary responsibility for the household and childcare. A 1982 study by the Institute for Sociology and Social Policy of the Akademie der Wissenschaften der DDR, for example, found that married women with children still spent around three times as much time on housework as did their male partners. Moreover, both sexes still appear to have accepted this as 'natural':

Neither men nor women have yet overcome the assumption that women have a 'natural' aptitude for housework. Both sexes accept the current situation with the over-burdening of women, but do not experience it as threatening to their relationship. In this context the generally higher commitment of men to the work process is put into the equation by women. Young people do not accept this attitude. They demand a stringently just division of household duties.[41]

Although there was a complex combination of factors involved, it appears from a number of recent studies that changes in work patterns, and particularly the prevalence of shift work, combined with the expansion of state childcare facilities to alter the character of family life and related assumptions about women's traditional responsibilities.

In the thinly populated, largely agricultural Prignitz area in the north of Bezirk Potsdam, for example, women who had worked in non-skilled agricultural production were threatened by the increasing mechanisation and specialisation of agriculture.[42] In the later 1960s and '70s, the SED mounted a massive campaign for enhancing women's qualifications. In 1968 a new factory producing women's woollen goods (Obertrikotagenbetrieb, OTB) was opened in Wittstock in which, following a relatively short six-month period of training, women were easily able to find employment. Indeed, because of the increasing emphasis on the production of consumer goods after the Eighth Party Conference, this was rapidly expanded. The factory operated three shifts a day, and women worked in large, windowless, stuffy rooms at a hectic pace, their levels of payment affected by quantities of output.[43] Quantity (fulfilment of the plan) took precedence over quality, and shops often returned goods as impossible to sell. Yet the OTB factory was further expanded in the later 1970s and '80s, with the construction of two new housing estate areas to accommodate increasing numbers of workers. In these conditions, worker turnover was relatively high, with around one fifth of the workforce leaving every year. Many women experienced work not as 'liberating', but rather as a process of subjection to authority and collective needs, and as increasing pressure to produce in order to receive payment. Nevertheless, in this relatively young and overwhelmingly female workforce, in which the average worker was in her mid-twenties, some women were able to rise to positions of authority and take on leadership functions. Young women found they had economic independence, and often earned more than their male partners. In the later 1970s and '80s, a whole set of new work-related institutions – childcare facilities, a medical centre with seven doctors, kitchens, a social centre, shopping facilities, even a hairdresser, as well as improved transport services – eased the pressures of combining motherhood and employment. Moreover, husbands often simply had to take over some domestic and childcare duties as a result of the exigencies of their wives' shift-work patterns. Thus, in interviews carried out after 1989, many women who had now lost their employment in this area remembered – despite the relative miseries of the pressurised and monotonous factory work – their former independence and social lives around the factory rather nostalgically.

Clearly the experience of employment and the relevance of gender depended greatly both on the nature of work, and on the question of whether the area of employment was predominantly female, male, or mixed. A comparison of a predominantly male office-machinery factory in Sömmerda and a predominantly female textiles concern in Leipzig, for example, has demonstrated that gender roles differed considerably.[44] In both factories, traditional sex stereotypes predominated in the 1950s. While these persisted in the male-dominated office-equipment factory, with men retaining the leadership positions despite the rising level of women's qualifications, in the predominantly female textiles factory women were more readily able to take on leadership positions vacated by male retirements. Yet even here the top positions in the Directorate were retained by men. There were higher chances of upward mobility, but in this traditionally somewhat dubious area of employment (where there were connotations of loose sexual morals going back to the nineteenth century, and where in the Third Reich forced labourers had been exploited) there was less social prestige and lower remuneration; by contrast, in the traditionally male-dominated factory, women enjoyed better status and material rewards, but had lower chances of promotion to leadership positions. Even promotion was hardly the product of active individual aspiration, since women had to be 'selected' to be 'furthered', in a rather passive sense, in the cadre system; and the somewhat ambiguous outcome would simply be more demands on a woman's time in terms of carrying out functions and attending meetings.

A similar, if slightly more depressing tale is told in a study of the 'last' workers in the textile industry in Niederlausitz, thirty of whom were interviewed in 1990–91, at a time when the textile industry was collapsing and unemployment was escalating.[45] As children, poverty and hard work were the central experiences of these women's lives: many had lost their fathers in the war, and their mothers from illness and exhaustion soon after the war; many had been brought up by relatives or in an orphanage. Employment in the textile industry was both hard and poorly paid. Difficulties in recruitment and domestic labour supply in this area led to the employment of migrant workers from Mozambique, Cuba and Vietnam in the 1970s and '80s. As far as women were concerned, poor pay and conditions were slightly mitigated by opportunities for regular skills training, and a few were able to rise up to the level of *Meisterin* (female Master) or *Ingenieurin* (female engineer); but work in this area generally was regarded with less esteem and carried lower social status than jobs in the coal and energy industries of the area. A wider report on the textiles industry carried out in 1961 had in fact commented adversely on the poor social repute of this occupation, noting that many functionaries responsible for occupational training were of the view that one could not ask parents to let their 'well-brought-up daughters work in such a morally degenerate industry'.[46] Nevertheless, however hard the combination of work and continuing poverty, and despite a general attitude of resignation, some of the women interviewed remembered with a degree of nostalgia the collective spirit of work brigades and camaraderie or togetherness (*Mitmenschlichkeit*).

In agriculture, women benefited from the growing social, educational and communal facilities and functions of collectivised agricultural enterprises; they enjoyed a degree of financial independence, with their own pensions and insurance schemes, and growing numbers (91.8 per cent by 1989) acquired some form of vocational qualification in relation to the increasingly specialised agricultural production methods of the GDR.[47] But despite the rising level of qualifications, and the increasing numbers of women in some form of managerial position, very few women attained real positions of leadership within agricultural cooperatives (LPGs): only 2.8 per cent of LPG Chairs were female in the 1980s. Interestingly, however, women in agriculture appear to have compared their position favourably with that of their mothers and grandmothers, and felt pride in their own economic independence, qualifications and social status; they do not appear to have felt the relevant comparison was with the positions of their male contemporaries and colleagues.

This sense of pride in their own achievements and massive social mobility in comparison with previous generations of women is evident, too, among the selected members of the first post-war generation interviewed in a unique study carried out by Western scholars in the later 1980s.[48] As male skilled workers had been promoted to leadership positions, women had acquired professional qualifications and filled the positions of skilled labour vacated by the men. While some of the interviews reveal that traditional gender assumptions about what was appropriate for 'women's work' persisted, even without much rational foundation, they also suggest that many women from previously disadvantaged backgrounds were quite content with their new status. Thus, for example, 'Dörtle Grothaus' (pseudonym), a skilled steel worker, comments on the widespread view in her factory that women were to be protected from 'men's work', even though no rationalisation for this could be given.[49] A woman of proletarian background, with a persistent fear of falling back into the 'underclass', Dörtle Grothaus appears to have felt she did well out of the new conditions of the GDR, and was able to lead a satisfied life as a 'modern' worker, wife and mother. Although she recognised she had no real power, she nevertheless felt she had a secure and valued position in life.

The question of attaining positions of power and authority was an ambiguous one. What is clear, however, is that in virtually every sphere of the economy, despite the increasing numbers and enhanced qualifications of women, they did not rise to positions of leadership in the same proportions as men. This is clear in even traditionally 'female' areas of the professions, such as education, health and social services.

For example, women made up 82 per cent of the total teaching profession in 1987. But among the leadership positions in the Ministry for Education (which was, of course, headed by a rather unusual woman, Margot Honecker), there were only four women, making up a total of only 8.9 per cent of departmental heads (*Abteilungsleiter*).[50] Not a single Rector of an Institute of Education (Pädagogische Hochschule) in 1986 was a woman, although there was one female Deputy Rector (making up a grand total of 2.9 per cent of deputies); only three of the Directors of Teacher Training Institutes (Institute für Lehrerbildung) were female, constituting a proportion of just over one in ten. The situation was only slightly better at the level of heads of secondary schools and sixth-form colleges (POS and EOS), with just under a third of these positions being held by women in 1983 (a total of 1,927 such jobs constituting 31.6 per cent) and rising to just over one third in 1986 (2,044 women making up 36.3 per cent of the total). In every section of the education system, women were better represented at lower levels than in the top jobs. In 1960, while nearly a third (30.4 per cent) of students at Berlin's Humboldt University were women, only 25 per cent of *Dozenten* (roughly the equivalent of British junior lecturers or untenured Assistant Professors in the US) were female, and 7.5 per cent of Professors were women (actually quite an impressive figure in comparison with West Germany at the time).[51] Even following the great expansion of educational opportunities and the rapidly increasing numbers of girls taking the higher school leaving examination (*Abitur*) and going on to higher education in the later 1960s, women who became academics tended to become assistants rather than leaders of collective academic projects.[52]

Similarly, in another traditionally 'female' and 'caring' area, that of health and the social services, 86.2 per cent of all employees in 1988 were women.[53] A total of 21,292 women were doctors, making up 52.6 per cent of all doctors. But a mere 12.8 per cent of those holding the top positions (*Chefärzte*) were women, and only 34.9 per cent of those on the slightly lower rung of *Oberarzt*. According to this report, a combination of gender stereotypes, sexist prejudices and women's own lack of self-confidence appears to have been involved. Often higher standards or expectations seem to have been set for female candidates for promotion than for men. Many males in leadership positions did not want women in positions of responsibility and authority. Many women, including those who had no children, lacked confidence in their own abilities and were dubious about whether they could combine motherhood and a demanding career.[54]

So women benefited massively from the strenuous campaigns of the 1950s and '60s to ensure they achieved similar levels of education and qualification as men and had comparable career aspirations, and they fully entered the East German labour force, their capacity to combine motherhood and employment greatly eased by the institutional and legal framework; but, with the exception of predominantly female industrial concerns, women did not rise to levels of leadership and management to the same extent as their male colleagues. Women continued to take primary responsibility for childcare and indeed also for domestic responsibilities throughout life, including care of elderly relatives, and to prioritise the needs of their families above those of the workplace.

Despite emphasis on 'emancipation', the attitudes of both men and women towards the fact of women working outside the home changed very much more than attitudes towards the domestic division of labour. There was increasing acceptance that women should take and retain paid work throughout their adult lives, rather than giving up after marriage or birth of children; but there was only a very slow and partial shift towards asking whether men should not also take an equal role as partners and parents in carrying some responsibility for the home and family affairs. And, given that women had to stretch themselves between two spheres, they by and large chose not to accept the overwhelming additional demands on their time that would have come with increasing responsibilities and promotion at work and in political life, which were extremely closely related.

By the later 1980s, many GDR sociologists, such as Barbara Bertram and her colleagues in Leipzig, explicitly recognised that the roles of women could not be rethought without a concomitant rethinking of the roles of men. They argued that, although rooted in biological differences, the gender roles of both men and women were primarily socially determined. As one (remarkable) text written by a team at the ZIJ put it: to achieve equality of opportunity for women and girls 'presupposed a rethinking of the development of *both* sexes'.[55] Considerable effort was devoted to exploring the attitudes of men and women in professional, political and familial spheres, and analysing what were held to be 'typical' patterns of behaviour for males and females.[56] The variety and energy of East German debates in the 1980s over women's roles, images, social-isation experiences and typical patterns of attitude and behaviour also became very evident in the 1990s, when the interaction of East and West German approaches occasioned lively debates.[57]

Issues of male and female sexuality were rethought to at least some degree even at the level of officialdom. For example, although it never ceased to be a somewhat sensitive topic surrounded by a degree of taboo, homosexuality was legalised in the GDR. Section 175 of the Criminal Code (Strafgesetzbuch), which had criminalised homosexuality, was barely used after the reform of the Criminal Code in 1957, and was struck out of the new Criminal Code of 1968. Section 175a, forbidding homosexual relations with minors, was replaced by Section 151, for the 'Protection of Youth'. In 1988 this, too, was struck out in the fifth amendment of the penal code.[58] Whereas in the 1950s and '60s gays and lesbians were generally perceived as 'abnormal' or 'ill', there was a more liberal climate in the 1970s and '80s. There is even a degree of sensitivity to be found in the official documents on this score: a Ministry of Health document comments, for example, concerning the possibility of AIDS appearing in the GDR, that homosexuals should be prevented from offering their services as blood donors 'without any personal discrimination'.[59] The real dangers of homosexuality, in the official view, lay in public health risks (such as already common infections such as Hepatitis B), and in social or 'lifestyle' aspects that were deemed to be politically suspect: 'through their relationships that transcend borders ... and through their being used to subversive ways of life and behaviour ... [and] through their desire to seek out exceptional anonymity in large towns, in particular also in the capital city Berlin'. About the only area of social life that was deemed to be 'free of homosexuality' was the People's Police, the Volkspolizei.[60] Organisations for the representation of gay interests were not possible within the formal political structure of the GDR: such groups were able to form only under the protective umbrella of the Protestant Churches in the 1980s. Nevertheless, there had been a clear shift in attitudes: being gay was no longer viewed as a potentially criminal condition, medical abnormality or moral abomination, but merely as one among a number of alternative lifestyles with links with the West that were viewed therefore as potential political threats.

There appear, however, to have been limits to the rethinking of men's roles. For example, control of reproduction continued to be seen as purely a female responsibility, as illustrated by the remarkable case of one Herr M.[61] This gentleman had already fathered several children, and was terrified of being trapped into further extra-marital paternal financial responsibilities, or even an unwanted marriage by the woman becoming pregnant against his will; on the other hand, as he pointed out, it destroyed any trust in a relationship if he used mechanical contraceptive measures despite the woman's assurances that she was taking the pill. Yet, as he disarmingly put it, 'I want to put all my energy into the strengthening of our Republic' instead of 'living under the permanent fear of creating more children'. Furthermore, this was a question of equal rights for men: 'The age of the Pill and of Abortion have only given women the possibility of making their own decisions about their lives and their bodies. Now as before, in such an important question as the creation of new life the man's life depends on either the accidents of biology or the will of the woman.'[62] Herr M.'s repeated attempts to obtain sterilisation were met with a notable lack of sympathy on the part of the medical authorities; there was simply no legal provision for routine male sterilisation. The argument was in the end taken to the highest levels: even top officials in the Ministry for Justice were ultimately involved, who resorted to invoking arguments from the practices of the Soviet Union and the writings of Lenin to support their case; ultimately, it seems, they succeeded in silencing Herr M. (or perhaps the Wall fell and his personal saga could be concluded under Western provisions) and sustaining the principle that male sterilisation could only be carried out under exceptional medical circumstances. In any event, even if this particular individual was remarkably unlucky in the degree of trust he was able to find in his intimate relationships, he nevertheless had a point about lack of equality for males. By the 1980s, not only lesbian relations but also different patterns of heterosexual relationship and types of partnership were being more openly discussed.[63]

Yet traditional conceptions of the allegedly feminine were still heavily represented by officially published works, even in the late 1980s. An encyclopaedia for women, *Kleine Enzyklopaedie: Die Frau*, for example, which was published as late as 1987, included articles on 'traditional' areas of women's interests, such as fashion, cooking and home care ('Furnishing the Flat' and 'Beautiful Consumer Goods that are Fit for Purpose', 'Cooking appropriately' and 'Clothes and Fashion') among those specifically on female health, legal and occupational issues.[64] An articulate minority of women challenged such perceptions; but changes were only partial and slow.

In general, despite growing discussion at least among a minority of citizens, and between at least some GDR sociologists, what appears to have changed is not so much conceptions of gender as such; rather, traditionally male areas, such as educational and occupational aspirations, were simply tacked on to areas that continued to be considered the female domain. Thus in general, rethinking was directed towards the question of making women more like men in the areas of work, while making little impact on traditional conceptions of female roles in the domestic sphere. On the other hand, before the notion of the unique 'double burden' of women is accepted too rapidly, the additional roles of men have to be reinserted into the analysis. For employment in an officially recognised job was not by any means all that men did either. Many men made a major contribution to the total income and well-being of their families by doing all manner of unofficial jobs in their 'leisure' hours, from do-it-yourself household maintenance, repairs and improvements, to participating in a far wider network of exchange of goods and services in the unofficial 'black economy'. There may have continued to be a gendered division of labour in the domestic sphere, but many men also bore a 'double burden' of a slightly different sort.

Gender and politics

Men also dominated the formal political system of the GDR. In the 1980s, no full members of the Politburo were women. There were only two female candidate members. Only one woman at this time held a ministerial post – and this woman was Margot Honecker (the wife of Erich Honecker) who held the post of Minister for Education from 1963 until the collapse of SED rule, and was a full member of the Central Committee from 1963 (a candidate member since 1950), but never a member of the Politburo. The woman responsible for women's affairs from 1961 to 1989, Inge Lange, was made a member of the Central Committee in 1964, and in 1973 became a candidate member of the Politburo, but was never promoted to full member. Former Politburo member Günter Schabowski suggests that Lange was not taken entirely seriously by Honecker: 'From time to time Inge Lange was the object of lightly ironic banter, if she in some context pointed to the interests of women. It would all be relatively temperate and, as far as those not involved were concerned, there was nothing too crazy about it.'[65] Even Schabowski's own post-unification description of this evident sexism – treating the very raising of women's issues as worthy of mirth rather than as a matter to be taken seriously – is itself indicative. The top of the SED – the ultimate power centre in the GDR – was almost unremittingly male and certainly male-dominated.

In the central state apparatus, women were very few and far between at the top. In 1986, apart from the sole female minister, there were 4 female deputy ministers, constituting 1.5 per cent of the total; 181 female heads of department, making up 10.2 per cent of this level of the hierarchy; and 685 female sector leaders, comprising 18.2 per cent of the total.[66] The situatiion with respect to percentages of women in higher positions improved somewhat at the regional and local levels of the state, although even here the picture demonstrated marked variations according to area. Thus only 1.3 per cent of those in charge of construction and planning at district level (*Kreisbaudirektor*) were women; and while women held a little under a quarter of the state posts with significant responsibility in most areas, they were somewhat better represented in the spheres of culture (37.9 per cent in 1982, 38.7 per cent in 1987) and youth (46.2 per cent in 1982, 48.2 per cent in 1987).[67]

Similarly, the further down the political hierarchies one goes, the higher the percentage of women becomes. While in 1949, fewer than 5 per cent of mayors were women, this rose steadily to 18 per cent in 1970, and more than 34 per cent by 1989.[68] The percentage of women correlated very closely with size of community, however. In 1987, while over half (51.2 per cent) of mayors of communities of fewer than 200(!) people were women, less than one in twenty (4.7 per cent) of mayors of communities between 10,000 and 20,000 were female, and 7.9 per cent of mayors of communities larger than 20,000, with a steady slide down the spectrum in between.[69] The absolute numbers of mayors in each size of community make for interesting reading, too: there were very many more small communities than larger ones, as represented in Table 1, which was prepared for Inge Lange and accompanied by detailed studies of the percentages of women in many other areas of East German society, with similar results.

Table 1: *Female mayors of towns and communities in the GDR in 1984 and 1987*[70]

Size of community	1984 number	%	1987 number	%
more than 20,000	5	5.7	7	7.9
10,000–20,000	6	5.6	5	4.7
5,000–10,000	12	6.8	13	7.6
3,000–5,000	39	14.4	44	16.1
2,000–3,000	44	12.7	48	14.4
1,000–2,000	217	20.5	232	22
500–1,000	506	25.6	531	27.6
200–500	1,017	37.3	1,060	38.2
fewer than 200	354	50.6	395	51.2

A similar picture emerges when one considers the statistics for female deputies to representative positions, such as assemblies at various local community, urban and district levels, compared to percentages in the national parliament, the Volkskammer. Nevertheless, the representation of women in these 'elected' positions always seems to have been markedly higher than one would expect in comparison to the Western participation of women in local, regional and national politics at the same time.

In 1953, for example, in the wake of the June Uprising, women represented a little over a quarter of those involved in discussions of the 'New Course': 27.4 per cent of representatives in the regional parliaments were women (279 out of a total of 1,019); 28.7 per cent of representatives on town councils (567 of 1,976) were women; 27.3 per cent of urban area councils (605 of 2,216) were women; and 25.1 per cent of representatives in district councils (1741 of 7,537) were women.[71] In the later 1950s, the percentage of women representatives at district, town and local level seems to have somewhat declined to around 17 per cent; but it rose steadily again thereafter.[72] Most ordinary women in the 1950s had neither the time nor the energy – nor arguably the inclination – even to attend political meetings. As a report of June 1959 noted, 'Particularly among the peasant women one has to notice that they have not bothered themselves much about societal development. This is because from early in the morning till late in the evening they have to work in the household and also in the fields and cowsheds. Only the men attend the meetings and other discussions.'[73] Those women who did become actively involved in politics found that demands were made on them from all sides, resulting in failure to fulfil their roles adequately. A report from the late 1950s draws attention to the fact that, 'In our opinion, the greatest hindrance to the success of the work of female people's representatives turns out to be the fact that virtually all these women also fulfil a whole series of often important societal functions quite apart from their activities as a representative.'[74] Once a woman was elected to the district council (Kreistag), she might well also be expected to hold functions in the DFD, the parents' association (Elternbeirat), act as an LPG-Chair, and so on.

But the situation changed markedly over the succeeding decades. A study of women in leadership positions in local government in the 1980s has provided an insightful analysis of the stages of women's increasing involvement in employment and politics over the years.[75] While the founding generation of *Trümmerfrauen* ('rubble women') had to focus on clearing the literal and metaphorical rubble of the war, the *Aufbaugeneration* (those building the new society) of the 1950s and '60s made the switch from merely wage labour to the acquisition of skills, qualifications and the notion of a career or profession rather than just a job. The *Enkelgeneration* ('grandchildren's generation') of the 1970s and 80s, products of GDR education and expectations, had a certain internalised self-understanding that included the notion of a career. The many female mayors of small communities in the 1980s were predominantly from this generation: their average age on becoming mayor was 32, and around 80 per cent of them were married, a far higher proportion than that in the general population. Their positions involved delicate negotiation between the needs of the community on the one hand – with which, given the generally small size, they were intimately familiar – and the demands of the SED and The Plan or The Task (*Aufgabe*) on the other. Tasks included checking on the well-being of elderly, frail or disabled residents, ensuring wood and coal supplies, and organising local festivals, rituals and the like, as well as bringing out the vote for the SED when required. However much there may have been frustrations and conflicting demands, holding a political office at this level could be very fulfilling, and indeed a position of more real power – in the sense of the capacity to put one's energies into genuinely improving the position of others – than serving at some higher level in the political bureaucracy.[76] Far from being prevented from rising further by some putative 'glass ceiling' (which undoubtedly did also exist), many women may have made a quite clear-sighted choice about personal priorities for spending their time.

What is perhaps of most interest about the many other statistics available in the GDR archival records, in some respects, is simply the mere fact that the authorities were so concerned about percentages of female involvement in different areas of employment and politics, and in particular in leadership positions. The extent to which they tracked female under-representation and discussed possible causes and remedies for the relative paucity of women in top positions is indicative of a genuine desire, at least in some quarters, to ensure that womens' talents were fully harnessed to building the new society – and not merely that their labour power was exploited at any level in economic production.

Moreover, as far as involvement in politics is concerned, the situation is perhaps a little more complex than simple statistics might at first sight suggest. Generally, the principle of exclusion in the GDR was related to political conformity rather than gender, and politics was very much predicated on the cadre-selection principle. Attempts at the politicisation of women in the official directions desired by the SED by organisations such as the FDJ and the DFD did not always succeed in a purely formal sense.[77] But the changes in women's lives and experiences had far more subtle and far-reaching effects on their levels of self-confidence and their assumptions about the normality of leading a life that was not purely bounded by the spheres of domesticity.

The ways in which women were capable of serious political involvement when it was a question, not of time-serving in a constraining and hierarchical apparatus with its own constrictions on real power, but rather in movements with a sense of purpose and ideals, became particularly evident in the course of the unofficial political movements of the 1980s. One has only to mention names such as Vera Wollenberger, Bärbel Bohley, Ulrike Poppe, or think of key groups such as Frauen für den Frieden ('Women for Peace') to realise that by the 1980s, women had not only found a voice – something that was not always easy for individuals brought up in a system in which there were only rewards for conformity – but also acquired the capacity for highly effective organisation, strategic and tactical skills.[78] Similarly significant developments in the exploration and articulation of women's roles, if tending in rather different directions, can be observed in the 'protocol literature' and in creative women's writing in the GDR, where a wide range of female authors – Christa Wolf, Brigitte Reimann, Maxie Wander, Irmtraud Morgner, Helga Königsdorf, Gabriele Eckart and many others – explored the historical complexities of female roles and possible alternative constructions of society that would allow for experiments in more genuine 'emancipation'.[79]

The extent to which large numbers of 'ordinary' women – those who did not make names for themselves in political groups that caught the headlines, or in literary works achieving international renown – nevertheless developed a degree of articulate self-confidence is also evident when one reads, for example, the mountains of letters that piled up in the files of a whole range of organisations. It is arguable that women were, in a more general sense, in fact far more politicised than purely statistical measures of numbers of women in high places might imply. Their willingness to speak in public meetings on a wide range of topics, to submit *Eingaben* on matters of personal concern, to argue for the right to have an abortion on demand, to extend their enjoyment of holidays, have increased time off for household duties, better access to part-time childcare and part-time jobs, or increased pensions, is illustrative of an active participation in the affairs of the day, in ways that might not be measurable in terms of occupying formal positions of power, but which should nevertheless not be overlooked as forming a significant part of the history of GDR society. Letters from women such as Frau Barbara C. of Rostock in 1988, who couched her appeal in terms of 'my rights as a working woman and a mother', indicate the extent to which women had by the later 1980s internalised the notion of equal rights, the lack of which had been such a cause for concern on the part of functionaries in the 1950s.[80] Such a sense of rights is evident across the generations by the late 1980s. One letter from older women in a DFD group in Oranienburg protested rights for pensioners in terms of the contribution they had made to the foundation and early years of the GDR: 'Why has the National Executive Committee over the years not argued more strenuously that the women who cleared the ruins after 1945, and who from the very beginning helped to build the GDR, should receive an appropriate pension?'[81] Another, from Dr Renate S., a research scientist in Rossendorf, gave a blast about the more general situation of women at the height of their careers: why were some working in a job below their level of qualifications because they could earn more in a less-qualified position; why were men and women not actually paid the same for equal work; why were women not arriving in the top positions? Dr S. sought to speak for her whole generation:

> We women embarked on our education full of optimism with respect to our future development. I personally was born in 1936 and since my youth I have been active in societal functions, in the last 25 years in the Women's Commission of our Institute, and in this capacity I have frequently taken part in Women's Conventions of the Science Trade Union [IG Wissenschaft]. For years we have been asking ourselves what has been happening in the course of time. When we started out in life, we were effectively promised the earth ['das Blaue vom Himmel versprochen']. In the meantime a great process of disillusionment has set in. Not only in our Institute but also in the women's meetings of the IG Wissenschaft one senses that the early momentum and vitality have been transformed into resignation and frustration ... Now here we stand with empty hands: career goals have come to nothing, and families are destroyed.[82]

Women such as these were not afraid to raise their voices and articulate demands for better conditions and social improvements. It was indeed in part because of such widespread willingness to voice critiques that the collective debate of the autumn of 1989, which swept up not only oppositionalists but also those who had been relatively loyal supporters of the regime but who saw the acute and increasing need for reform and improvement, contributed to the collapse of the GDR and reunification with the West.

In the event, unification inaugurated massive changes for women, not all of which were unambiguously 'liberating' even in the Western sense of the word. Over 70 per cent of women rightly feared that women's employment prospects and childcare facilities would deteriorate rather than improve as a result of unification.[83] With unification came the collapse of the infrastructure of state-run childcare facilities; with the collapse of East German industry, women were laid off faster than men, such that a disproportionate percentage of the unemployed in the 'five new *Länder*' were female (and there was a larger pool of hidden female unemployment among those who did not feel they could register for work); the traditional ideals of female domesticity and consumerism were reinvoked, despite the fact that many East German women registered a sense of isolation and loss of social identity with the loss of the workplace environment. The right to abortion was challenged as the West German constitution, with its prohibitive stance, formed the basis for the accession of the East German *Länder* to the new enlarged Federal Republic, leading to two years of uncertainty, debate and compromise. And over a decade later, many ordinary women in the eastern part of Germany were looking back with nostalgia to the days of seamless childcare, educational and training opportunities, subsidised holidays and secure careers. There was little point in having the formal freedom to take a holiday in Spain if one lacked even the means to travel out of Saxony.

Interpretations of gender in the GDR

Gender provides an intriguing topic for analysis of some key interpretive questions concerning the GDR. For one thing, the initial political barriers to understanding SED policies (and their failures) are relatively low: apart from out-and-out misogynists, there are few observers who start from a position of principled opposition to all and any attempts to raise the career aspirations and achievements of women (as well as men). Thus, the 'repression thesis' is harder to sustain when in this case, for once, many Western historians can sympathise with the ideals of those who were trying to alter the perceptions, values and aspirations of women. Exasperation at the 'resistance' of women who stubbornly continued to believe that they had no future after leaving school at the earliest opportunity other than to pursue the best possible marital match and then live a life subordinated to the needs of husband and children, seems to many Westerners more readily understandable than many other aspects of the SED project for future society. The general arena of discussion is hence less beset by extra-historical mines and booby-traps than are the more directly 'political' areas, even if the conclusions reached (with respect, for example, to the extent of 'emancipation' possible within a dictatorship) often remain highly contentious.

SED policy-making was never monolithic on the question of women or gender more generally: unexamined assumptions about the primary responsibility of women for reproductive and nurturing functions were continuously held by some of those in power, while others repeatedly argued for change; and an underlying theme at all times was that of women's contribution to the building of a socialist society, however differently this might be interpreted in terms of specific social policies in practice. The standard periodisation in terms of an earlier, idealistic phase focusing on 'emancipation' under Ulbricht, and a later, more pragmatic phase focusing on what might be called the 'unity of production and reproduction' under Honecker, thus requires some revision. Nor is the story easily written according to the standard top-down/bottom-up scripts of totalitarian theorists. Often we have pressures coming from below for changes in the position of and opportunities for women, which were taken up by some but not all of those in positions of power; and we can sympathise more easily with the frustrations of at least some of those SED functionaries seeking to raise the aspirations of young women beyond domestic bliss (or otherwise) at the earliest possible moment on leaving school.

The roles of women themselves in negotiating change – as indeed the roles of 'ordinary people' more generally in the development of GDR history – are, however, often greatly understated. Totalitarian theorists suggest that women were unable to represent their own interests, and that the official women's organisations in fact merely represented the exploitative and repressive interests of Party and state.[84] But this view more or less ignores the role played by women in raising their voices over certain issues, such as the Abortion Law of 1972, or the more frequent complaints regarding the difficulties of everyday life (housing, childcare, food supplies and so on). It understates the very real concerns of SED policymakers – whether female or male – in seeking to redress such difficulties. It underemphasises the genuine desire for female emancipation, which was a permanent, if at times submerged, strand running through SED thinking on this issue. And it grossly understates the role played by large numbers of women in many areas and at many levels of East German cultural and political life.

Some major interpretive questions remain, in part because the significant moves towards a rethinking of gender roles were in practice both partial, and attempted under the doubly constraining conditions of a political dictatorship with an ailing economy. The legal position of women with respect to such matters as rights within the family and at work, marriage and divorce, insurance and pensions, and control over reproduction, was undoubtedly improved in purely formal terms. The high participation of women in the paid labour force also signalled a significant move in the direction of some form of 'female emancipation', made possible by generous state maternity and childcare provisions, in that – however disagreeable the work – women gained a degree of real financial independence, experience and self-confidence that had not previously been so widely enjoyed. However, it is not always easy to evaluate patterns of change. For example, is the continuing under-representation of women in the higher reaches of politics and in positions of responsibility in the economic sphere primarily a consequence of some communist version of the 'glass ceiling', or rather an indication of the good sense of women choosing to evade even more overwhelming burdens of responsibility, and having the wisdom to concentrate on areas in which they could be most effective? Furthermore – as at all times – it is important to remember that the experiences and aspirations of 'women' varied dramatically according to their positions in the stratification system. Articulate and relatively privileged women writers such as Christa Wolf had very different experiences of what it meant to be a woman in the GDR than did, say, a woman working on a collective farm, in a textile factory, or a large industrial concern. The majority of women continued to lead extremely hard lives, concentrated predominantly at the lower levels of any hierarchy, where they had lower social status and less control over their work than did their male superiors; and they continued to rush around in an often-frenzied attempt to accomplish, in addition, the majority of mundane tasks required to keep families and households functioning. Meanwhile, male gender roles were rarely, if ever, explicitly challenged or significantly shifted.

Even so, the construction of gender and the social determination of women's roles changed in quite remarkable ways over the course of forty years. The experience of unification served to underline the ambiguities of gender roles in the GDR. The sudden removal of crucial institutional supports and an effective rejection of women from the worlds of work and politics simply heightened a sense of nostalgia for what had been lost, quite apart from the gains in terms of formal political freedom. Although conditions for women in the GDR had been far from perfect, and at the time experienced by many as a 'double burden', any notion of real 'emancipation' would have been better served if the introduction of political democracy had been accompanied by a continued movement towards equalisation of responsibilities in the domestic sphere, and a wider rethinking of the roles of both men and women not only as producers but also as equal partners, parents and citizens.

Part II

Class in a classless society:
Power, work and social inequality

Chapter Eight

The withering away of the state? Ruling elites

The alleged 'ruling class' – the workers – were not the ruling class. Although the 'peoples' own factories' were at least formally owned 'by the people', all key decision-making was concentrated at the top of the political pyramid, by members of a party ruling, on good Marxist-Leninist principles, 'on behalf of the people'. Power, which also entailed effective control of economic resources, replaced ownership of property as a key determinant of stratification under East German communism. Analysis of power and political processes is thus indispensable to any understanding of the system of social inequalities in the GDR.

It would be easy enough, then, simply to assert that power displaced class. But it did not, in any simple sense. While power was a key determinant of social stratification, participation in the exercise of state power spread, as we have seen, in all manner of ways beyond the rather small group who can be characterised as the core ruling elite. Moreover, it was possible for participants in the extended power structure to have straddled a whole variety of positions with respect to occupational class and to consumer lifestyle. It was not merely possible to rise high in the power structure from a very humble origin in the socio-economic structure; with the officially ordained inversion of the traditional class-prestige hierarchies of bourgeois capitalist societies, it was indeed easier to rise up in the power hierarchy from a working class or peasant background than from a bourgeois background. Although to a greater degree in some periods than others, a very high value was placed on being able to claim humble social origins, even when this meant stretching the truth of the biographical details rather far. The duality of power structure and social stratification, and the inversion of inherited prestige hierarchies, thus further complicated the class structure of the GDR.

Life at the communist court

The small East German power elite had a highly distinctive lifestyle. Being a member of the power elite effectively determined every aspect of one's personal life; there could be no real private life untouched by the conditions of service to the Party.

The most important individual members of the political elite lived, for security reasons, in secluded and well-guarded residential settlements. From 1945 to 1960 members of the then political elite lived in the rather comfortable, spacious old villas (indeed suspiciously bourgeois in character) with their pleasant gardens around the Majakowski-Ring in the northern Berlin suburb of Pankow, close to the Soviet military headquarters. As well as the real power-holder and SED leader Walter Ulbricht, residents of this horseshoe-shaped road (hence 'Ring') included former SPD leader and Prime Minister Otto Grotewohl (1894–1964), and the first and only President of the GDR Wilhelm Pieck (1876–1960, a veteran of socialist struggles in Germany before and during the First World War and a founder member of the KPD in 1918–19), who were joint Chairs of the SED until 1954.

Despite some natural advantages – flanked by a park, a stream and some insignificant side roads – the Majakowksi-Ring complex proved difficult to guard effectively. In 1960 top members of the political elite were moved to the more secure, walled-in residential settlement, the Waldsiedlung Wandlitz, a highly exclusive compound in the woods north of Berlin, about two kilometres from the small town of Wandlitz. The dubious 'privilege' of being selected to reside in Wandlitz was a clear indication of top political status in the GDR. Altogether a total of thirty-nine people were at one time or another residents of this compound by virtue of their own political status (rather than in another capacity such as family members or staff). Apart from Erich Honecker's wife, Margot Honecker, who might or might not have qualified for residency in her own right, only two were female: Edith Baumann (1909–73), and Ingeborg Lange (born 1927). This is symptomatic of the deep-rooted attitudes about gender and the essential patriarchy of the GDR gerontocracy.

Wandlitz was widely known as 'Volvograd' because of the prevalence of the western chauffeur-driven Volvo cars carrying functionaries to and from their homes here.[1] The enclosed inner compound was where the top political functionaries lived; it required the equivalent of a high-security 'visa' to gain access to this area, even for the family members and servants of functionaries. The permanent staff serving this elite, who all worked under conditions of military service – even cooks, cleaners and chauffeurs – lived in a separate outer compound, also enclosed.[2] The tightly guarded Wandlitz settlement was complete with its own social club and swimming pool, shops stocked with Western goods, a health clinic, laundry, kindergarten for functionaries' children, fully equipped bunkers in the event of warfare, a petrol station for free re-tanking of private vehicles (including those of the functionaries' visiting relatives), and even a veterinary practice for family pets. Scattered around the neighbouring countryside were hunting lodges and country retreats, again serviced without question by the Wandlitz staff; the leisure pursuits of the SED elite ironically bore considerable resemblance to those of the former Nazi political elite, notably Hermann Goering, whose hunting lodge of Carinhall was in the same area as the leisure retreats of the Wandlitz elite, including Honecker's hunting lodge at Wildfang, Mittag's house at Trümmersee, and the SED holiday homes at Dölln and Schloss Hubertusstock.[3] Honecker's own passion for hunting was so great that he ensured that the regular formal Tuesday Politburo meetings finished promptly enough to give him time for an afternoon's hunting. Much (unfortunately for the historian, un-minuted) political business between key individuals, such as Honecker, Mielke and Mittag, was also transacted in the course of these hunting jaunts.

In comparison with the average relatively affluent North American suburb, let alone anything approaching the Kennedy compound in Massachusetts or the Bush ranch in Texas, Wandlitz was a miserable example of petit bourgeois modesty. But for anyone familiar with GDR conditions – a country in which petrol stations were so few and far between that they actually earned an explicit entry on GDR maps; in which shopping could take hours of patience, skill and insider knowledge and became a socialist version of hunter-gathering in itself; and in which scarce Western goods were a constant source of popular dreams and desires – this modest settlement inhabited by the power elite would appear to be the height of hypocritical luxury.

Membership of the top political elite clearly had its privileges, but the lifestyle also illustrated wider problems of the GDR's small ruling class. Being selected on the cadre system meant extremely long working hours, and total submission to Party discipline; it meant serious constraints on any conception of personal freedom to choose a career path, or lead any semblance of 'normal' family life. Günter Schabowski (born 1929), who became a member of the Politburo relatively late (1984, followed in 1985 by becoming First Secretary of the important Berlin *Bezirk* or Regional Administration), describes the relatively isolated lives led by residents of Wandlitz, who had neither much time nor inclination to socialise with other members of this elite outside working hours. Since they did not even need to mow their own lawns, there was no occasion for informal contact in leisure time; more importantly, it was in any event politically undesirable for informal 'friendships' to spring up that might then raise the suspicion of providing the kernel for political cliques or 'fraction-building', a major sin in this paranoid party. Schabowski only ever saw the inside of one other house in the Wandlitz compound, and even went out of his way ('jumped sideways into a bush') to avoid Honecker if their paths happened to cross while Schabowski was out walking his dog (who allegedly might have pounced up at Honecker, for reasons unspecified).[4] As a somewhat younger member of this political elite, Schabowski did not share the enthusiasm for hunting and hunting lodges that was characteristic of the wider milieu from which older members either came or to which they aspired.

Common to all residents of 'Volvograd' were not merely the privileges (from special soap to servants), but also the highly constrained working atmosphere in the Berlin headquarters of the Central Committee of the SED in which the key members of the Politburo and Central Committee and their assistants worked. Driven in every day to their offices in the highly guarded and rather faceless grey-brown building, originally built in the 1930s as the home of the German Reichsbank, and close to the ostensible centre of 'people's power' in the brash new Volkskammer, the power elite was effectively both living and working in almost total isolation from the rest of society. Arguably the most isolated of all, at least in daily work practices, was Stasi chief Erich Mielke. He did not even have the dubious pleasure of working in the same central Berlin building as the others, presiding as he did over a suite of offices in the massive and intensely forbidding Normannenstrasse headquarters of the Stasi in the Lichtenberg district of East Berlin, and thus missing out on the apparently highly constrained communal daily lunches in the SED headquarters canteen in which Honecker held informal court.

The power elite

A very small group of people – mostly men – dominated the history of the GDR from beginning to end. From being a small group of highly committed communists and social democrats, determined to rebuild Germany on anti-fascist foundations after the war, the power elite in the GDR developed into a professional ruling caste. This shift corresponded, somewhat imperfectly, to a generational shift in class origins: early powerful figures in the left-wing socialist and communist movements had tended to come from often very poor backgrounds, and had suffered the miseries of the First World War and the Weimar years; those who succeeded in gaining entry to the (increasingly ageing) political elite of the later years of the GDR belonged to a new breed of rather better educated, more highly qualified Party apparatchiks.[5] The increasingly reclusive, privileged lifestyle and ever more ritualised rhetoric of the

GDR power elite became, eventually, the butt of the population's humour and sarcasm. But in contrast to the Nazi upwardly mobile Party elite, who hailed from petty bourgeois backgrounds, and who constantly had to contend with the continuing power and prestige of traditional elites – old aristocrats, conservative nationalists, the military, powerful figures in finance and industry – this new political elite of the GDR managed to gain and retain control of the diverse areas of military and economic as well as political power. It had perhaps taken Hitler's destructive drive to shatter the previous hold over German society and politics of traditional elites, but it took the East German communists, backed by Soviet force, to consolidate a new system entirely, leaving, eventually, barely a trace of the old hierarchies of inherited prestige and privilege. The emergence and successful reproduction over four decades of the new power elite, successfully ousting previously privileged classes, marked a very deep break indeed in German social history.

The GDR political elite proper was relatively small, with key individuals often holding multiple positions in both Party and state apparatuses, either simultaneously or consecutively as they rose up the various hierarchies over the course of a career. The formal institutional structure – an effective pyramid of power – has frequently been described, and needs only a brief sketch here.[6] At the top of the power hierarchy was the Politburo of the SED, where all key decisions were made. The wider political elite included the members and candidate members of the SED Central Committee, the heads of the various Departments (*Abteilungen*) of the Central Committee with special areas of responsibility, and the First Secretaries of the fifteen Regional Administrations (*Bezirke*) that replaced the five *Länder* in 1952 – who would in any event be members of the Central Committee and possibly also of the Politburo. It also included the members of the leading organs of the key mass organisations, notably the FDJ and the FDGB; some of the key positions in the economy, particularly the General Directors of the most important *Kombinate* or major industrial combines; and the most powerful positions in the repressive and security apparatus, the Ministry for State Security (Stasi) and the National People's Army (NVA). In contrast to the chaotic, 'polycratic' system of the Third Reich with its many competing and overlapping centres of power, this system was at least in principle streamlined and well organised. In practice, as we shall see in a moment, the complexities involved in the diffusion of power did not simply reflect the theories of either 'democratic centralism' (the official Marxist-Leninist version) or the various models of totalitarianism that are the direct anti-Marxist equivalent of the democratic-centralist model.

The situations and lifestyles of these groups differed somewhat according to the peculiar demands of their situation. The top political elite – and particularly the members of the Politburo – dealt with just about everything, from the vital to the trivial. It was in part their wilful determination to take responsibility for all areas of life – from supplies of oil and industrial equipment, to washing machine spare parts, coffee and toilet paper – that led to eventual widespread criticism of the system as a whole in principle, and not merely of certain shortcomings in practice. A great deal of power was concentrated in the hands of a very small number of people. To achieve membership of the political elite involved total acceptance of Party tasks, total submission to Party discipline, and total commitment to the Party's purposes. Beyond the level of the top elite, the submission to Party discipline was greater, the privileges and power correspondingly less.

From the moment the so-called 'Ulbricht group' was flown in from Moscow, in the closing days of the war, Soviet power effectively underwrote the actions of the Communist Party in the GDR.[7] Formed from the merger of the SPD and the KPD in April 1946, the SED was the leading force in GDR politics. Becoming a Stalinist 'party of a new type' in 1948, and following the foundation of the GDR as a separate state in October 1949, the SED and hence the GDR was effectively led by its General Secretary or (as renamed following the upheavals of June 1953) First Secretary. Whatever the nuances and shifts in the precise character of the power relationships at the top, the SED leader remained the central cornerstone of the SED power elite over four decades.

In the first years of the GDR's existence, SED leader Walter Ulbricht faced not merely the wider uncertainties about the character and future of the GDR itself, but – in part related to these wider issues – also a number of internal struggles within the Party leadership.[8] Challenges to Ulbricht's authority on the part of Wilhelm Zaisser and Rudolf Herrnstadt in 1953 were deflected, in part because of the power changes in Moscow, in part because any change in leadership at this time would have looked like an admission of weakness in the wake of the June Uprising. Further supposed factionalism in 1956 and 1957–8 was successfully nipped in the bud. Ulbricht's position in the 1950s was secured not least through the apparently loyal backing of his young supporter and protégé, Erich Honecker, leader of the FDJ and then Secretary of the newly created Security Commission reporting directly to Ulbricht, and, from 1958, Secretary of the Central Committee and a full member of the Politburo. This early period was one characterised by very obvious and brutal repression of alternative voices, particularly in the late 1940s and early '50s, in the period of 'high Stalinism'. Massive popular discontent and opposition were manifested in the June Uprising of 1953, and again in a more muted fashion in the rumbles and echoes of 1956; meanwhile, the system of state and political functionaries in the provinces, and the apparatus of security and surveillance, were far from securely established.[9]

The atmosphere changed with the building of the Wall in August 1961. In the early 1960s, following what appeared to be a secure establishment of a position of unquestioned power, Ulbricht began to take advice from a larger body of experts, appearing even to relish the exchange of ideas and debate thus opened up. The Central Committee was no longer merely an 'organ for acclamation and declamation', but – even perhaps from as early as 1959 – an arena for consultation with invited guests and working groups (*Arbeitsgruppen*) working in specific policy areas.[10] A partial 'exchange of elites' took place as younger, educationally more qualified cadres were recruited in an era laying great emphasis on specialist credentials.[11] Simultaneous and partially contradictory processes of a degree of decentralisation in terms of the increased role of technical experts in different areas, and yet increased centralisation of power and final decision-making in Ulbricht's own hands as the 'supreme father figure' were evident at this stage.[12]

From the mid-1960s onwards, Ulbricht was constantly flanked, in part challenged, and ultimately outflanked by his 'crown prince' and – increasingly – rival, the younger Erich Honecker.[13] Brought in 1971 to 'resign' on grounds of age and ill-health, as a result of Honecker's active machinations over a considerable period of time, Ulbricht managed to potter on in a rather displaced role as Head of the Council of State until his death at the age of eighty, two years later – barely given adequate official notice due to the greater importance attached to the Tenth World Youth Festival taking place in Berlin at the time. Honecker then sought to expunge Ulbricht's image almost entirely from the historical record, and certainly from the pantheon of great leaders, not merely having memorials, favourable references and pictures of Ulbricht removed from historical accounts, but even going so far as having Ulbricht's former house in the Majakowski-Ring razed to ensure there could be no physical shrine for potential Ulbricht-supporters to worship at. In his turn, Honecker set up something of a leadership cult, representing himself as the great new hope for the GDR, paying considerable attention to appropriate 'photo opportunities' in a manner worthy of any US President, and keeping close control of all references to himself in the daily Party newspaper, *Neues Deutschland*. Although in many respects the early 1970s did see certain new initiatives, and certainly new emphases in continuing policies, the extent of the presumed caesura of 1971 was greatly exaggerated by Honecker to promote his own role. Recent historical research suggests far greater continuities between the mid-1960s and mid-1970s than had previously been thought, in part of course because of Honecker's own role in the later Ulbricht period, despite his own determination to present 1971 as a clean break, in part for other reasons.[14]

The role of SED leader was clearly one of immense power and significance, but it was so by virtue of its location in the political system, and thus it differed somewhat from the character of Hitler's power in the preceding Nazi dictatorship. Neither Ulbricht nor Honecker held their positions on the basis of any identifiable personal 'charisma', in the Weberian sense of a personal relationship between leader and followers; rather, both were there by virtue of their place in a routinised, bureaucratic Party system.[15] Ulbricht and Honecker, for all the differences in their individual personalities, were fundamentally apparatchiks, sustained in (or ousted from) their positions in part through the (changing) interests of the USSR leadership in the Cold War context.

Both Ulbricht and subsequently Honecker were surrounded by a few key decision-makers, although the circle was drawn ever more tightly in the Honecker era. In particular, the spheres of political power, repression and control of the economy were all very closely connected.

A central figure in the very small group of powerful men was the Stasi chief Erich Mielke (1907–2000). The State Security Service (Staatssicherheitsdienst, or Stasi), formally founded in February 1950, seems to have been caught rather unawares by the 1953 Uprising, but subsequently experienced exponential growth to become a major if shadowy power in the land, responsible not merely for 'defensive' spying abroad and general surveillance, but also for identification, proactive intervention and instant 'throttling' (to use the rather unpleasant term deployed in an early Stasi order) of any kind of suspected domestic dissent or potential political opposition.[16] The first head of the Stasi, Wilhelm Zaisser (1893–1957) was a casualty of political ructions in late 1953, as was his successor Ernst Wollweber (1898–1967) in 1957, when he was replaced by Erich Mielke. Mielke, who had cut his political teeth in a relatively minor capacity in the communist resistance to Hitler (including involvement in the murder of two police officers at a demonstration in Berlin in 1931, for which he was eventually brought to stand trial in the 1990s), served continuously as Minister for State Security from 1957 right through to 1989. In the Honecker period Mielke was one of the three single most powerful men in the GDR. From 1971 Mielke was a candidate member, and from 1976 a full member, of the Politburo; he had regular private meetings with Honecker to discuss the details of security policy, and his Ministry for State Security was alone exempted from the stringencies of economic planning and accountability, allowing it to expand exponentially in the era of détente and porous borders in the 1970s and '80s.

The third in the triumvirate of most powerful men in the latter half of the GDR's existence was Günter Mittag (1926–94), who was, apart from Honecker, the single most important figure in the all-important arena of economic decision-making. Mittag was effectively the GDR's economic tsar, holding numerous key economic positions including: control of a veritable empire of departments of the Central Committee's Secretariat for the Economy (personally in charge of no less than nine of the thirty departments); Chair of the Economic Commission; Chair of the Politburo working groups dealing with the balance of payments and with West Germany; Chair of the Parliament's Committee for Industry, Building and Transport; and a member of the Council of State; as well as having huge powers of patronage through his position with respect to nominations to positions of particular political significance (the so-called *Nomenklaturkader*). Mittag appears, by virtue both of his extraordinary empire of powerful positions and his very close personal relationship with Honecker, to have been the ultimate decision-maker with respect to setting priorities, determining the balance between heavy industry, consumer goods, education and training, the health system, the construction of new homes, military expenditure and other projects. He also appears to have had an aggressive, bullying manner, siding with Honecker but otherwise brooking no opposition or debate.

Others, too, were important, though without quite the ultimate power of this triumvirate. Certain individuals held notable positions, particularly with respect to the vital area of economic policy formation. Harry Tisch (1927–95), Chair of the Executive Committee of the FDGB in 1975–89 and a member of the Politburo throughout the Honecker period (candidate member 1971–5, full member thereafter), played an increasing role with respect to social policy decisions affecting the workforce, in a form of 'authoritarian corporatism'.[17] Gerhard Schürer (born 1921), Erich Apel's successor as Chair of the State Planning Commission from 1965 and in 1973–89 a candidate member of the Politburo (briefly serving as a full member in late 1989), played an expert but arguably politically subordinate role in economic developments; his informed warnings about the impending path to bankruptcy appear to have been readily ignored by the political heavyweights. An increasingly crucial role in shoring up and camouflaging the collapsing economy was played by Alexander Schalck-Golodkowski (born 1932), who was, among other responsibilities concerning the economy and international trading, technical and cultural relations, from 1966 leader of the all-important and euphemistically entitled Commercial Coordination Sector (Bereich Kommerzielle Koordinierung, or Koko), formally responsible to Günter Mittag. Schalck was responsible for the vital areas of imports and foreign hard currency, and instrumental in attaining the massive credit deals with West Germany in the early 1980s. After the collapse of the GDR, these and other protagonists bickered about degrees of responsibility for failure to take control of the GDR's mounting economic difficulties, Mittag and Schürer in particular disagreeing over each other's characterisations of their roles. The burden of evidence suggests, however, that despite some differences of viewpoint (Mittag having been closely associated with Ulbricht's reform programme) primary responsibility lay with the two most powerful men in this area: Honecker and Mittag.

Circles of power

These were the most important people in the power elite. But there were others in a wider ruling elite as far as the exercise of real power was concerned, numbering perhaps somewhere in the hundreds. The patterns of recruitment, social profiles and lifestyles of these wider groups in the ruling elite varied according to the type of power in different spheres of activity.

The officer corps of the NVA and the top figures in the Stasi, who also held military ranks as generals, were of necessity the most isolated from the wider population.[18] They appear to have compensated for the lack of high, visible public status through privileges in terms of housing, holidays and schooling for their children, as well as by copious indulgence in titles, medals, awards, ceremonies and uniforms, in a form of symbolic back-scratching to reward achievement and express mutual esteem.[19] They were at least not widely known or recognisable: powerful figures in the Stasi, such as the foreign spy chief Markus Wolf, or the shadowy intermediary on church affairs, Seidowsky, managed to keep their identities totally secret for extremely long periods of time.[20]

By contrast, the position of the Regional First Secretaries, or 'Regional Princes' (Bezirksfürsten) as they were popularly known, was highly visible. After a period of relatively rapid turnover in the 1950s, from the 1960s a new generation of more highly qualified, better-educated individuals took up these vital leadership positions in the provinces. Quite apart from the tensions involved in holding elite status, these individuals were also caught in a series of contradictions between their professional expertise and the autocratic political system.[21] Their position became increasingly difficult in the course of the 1980s, with growing economic and political problems with which to contend. Some appear to have been more capable of exploiting a degree of regional autonomy than others, although the position was always one of some tension, as the experience of the somewhat reform-minded First Secretary of Dresden, Hans Modrow (favoured by Gorbachev, disliked by

Honecker), clearly demonstrated. A similarly uncomfortable position of a high degree of visibility and responsibility for unrealistic levels of productivity and plan fulfilment, combined with acute awareness of local difficulties, shortages and real (im)possibilities was characteristic of the General Directors of the industrial combines, who were also part of the political 'nomenclature' system (in which individuals were thoroughly vetted and nominated into particularly significant posts) and answerable directly to Mittag. Here, too, there appears to have been something of a turnover of personnel in the later 1960s, followed by a period of remarkable continuity in Combine Directors.[22]

The total membership of the political elite proper, or 'ruling class', if 'class' it can be termed, was, even including these wider circles of those exercising significant power in the military, political and economic spheres, still exceedingly small. Far wider numbers were, however, involved in the daily exercise of power and the running of the state, ranging from the political and economic hierarchies, through state bureaucrats to grass-roots functionaries and those who held honorary positions in one or another political or social organisation.

If the capacity to exercise real decision-making power is the determinant of the GDR's 'ruling class', then it was a very small class. If being a functionary of the state in one way or another, and thus 'tainted' by proximity to the centres of power is held to be the key, then this was a dictatorship in which a very large number of people participated, although the vast majority of them held little real power and were barely distinguishable from many fellow citizens in terms of lifestyle and privileges. Indeed, in many respects intermediate level functionaries were worse off than their apolitical neighbours, for with participation in the state system at these lower levels came not so much privileges and perks, as pressures and stress, along with a lack of personal control over their own careers and prospects, and compounded by exclusion from the various strategies for improving one's lifestyle through Western contacts or 'connections'. Moreover, in practice local functionaries often represented the interests of people at the grass roots in both local-level conflicts and in relation to superiors higher up in the political hierarchy. The complex web of cross-cutting conflicts, and the often intermediary role of middle-level functionaries, further complicates the picture the further removed people were from the power elite proper. There is thus no neat overlap between the system of social stratification and the question of participation in power.

The extension and exercise of power

Distinctions may usefully be made between those who actually made the decisions, those who assisted in the preparation of decisions, and those who were charged with the responsibility for carrying them out.[23] In addition to the very small circle of the power elite proper were wider groups of people who held positions in which they could exercise power, even if they were not always fully involved in top-level decision-making. Common to all of these was a degree of isolation, and total prioritisation of the 'Party task' over any freedom of choice in their private lives. But according to precise location in the apparatus and system of power, the lifestyles of each of these groups differed considerably. And in each area – repressive, political, administrative – there were additional hierarchies, with those at the top living under very different conditions of constraint and privilege from those 'on the ground'. Some were in effect members of the extended ruling elite, others held far less elevated positions in the power structure, or were involved in the web of complex, overlapping hierarchies in ways that allowed them to exert different types of influence through different avenues of power. The full extension of power in the GDR is revealed when one considers the different areas in which the new power elite exerted control: administrative and political, social and economic, manipulative and repressive.

A fascinating account by Manfred Uschner provides glimpses into the constrained lifestyle of the functionaries who worked in the central power house in Berlin. There was no open job advertisement for a position such as Uschner's; rather, following extensive undercover investigation by Party and Stasi of one's background, credentials and political reliability, one would be approached with what was less an offer of employment than an offer of 'an honour, an honourable duty and a vocation', which could not be refused. 'One had to accept with gratitude the "Party task". Any other response would have been seen as blasphemous and interpreted as an attitude hostile to the Party.'[24] Once in, one could not resign without serious personal and professional consequences: there was no way of getting out and still rescuing some kind of appropriate career. But if one remained within the organisation, there was neither job security, nor clear promotion hierarchy; even a relatively high-level functionary was totally at the mercy of the political winds blowing around the Party apparatus at any given time. What in capitalist societies would be seen as 'human resources policy' was in the GDR an extension of political cadre selection and training, including 'the identification of absolutely reliable Party members who were "bound to class and party", initial "testing" at the lowest level, and then step by step, according to performance, "preparing" for higher functions'.[25] Career trajectories were recounted in a curious use of the passive voice, apparently lacking in space for individual decision-making and personal initiative – 'But soon, as a "Party mission", I was ordered back to my old institute' – accompanied sometimes by not-so-veiled threats of being sent 'to work in the brown-coal mines' (or more generally, in manual labour) if one did not accept the 'Party task'.[26] Within the 'second floor' of the Politburo office block, these largely anonymous functionaries appear to have led highly pressurised lives, with long hours of work and high rates of stress, illness and breakdown.

Few seem to have felt they had full opportunities to express their views, although the degree to which the atmosphere was oppressive or one of relatively open debate is the subject of some dispute among former functionaries. Claus Krömke, a former personal assistant to Günter Mittag – whose suite of offices was a little distant, on the fourth rather than the second floor – claimed that there was 'in fact an objective [*sachliche*], friendly, sometimes perhaps even too-friendly working atmosphere in this Party apparatus'.[27] Yet even Krömke agreed that the situation was riddled with sensitivities, taboos and severe constraints on raising any kind of independent critical voice. A far more damning account is given by Erhard Meyer, answerable to Mittag as former section leader of the ZK Department of Planning and Finance.[28] He recounts the dictatorial manner in which Mittag instilled fear in all around him, controlled information, and bullied his subordinates, with an empire reaching not only through the central Party and state departments but even directly into the heart of the GDR's industrial combines and factories through the system of General Directors and dedicated ZK Party Organisers with a direct line from Mittag to the workbench. The sole area of economic policy that seems to have been out of Mittag's aggressive and absolute control was that of Honecker's beloved social policy subventions: basic prices, rents and transport subsidies.

For lower level political functionaries, the record is a mixed one: the pressures much greater, the power much less, than for those functionaries who were genuinely members of the ruling elite. In the early decades the functionary system was far from stable, and proactive intervention from above was constantly required to monitor turnover and performance of local functionaries.[29] But by the 1980s, at least some of these functionaries appear more as representatives of the people than emissaries from the centre; or, at the very least, their positions were those of precarious intermediaries, damned whichever direction they faced.[30]

A 'reportage' by Landolf Scherzer, for example, of a month in the life of a local district (*Kreis*) First Secretary, Hans-Dieter Fritschler, provides fascinating vignettes of the local people and the numerous demands made on the man in charge of the Bad Salzungen district in the later 1980s.[31] Ricocheting between visits to factories with appallingly outdated equipment and unhygienic working conditions, residential areas of collapsing and dilapidated housing, contentious construction sites, military barracks with inadequate food and facilities, the homes of individuals in need of personal support or birthday greetings, and lengthy political meetings with prepared type-written speeches and much alcohol, Fritschler appears as the hard-working servant of the people. His wife barely sees him, and their lifestyle is so modest as to be virtually indistinguishable from that of their neighbours (except that, uniquely, they could not enjoy or exploit the numerous ways of circumventing or 'playing' the system). This is hardly the embodiment of state power and repression. One gains the impression of a highly committed individual seeking on the one hand to justify the virtually unjustifiable and defend in public the 'unity and determination' of the Party, and on the other to shore up a visibly collapsing system through sheer dint of hard work and the exploitation of personal connections and friendships at all levels of the political hierarchy. Fritschler emerges from Scherzer's account, and from his own post-*Wende* analysis, as more of a real intermediary, a genuine representative of the people to 'those on high', than a representative of the Party state to the people. Ultimate power remained with the centre, and indeed even at the centre, in Berlin, with Mittag and Honecker, and not with those seeking to put the case that came from the provinces. Thus, for example, Fritschler made representations on behalf of the people of Bad Salzungen to Politburo members Horst Sindermann, Erich Mückenberger and Werner Jarowinsky, protesting against a proposal to replace a relatively new and efficient heating-oil production plant with an environmentally destructive brown-coal works that would also destroy the local tourist industry. The case was put forward by Sindermann to the economic commission of the Politburo, led by Günter Mittag, where it was peremptorily dismissed. There was a similar experience with proposals to increase crop production with vegetables that, in the view of local agricultural experts, could not and would not grow on the local soil in the particular geographical conditions of the area; the expert knowledge of farmers, as represented by Fritschler, was simply rejected out of hand.[32]

Local mayors, too, seem to have been caught in a web of tensions: they were responsible for bringing in the vote and representing the needs of the Plan, as well as having all manner of mundane duties in everyday life, from visiting elderly and disabled residents, to ensuring adequate energy supplies and participating in local festivals.[33] They had to engage in political networking and the exploitation of influential connections in order to try to 'organise' scarce goods and materials for their locality, as well as performing genuinely representative functions on behalf of their communities. Mayors, as with other key political positions, were selected by the cadre mechanism, rather than through individual initiative, democratic election and open competition; yet they do seem to have been, on the whole, remarkably rooted in and committed to their local communities, whose needs they knew intimately. In 1989, only a little over three quarters (77 per cent) of local mayors were members of the SED; 21 per cent were members of a bloc party, and 2 per cent were members of no party at all (in the circumstances, a remarkably high percentage!). More than one third (34 per cent) were women, with a higher percentage of women mayors serving in small communities, where they were often perceived as 'the "soul" and "organisational talent" of the community'.[34]

Paid functionaries at the lower levels were vital to the implementation of SED rule. Explicit intentions with respect to local representatives and their modes of procedure were, even from a Western democratic viewpoint, in principle highly laudable, even if inevitably tinged with the characteristic tone of GDR didacticism. As one 'information document' (*Information*) of the Agitationskommission beim Politbüro put it, commenting on the 1973 Draft Law for the local representative bodies and people's representatives in the GDR, it was essential to devise a better method of informing deputies about local problems, and also of 'informing citizens in a timely and comprehensive manner'. It was essential to develop

> continuity of cooperation between the people's representative bodies, factories, agricultural co-operatives and residential areas, in particular in respect of the improvement of political-ideological work and the more effective deployment of the means and materials for the improvement of working and living conditions in residential areas.[35]

This characteristically combines the determination to influence citizens in the 'right' direction with the paternalistic concern for their well-being. There is an implicit assumption that citizens' interests are entirely in line with those of the state; they merely need to be made more aware of this fact.

Elites and power in East German society

The character of 'elite status' in this curiously inverted system was exceedingly ambiguous. Recent research suggests that those who took advantage of the peculiar opportunities for genuinely elite status in the GDR were not very different from careerists and the upwardly mobile in other industrial societies. There was, however, one unique feature of the elites in the GDR: they could not explicitly claim elite status.[36] Part of the cultural currency of GDR political culture was the claim to be working class, hence it was impossible, indeed counterproductive, to indulge in any form of explicit self-representation as an elite. Instead, one had to pay lip-service to the anti-elitist, egalitarian ideals of the 'workers' and peasants' state'. But one could openly claim, and flaunt, political awards and allegiances, as the vast multitude of lapel badges and pins left over as the material debris of the Party state readily attest.

Power was in some respects the key to social stratification in the GDR, and the power elite was the ruling class. This was a tiny class in the GDR, with a quite distinct social profile. But if the extended exercise of power was also diffuse and dispersed, the class structure below the level of the power elite was more closely rooted in differences of occupation and education, as becomes evident when looking at the fates of the old middle classes and new socialist intelligentsia, and at the alleged 'ruling class' of workers and peasants.

Chapter Nine

Cultural capital: From bourgeoisie to socialist intelligentsia

The diverse 'middle classes' of the GDR were caught in a tangle of historic and contemporary contradictions. The property-owning middle classes or bourgeoisie (*Besitzbürgertum*), historic oppressors of the proletariat, were the very embodiment of the capitalist system: anathema to the new society, ripe for dispossession. Yet nevertheless, a degree of managerial and economic expertise was required to run an efficient modern economy. Professional groups – earlier known as the 'educated bourgeoisie' (*Bildungsbürgertum*) – were similarly essential to the project of developing an efficient industrial state, even one under communist colours. Without appropriately qualified teachers, doctors, scientists and engineers, the GDR could not hope to run a modern economy or train and treat an educated and functioning workforce. Yet precisely these sorts of group had also been, in various degrees, pillars of the Nazi state. Without creative intellectuals committed to the construction and transmission of public systems of meaning, the SED could not 'bring culture to the masses' or seek to transform the remnants of 'bourgeois ideology' and 'false consciousness' among a population emerging from the ruins of Nazi propaganda and capitalist ideology. Yet creative intellectuals had a tendency towards autonomous thought and critique. Thus a massive transformation in either mentalities or personnel, or both, was necessary for producing the new 'socialist intelligentsia' of a modern communist state; and there existed a constant tension between the demands for conformity and commitment on the one hand, and the autonomy required for genuine creativity and innovation on the other. In all areas, one form of 'middle class' was ultimately replaced with another, though with very different degrees of rapidity or tardiness, draconian measures and enticements, pressures and privileges.

The East German 'intelligentsia', if such a word can be used at all, was therefore far from being a homogeneous group with common characteristics and outlook. Some Western scholars have suggested that the term 'intelligentsia' should not be used at all in this connection.[1] The 'socialist intelligentsia' even constituted a conceptual problem for GDR social theorists. Despite the fact that functionaries had for years been making observations in political reports on the political attitudes and opinions of the 'intelligentsia' as though their identification were more or less unproblematic, East German sociologists considered the very labelling of these educated groups – who were clearly not a 'class' in the Marxist sense – to be a highly contentious and controversial issue.[2] It is, however, useful to indicate those groups whose occupational position depended on a professional education and qualifications, or whose 'products' were the outcome of primarily intellectual rather than physical labour, and who were in many respects distinctively different from both the power elite and the industrial and agricultural working classes.

According to GDR sociologists, who were far from comfortable in admitting this group as a 'class', the 'stratum' (*Schicht*) of the 'intelligentsia' (*Intelligenz*) made up fully 15 per cent of the population in 1985.[3] The groups within this stratum were characterised by wide variations in status, lifestyle and relations with the state. They differed, too, in the extent to which they were affected by radical social revolution in the early post-war years or experienced more gradual processes of change over a longer period of time. The variegated transformation of the German middle classes and the eventual emergence of a socialist intelligentsia were nevertheless central to the making of the distinctive character of East German society.

Patterns of radical upheaval and rapid transformation

Some middle-class groups were subjected to very rapid, radical transformation, through far-reaching changes in structures or personnel, or both. This was particularly the case with respect to shifts in the economy from private to state ownership of the means of production, and in relation to groups that were ideologically fundamental to the construction of the new communist project such as teachers and lawyers.

The propertied bourgeoisie and large landowners were clearly doomed for destruction according to the Marxist scheme of history, and further damned by their alleged role in sustaining the Nazi or 'fascist' regime. Although for largely pragmatic reasons the actual record in the period of Soviet occupation is more complex and patchy than pure theory might suggest, these groups were radically affected by the expropriation of private ownership of the means of production and a swingeing tax regime in the later 1940s and '50s.[4] Many of those who lost their land or their enterprises fled to the West; others sought

to survive as best they could under the new regime. The economically relatively insignificant remnants of a propertied bourgeoisie were to be found
among the few remaining small traders, craftspeople, independent participants in enterprises half-owned by the state, and the self-employed, some of
whom survived even Honecker's attempted final blow – effectively an
economic own goal – in 1972.[5] By the 1980s, the few remaining survivors of
these policies had begun not only to be accepted but even in some respects
welcomed as an addition to national productivity, particularly with regard
to such crucial items for the national well-being as garden produce, honey
and eggs.

In the place of the old propertied bourgeoisie was, in part, an entirely new
breed of economic functionaries. At one level, many of the new economic elite
were politically committed participants in the new regime: managers of
individual enterprises and larger combines, increasingly well-educated Party
apparatchiks transmitting orders from the centre and cooperating with local
functionaries of the FDGB and other state representatives (including the Stasi)
to try to run a modern economy. Thus, with the transformation of capitalism
into a form of 'state socialism', the new economic managerial class that
replaced the propertied bourgeoisie was part of the wider circle of the ruling
elite: at the very top levels, indeed, particularly prominent individuals were
part of the political 'nomenclature' system. In very simplistic terms, therefore,
the difference between the roles of the economic elites in the preceding capitalist system and in the GDR was that in the latter, political commitment and
managerial power became far more closely interrelated.

The position was, however, rather different with respect to the 'educated
bourgeoisie', who could neither be 'eradicated' – at least in formal terms, as in
the case of the property-owning classes – nor even always easily transformed
with respect to political commitment to the new regime. In some areas, political commitment was far more important than specialist expertise; in others,
the situation was completely the reverse. The histories of different professional
groups thus varied dramatically, as a comparison of key professions will
rapidly make clear.

Education was a highly sensitive area politically, given the importance of
socialising a new generation of 'socialist personalities' – and this in a context
where the teaching profession was inherited from a previous regime of quite
different ideological outlook. The Third Reich had been no less interested in
stamping its mark on the rising generation than was the new communist
regime, and the Nazi culling of the teaching profession from 1933 onwards,
with the systematic exclusion of Jews, socialists and anyone else inclined to
query the values and curriculum of Nazi Germany, had left its mark on the

political profile of the teachers remaining in post by 1945. It has been estimated that no fewer than 28,179 of the approximately 40,000 teachers in the
Soviet Zone of Occupation, or just under three quarters (71.6 per cent) of
teachers, had been members of the NSDAP.[6] In Thuringia, the figure seems to
have been as high as a staggering 97 per cent.[7] There was therefore considerable debate as to whether only seriously tainted, active former Nazis should be
sacked, with 'nominal' former members of the NSDAP retained in their posts
for the time being. In the event, a somewhat confused process of firing and
hiring produced considerable variations from one area to another; but the
general thrust of official policy was to train, as rapidly as possible, a whole new
generation of *Neulehrer*, or 'new teachers'.

There was thus a very high turnover of teaching personnel in the early post-
war years, with the extremely rapid training and appointment of young and
inexperienced individuals. Some of these were young men returning from the
front, often without any relevant higher education or training; others were raw
school leavers, equipped merely with the knowledge acquired in their own
education in the Third Reich. In March 1947, there were still 16,332 former
Nazis working as teachers in the Soviet zone; but by April 1949, *Neulehrer*
made up over half of the teaching profession, and by 1950, around 80 per cent
of all teachers were newly trained.[8] The effect was a radical change in the
age profile of the teaching profession: while 70 per cent of the male teachers
already in post at the end of the war were over fifty years old, in the Jena
area, for example, the average age of the new teachers was around twenty-five
or twenty-six, and only 9 per cent of *Neulehrer* were over thirty-five years
of age.[9]

The main relevant criterion for becoming a *Neulehrer* was lack of any political taint. The vast majority were, at least to begin with, apolitical: in Saxony,
for example, in December 1945 only 3.7 per cent of new teachers were
members of the KPD, and 7 per cent belonged the SPD, while as many as 85
per cent belonged to no political party at all.[10] Some in the event became
politicised in the desired direction of socialism as a result of the heavily ideological training courses: more than half of the graduates of the courses run in
1946 joined the by-now 'unified' party of communists and social democrats,
the SED.[11] Training courses were initially extremely short, varying in length
from two to six weeks, and in a few areas up to two months, before a young
person was put in charge of a school class.

The situation in which new teachers found themselves was hardly guaranteed to entice people into the profession. The children put in the charge of
these newly qualified teachers were often extremely poorly clothed, lacking
particularly in adequate footwear, desperately hungry, ill-housed, and often

suffering traumas at home with problems of fathers, elder brothers and uncles held as prisoners of war, missing or dead. The teachers themselves often lived in highly primitive conditions, having to engage in manual labour after school hours to augment an inadequate salary, and, in the absence of alternative accommodation, pulling out a bed in the schoolroom to sleep. A general, undated report from about 1950 on the situation in schools bemoans problems not only with the training of teachers, but also with inadequate supplies of appropriate schoolbooks, the lack of teachers in specific subjects (notably Russian), and bad food – without even a mention of probably one of the greatest problems at this time, the appalling physical condition of schools in many areas.[12] Even around 1960, teachers were still suffering from an acute shortage of decent housing: in one case, 'an adapted cowshed was made available to the teacher'.[13]

Sometimes politically committed teachers could have what appears to have been a quite amazing effect on their pupils. Brigitte Reimann, for example, seems to have undergone a remarkable conversion experience from belief in God to belief in communism in the space of three years or so. In her letters to a former school friend who had moved to the West, in the summer and autumn of 1947 there is much evidence of strong religious beliefs and quite unproblematic mention of God (to whom she prays, and whom she thanks for the safe return of her father from a prisoner-of-war camp).[14] By 1950 there is evidence of strong political commitment to the new regime, with Reimann running around from one meeting to another, enthusing about the Deutschlandtreffen, a massive international congress of young people in East Berlin, warning her friend not to believe in Western propaganda, and sketching-in her mad schedule of political activities, from the political 'circles' or literary discussions in the Club House, through the FDJ meetings, to the activities of the German-Soviet Friendship Society (DSF), of which she was the First Secretary for her school.[15] This frenetic round of activity and political commitment seems to have developed in large measure as a result of the influence of her young teacher, Ilse, whom Reimann describes as 'still quite young and also a member of the FDJ. But despite her youth she is colossally well educated, and above all a marvellous comrade, who treats us pupils as equals, and without whom our FDJ work would soon collapse.'[16] The number of people who earned an entry in the posthumous *Wer war wer in der DDR?* ('Who was who in the GDR?') who had formerly been a *Neulehrer* also provides testament to the effect this training and experience had on a generation of young adults who subsequently went on to take up prominent positions in the GDR.[17]

But this appears to have been only half the story. Despite the fact that the school was a prime locus for ideological pressure, the grip of the state through its front-line representatives was never entirely secure. Many *Neulehrer* did not survive the physical privations and increasing ideological pressures for very long. By 1954, around 70,000 teachers had left the GDR for the West, of whom it is estimated that no fewer than 30,000 were former *Neulehrer*.[18] Meanwhile, former Nazi teachers were gradually rehabilitated, reducing the percentage of the profession who were *Neulehrer*. Even some of the younger teachers in the 1950s and '60s showed the continuing influence of their own socialisation under Nazism. But the problems continued. In Neubrandenburg in early 1962, teachers were allegedly avoiding 'basic political questions' ('politische Grundfragen'); in Klein-Halle even the School Director refused to use the word 'socialism'.[19] Teachers in the 1960s suffered a massive overload as far as hours of work were concerned, not even taking into account the numbers of additional functions many of them took on with respect to activities in the FDJ and other organisations.[20] In the 1970s, there were complaints about the increasing turnover of teachers, with many giving up because of 'excessive demands, pedagogic failures and health problems', and about the fact that, while the teaching profession itself had an increasing proportion of younger teachers, the average age of those who were Party members among the teaching profession was steadily rising.[21] In 1980, a general report on new trainees for the teaching profession indicated that, while the student trainee teachers showed high levels of interest in developments in Poland (political strikes, the Solidarity movement), large numbers did not express the 'right' opinions on this. There was a regrettable 'contradiction between the political knowledge at their command and their personal willingness to act, such that for a considerable number it was still [note the ever-optimistic *noch*] difficult to reconcile their personal interests with those of society'.[22] With teachers like these, perhaps it was scarcely surprising that a degree of independent thinking and individualism was able to develop among the schoolchildren of the 1980s. Yet the Ministry of People's Education (Volksbildung), in 1963–89 under the control of Margot Honecker, was among the most politicised of all, and teachers were at the front line of the supposed indoctrination attempts of the SED state.[23]

If teachers at school level were crucial to the transmission of new attitudes and beliefs among the younger generation, necessitating rapid turnover, university staff and members of professions where long periods of specialised training were necessary were subject to rather different considerations. In the case of lawyers and judges, political considerations similarly outweighed any worries about technical training. The legal system of Nazi Germany had been from the very beginning subjected to massive political abuse: Jewish, socialist and other 'undesirable' groups had from the spring of 1933 been excluded from the legal profession; Hitler himself had from the outset demonstrated a total disregard for the rule of law, despite his spurious 'legalisation' of acts of violence (as in the *post-hoc* 'legal' justification of the murders carried out in the 'Night of the Long Knives' in the summer of 1934); and by the end of the regime the legal system was so subverted to political ends that, in the winter of 1944–5, around 5,000 people were sentenced to death and executed after the most perfunctory 'trials' in the 'People's Court' under the notorious Roland Freisler. It is arguably scandalous that there were such massive continuities in the legal profession in the Federal Republic of Germany in the 1950s, with evidence even in the various concentration-camp trials of the late 1950s and '60s of extraordinarily lenient sentences for some of those who had been perpetrators in the Nazi regime. Such continuity in the legal profession was not the case in the Soviet zone and GDR; but there was a new form of subversion of law to political ends, although of a very different ideological colour.

Despite a brief moment that saw the re-establishment of a form of 'legal state' (*Rechtsstaat*) in the different *Länder* of the early occupation period, the legal system was very rapidly the object of political attention. Radical early weeding left massive holes in the profession, which were filled by speedily trained and politically reliable 'People's Judges' (*Volksrichter*), somewhat on the lines of the *Neulehrer*, and the legal system as a whole came under increasing political pressure. This radical turnover was the subject of bitter criticism by contemporaries, who denounced the dismissal of their former 'specialists with experience, good educators and models' as well as their 'good old judges and lawyers', and claimed that the new system 'ignores all human rights and violently oppresses the freedom of the citizen', conveniently forgetting that at this point the new communist regime was merely repeating, under very different political colours, the strategies of the preceding Nazi system.[24]

The political abuse of the legal system was most visibly flagrant in the early 1950s, with the show trials presided over by the formidable Hildegard Benjamin, Vice President of the High Court in 1949–53, and then Minister of Justice 1953–67. There were marked variations with respect to the character of proceedings in different areas of the law, not all of which were directly subordinated to the whims of the SED elite or the Ministry for State Security; but, all due qualifications notwithstanding, it is undoubtedly the case that the legal profession in the GDR became very much a loyal servant of the state, with political considerations capable of overriding notions of justice in the Western sense throughout the history of the GDR.[25] The subordination of at least some areas of legal decision-making to crass political considerations was the object of overt critique in novels such as Christoph Hein's *Der Tangospieler*.

Patterns of gradual turnover and generational change

In the case of other professions, an equally compromised Nazi past was only part of the wider picture, and other considerations came to the forefront.

The case of medicine provides an interesting demonstration. As one university professor commented as late as 1961, 'we don't have the old lawyers, the old teachers, etc., anymore, but we still have the old doctors, and this situation should have been dealt with a long time ago.'[26] But it was not so easy to know how the medical profession should have been 'dealt with'. Doctors were crucial to public health, particularly in the appalling conditions of near-famine, widespread disease and periodic epidemics of the early post-war years. In some areas, overcrowding in the remaining habitable dwellings among the ruins was exacerbated by the influx of refugees, who were forced to live in increasingly insanitary conditions, with resultant waves of infection. Disinfectants and medications were in extremely short supply, as were doctors to tend to the sick. This was no moment to worry about political credentials.

Yet the medical profession had been peculiarly nazified in the Third Reich. The atrocities of the 'medical experiments' committed in Auschwitz and other concentration camps by the notorious Josef Mengele, Carl Clauberg, Horst Schumann, Sigmund Rascher and many others, are of course well known: injecting women's wombs with formalin to cause inflammation, scarring and hence infertility; infecting people with deadly diseases such as typhus; torturing and murdering twins in the interests of 'scientific experiment'; immersing prisoners in freezing water for hours to see how long they could endure hypothermia before the inevitable death. All these were horrific and almost unthinkable evidence of the Nazi lack of respect for human life and total lack of compassion on the part of individual 'scientists'. But the active and fundamentally murderous racism of Nazi Germany was not limited to the extremes of brutality, torture and murder practised against inmates of concentration camps. Racist thinking and practices permeated medical practice far more widely in Nazi Germany, even with respect to the 'Aryan' population of the German 'folk community': for example, ordinary doctors in general practices participated in 'marriage guidance' on eugenic lines, giving advice on suitable partners with whom to reproduce, or signing compulsory sterilisation papers for those deemed by the state to be unfit to have children because of real or alleged 'hereditary conditions' ranging from 'feeble-mindedness' to 'hereditary alcoholism'. The vast majority of doctors who stayed in post in the Third Reich were hence to a greater or lesser degree active carriers of Nazi racist views and practices, and the majority were at least nominal members of the NSDAP, whatever their subsequently professed lack of responsibility for the extremes of concentration camp 'medical' practices.

Medical expertise and related scientific knowledge could, however, not be rapidly acquired by a new generation straight after the war: there was thus no possibility of radical denazification of the medical profession by introducing training courses of a few weeks to produce 'new doctors' on the lines of the *Neulehrer* programme. It was not possible simply to dismiss trained medical personnel with tainted pasts from their jobs before adequate replacements had successfully gone through the lengthy training process; and nor could those doing the training readily be replaced. One strategy was to send former Nazi doctors on a form of 'labour service' to difficult areas characterised by very high rates of disease, where their expertise was vitally needed. Often doctors were in fact able to make new lives in these areas, where their Nazi past was not generally known, and many settled in the new environment. By 1949, fewer than 15 per cent of the medical profession had irrevocably lost their positions as a result of denazification measures.[27] Those replacing them were often very elderly, and brought back out of retirement; a very small number were returnees who had been forced out by the Nazis after 1933. But the vast majority of the medical profession in the Soviet zone and early years of the GDR were individuals who had been actively involved in sustaining the Nazi 'racial state'. In the academic sphere, the proportion of former Nazis actually rose slightly in the period 1947–57, only beginning to decline somewhat by 1961; even at this time, a mere third were not in any way coloured by a politically suspect past, while as many as one in five seem to have been very active former Nazis (in the category of 'heavily tainted' or 'schwer belastet').[28] A report from December 1959 similarly estimates that

> Around 80 per cent of the old medical intelligentsia, that is 30 to 40 per cent of the total medical intelligentsia, were more or less active fascists in the Nazi period, or held high grades in the fascist army. There is no other group among those classed as intelligentsia that reveals such a high percentage of former active Nazis as do the medical intelligentsia.[29]

The percentage of former Nazis in the medical faculty of the University of Halle was as high as 84 per cent; among professors, the figure rose to 87 per cent.[30]

If the SED recognised the urgent need for doctors and university teachers of medicine, their approach to them was at best ambivalent. On the one hand, they were treated very generously (by GDR standards) in terms of salary and working conditions; on the other hand, their children were discriminated against in school, and prevented from entering higher education. Doctors complained about the inadequacy of buildings and technical resources, about obstacles placed in the way of their attending medical conferences in the West, and about sheer overload. What denazification had not achieved by way of culling the profession was, however, made up for by the still-porous border with the West before 1961. In the 1950s, doctors were easily able to flee West, where they would not only find better career prospects for themselves but also would not find their children subjected to massive disadvantages in terms of educational prospects. Between one fifth and one third of doctors sent their children to study in the West in the 1950s.[31] Others decided to remove themselves and their families entirely. Around 7,500 doctors left for the West before 1961, about half of whom left in the period after 1954; by 1961, around 8,740 doctors living in the Federal Republic of Germany had come from the GDR; and somewhere in the region of 1,474 dentists left between 1954 and 1961.[32] By January 1962, the 50,000 residents of Meissen, for example, would have been well advised to look after their teeth, on the grounds that prevention was better than (failure to) cure: of the grand total of 13 remaining dentists, after three had fled to the West and two had died in the previous four years, no fewer then seven were aged over sixty, and two were well into their seventies; a mere four of the 13 dentists still officially on the books were actually fit to practise full time, the others being reduced to part-time work since they were suffering from various serious illnesses, heart problems and severe physical disabilities.[33]

The SED was thus caught in a difficult situation: constantly complaining, yet also needing to retain medical expertise. Functionaries complained about the unwillingness of doctors to work in rural areas, their 'individualistic' and 'careerist' perspectives, and their tainted Nazi pasts. As one report summarised it in 1956:

> The med. intelligentsia has personal concerns in relation to their children's studies, spending holidays, visiting West German and foreign congresses, the question of housing, etc. They consider that, given current conditions for practising medicine in the [German Democratic] Republic, the possibilities for personal and professional development are unsatisfactory. Our current organisational system gives the experienced doctor too little chance of fulfilling any wish for independent responsibility, as was previously the case in Germany and as is now possible for doctors in West Germany with their own practices.[34]

A report of 1961 suggests that doctors were leaving for the West, 'not for financial reasons by any means', but rather because of 'the search for the satisfaction of personal needs, which currently are difficult over here (new flat, television sets, car, etc)'.[35] The ultimate solution was of course to seek to 'grow' a replacement medical profession, through the education system, ensuring that the next generation of doctors and medical professors would be politically reliable and committed to the general good, as interpreted by the SED, rather than their own individual careers and opportunities.

But even this was problematic, given the wider influence exerted by those entrusted with the literally vital task of teaching the next generation of doctors. This point was also not lost on somewhat-alarmed contemporaries:

The majority of professors adopt a 'wait-and-see' [*abwartend*] approach to government politics because they are not convinced of the victory of socialism ... [T]he majority of these old professors cooperated actively with the Nazis and then withdrew into an 'un-political' attitude after 1945.[36]

And it was their influence that threatened to blight the next generation:

The situation in the up-and-coming scientific generation reflects the ideological uncertainties among the teaching body. Until recently the selection and also the training of the next scientific generation were entirely under the control of those holding teaching positions.[37]

There was, moreover, a traditional conservative-bourgeois subculture among university students that was hard to combat for the 50 per cent or so of students in the late 1950s who came from working-class and peasant backgrounds. Among these members of previously under-educated social groups, catapulted suddenly into a quite unfamiliar milieu by Ulbricht's policies of fostering the rapid upward social mobility of disadvantaged groups, there was still a certain deference to traditional notions of bourgeois culture and concomitant aspirations with respect to attitudes and lifestyle:

Through their self-confidence and arrogant demeanour, acquired through upbringing in the parental home, and because of their favourable material situation, [middle-class students] exercise great political and moral influence on the students [from poorer backgrounds]. In the course of their studies, many workers' and peasants' children attempt to make such ways of life their own.[38]

Thus, students from working-class and rural backgrounds were easily influenced, not only by their nazified generation of teachers, but also, to a considerable extent, by the middle-class students who were their peer group.

Over time, nevertheless, new generations of doctors and teachers of medicine were produced within the GDR who were distinctively different in social profile and outlook from the older members of the profession. As more women entered medicine, so there was more sympathy with particularly female concerns, such as that of the claimed right to abortion. With changes in the structure of the medical system, there were eventually concomitant changes in the attitudes of professionals. Once the border was closed, doctors were rewarded with honours, titles and, for the truly committed, the status of 'travel cadre' with permission to travel to congresses or scientific conferences in the West. But the basic credentials in terms of medical knowledge and expertise were never compromised, nor could they be compensated for, by political commitment. Unlike the situation in the Soviet Union, where medicine was abused for political purposes as in the 'psychiatric treatment' of dissidents, there appears to have been relatively little such abuse in the GDR, with apparently only a small number of cases of the administration of inappropriate drugs or treatments – although even 'only a few cases' are too many.[39] Among the wider medical profession, the traditional milieu of the German educated bourgeoisie remained remarkably persistent. Hierarchies within clinics and hospitals, with the supreme authority of the 'big man' at the top, appear to have remained intact; so too does the privileging of certain patients over others, and the patronising approach that tended towards treating patients as objects rather than subjects, not privy to the details of their own illnesses, particularly in respect of cancer.[40]

The case of medicine was perhaps peculiar given the unique combination of life-saving skills and knowledge with a highly compromised political past. In other professions, the balance was quite different: journalism, for example, was particularly close to political imperatives, while other subjects were to a greater or lesser extent less politically relevant. It took over two decades to transform the university teaching profession generally, with considerable variations across different subjects. By the mid-1960s, among university teachers, law – for reasons described above – was the most 'proletarianised' profession (in 1965, 51.3 per cent of lawyers supposedly came from a peasant or working-class background), while medicine and theology remained the most bourgeois in terms of class backgrounds. It was only by the mid-1970s that most members of university staff came from what were at least claimed to be non-bourgeois backgrounds.[41]

University staff – and indeed also students – were not easily satisfied with their conditions of work, for reasons that will be recognisable to academics everywhere. University teachers wanted to be able to confer with colleagues across borders, on the grounds that 'science knows no [geographical] boundaries'.[42] They wanted more foreign language teaching – particularly English, as the international language of academic specialisation – and more chances for 'world-openness'.[43] The situation with respect to secretarial help was 'more than catastrophic', since secretaries could earn more in industry.[44] There was a lack of apparatus, instruments and other essentials obtainable only from the West. Academics were also irritated by apparently being disadvantaged in the allocation of housing, with other groups – such as practising doctors – getting priority in obtaining scarce flats.[45] A comprehensive catalogue of complaints from the University of Greifswald in January 1960 pretty well summarised the situation of academics across the GDR at this time.[46] They were angry at the fact that administrators cut Western titles from the library holdings without consulting academics about what was truly important in their field. They were bothered by the difficulties of getting their own work published, and obtaining relevant publications. They were annoyed at bureaucratic overload, with 'organisational work' taking up between two thirds and four fifths of their time, leaving little time for serious academic research. They were critical of the fact that technical assistants were paid so little they could earn more as teachers. They would have liked more opportunities for open-ended intellectual discussions about art, culture and science without political constraints. The health of academics was allegedly 'extremely bad' because of the 'psychological burdens' from which they were suffering. As one academic summarised it: 'You can manage very well without the odd orange and such-like, but what is wearing us down are the bureaucratic obstacles to scholarly work and the ignoring of our wishes that could be fulfilled.'[47]

It nevertheless remained the case that there was a peculiarly traditional bourgeois milieu and lifestyle among many of the academic elite of the GDR, even among the most politically committed. Conditions in the research academies were also in many respects better than in the 'front-line' teaching universities. And one has only to take a brief glimpse at the copious outpourings of that prickly doyen of SED historical writing, Jürgen Kuczynski, to gain a sense of the extraordinary continuities in the lifestyle of the German educated middle classes across the capitalist–communist divide.

There was one professional group that was even less dependent on the state for professional education and employment: ministers of religion. Even here, however, the new political circumstances of the GDR stamped their mark. Many individuals indeed found themselves entering a career within or in the environs of the Church precisely because they had been inadequately conformist at school and had found theology the only area of study remaining open to them; the oppositionalist Pastor Rainer Eppelmann is perhaps the most well-known example. Ministers of religion held a unique position in the GDR: both totally unnecessary, as far as the long-term communist project was concerned (with the ultimate death of religion a fixture on the official world-historical agenda) and yet at the same time in all sorts of respects essentially unassailable. Thus clerics, an alleged remnant of bourgeois society, remained a contested and uncomfortable island in GDR society. Catholics, in a minority of around one million among the predominantly Protestant population of the GDR in the late 1940s, fairly rapidly regrouped and transformed their institutional structure in order to develop a sustainable *modus vivendi* with the regime.[48] Catholic priests, particularly in those rural areas that remained relatively untouched by major economic changes, found ways to preserve a quite strong Catholic milieu across forty years of an atheist regime; the situation was different where, for example, the introduction of extensive brown-coal mining destroyed whole villages and disrupted rural life.[49] Protestant pastors represented initially the vast majority of the East German populace (around fifteen million of a total population of seventeen million). Although the size of Protestant congregations had dwindled substantially by the later 1960s, the institutional structure and property of the Protestant Churches remained intact, and, even after the formal institutional separation from the West German Protestant Churches in 1969, they continued to benefit from considerable West German financial and moral support. During the course of the 1970s, considerations of the role played by church hospitals, homes for the elderly and disabled, orphanages, and social outreach work with alcoholics and 'asocials', combined with wider considerations of international recognition and domestic political co-option (not least through extensive infiltration by the Stasi) to culminate in the famous Church–State agreement of 6 March 1978. The relatively de-centralised organisation of the Protestant Churches meant that, in the 1980s, central church authorities were unable to control the more dissident spirits at the grass roots, where certain pastors felt it was important to sustain a space for open discussion and debate. Thus the structural position of the Church and the local role of pastors proved to be crucial in providing the conditions for the growth of dissent in the 1980s, and hence in the domestic origins of what was sometimes dubbed the 'Protestant Revolution' of 1989.[50] Ministers of religion constituted, then, one very significant yet allegedly anachronistic social group among the 'remnants of the bourgeoisie'.

Uncomfortable comrades: The cultural intelligentsia

Autonomous artists, writers and thinkers who were not dependent on a regular income from some form of institutional employment, were far more problematic in many respects. They also constitute an exceedingly diverse set of groups – or indeed individuals – with opinions ranging from the ultra-supportive to the utterly critical.

On the one hand, members of the new 'cultural intelligentsia' were vital in the task of putting across the appropriate images and fostering whatever was currently considered to be the right kind of cultural life. Many prominent opponents of the Nazi regime decided after 1945 (often returning from exile abroad) to settle in eastern Germany, thinking this would be the 'better' Germany. Anna Seghers, Bertolt Brecht, Johannes R. Becher and others provided a lead in articulating utopian visions of a new society – which in some cases did not always preclude critical comments on the current state of affairs, as in Brecht's notorious poem occasioned by the 1953 Uprising in which he ironically asked whether, in view of the difficulties, it might not be better for the government to dissolve the people and elect a new one. At less elevated levels, those larger numbers of the cultural intelligentsia who were in one way or another closely dependent on the regime for their jobs – journalists, radio and television producers, film-makers, actors, directors of theatres, conductors of orchestras and the like – were relatively easy to select, promote and keep an eye on through the cadre system. Thus the reliable could be fostered, the less reliable disciplined and if necessary removed from their professional means of livelihood. It was more difficult to know how best to deal with those creative writers, poets and artists who were more independent, and who often enjoyed a degree of prestige and publicity in the West, making disciplinary measures more problematic and arguably counterproductive.

The history of dissident intellectuals in the GDR attracted a great deal of attention in the West well before 1989, in part because critical or semi-critical texts produced in the GDR were often published and indeed widely publicised in the West, in part because prominent dissidents themselves very often landed up physically in the West, a favourite strategy of the regime being to export troublesome spirits to the capitalist side of the inner-German border. Thus Rudolf Bahro, for example, author of *The Alternative in Eastern Europe* (1978), eventually became a leading light in the West German Green Party; the guitarist and singer Wolf Biermann found himself involuntarily exiled in 1976; and the well-known actor Manfred Krug gives a chilling account of the way in which he was effectively frozen out of any kind of professional career following his failure to recant his protest against the expatriation of Wolf Biermann.[51] Significant numbers of less well-known writers and musicians were also forced or 'encouraged' to accept exit visas to the West, particularly in the later 1970s and '80s, frequently following prison sentences for a variety of alleged offences, including the trumped-up charge of offending against the GDR tax regime by publication in the West.

Among lower-level cultural functionaries, and those who were in one way or another essential to the production and dissemination of culture but whose names never hit the international headlines, the situation was also rather mixed. A snapshot of cadre reports from 1969–70 on those involved in film and television production, and those working in publishing houses, for example, reveals a startling proportion of individuals who were not merely themselves not of the appropriate or desired working-class background, but who even 'disdained' or 'were contemptuous of' the 'leading role of the working class'. Only 13 of the 39 members of the leadership collective in the Mitteldeutscher

Verlag were members of the SED, and only five of the 15 lectors – effectively censors – were members of the SED. The lectors were allegedly 'politically unreliable and in part indifferent . . . [and hence] not in a position to help writers in political debates in order to pick up and work through the new problems of our societal development'. This was allegedly because they 'do not proceed in their work from a class standpoint, because they themselves do not possess a clear political position and allow themselves to be led by petty bourgeois ways of thinking and behaving'.[52] The Dresden Philharmonia Orchestra in 1970 had a total of 131 members, of whom only 13 were members of the SED; 17 former members had fled the Republic while on tours in the West, including four after 1961. Even the trade-union leaders in this orchestra refused to join the Party, and the 'political development of the musicians had not fully kept pace with the high demands of the cultural-political and artistic effectiveness of the orchestra'.[53] A report on this orchestra a few months later came to the conclusion that they represented 'the standpoint of the "just-a-musician", not having recognised the class character of art . . . Petty bourgeois lifestyles predominate among these members of the Philharmionia'.[54] Interestingly, the majority of those to whom the reports refer were of the generation to have experienced the Third Reich at first hand, having often served in the 'fascist army', as it was scathingly referred to, and a few had been members of the NSDAP; there were, for example, six former Wehrmacht officers and four former NSDAP members in the State Committee for Television.[55] More generally, reports of the 1960s repeatedly refer to the ways in which different members of the cultural intelligentsia at these less elevated levels tended to adopt a distanced and 'wait-and-see' approach (*abwartend*).

Yet even in these areas, the generational shifts of the 1970s and '80s had their effect. The extent to which East German culture was by and large no longer the object of direct political controversy in the mid-1980s can in part be illustrated by a contrast case. The First Secretary of the Verband der Film- und Fernsehschaffenden der DDR, Professor Peter Ulbrich, attended a meeting of the Fifth Congress of the Filmverband of the Soviet Union in Moscow in May 1986 – a meeting also attended by the Soviet Union's then still relatively new leader, Mikhail Gorbachev. Ulbrich could hardly contain his surprise at the critical atmosphere, the very open discussions, indeed heated debates, about the perceived dire state of Soviet films and documentaries; his report is drenched with amazement and shock at the tumultuous character of the discussions at the Congress, which clearly contrasted sharply with his experiences of comparable gatherings in the GDR.[56] The lively interest among the GDR creative intelligentsia in developments in the Soviet Union is confirmed in other reports of the time.[57]

Interpreting the role of the East German intelligentsia

So while the 'bourgeoisie' in its capitalist form disappeared, and its remnants were viewed with constant hostility and suspicion, new forms and variants of the educated middle classes or 'socialist intelligentsia' emerged. These were not captured well in the GDR's own (changing, and inconsistently applied) system of social classification; nor did GDR social scientists and political theorists ever quite decide what to make of the role and historical mission of different groups among the new intelligentsia. As with other areas of social stratification, following a period of rapid transformation in the first decade and a half after the end of the war, a new system emerged in which working conditions, income, status, lifestyle and power were recombined in a variety of ways, with marked variations from one group to another.

Professional groups – doctors, lawyers, architects, teachers, scientists, engineers, journalists, ministers of religion, film makers, artists and writers – were highly diverse both in the character and implications of their activities and in the degrees of strategic importance or potential challenges they posed to the regime. While some, such as Catholic priests or Protestant pastors, were unambiguously to be considered historical 'remnants', others were ever more products of the new society. And the records indicate that there was little sense of any common 'class consciousness' across these very diverse groups, many of whom seem to have been very willing to bicker about the relative privileges they felt were enjoyed by others but not their own particular group.

Meanwhile, the relationships between well-educated members of the intelligentsia and the often less well-educated, less intellectually adept and less articulate functionaries of the SED and the mass organisations were often somewhat problematic. The inverted hierarchies of political power and cultural capital clashed, as new power relationships displaced the old power of education and yet power-holders were unable to engage in an argument on equal terms. Functionaries might experience being 'laughed out of court' ('verlacht'), and as one report of 1961 commented:

> In dealing with basic questions of politics and cultural politics, we are often lacking in appropriate discussion partners. It is still very much the exception if leading functionaries from the Party and state apparatus or from the FDGB organs are able to appear in front of the artistic and scientific intelligentsia. If that does on occasion occur, then generally only in large gatherings, which do not permit any genuine discussion to develop on the part of the artists.[58]

Although this problem receded somewhat over time, with the increasing educational qualifications of functionaries in the 1970s and '80s, the intrinsic tensions between political ideologues constrained to toe the Party line, however well educated, and those whose vocations involved the exercise of their critical capacities, never entirely dissipated.

At the same time, there were also persisting tensions between the intelligentsia and ordinary workers and employees, rooted in a number of disagreements over perceived privileges – for example, in the distribution of holiday places, or permission to travel – as well as in inherited notions of status. Yet in a society in which there were only relatively modest differences between income levels, professionals often earned little more than some of their less well-educated, working-class compatriots. They did not necessarily have better access to the almost random distribution of personal 'connections' that were necessary for 'organising' scarce goods and materials (particularly when these were to be 'liberated' from a building site), nor were they necessarily better off with respect to Western contacts and access to foreign currency (although those favoured with 'travel cadre' status might be). Thus status and 'connection'-dependent aspects of lifestyle were very often at odds with the inherited 'cultural capital' and characteristic lifestyles and milieu of professional groups. Officially accorded lower prestige than the heroised (masculine, muscular, manual) working class, professionals were often officially portrayed as effete, vacillating intellectuals having to make uncomfortable compromises with the authorities.[59]

Yet in all sorts of respects, members of the socialist intelligentsia and their families managed to enjoy better 'life chances' than manual working-class compatriots: they had on average longer life expectancy, access to better housing, and a greater likelihood of their children being successful in school. And, following the early decades of massive societal change and the exchange of elites, by the 1970s and '80s the new socialist intelligentsia was beginning to reproduce itself. Just as in Western societies, many of those born into privileged and well-educated households found it easier to do well in the educational system, to play the parameters of the system, and to enter the ranks of the next generation of intelligentsia. This, too, bothered GDR sociologists, although they ran out of time before they were able to find any kind of solution.

Chapter Ten

The un-making of the German working class (and peasantry)

Whatever the official re-designation in terms of 'strata' rather than 'class', consciousness of class differences remained a live topic in the GDR. In Brigitte Reimann's novel about a young female architect, *Franziska Linkerhand*, the protagonist repeatedly registers her relative social isolation from the proletarian cohabitants of the hostel in which she is billeted while working on the construction of a new town in the south-east of the GDR (based on the real example of Hoyerswerda). A young proletarian blonde accuses Franziska of 'being just one of the intelligentsia'; Franziska rages against the working-class women with their bleached hair showing dark roots, their bitten-down fingernails, their premature wrinkles and tendency to drunkenness; she rages, too, against herself, for wanting their friendship. She rages against one particular working-class 'clan' (a family with whom she had earlier been intimately connected) with their hatred of 'the educated', and their

> dumb suspicion of 'them up there', anyone who is different from them, and their sentimental robber ballads, their nick-nacks, little porcelain dogs and marzipan pink nymphs with small greyhounds, and the coloured pictures above the beds in the bedroom . . . once, at a birthday party, she had to throw up when the sister, doubled up with laughter, came in carrying boiled sausages in a chamber pot.[1]

The sharply drawn picture is one of persisting difference between the educated daughter of the old bourgeoisie and the raucous, lewd, hard-bitten masses with their distrust and dislike of those who were better educated. Even the time and manner of death in the different social classes are brought to the reader's attention: in Franziska's bourgeois background, people like her grandmother died a dignified death in old age; among the workers whose stories she has to listen to, all manner of tragic tales of accidents and injury lead to premature and violent departure from the world of the living.

Yet even the character and status of the 'working classes' changed over the forty years of East German society. While older workers may have retained a strong sense of working-class identity, often forged in the deprivations and struggles of the 1920s and '30s, among younger East Germans the character of class identity began to shift and diversify. Once one starts to disentangle the different aspects of class formation, a picture emerges of a set of processes through which, while the concept of 'working class' was vastly extended, the practices and experiences of everyday life cut across earlier forms of class solidarity. Distinctions between different types of work remained, but were overlaid by other inequalities; there was an unravelling of the strands that, when run together, might form a coherent wider working-class identity.

The GDR was officially designated the 'workers' and peasants' state' (*Arbeiter- und Bauernstaat*), a title even enshrined in the GDR constitution of 1974. In what has been termed a 'worker-society', everyone was or at least claimed to be working class.[2] This class was heroised in official imagery and ideology: even the top Party functionaries claimed working-class status if they had so much as spent two weeks on a training course for some manual occupation. The greatest status was attached to being a member of the working classes, in contrast to Western industrial societies of the time (as in Britain, where the 'we're all middle class now' slogan became popular in the post-war era). But at the same time, the things that tend to make for class formation and class cohesion – certainly in the classic heyday of class society in the nineteenth and early twentieth centuries – began to fall apart. For a strong sense of collective class identity to exist, several different criteria have to correlate very closely with one another: type of employment and relationship to the employer; a bundle of common inequalities, in contrast to other classes, to do with income and lifestyle; and a common consciousness of collective character and collective interests in opposition to other classes.[3] But while the notion of the 'working class' was almost grotesquely expanded in GDR official ideology, in what might be called the 'lived experience' of East German workers there was an uncoupling of many of these features, and a dissolution of 'class' bonds. The notion of 'working class' was at one and the same time grossly inflated, imbued with massive cultural-political significance, and simultaneously dissolved by the transformation of factors determining lifestyle and collective experience. These processes took place alongside a revolution in social relations on the land and a transformation in the nature of the East German peasantry. In the process a new collective identity emerged: that of 'ordinary' East Germans.

Images and self-images

Officially heroised, images of the East German working class and its glorious struggles of the past were ubiquitous. In political propaganda, statues and posters, pictures in children's books, prominent members of the politically organised communist working class had their praises sung. Heroic battles against the inequalities of capitalism and the repressions of fascism were recounted in history books, in exhibitions and at memorials to the defeat of Nazism. Names of key individuals were enshrined both physically, as in the shrine to Ernst Thälmann in Buchenwald concentration camp, and symbolically, in the names of streets, schools and youth clubs, and organisations such as the 'Thälmann Pioneers' for children.

And the working class was represented as continuing to struggle in all sorts of ways to build a better society on the ruins of the defeated past. Periodic campaigns such as the Hennecke movement were intended to induce others to do likewise. In creative literature, strenuous attempts were made from the later 1950s – marked by the first Bitterfeld Conference of 1958 – to forge closer links between literary output and the lived experiences of workers at the production face. Novels such as Brigitte Reimann's *Ankunft im Alltag* (1961) and Christa Wolf's *Der geteilte Himmel* (1962) portrayed members of the industrial working class both owing much to the new state, and seeking to make their own active contribution in the ongoing struggle to build a better future. Many films from the East German DEFA studio portrayed muscular male working-class heroes, such as Balla in *Spur der Steine* (1965), or extolled the intrinsic authenticity and fundamental morality – despite, or perhaps in face of, all manner of temptations, setbacks and challenges – of young working-class female protagonists such as Maria in *Das Kaninchen bin ich* (1965), or Paula in *Die Legende von Paul und Paula* (1973). (While the last of these was a commercial success, the first two were banned in the cultural slaughter of the Eleventh Plenum of 1965; but the portrayal of the key roles, particularly those of female protagonists, was nevertheless indicative of a dominant trend.) To be a member of the working class was to be on the winning side in the battles of the past and the ongoing efforts to build a better future.

To be a member of the working class was not merely a high accolade. Particularly in the early period, from the later 1940s to the early 1960s, it was a vital ingredient in upward social mobility. The opportunities offered by a combination of demographic and political factors were indeed unprecedented. Losses of manpower in the war, massive migration westwards in the period before the construction of the Wall, and political discrimination against those of a bourgeois background and conservative outlook meant that individuals with working-class origins and left-wing political credentials had extraordinary opportunities. Educational qualifications or specialist expertise were at this time relatively unimportant. In the 1950s, as many as 50 per cent of those entering the socialist 'service class' had neither the basic school leaving certificate (*Mittlere Reife*) nor the higher level *Abitur*.[4] Initiatives such as the 'Workers' and Peasants' Faculties' (Arbeiter- und Bauernfakultäten) and evening classes provided additional opportunities for acquiring qualifications later in life for those who had come from backgrounds where further and higher education were almost undreamt of. Even in the 1960s, and as late as the 1970s, reorganisation of the economic structure combined with the effects of earlier migration to allow continued upward mobility for people of humble backgrounds.

Yet with enhanced significance came inflation of the image. Everyone who could do so – even members of the political elites – claimed to be a member of the working class, making exact calculations rather difficult. While official statistics suggested that somewhere between a half and two thirds of political functionaries came from working-class backgrounds in the 1950s and '60s, scholarly estimates suggest that a mere one in five, or 20 per cent, really did come from working-class backgrounds.[5] And while top functionaries claimed identification with official images of the working class, as far as wider members of the East German population were concerned, self-images of the working class or constructions of what one could take pride in were rather different. Oral history research suggests that by the 1980s, far from seeing themselves in terms of the heroic resistance fighters and builders of the new utopia of official imagery, people's self-perceptions revolved around quite another cluster of attributes. These included a continued pride in one's own work, and individual capacities as a worker, rooted in long-standing German traditions; and pride in the role of 'individual organiser', capable of exploiting 'connections' to acquire scarce goods and services, very specifically related to strategies for survival and enhancement of one's own circumstances within the GDR.[6] With such shifts in self-image came shifts in relationships to the 'workers' and peasants' state': in the 1980s, there was a decline in openly admitted loyalty among manual workers to 'their state', alongside evidence of instrumentality – using professed loyalty to obtain individual privileges or promotion – rather than genuine commitment to the state.[7]

The extension and dissipation of class images are closely related to wider changes in the character and experience of those who might by virtue of the nature of work and life in the GDR be thought to come under the contested category of the working classes. On examining the bases of community and conflict, and patterns of lifestyle and consumption, it rapidly becomes clear that the lives of ordinary workers in East Germany were affected by far more than merely their place in the division of labour.

The changing shape of industrial and agricultural labour in the GDR

To some extent, the 'un-making of the German working class' had begun already in the Third Reich. The processes of individualisation that were to become more marked in the course of GDR history had already been fostered in the Third Reich by the destruction of independent collective institutions and by Nazi economic and racial policies. During the twelve years of Hitler's rule, significant changes took place with respect to the working class.[8] Independent trade unions, which had barely won official recognition with the birth of the Weimar Republic in 1918, were subsequently significantly weakened by loss of members and finances during the Depression following the Wall Street Crash of 1929. After Hitler's assumption of power in 1933, independent trade unions were formally abolished following the traditional May Day labour celebrations and replaced by the German Labour Front (Deutsche Arbeiter Front, or DAF) under Walther Darré. Thus, while older workers in the GDR could still remember the days of trade unions that genuinely acted as workers' representatives in the early 1920s, 'younger' workers – effectively anyone born during or after the First World War – had little or no experience of such collective representation. From late 1932, when the economy showed the first signs of recovery (even before Hitler's appointment as Chancellor), to the later 1930s, mass unemployment gave way to a shortage of skilled labour in Germany. By the later 1930s, in part simply because of working longer hours, there was a rise in average wages; but this varied in different segments of the labour force, with skilled workers earning significantly more than their unskilled counterparts. Further internal differentiation was introduced through Nazi racial policies: during the later 1930s and even more so during the war years, new racial hierarchies entered the German workplace. With the influx of millions of foreign labourers – as many as three million in 1941, rising to seven million in 1944 – who fulfilled largely menial and subordinate roles, many German workers acquired unprecedented levels of supervisory experience. 'Achievement', or *Leistung*, became one of the key principles and continuing bases of pride among the skilled sections of the German labour force.

In the GDR, new sources of differentiation within the workforce developed, as a result of a combination of interrelated processes. Many skilled workers left for the West before 1961, compounding the already devastating demographic effects of the mass casualties incurred in the war years and leaving a serious shortage of manpower in post-war East Germany. This played a significant role in the campaigns for the retention and further encouragement of women in the labour force, with consequences not merely for the social mobility and increasing internal heterogeneity of the working classes, but also for gender roles in the GDR.[9] Meanwhile, although foreign labour was an important element in the GDR, with workers from countries such as Mozambique and Cuba, as well as the traditional sources of labour supply in the form of Polish migrants, the GDR did not rely on foreign labour to the extent that the Federal Republic did from the 1960s onwards, with its so-called 'guest workers' (*Gastarbeiter*). By the 1980s, there is some truth in the view that the guaranteed right to work in the GDR served merely to disguise a surplus rather than shortage of labour, with an element of idling at work in place of the combination of widespread unemployment and overwork for the rest characteristic of capitalist economies in the 1980s. The labour force itself was increasingly heterogeneous, with fissures running along a number of different lines.

Older sectors of heavy industry were further developed and expanded, with rapid growth in certain areas. The traditionally industrial area of the Lausitz region, for example, in which nearly one third (32.7 per cent) of the workforce had been unemployed in 1933, had experienced economic regeneration in the 1930s, producing considerable popular support for Hitler. Its industrial potential was to be further exploited in the GDR: in 1950 the Lausitz region already produced over a quarter (27.5 per cent) of the GDR's brown-coal supplies; by 1965 it was producing somewhat under one half (45.3 per cent).[10] Alongside the expansion of brown-coal mining and associated processing went the expansion of chemical industries, machine construction, metal and concrete works, and the growth of glass and textiles industries, with the building of vast new industrial complexes and associated new satellite towns for workers.[11] Thus the labour force was constituted in part of older working-class communities; in part of newer sections of the workforce, with many workers commuting from primarily agricultural areas where their partners (generally wives) might still work a plot of agricultural land to enhance the family income and larder; and in part of workers in new towns, many of whom might have relocated or migrated from a considerable distance. Additionally, in some enterprises high proportions of refugees from further east in post-war Europe added to the internal heterogeneity of the labour force. Industry was further differentiated by a range of other factors.

In the rather special case of the Wismut uranium-mining industry, massive disregard for human health and safety was combined with relatively high wages and social benefits at work in this highly secretive and dangerous area of production.[12] Workers were, particularly in the early post-war years, often pulled in to work in this area very much against their will. There were reports of labourers on building sites being threatened by withdrawal of preferential ration cards and additional supplies of cheese and cigarettes if they did not go to work at the Wismut mines; some who were technically without employment managed to escape by pretence of having other work, while others found they were more or less 'kidnapped'.[13] For those unlucky enough to have begun work at the Wismut, there were many who tried to get out again, and consequently high rates of labour turnover; among those who remained, there were high levels of acute dissatisfaction with living conditions. Complaints included the fact that as many as ten men might be forced to sleep in one small room, with insufficient numbers of blankets; inadequate supplies of food were compensated for by workers 'drinking away' all their weekly wages on payday; the lengthy journeys on organised transport between barracks and workplace were 'catastrophic'; large numbers of former Nazis were sent by the labour exchanges and factories to do labour service in this area; youngsters aged in their late teens were not 'protected' in any way; and there was not merely criticism of the many former Nazis who appeared to remain still in positions of immediate authority, but also widespread fear of the Russians, who were ultimately in overall charge.[14] While material problems seemed to have been less pressing a decade or so later, complaints about the influence of former Nazis were still rife in the mid-1950s.[15] By the mid-1960s, the complaints about 'lack of clarity' ('Unklarheiten') on issues such as the division of Germany – precipitated, for example, by the decision of the International Olympics Committee to allow teams from the two German states to compete in the Mexico City Olympics – were sufficiently routinised for one to have the impression that here, as elsewhere in the GDR, processes of 'normalisation' had set in. Complaints were now about the lack of freedom to travel to the West, rather than about former Nazis in high places, or about conditions in Wismut itself.[16] Later, of course, Wismut repeatedly surfaces in the records in terms of work-related diseases and early retirements.

Meanwhile, wider shifts were taking place in the character of the workforce across the GDR more generally. Over the years, traditional branches of heavy industry, chemicals production, and long-standing highly specialised areas such as optics (for which Carl Zeiss Jena had a long reputation), were increasingly complemented by the expansion of fields such as machine-tools manufacture and the growth of the new field of microelectronics. By the 1980s, Honecker placed enormous and totally unfounded faith in the GDR's capacity to compete in a world market in the field of computers and the microchip; this development sat uneasily alongside the simultaneous expansion of the massively polluting brown-coal mining, which destroyed wide swathes of the countryside in a search for cheap domestic energy following the oil crises of the 1970s.

The rather gradually changing shape of the industrial working classes was paralleled by arguably even more striking transformations with respect to the conditions of those who worked on the land.[17] In the autumn of 1945, the expropriation without compensation of landed estates of over a hundred hectares in size caused massive misery for those landowners who lost their ancestral estates. The official 'legitimation' was that the landowning aristocracy was part of the 'military-imperialistic-capitalist' complex of oppressing classes that were ultimately to blame for the rise of 'fascism' in Germany, in the particular shape of the Hitler regime. While many of these landed aristocrats had indeed been more or less active or passive supporters of Nazism, contributing their sons to the officer class of the Nazi army, a few individuals had participated in the conservative-nationalist resistance circles associated with the July Plot of 1944. Little regard was had for such niceties, however. While the situation varied slightly from place to place, under the controlling hand of the Soviet military administration, local political functionaries ensured that most landowners were unceremoniously evicted without any regard for their individual political past. Many were sent to camps or detention centres from whence some managed to make their way to the West; others were 'resettled' at some distance from their home areas, to ensure that there was a radical break with any paternalistic relationships or traditional sense of deference and mutual responsibility in villages that had lived under the sway of a particular landowning family for centuries. While individual former aristocrats did continue to make their lives in the GDR, the Junker class as a whole simply disappeared as a result of this land reform.

In its place, accompanied by many small ceremonies with a carefully orchestrated festival atmosphere, a whole new class of land-owning peasant proprietors of plots of around five hectares was created. Under the typical rhyming slogan 'Junkerland in Bauernhand' ('Junker land into the hands of peasants'), small areas of land were parcelled up and handed out to agricultural labourers, refugees and other deserving members of rural society. While this may briefly have stimulated a real sense of gratitude in some quarters, such feelings were generally short-lived: people soon discovered that their new small peasant holdings were economically non-viable. New peasants lacked the necessary machinery, equipment, buildings and animals, and they were very soon struggling with high rates of debt. The situation of those who were simply paid as wage labourers in agriculture was arguably even worse, with very low levels of qualification, pay and conditions, poor housing, inadequate food, and high rates of illness. Not surprisingly, many made the most of the high rates of mobility and simply left the land: while nearly one million (988,000) worked as agricultural labourers in 1946, the figure was barely more than a third of this number (378,435) by 1952.[18] In the course of the 1950s, many more fled the land: not only expropriated landowners, but also independent small peasants escaping pressures for collectivisation, and former expellees and refugees who had failed to settle permanently in the villages in which they had at first landed.[19]

Larger farmers initially found they had considerable power to control the food supply, and to lend out machinery, but from 1948, they faced a barrage of new restraints, including the reform of taxes in favour of small farmers, and the founding of a new political party, the Democratic Peasants Party of Germany (DBD), which to some extent sought to present communism with an agrarian face to rural communities that had a mere decade and a half earlier voted in large numbers for the Nazi Party. In 1950–52, around 5,000 large farmers simply abandoned their farms and many fled to the West while the inner-German border was still relatively open. This highly unstable situation formed the background to the first wave of the collectivisation of agriculture: the introduction of LPGs, announced at the Second Party Conference of the SED in July in 1952, was thus in large measure an attempt to deal with a snowballing domestic crisis on the land, and not merely a response to changes in Soviet policy and the collapse of Stalin's initiatives for reunification in the spring of 1952.

The growing crisis in agriculture played a role in the unrest of the following months, culminating in the June Uprising of 1953 and the consequent relaxation of earlier attempts at rapid social change. But enforced collectivisation was resumed in 1960, in a climate of optimism about the prospects for world communism (with the Soviet Union's successful Sputnik space mission) and Ulbricht's pronouncement that the GDR would 'overtake West Germany without catching up' ('überholen ohne einzuholen', one of the odder slogans produced by this slogan-prone regime). Following this enforced collectivisation, only a small percentage of agriculturally productive land remained entirely in private ownership. The rest differed according to type and degree of property-ownership. The so-called VEGs (Volkseigene Güter) were state-owned farms (or rather, the euphemistically entitled 'people's own' farms), based on property expropriated by the state from previous landowners. There were in addition three different types of LPG, or agricultural cooperative, ranging in type from those in which all land, livestock and equipment was held in common, to those where only the land was farmed collectively but machinery and animals remained private property. While the former type predominated in northern areas, the latter, least collective form was more common in the southern part of the GDR.

It took some years before the new organisation of farming became in any way routinised, with the breaking of traditional, fiercely independent attitudes among small farmers and the emergence of new forms of cooperation and conflict resolution in agricultural collectives.[20] Yet agriculture, in a modest sort of way, was arguably one of the few success stories of the GDR, at least from the mid-1960s to the mid-1970s. It already had a better record than industry by the late 1960s, making a growing contribution to a relatively autarchic provision of food to the East German population.[21] In the 1970s, livestock farming and plant production were separated and agricultural workers increasingly developed specialised qualifications in one or another area of agriculture. With growing specialisation and 'giganticism' in farming in the 1980s, however, came increasing inefficiencies in production. Specialisation and the separation of animal and crop production proved to be less viable, particularly in the context of far wider economic problems.

The character of rural society had thus, over four decades, been dramatically transformed – despite superficial continuities in the physical appearance of the small villages that dotted the East German countryside without any evidence of the commuter sprawl or second home syndromes of rural areas in Western societies. In the GDR the LPGs, with their bases in the larger and more important villages, came increasingly to dominate the local region as the chief employer; the agricultural cooperative became the social, cultural and political centre of village life, and the chairmen of LPGs were often as important as the local mayors in organising support for the local community in terms of finance, materials and support for leisure activities. The large villages at the hub of LPGs were also better provided with childcare facilities, public transport links, shops, schooling and medical services than were less important villages.[22] Village life changed in a number of interrelated respects, as the varied centuries-old breeds of independent peasants with emotional ties to a particular family plot of land, and large landowners and workers closely tied to a particular estate, disappeared with collectivisation. Fewer people worked on the land; they acquired qualifications and specialised in a particular area of agriculture, and they worked over a wider area, often commuting some distance from their home to the place of work. Others living in rural areas became commuters to towns or new industrial areas.

With mechanisation and the changing structure of the economy in the 1970s and '80s, both the agricultural and the industrial workforces were further differentiated in a number of respects. More women were drawn into the labour force; and although younger GDR women were increasingly well qualified, the upward social mobility of the East German male working class may well have taken place at the expense of older, unskilled females.[23] By the

1980s, among those aged over sixty, many males of 'genuine' working-class backgrounds had risen to management or functionary positions, with higher proportions of women in the lower levels.[24] But during the 1970s the principle of 'achievement' (*Leistungsprinzip*), educational qualifications (at the very least, the *Abitur*) and 'societal engagement' ('gesellschaftliche Engagiertheit') had, for most younger people, taken the place of a working-class background as a prerequisite for social mobility.[25] Many people felt their chances for betterment lay outside the workplace, in the areas of lifestyle and consumption, on which more in a moment.

By the 1980s, the vast structural opportunities for upward mobility of earlier decades had dried up. The consequences of changing patterns of and possibilities for social mobility have been much discussed: some have suggested that while older generations felt they had a personal 'stake in the system' and were grateful for the opportunities made available in the 1950s and '60s, younger people hitting the 'mobility blockages' of the 1980s allegedly experienced a greater degree of frustration.[26] But on balance it would seem that the frustrations experienced by the vast majority of East Germans in the 1980s were about far more than just 'blockages' to mobility. At a time when holding a position of greater responsibility with little real power simply meant being on the receiving end of a rising barrage of complaints from all sides about deteriorating conditions and shortages, blocked opportunities for 'upward social mobility' were far from constituting the primary concern or most significant source of frustration for most people. And these frustrations, as we shall see, were shared widely across all manner of groups within East German society.

Forms of collective organisation and conflict resolution

The changing profile of the East German working classes was further affected by the distinctive character of the collective institutions that might potentially have formed a basis for collective class consciousness – but in the event did not, or barely did so. Changing relations of power within the economy, and the representation of interests at the micro level, in the event further assisted trends in the atomisation of the East German working class.

The removal of economic enterprises from private ownership into state ownership, which was largely complete with Honecker's final assault on private ownership in 1972, meant that economic management in the overwhelming majority of enterprises was pervaded at all levels by the SED. The nomenclature and cadre system ensured that SED people were in key decision-making positions at all levels in the hierarchies of state-owned industrial enterprises. If expertise was crucial to economic management, then great pressure was exerted to ensure that relevantly qualified individuals would join the Party and submit to Party discipline. By the 1970s and '80s, non-Party people were in high positions only in exceptional circumstances, and in very small and relatively unimportant enterprises. Among the wider labour force, SED membership varied: while it could be as high as 25 per cent in the traditional heavy industry enterprises, it might be barely more than 10 per cent in smaller enterprises and particularly in those with a high proportion of women in the workforce. The dubious benefits of belonging to the SED included the requirement of attending innumerable meetings, attending periodic Party 'schools' (the Parteilehrjahre), and living in the constant shadow of Party disciplinary control (through the Parteikontrollkommission) and potential punishments for infringements of Party discipline.[27]

In face of Party control of economic management and production 'on behalf of the people', there were officially no legitimate grounds for worker protest against 'their own' Party representatives in 'the people's own enterprises' (*volkseigene Betriebe*), and hence, at least from the point of view of official propaganda, little obvious role for any trade union conceived as representative of workers' interests against management. The official trade union organisation, the FDGB, with over nine million members in the 1980s, covered more or less 100 per cent of the adult population.[28] It was, as has been frequently pointed out, a state-run organisation effectively representing the supposed 'true' interests of the workers as conceived by 'their vanguard party', the SED, rather than a trade union in the sense of the independent collective representative of freely associating workers as in capitalist democracies. The structural continuity (despite stark differences in ideology) with the Nazi German Labour Front (DAF) is of course evident, although it has been suggested that the latter was better at 'selling' Nazi economic policies to the then German working classes than the FDGB was at putting across SED policies to the GDR labour force.[29] In any event, the Nazis had already done the preliminary work in terms of the destruction of strong independent trade unions; the FDGB in this sense at least had a fairly easy ride.

While there were indeed widespread complaints among East Germans about the FDGB not being truly representative of their interests, it was not all a 'top-down' story. In many incidents, the FDGB took very seriously workers' complaints about poor working conditions or bad management, and it frequently did genuinely serve to represent workers' interests against those of local managers, particularly when there were disputes about health, safety, working conditions, the availability of tools and materials, or the lax character of management, where the parameters and battle lines were not necessarily entirely clear. Moreover, from the perspective of most working people, membership was in large part also about 'perks', particularly holidays. The organisation of regular holidays within the GDR was more or less the monopoly of the FDGB; going to an FDGB holiday home was for many people the only chance they had of going on holiday at all.[30] The massive membership of the FDGB was thus not – or not merely – one arising from a degree of coercion or pressures for conformity. It became for many people not only taken for granted, but also something out of which one could potentially gain tangible personal benefits, however much one might criticise its functionaries as representatives of Party and state.

In a rather different way, another form of collective grouping, that of workers' brigades, did come to act, at least at certain times for limited numbers, as a more genuine representative of collective interests – although the moment they began to take on the appearance of quasi-independent union functions, their activities could be curtailed or indeed brigades could be entirely disbanded. On the one hand, therefore, workers' brigades were periodically fostered and officially encouraged; on the other hand, the brigade movement seems at times to have developed a momentum of its own, with a degree of autonomy and capacity for exerting some pressures on at least local issues.

In 1947–8, youth brigades were started in the Soviet zone; and from 1950, workers' 'production brigades' were introduced, based primarily on the Stakhanovite Soviet model of the 1930s. The primary purpose was to try to increase productivity by collective team efforts, initiatives and (self-)discipline, in competition with other brigades. They were even seen as a mechanism for inculcating new norms of 'socialist morality'. By the end of 1950, there were more than 98,000 brigades, encompassing perhaps 663,000 workers.[31] From 1958, many of these produced 'brigade diaries' (*Brigadetagebücher*), which have proved to be a rich source of information on their attitudes and activities, if read appropriately.[32] In the course of the 1950s, the brigade movement began to flourish to such an extent that they provoked charges of 'syndicalism'; nevertheless, following a brief clampdown, they were relaunched and became a fixed part of the landscape of economic enterprises from the 1960s right through to 1989. Their numbers expanded greatly in the Honecker period: by 1988, as many as 5,500,000 people (nearly two thirds of all workers) were members of a brigade.[33]

Intended initially as a means of raising productivity and exerting a degree of self-discipline, many brigades developed a rather wide range of social, cultural and representative functions. They have sometimes been described as akin to families, organising birthday celebrations, visits to exhibitions, theatre performances and other outings, and keeping a pastoral eye on those members who were suffering from physical ill-health or personal problems.[34] Brigades made up predominantly or entirely of women seem to have been particularly geared to the communicative and social functions. But they also seem to have fulfilled a role somewhat akin to that of an independent trade union, exerting pressure on behalf of their members for higher wages and premiums and improvements in working conditions. By the early 1960s, many brigades were in charge of their own finances, and appear to have been displacing the FDGB as the organisation with which factory managers would directly deal in order to sort out difficulties and conflicts on the shop floor.[35] Indeed, in the representation of factory life in the early 1960s portrayed in the film *Spur der Steine*, there is no sign whatsoever of the FDGB: here, the brigades – particularly in the figure of the Brigadier Balla – appear to be the only vehicle for representation of the collective interests of workers.[36] Whatever their origins, it is clear that brigades ended up playing some form of intermediary role between management and workers.

Yet this intermediary role was one that was only possible within certain parameters. Brigades – much like the enterprise's functionaries with whom they were dealing – could not hope to tackle the big problems beyond the scope of any particular enterprise; they could only deal with 'everyday problems', and seek to achieve minor improvements in the living and working conditions of their members on a very local scale. And they were essentially small, isolated and rather weak units of a highly segmented labour force, within a wider framework of the powerful organisations and official institutions of the GDR. Thus, while they performed a wide range of valuable functions for their members on a local level, and arguably sustained forms of local collective consciousness (more so in some conditions and at certain times than others), brigades were hardly vehicles of any collective working-class consciousness in the GDR.

Nor was strike action, at least not after the suppression of the uprising of June 1953. It has been cogently argued that unofficial work stoppages (to use a somewhat long-winded but more accurate label, since 'strikes' were not officially permitted) provided the East German working class with an effective 'veto power' against SED policies.[37] Certainly the fear of 'another 17.6.53' was an ever-present worry in the minds of the SED and Stasi leadership, right up to the very end, as Stasi chief Erich Mielke's comments in the turbulent autumn of 1989 clearly demonstrate. But, from a slightly different perspective, it is far less clear that strikes constituted any kind of basis for working-class consciousness for collective solidarity on any significant scale. For one thing, such work stoppages were, after the suppression of 1953, purely local events; even in 1956, when there were stirrings of unrest in the context of troubles in

Hungary and Poland, strikes were sporadic and ill-coordinated. For another, there is some evidence to suggest that, on virtually every measure, the scale and significance of strikes declined in the period from the 1960s to the 1980s. The total numbers of strikes per year appears to have declined; the average number of people involved in each work stoppage appears to have become smaller; and unofficial work stoppages appear to have waned in significance as a means of expressing protest and exerting pressure for improvements. In place of – and on occasion in addition to – collective strike action, the generally more individualistic form of *Eingaben* appears to have become more prevalent as a means of venting grievances and seeking improvements.[38]

In other ways, East German workplaces did appear to provide an important basis for the development of collective identities – at least in the 1960s and early '70s. As the location for many social activities, and supplier of many services – ranging from daily canteen meals and transport for shift work, to health clinics and childcare facilities – the enterprise was for many East German workers the centre of more aspects of life than might be assumed from a Western perspective. In some respects, East German enterprises continued long-standing traditions in Germany of the paternalistic employer, and the development of new GDR work-based health and childcare provision was of major pragmatic importance for many individuals. This was most of all the case where work, canteens and outlets for provisions, cultural organisations, housing, health care, childcare, social and sporting facilities – in short, facilities and activities covering or catering for most aspects of life – were all closely bound up with one major industrial enterprise, such as the EKO (Eisenhüttenkombinat Ost) in Eisenhüttenstadt. Yet, paradoxically, with the 'unity of economic and social policy' under Honecker came developments that started to erode the centrality of the enterprise. Improvements in the provision of family housing, the growth of car ownership, and the near saturation of GDR households with televisions receiving Western stations, all tended in the long term to marginalise the role of the enterprise as a locus of collective solidarity and social life.

What members of the different groups that formed the East German working class had in common was exclusion from the real decision-making processes in the workers' and peasants' state. Yet surprising numbers, as we shall see, did actually participate in some way in the exercise of power as functionaries for mass organisations or in honorary capacities of one sort or another. Even at the lowliest levels of the workplace, unofficial informers for the Stasi might feel they were able to perform an important function, or that their individual worth was in some way recognised. And a key task of the Stasi was to ensure that the potential bases for collective action in opposition to management (or the state, or the Party) did not develop such that there was little or no public discussion of even major causes for collective concern; that strikes were prevented and individual 'trouble-makers' or 'ringleaders' rapidly isolated and disciplined; and that all 'untoward incidents' – whether acts of suspected sabotage or arson or genuine accidents – were thoroughly investigated and dealt with. This prevalence of the Stasi in economic life further complicated the possibilities for collective action and the development of any kind of collective identity among the East German working class.

It is, of course, true that the Stasi's primary focus was less on economic enterprises than on political opposition groups, the Churches, and the activities (real or imagined) of the 'class enemy' at home and abroad.[39] But the maintenance and enhancement of economic productivity was crucial to the success of the East German socialist experiment. Thus the extent to which different areas of employment were exposed to Stasi infiltration varied in relation to degrees of economic and/or political significance. If the product was of considerable value in terms of hard currency exports and specialist knowledge (as in the case of microelectronics), then the saturation with Stasi informers was likely to be particularly high. Similarly, if working conditions were particularly dangerous, with a combination of outdated equipment and serious hazards to the immediate or long-term health of both workers and local residents – as in the Buna chemical-industrial complex – then the Stasi's concern was less to address the root causes of preventable accidents and environmental pollution than to seek to ensure that knowledge of their effects did not become public and that there was as little discussion as possible of such issues: in short, to prevent the increasingly disastrous state of the GDR economy in the 1980s from turning into a political problem for the regime. In this, of course, it was notably unsuccessful. The Stasi was also present in force where there were significant clusters of *Reisekader*, those who had permission to travel abroad, for example to market products and organise trade agreements in the West. Nor, in this paranoid state, could even the SED's own cadres and those selected through the nomenclature system be entirely trusted: thus even such high-standing economic functionaries as Wolfgang Biermann, General Director of the Kombinat Carl Zeiss Jena, were surrounded by unofficial informers for the Stasi.

In sum, for a variety of institutional and political reasons, workers in the GDR were not able to engage in much by way of independent collective organisation or action in the representation, defence or furtherance of their collective class interests. Even where such organisation was possible, as in the case of the brigades, it was only with respect to limited issues that could be dealt with at local level; and only to the limited extent permitted at any given time. Thus, in so far as collective identities formed, they were not in the sense of a broad working-class identity in opposition to another class. Rather, such collective identities as formed were related to more specific groups: those based in particular types of work; particular brigades; or particular economic enterprises, with their associated patterns of social life. This was not exactly individualisation (akin to Marx's famous analogy of 'potatoes in a sack'), but rather the atomisation of small collective units at the base of society.

Income, lifestyle and consumer socialism

In Western capitalist societies, class in the sense of type of labour (manual, white-collar, service, professional and so on) tends to correlate very closely with income and lifestyle. It is certainly the case that significant class differences in income and lifestyle persisted in the GDR. The East German 'service class' continued to earn around one third (30–40 per cent) more, on average, than members of the working class; and they had higher levels of ownership of desired consumer goods such as cars. Only one quarter (25 per cent) of working-class households had access to a telephone, compared to 60 per cent of service-class households; and far more members of the service class visited theatres, museums and read books than did their working-class counterparts.[40] 'Cultural capital' and differences in interests and milieus continued to be of major importance – indeed, increasingly so with decreased structural chances for social mobility and a degree of 'closure' of the new GDR service classes in the 1980s. But nevertheless, in the GDR the strong relationships between class, income and lifestyle characteristic of capitalist societies started to uncouple, for a variety of reasons.

Official policies led to a degree of levelling of incomes and even to a degree of inversion of traditional income and status hierarchies. The introduction of and increased emphasis on 'performance wages' (*Leistungslohn*) in the 1960s, and the general levelling of incomes and replacement of material incentives by non-material rewards such as honorary acknowledgements and related medals (which also underwent an unimaginable degree of inflation) in the 1970s, meant that wages and type of work no longer correlated in the ways characteristic of the West.[41] By the 1980s, qualified East German *Facharbeiter* – workers with a particular craft specialism – could earn as much as and in some cases more than more qualified and highly educated members of the technical intelligentsia, such as engineers. The latter could console themselves that they could indulge their intellectual interests, and possibly had a greater degree of control over their work; but neither higher income nor higher official status were any longer available as incentives for the longer period of education and acquisition of qualifications through the examination process required to enter these more professional categories.

Furthermore, while income differentials between different types of job remained, the heavy involvement of women in the workforce and the conse- quent widespread prevalence of two-income households – in which high earners showed a remarkable tendency to marry lower-earning partners – meant that overall 'household' or 'family incomes' did not vary quite as widely as individual wages.[42] Oddly, the re-evaluation of the meaning of 'working class' in the GDR seems to have made it easier for couples to choose their partner across the kinds of class divide that act as invisible barriers to romantic love in capitalist societies: thus while East Germans appear to have shared the Western notion that professional males could (and possibly even should) marry women with less demanding jobs and lower career aspirations, in contrast to the West, East German male manual labourers seem to have felt no inhibitions about marrying better educated professional females (and of course vice versa).[43]

Price policies and the massive state subsidies for basic foods, rents and transport meant that, beyond a basic minimum level (below which under- privileged groups such as pensioners certainly fell), the level of wages and salaries actually made little real difference to real purchasing power. Even after the price reforms of the 1960s – somewhat belatedly and half-heartedly asso- ciated with attempts to make the New Economic System viable – incomes still outstripped prices by a considerable margin.[44]

What did make a difference to people's lifestyles was the (sheer lack of) availability of desired consumer goods. This raised two other factors to a status of crucial importance. First, 'connections', often known as 'Vitamin B' (for *Beziehungen*): if one had a good relationship with a network of individuals in key positions – workers who could 'liberate' crucial parts and materials from their places of work; shop assistants who could 'bend under the counter' to pull out scarce items (*Bückwaren*); car mechanics, plumbers, electricians and other handymen who could assist in repairs and the more complicated aspects of a DIY job – then life was made a great deal easier. 'Friendships' would be cultivated with those potentially of assistance, in a society where such mutual aid was a key ingredient in creating the physical preconditions for material well-being. And workers with skills were of course particularly in demand in such a situation. Secondly, access to Western currency was of comparable importance – even encapsulated in the quip (variously attributed to the guitarist and singer Wolf Biermann, and the dissident thinker Wolfgang Harich) that, in contrast to Marx's original reference to individual needs, the operating slogan of 'actually existing socialism' ran along the lines 'from each according to his ability, to each according to the residence of his aunt'. Deutschmarks could open a lot of doors, both unofficially and, increasingly, also officially in the state-fostered pockets of Western consumer society.

Ironically, the classes that could not participate fully in the developing consumer society of the GDR were precisely the politically privileged functionary classes. By virtue of their positions, they could not have Western contacts, and hence they had no access to Western currency and the associated use of the Intershops. If they were high enough in the political hierarchy, of course, the position was quite different: provisions for Politburo members in Wandlitz and in the central bureaucracies in Berlin were rather special. But below this level, East Germans with a degree of political responsibility and visibility were excluded by virtue of the communist rules of political correctness from the modest oases of consumerism that the GDR of the 1970s and '80s was able to offer to 'ordinary' workers with appropriate incomes and connections. All this, then, further complicated the class structure of the GDR.

By the 1980s, many workers not merely felt there was no positive financial incentive to seek further qualifications and upward mobility, but there were also significant disadvantages to so doing. Increased responsibility at work would merely bring increased pressure for achievement in a context in which productivity was constantly frustrated by wider economic forces beyond the individual's control, and upward mobility was further associated with the need to adopt a more puritanical lifestyle. So to the closure of class mobility that was developing for other reasons – social exclusion, the inheritance of 'cultural capital' – came a degree of positive 'abstention' (*Verzicht*), or conscious decision to count oneself out of a rat race in which there were few obvious advantages and many disadvantages, and to focus rather on other goals in life: improvements in the private sphere. But even for those who chose to remain apolitical 'ordinary workers', enjoying the benefits of relatively high status and wages in relation to prices, the officially fostered consumerism of the 1970s proved to be a liability in the 1980s. For the effects of novelty, potentially stabilising in the short term, could not be sustained over the years, and the more East Germans participated in global trends – watching Western advertisements for Western consumer products – the more they were aware of the inadequacies and shortcomings of the limited supplies at home. The banana may have been overstated as a symbol of 1989, but it certainly played a role in growing public discontent with a system that had effectively made an unwritten pact with the Western consumerist devil and then found that it simply could not deliver the goods.

Part III

The participatory dictatorship

Chapter Eleven

The honeycomb state:
The benign and malign diffusion of power

The boundaries of the state in the GDR are harder to define than one might at first think. The real fissures ran, not so much *between* 'regime' and 'people', but rather *within* the very large complex of Party and state functionaries, only a small fraction of whom can be held to be genuinely members of an elite or 'ruling class'. What is really quite remarkable about the GDR is the way in which extraordinarily large numbers of people were involved in its functioning, who were implicated in a complex web of micro-relationships of power in every area of life, serving to reproduce and transform the system. Very large numbers of people acted as honorary functionaries in a wide range of organisations, in a manner that, by the 1970s and '80s, was more or less taken for granted by a very significant proportion of the population. They participated in and sustained the system; they took on, embodied and enacted roles, and played within the rules and parameters of the system; yet their participation in the micro-structures of power, while very often conferring on them privileges and opportunities as individuals, did not serve to displace their class positions as defined by the occupational structure.

Closely related are questions concerning the ways in which the character and shape of the 'state' changed over forty years. Far from 'withering away', as Marx envisaged might happen in his dream of pure communism, the state grew enormously in the 'actually existing socialism' of the GDR. But it grew in two quite different ways. On the one hand, ever larger numbers of people participated in the broader formal and informal political systems of the GDR, thus serving to 'normalise' the initially strange and forcibly imposed structures of power. On the other hand, while perhaps decreasingly obvious in everyday life, the repressive and malign aspects of the exercise of power through the practices of the Stasi also grew exponentially. With the expansion of the state, processes of normalisation and enhanced means of surveillance and repression went hand in hand.

There are, therefore, a whole set of questions concerning the diffusion and variety of forms of power; and it is crucial to distinguish between repressive, coercive and manipulative means of exerting power, and more routine, widely accepted methods, which were 'carried' by increasing numbers of people with barely a second thought. To use Max Weber's terminology, the balance between 'power', in the sense of the 'capacity to exert one's will against the will of others', and 'authority', in the sense that commands are likely to be obeyed (for whatever combination of reasons), is more complex than at first one might think. In the GDR, from perhaps the mid-1960s to the mid-1980s, the two aspects grew hand in hand. It was only with the growing economic and related political crises in the whole Soviet bloc in the mid- to later 1980s that ever more people began openly to question the fragile consensus that had, at least among significant numbers of citizens, been growing in the course of the 1970s; and even the enhanced domestic power of repression was not sufficient to shore up the fragile system of authority in the altered international circumstances of autumn 1989.

These partially contradictory, or at least simultaneous and very different aspects of the growth of the East German state, are crucial for understanding the people's paradox. It was possible both to have participated in the structures of power, and yet simultaneously to have been openly critical of the regime – even well before 1989. It was possible both to have participated in the structures of power, and still not have been part of the ruling elite. It was possible, in other words, to have occupied a position that was simultaneously located in 'state' and 'society': in the extended 'societal state', a system sustained through myriad micro-relationships of extended power and authority, the dichotomy between 'state' and 'society' simply does not hold up; the battle lines are more complex and difficult to delineate.

Implicated and committed? The participatory system at the grass roots

Implausibly large numbers – perhaps one in six of the population – were involved in one way or another in what might be called the micro-systems of power through which GDR society worked. This system cannot be described in terms of an extended 'state' that was 'doing something' to a 'society' conceived of as separate from the 'state': rather it was the very way society as a whole was structured. Life in the GDR, in just about every respect – including not only the obvious areas of the economy or the education system, but also housing and leisure – was organised in ways that were at the same time dependent on central policy decisions and on the practices of innumerable people who were active participants in the maintenance and functioning of the system on the ground.

There were perhaps as many as 300,000–400,000 key functionaries, or around 3 per cent of the adult population, 'who played a really important role in the exercise and securing of power', and a very much larger group still of between one to two million adults overall – perhaps around 8–16 per cent of the adult population – who played a significant role as a functionary in one or more of the mass organisations, political parties and regional and local representative institutions such as the Stasi, the Army and the People's Police (Volkspolizei), and the state administrative and economic apparatus.[1] Beyond this, there were numerous citizens who took up occasional positions as honorary functionaries on behalf of one or another 'good cause', such as cultural activities in factories or helping with children and young people in holiday camps or youth clubs; and a rather more shadowy but highly signifi-cant figure of those who cooperated as 'unofficial informers' for the Stasi. To lump all these together as part of the 'political elite' would be utterly wrong; to castigate all of them indiscriminately as 'perpetrators' or 'accomplices' or 'fellow travellers' would also be inappropriate. Even to try to call them all representatives of the 'state', rather than members of 'society', would be to make an artificial distinction that does not adequately depict the situation on the ground. They were of course essential to the 'functioning of the regime', but it has in some way also to be understood that, perhaps from the 1960s onwards, this was increasingly a matter of the way GDR society worked, in a very banal and day-to-day manner. Large numbers of people over time became involved in the system, in one way or another, almost as a matter of course.

There were quite simply an enormous number of functions that could be occupied by persons in a very wide range of social positions. For example, a study carried out in March 1960 of 252 teachers in 17 schools found that, between these 252 teachers, there were no fewer than 374 functions. Only 61 teachers held no functionary position at all, while 184 held between one and four functions each; four held five functionary positions, one had six, and a poor two teachers each had as many as seven different functionary positions to juggle in their 'free time'.[2] This commitment to the exercise of social func-tions was on top of workloads in their primary occupation as teacher ranging from between 43.5 hours per week at the lowest end to over 110 hours claimed at the highest end. Functions included positions in a variety of relevant organ-isations, among which the most important were the FDJ and Pioneer organi-sations for young people and children (57); the National Front (27); the German Society for Gymnastics and Sport (DTSB, 15); the German–Soviet

Friendship Society (DSF, 10); the Democratic Women's League of Germany (DFD, 10), as well as a variety of other social and pedagogical organisations.

Functionary positions were far from being the prerogative of particular social groups such as teachers, already in a position of some authority. Rather, they were spread across every organisation and covered every area of life. In December 1979, it was estimated that over 650,000 (28 per cent) of the then 2,300,000 members of the FDJ, covering the full range of sixteen to twenty-five year olds, held a functionary position. Nor did being a functionary necessarily entail complete political or ideological commitment. A study of FDJ members in the districts (*Bezirke*) of Karl-Marx-Stadt, Leipzig, Magdeburg, Berlin, Erfurt and Dresden, who were already employed rather than still being students, found that fewer than half (44 per cent) of those holding functionary positions in the FDJ were members of the SED; and that while the proportion of those who were explicitly committed to the official 'worldview' of atheism was declining, the number of those who were either definitely religious or agnostic was rising. Less than one in five of these functionaries was *not* involved in any other organisations and societal activities; one quarter were involved in at least three or four other organisations, and fully one quarter held at least one other functionary position in another organisation.[3] Whichever area one looks at – trade union organisation in factories, the committees running collective farms (LPGs), the honorary helpers of the People's Police – there were innumerable possibilities for engaging in service to the community on the part of ordinary people in all walks of life.

People became involved for all sorts of reasons, including a genuine desire to help with, for example, the work of a local club for children or the equivalent of a parent–teacher organisation in a school. But there was more to the functionary system in the GDR than simply the concept of 'active citizenship' that inspired much similar paid or voluntary work in Western societies at this time. There was also to some degree an unwritten pact, or informal understanding, that active commitment to the GDR system as evidenced by societal engagement and particularly service as a functionary would be 'rewarded' with small privileges and opportunities in a situation characterised by scarcity. This becomes very evident when one looks at letters from citizens who were frustrated in some way in the achievement of particular goals, or whose expectations, which they had assumed to be fully justified, had not been met. It is in these 'breaks' in the unspoken agreement that the nature of the latter can be most clearly perceived. Needs ranged from gardens, holidays and housing, to pensions and other perks. When resources were insufficient to meet the full spectrum of demand – as they virtually always were – then appeals would be made to the active contribution an individual had made to the system as a major reason why the satisfaction of their needs should take precedence over those of others. And from the official side, those seen as the 'deserving' and the actively committed took priority over more passive citizens with fewer perceived needs, dependants or claims to reward.

Thus, for example, in the summer of 1975 one Frau Hildegard B. of Magdeburg was desperate to buy a small allotment garden in which she and her husband could relax.[4] Having agreed a price of 2,000 Marks for a suitable garden, she was shocked when it was suddenly put up to 3,300 Marks. The shock was all the greater because she had been waiting endlessly for a garden, had constantly been informed that she was next in line for the next suitable garden to become vacant, and each time one did come up it was given to someone else. Her letter – long, hand-written on square exercise book paper – lists all her contributions to the system over many years until retirement: 'as a comrade [*Genossin*, or SED party member] and for years Chair of the Factory Trade Union Executive Committee', as someone whose children are also now 'comrades and functionaries', and who has been active in a socialist brigade, held innumerable functions and has received all sorts of honours (*Auszeichnungen*) for her services to the system. It ends on a rather sarcastic, bitter note: 'But just a garden for well-deserved relaxation, a garden that would be looked after and tended lovingly, that we don't deserve.'[5] Interestingly, the letter in response to Frau B.'s complaint from the Chair of the Magdeburg District section of the Verband der Kleingärtner, Siedler und Kleintierzüchter (Association of Small Gardeners, Settlers and Small Animal Breeders) explaining the priorities determining decisions in allotting gardens, confirms the underlying principle of privileging those who actively contribute to the system, but in his case the potential future contribution appeared to weigh more heavily than reward for past contributions. Those who, from Frau B.'s point of view, had 'jumped the queue' included: 'a family with two children, the husband an *Aktivist* several times over, who already while he was waiting following his application contributed actively to common tasks in the branch'; and an 'agricultural specialist with a diploma, who has worked for the GDR in Africa, and who declared himself prepared to contribute to the branch in the capacity of specialist [*Fachwart*], which we were looking for.'[6] In the end, Frau B.'s claims were recognised by Dr Fritz Rösel of the National Executive Committee (Bundesvorstand) of the FDGB, to whom her original letter had been addressed; and she was offered the opportunity to obtain a garden in a different branch where the underlying 'misunderstandings' giving rise to her complaint would not prove an uncomfortable social legacy.

Similarly, Herr Werner L., forced into early retirement because of silicosis acquired through working in the Wismut uranium mines, and seeking an additional pension of 100 Marks a month, does not simply rest his case on the rules for retirement on medical grounds caused by work-related illness. He points out that while employed at the Wismut mines he was a member of the 'workers' militia' (*Kampfgruppe*) from 1952; that he was subsequently a functionary in the paramilitary Society for Sport and Technology (Gesellschaft für Sport und Technik, GST); and that he still sees it as his 'duty to our youth to continue to prepare them thoroughly for their tasks in the National People's Army and the defence system', believing that in this way he can 'also help to contribute an important foundation for the construction and protection of our Republic'.[7] Another former Wismut worker, Herr Kuno S. of Gera, is keen to have a special holiday to celebrate his silver wedding, and he and his wife have set their hearts on a trip to Yugoslavia. In his letter appealing to the FDGB Executive Committee about difficulties arising with the permission for this trip, he points out that for 22 years he has held 'major official functionary positions in the Youth Association and in the Party'.[8]

Those who had not made the necessary contribution to GDR society by even formal membership in, let alone active service to, a relevant organisation might find themselves quite simply excluded from any of the benefits and privileges such commitment could bring. Thus the unfortunate parents of Herr Bernd W., despite now being pensioners, were not entitled to enjoy a holiday in FDGB holiday homes even in the depths of the low season when many spaces were available, because in their earlier employment they had not even been members of the FDGB.[9]

Failure to obtain desired goals might elicit a veiled threat of withdrawal of goodwill and 'resignation' from the implicit compact. Frau Angela J., an employee of the Schwerin radio station seeking in October 1989 more flexible working hours to help with childcare duties (and clearly unaware of the historic changes about to overwhelm the GDR), makes this generally tacit understanding quite explicit:

> In all the years I have been employed in the radio station, I have never shied away from being actively involved in societal work for my enterprise. I was for years the FDJ Secretary, and since 1986 I have been working with the Party Leadership in our branch organisation. I have just been elected as the Chair of the Parents' Committee (*Elternaktiv*). I do not wish unduly to make too much of my societal activities, but nevertheless I do expect some sort of reciprocation. If personal interests are not taken into consideration by the enterprise, then the motivation to be socially active decreases markedly.[10]

The vast majority of these functionaries were, for a variety of reasons, exercising their (extended) power in order, at least as they saw it, to do something *for* people: to contribute to what they conceived of as the public good. The same could not unequivocally be said about those who cooperated with the secret State Security Service, the Stasi: they, by contrast, were exercising or facilitating the power to do things *to* people. And what was being done to others was generally without their knowledge, certainly without their consent, not in their expressed interests, and very often actively to their detriment. This was, in short, a very different type of 'complicity' in a very different area of the extended 'societal state'.

The malign exercise of power: Unofficial collaboration with the Stasi

The highly formalised system and the sheer extent of the regularised network of unofficial informers for the East German State Security Service was unique in twentieth-century dictatorships, whether of the capitalist or communist variety. By way of comparison, the Gestapo employed 7,000 officials for a total population of 66,000,000 in Nazi Germany; the Stasi employed over 91,000 full-time staff in a GDR population of about 16,400,000 in 1989.[11] Unlike the Gestapo, which relied heavily on the sporadic willingness of many Germans to inform voluntarily on neighbours with whom they might have a personal score to settle, the Stasi developed a highly organised system of enrolling and directing the regular activities of large numbers of citizens, seeking not merely to gain an insight into, but even to intervene actively and alter the character of any imagined, potential or actual oppositional activities in the GDR. To this end, an extraordinary system of official guidelines and procedures was developed, with a formal categorisation of different types of unofficial collaborator, and detailed instructions for the relevant procedures for training, meeting, reporting, analysis and controlling of informants.[12] Such a system could only work if very significant numbers of people were, indeed, willing to act as informants in this highly organised way.

The number of informal collaborators, or IMs (*inoffizielle Mitarbeiter*), exploded over the years. In the mid-1950s, there were between 20,000 to 30,000 informants. Thereafter the figure rose steadily, reaching around 100,000 in the crisis year of 1968; and with the more porous borders of the GDR following *Ostpolitik*, the size of the Stasi mushroomed. The highest point was attained with a total of around 180,000 unofficial informants in 1975 – ironically, perhaps the year in which the GDR also scored highest in terms of the rather nebulous question of popular support (or perhaps better: widespread hopes for improvement and willingness to contribute to such potential improvement). Thereafter, the figures remained fairly steady, fluctuating between 170,000 to 180,000 – an average ratio of one informer to every 60 or so adults, although distributed more thinly in some areas, in greater concentration in others – with an annual turnover of about one in ten informants dropping out or being dropped and replacements being recruited.[13] Most relationships appear to have been broken off because the Stasi found the informant was not, or was no longer, being useful; only around one in five informers initiated the termination of their services themselves. Cumulatively, assuming an average turnover of around 17,500 informers each year, this means that in the Honecker era perhaps somewhere in the region of 500,000 East Germans at one time or another informed on their fellow citizens. Only in the later 1980s did the Ministry for State Security register greater problems with the recruitment and retention of unofficial informants – precisely at the time when popular dissatisfaction was also visibly growing. From 1986 onwards, those leaving the informal service of the Stasi outnumbered those agreeing to take up a commitment to be an unofficial informant, posing a considerable problem not only for the surveillance of the population at a time of increasing unrest, but also with respect to the intended 'secrecy' of the methods and means employed by the Stasi, knowledge of which thus inevitably seeped out among the wider population.[14]

It seems nevertheless to have been relatively easy to recruit willing informants, on the basis of a considerable variety of motives. At one end of the spectrum, many informants were committed and loyal citizens of the GDR who were genuinely convinced that it was important to keep a watchful eye out for what they held to be the subversive activities of dangerous 'enemies of the state'. For them, 'security' meant precisely that. A fairly high percentage of informants were members of the SED; in 1962, for example, in the administrative district of Neubrandenburg, as many as 40–50 per cent of IMs were members of the SED.[15] Some informants were employed in positions in which it would appear routine or simply 'part of the job' to inform, such as members of the police and armed services, or those occupying elevated positions within factories and business enterprises. The problem, however, of relying only on loyal and publicly committed citizens was that they often did not have obvious or inconspicuous means of access to the sorts of circles that were deemed worthy of surveillance. Thus far wider groups had to be brought into the network of informants.

In probably the majority of cases, the informant was persuaded into cooperation through a combination of feeling important, being attracted by small advantages, social rewards, material inducements or by a sense of adventure and stimulation to break an otherwise routine existence.[16] Attempts were made to recruit promising youngsters while still at school: teenagers might find themselves being called into the head-teacher's office and being left alone to talk with a visitor, and might be flattered by the attention devoted to them; they might also feel a sense of some relief at having high-level support and a clear career path mapped out for the future. While surveillance and reporting were important in every area of East German life, including among young people still at school and apprentices and workers on the factory floor, some areas were clearly politically more important, or potentially problematic, than others. Particular attention therefore had to be paid to placing or recruiting appropriate people in areas such as the 'alternative culture' of the Prenzlauer Berg 'scene' – where as an IM the supposedly dissident poet Sascha Anderson wrought havoc with the lives and relationships of his supposed 'friends' – and among the peace activists and human-rights campaigners in the church circles of the 1980s. In some of these cases, the IM might even feel (or later claim that they had felt) that informing was a legitimate method of communication, and that they could thereby contribute to making the regime understand better the concerns of people on the ground, or even 'protect' the interests of dissidents. Some informants in the dissident scene, such as Knud Wollenberger, informing under the code name IM 'Donald' on his wife Vera Wollenberger and her friends who were active in the unofficial peace movements of the Protestant Church in the 1980s, later claimed this as an attempted justification of activities that put people in serious danger.[17] A not dissimilar defence was used by Manfred Stolpe, a prominent churchman in the GDR and later Prime Minister of the Land Brandenburg in post-unification Germany, with respect to his frequent regular contacts with Stasi officers.[18] In probably the vast majority of mundane cases in less fraught areas – and only the tip of the iceberg has been touched by the now notorious cases that received so much media attention in the 1990s – motives were probably far more banal.

Something in the order of less than one in ten collaborators was in some obvious way 'coerced' into informing; on the Stasi's own figures, only 7.7 per cent of informants were recruited through a process of clear coercion, although this figure hardly takes into account the more diffuse feelings of fear, guilt, dislike of the situation but failure to see any realistic alternative, which probably account for a very much larger number of cases in which 'coercion' might arguably be too strong a word, but in which the informant would undoubtedly have preferred not to have been caught in a threatening situation in which this seemed the only viable option to 'choose'. Perhaps bullying would be an appropriate term to account for many such cases. Informing could, for example, be a means of ensuring better conditions or a shorter prison sentence, as in the case of informers within the prison cells of the horrendous Stasi prison at Hohenschönhausen, often at the expense of other prisoners.

Concern for the well-being of an imprisoned partner could also be used by the Stasi as a ploy to gain or retain a person in a key position as an informer, as was attempted in the case of the writer Brigitte Reimann.

Much of the evidence about professed motives comes from confessions and interviews carried out after 1990, with all the attendant methodological problems. But Reimann's private diary entries at the time she was actually contacted by the Stasi are highly revealing of the complexity of motives and the mixed feelings – a combination of a sense of idealism, of being flattered and intrigued, as well as a little dubious and ultimately angry and fearful – which could be aroused by such contacts. In September 1957, on the first approach by the Stasi in the form of one Herr Kettner, Reimann was only too well aware of the fact that she was being psychologically manipulated; yet she allowed herself to be 'almost convinced' by the 'idealistic goals' of the Stasi. At the same time, she was 'attracted by the adventure' and 'had to keep laughing about this game of playing Indians – code names, secret apartments, and so on'; and she was also genuinely attracted by the prospect of being able to contribute to the task of 'liberating the good, clean kernel of socialism from all the muck clinging to it'.[19] At this time, she agreed to inform under the code name of 'Caterine', on the condition that she would give just general reports of prevalent views and current opinions without mentioning any names, and signed the agreement accordingly, joking to herself that she had already broken the duty of strict secrecy by confiding in her diary. But in December 1957 Reimann's then partner Günter was arrested and her relationship with the Stasi became far less of a laughing matter. By 25 January 1958, Reimann's diary entry is far from light-hearted:

> I've got to make a break with the Stasi, there's nothing for it. They have tried to blackmail me . . . They promise me that Günter will get probation and that I will be allowed to visit him more often than is really allowed . . . and that they will smuggle in letters from me . . . Good God! What swines they are! They are speculating on my emotions . . . In recompense I am to deliver reports on our writers . . . This dreadful decision: either to help my most beloved and for this to perform spying services – or to jump off and leave Günter to his fate . . . I don't even know for certain what Günter would think about the whole thing.[20]

It was relatively easy for individuals approached by the Stasi with a view to informing to avoid being ensnared, although inevitably anyone in this situation would worry about potentially adverse consequences in both employment and private life. A common method of avoiding entering an agreement to inform was simply to break the demanded code of secrecy by telling someone else of the approach – a family member, a colleague or a friend – on hearing which the Stasi would immediately drop the potential informant. Another was simply to refuse. It was also possible just to deliver 'information' of mind-numbing uselessness, and thus be dropped.

For many, the impact of Stasi surveillance and interference with their lives was devastating.[21] In the case of members of the dissident political scene, a classic Stasi ploy was to initiate the breakup of previously harmonious relationships by sowing the seeds of mutual suspicion and distrust; the reputations of morally upright dissidents (such as pastors) might be destroyed by casting suspicions over their fidelity; the children and relatives of dissidents might be subjected to harassment and personal disadvantage. Attempts to come together to discuss lyric poetry or other writing critical of the state, to listen or play whatever was designated as politically subversive music, to engage in organised protests, could land an individual in prison for indefinite periods of time without any apparent possibility of resorting to legal rules or appeals to human rights. People could emerge with their health, self-confidence and future working lives damaged beyond recovery.

At the extreme, there are suspicions that the Stasi not only initiated well-attested murders and attempted murders of a number of individuals but also attempted more subtle methods of causing long-term ill-health and death from less easily identifiable causes, such as cancers caused by exposure to sustained high levels of radiation.[22] The subsequent serious illnesses and premature deaths of dissidents such as the novelist Jürgen Fuchs, and the author of the critical analysis of *The Alternative in Eastern Europe*, Rudolf Bahro, have been linked by some to the suspicion of exposure to extraordinarily high and sustained levels of X-rays while waiting for interrogations, and being strapped to unpleasant chairs in small prison cells in front of mysterious closed boxes – boxes that, along with their mysterious apparatus, curiously disappeared after the collapse of the SED system.[23] There have also been suspicions that symptoms of mental illness were actually created by 'medical' treatment, as in the case of Pastor Heinz Eggert. Eggert, who fell ill while on a family holiday at the Baltic in the summer of 1983, sought medical help for a depressive psychiatric illness and was treated in a closed psychiatric institution by a doctor who was also a Stasi informer. His later fears that medications administered actually produced and exacerbated the symptoms of illness have on further investigation proved to be without adequate foundation; the Stasi's crimes in this case consisted rather of persistent harassment of family and friends while Eggert was ill, and breaching of medical confidentiality to report on his illness and thus to discredit him.[24]

It is difficult to assess the impact of reporting on those who were subject to routine surveillance, or who simply knew they might be reported on if they stepped too far out of line. Where no apparent damage was done by anodyne situation reports, and where the vast majority of the populace were aware of the existence of the Stasi, it appears to have been simply taken for granted as a fact of life, in light of which certain precautions had to be taken (which for some individuals undoubtedly meant major restrictions on their activities, whereas for others the impact barely registered). Undoubtedly the codes of secrecy and manipulation had an effect on the character of inter-personal relationships, but trust and friendship still were possible for most people most of the time. The personal consequences of Stasi informing in these cases often proved infinitely more explosive in the 1990s, once the files were opened and the identities of former informers were revealed.

Claudia Rusch, for example, whose mother was close friends with the well-known dissidents Katja and Robert Havemann, grew up with Stasi surveillance as a fact of life. Claudia was just five years old when Wolf Biermann was expelled, and Robert Havemann placed under house arrest; she now rapidly became used to the presence of the Stasi:

> Suddenly the Stasi were everywhere, men in uniform or everyday clothes. They sat in Lada cars parked in front of the house, they observed us, they followed us, but they were not allowed to talk to us. Sometimes they hid like hares behind the trees.
>
> I did not understand why Robert was constantly to be seen on television and was now no longer allowed out of the house, why police barricaded the street and would no longer allow my mother to see Katja.
>
> But I quickly got used to it. I am still aware that at that time I did not really find the presence of the Stasi threatening. For me, the eternally waiting men were reassuring. They kept an eye on me [in the benign sense of 'looked after me']. Just as in the sense of the Stasi-ballad: bodyguards.[25]

Perhaps these were merely the innocent perceptions of child who was herself in no real danger. And, despite her close connections with the dissident scene, Claudia Rusch had happy memories of her own 'free German youth' in the 1970s and '80s. With the opening of the Stasi archives after unification, however, the unsolved mystery of her grandfather's premature death in 1967 at the age of 42, in a damp interrogation cell of the Stasi prison in Rostock, precipitated far greater emotional agony. Searching desperately around the variety of clues to possible identity – symbolic cover names relating to trees, personal information and particular incidents, the length of time the informant had known him – Claudia and her mother came aghast to the unwilling suspicion that the informant could only have been Claudia's grandmother, following the collapse of their marriage in 1962. Claudia and her mother contemplated with agony the possibility that such a close family member could have betrayed another. They could not actually believe it of her; and yet:

> that was the real strength of the State Security: to produce the effect that millions of people behaved towards one another with anxiety, self-control and suspicion. They ensured that if you told a political joke you automatically lowered your voice. Anticipatory obedience spread through every sinew of society and intimidated a whole nation.
>
> But not my Grandma. She would never have betrayed us. We were her family. Or at least, everything that was left of it after the war.
>
> But perhaps after all? Had she first informed on her husband, and then on her daughter . . .? How badly can one misjudge a person? How far can emotional betrayal go? What can one still believe, if that was true?[26]

Ultimately – and purely because of her mother's chance remark to a very close friend and confidante, a psychologist to whom she had turned for advice in this emotional turmoil – it turned out that the informant was not, after all, the grandmother. Ironically, it was the close friend, the psychologist, who confessed purely because the mother had, falsely, claimed that she would in any event find out the identity of the informer within a couple of weeks from the files. This confession from the former confidante brought to a total and utter end a friendship that had lasted thirty years or more.

It was not merely friendships that might be broken by post-unification revelations from the files. Curiously, the fear also existed that one's own biography might be presented in such a totally alien light that one's very identity was challenged. As the dissident Lutz Rathenow put it, the unwillingness on the part of a former acquaintance, Frank-Wolf Matthies, to look at his Stasi files was based in 'the fear that one's whole life would in retrospect appear to have been steered from outside'.[27] This challenged the very conception of the self-made life so central to post-Enlightenment thinking about the individual.

Informal collaboration with such a malign organisation was thus a very different matter from voluntary help with a women's group, a stamp-collecting society or a children's camp in the summer.

The diffusion of power in East German society

Participation in the multiplicity of little honeycomb cells of the many overlapping and intersecting elements in the GDR networks of power and social organisation was thus very widespread; but, as we have seen, the power elite proper was very small, with real power concentrated in very few hands. At the lower levels of society, participation in the structures of power – often on a voluntary and temporary, if time-consuming, basis – did not displace primary occupation as determinant of social status; at the higher levels, it was the principal determinant of status. And as far as secret collaboration with the Stasi was concerned, the extended exercise of power was very different in character and implication from that in more visible areas of the societal state. Power was by no means a matter purely of formal position in the system; nor did it overlap neatly with social stratification, except at the very top.

There was a variety of privileges for those who were prepared to make a 'positive' contribution to the running of the state. At the lowest level, the little networks of favours, of preferential treatment in relation to scarce goods and services, and of generally being 'in good standing', could make a quite considerable difference to the patterns of daily life and the chances of achieving a holiday, a change in working hours or conditions, or an improvement in housing conditions or leisure facilities. For shorter or longer periods of time, unofficial collaboration with the Stasi could bring all manner of large and small privileges and rewards, financial, material and psychological. Positive participation in the business of the state, whether malign or benign, in a paid or an honorary capacity, could also be a long-term investment against the miseries of poverty in old age. There were significant additional financial contributions, over and above the regular state pensions, for those who worked in the state administration, the parties and mass organisations, served as Chair of Collective Farms (LPGs), or – to take an example much higher up the hierarchy of the paid functionary system – as General Directors of major industrial concerns.[28] There were also politically justified 'pensions of honour' (*Ehrenpensionen*) for 'fighters against fascism' and 'those persecuted by the Nazi regime' ('Kämpfer gegen den Faschismus and Verfolgten des Naziregimes'), as well as for people who had served for twenty-five years or more as members of the 'citizens' militia groups of the working class' ('Kampfgruppen der Arbeiterklasse'). These higher pensions were the outcome of political decisions for preferential treatment of specific groups, irrespective of the individual's actual social class position with respect to type of work (manual or non-manual, professional and so on). Pensioners were otherwise the absolutely poorest group in the GDR; seen as non-productive drains on state resources, they alone had the privilege of freedom to travel to the West – if they could find anyone willing to pay for them.

Thus significant numbers of East Germans were in one way or another implicated in the extensive and very varied system of the extended exercise of power, a system that massively expanded the loose metaphorical boundaries of the state well beyond the narrow group of the ruling 'power elite' proper. This is in part why sharply drawn distinctions between 'state' and 'society', 'regime' and 'people' are so difficult to apply, and actually so misleading with respect to the GDR. While there was indeed a massive concentration of power at the top, the people's paradox is in part explained by the fact that those 'below' did participate in the running of their state in many respects. Moreover, while functionaries at the grass roots had very little real power or influence 'upwards', they did often seek genuinely to represent local people's concerns. Thus the 'state' was experienced at the base as at least partly benign, if often also risible. People's representatives were to some extent a part of local communities, and power spread like a dye through the wider fabric of society, colouring great patches of all areas of professional occupation and social activity, in some areas visible and benign, in others dark and disturbing.

Chapter Twelve

In place of a public sphere?
'Discussions', cultures and subcultures

It is well known that around three and a half million people fled East Germany while it was still possible to do so in the 1950s and that very large numbers were involved in the popular uprising of June 1953 and in other forms of active protest and opposition to the East German regime over the years, including widespread protests in 1968 and the growth of a variety of forms of political dissent in the 1970s and '80s, well before the mass demonstrations and stampede to the West of autumn 1989.[1] But what has often been less seriously explored is the way in which there was space for some form of discussion within the system itself; and the implications of such channels of discussion for people's experiences of life in the GDR. This system arguably only really came into its own following the building of the Wall and the securing of a rather different, self-contained – or imprisoned – society. Yet it was important for the stability of the GDR, particularly in the middle decades, and it played a role, too, in the climate of open critique that ultimately contributed to the downfall of the GDR.

Clearly there was no 'public sphere' in the GDR in the Western sense. Newspapers, television coverage, social and political organisations, were all in one way or another ultimately controlled by the SED; the borders of permissible debate and behaviour were as closely policed as were the physical borders of the country itself. Those who stepped too far out of line were subjected to a variety of measures for disciplining, metaphorically having their 'spine broken' (to use a favoured German expression for forcing people into a submissive mould), manipulation, bullying, or, at the extreme, severe and often arbitrary punishment including incarceration under appalling conditions in the Stasi prisons. Human rights to freedom of speech and freedom of association were clearly not priorities on the SED agenda, and the breaches of human rights in the GDR are well known. On some of the more critical accounts, personalities in the GDR were 'deformed' by a peculiarly constraining, repressive if paternalistic system of rule.

But this did not mean that there were no forums for any kind of collective debate about the character and future of East German society, or for the development of different subcultures and lifestyles. The bases, channels and outlets for such debates were always subject to varying degrees of political control. But far from being 'laid to rest', or repressed into dumb conformity, East German society was constituted by a rich variety of voices – not all of which, of course, were given equal space for expression, but which nevertheless played a role in the life experiences of perhaps the vast majority of 'ordinary' East Germans who did not seek to challenge and change the system but rather made their lives within the boundaries of the permissible.

None of this should be overstated: the GDR was no democracy in the Western sense of the term. But the story of political dissidents and opposition, which has rightly received much attention since 1990, has tended to displace from view the simultaneous story of constructive input on the part of very large numbers of ordinary East Germans. There was a curious combination of dissent and opposition, and constructive (if often disgruntled) critique; both aspects – or rather the full and often ambiguous palette of colours and shadings of critical participation and reaction – need to be held simultaneously in the picture. Recognition of the (limited) spaces for discussion and debate is an important ingredient in explaining the 'people's paradox': many East Germans did feel they were at least on occasion able to have a legitimate voice in matters of collective rather than merely individual concern, and that they could play an active role in shaping their own social environment and suggesting improvements for the future; and yet at the same time that they critiqued the GDR for very real shortcomings. Many East Germans also had a sense of being able to 'make their own lives', in the sense of abstaining from participation in the East German variety of the rat race, and simply opting for alternative lifestyles in ways that they found personally fulfilling.

'State poets', critical spirits and cultural interventions

Intelligent people in any kind of regime – whether capitalist or communist – do not appreciate being constrained, controlled or hoodwinked by political and media manipulation. And there were plenty of people in the GDR who had a relatively low opinion of flat-footed functionaries and dull ideologues, but who retained a dream of a better form of socialism – or, at least, felt there was greater opportunity for developing this in the East rather than the West.

The choice – or rather, the feeling that it was not so much a choice but merely a question of which regime was 'the lesser of two evils' – could be agonising for individuals. Victor Klemperer, having miraculously survived throughout the Hitler regime, was under no illusions about the character of the GDR; but he was even more bitter about the failure of the Federal Republic to deal with the Nazi heritage. As he noted in diary entries in April 1958: 'Personally, I find the people in Bonn hateful; but the pig-headed hostility to culture, the lack of education and the tyranny of the Party here daily get on my nerves.'[2] He continues by criticising 'the blatant battle for culture [*Kulturkampf*], the blatant education policy, the blatant arse-licking [*Arschkriecherei*] of the LDP, the CDU and NPD ... [It's just that] Bonn is *even* more hateful to me than "Pankow".'[3] He summarises the situation in the two German states of the late 1950s, weighing different aspects and levels of disagreeability against each other:

> Everywhere 'flight from the Republic' [*Republikflucht*], particularly among doctors, university professors, the intelligentsia. The battle for culture, the passport law, the tyranny, the pressures on conscience, the way children are torn apart – it's Nazism through and through. And in the Bonn state an open Hitler regime, ministers and generals from the Hitler state – but in general the individual lives in somewhat greater freedom ... [and] can express opposing opinions in the newspapers, whereas here the press etc. are closed off to individuals – but over there Hitler supporters can also openly pursue their hate campaigns etc. etc. Vile, and always the same and every day even more vile.[4]

Clearly there was a gulf between those in positions to impose the dumb ideological tenets of the new regime and those more critical spirits trying to think through ways to a better form of society. For the latter, the choice for the GDR was very often a critical choice for what they perceived as the lesser of two evils, and compromises were constantly essential to maintain any kind of discussion.

Members of the cultural intelligentsia – the core of which was actually only a rather small group of people – who were in principle committed to at least some version of the communist project found it possible in a number of ways to seek to have an input into internal debates. Christa Wolf, Stefan Heym and others repeatedly – but always within bounds – made critical interventions in debates about the character and future of the GDR. At times such interventions seemed easier, at others there were stronger restrictions, as periods of liberalisation (the period 1963–5, the early 1970s) were followed by periods of clampdown (the Eleventh Plenum in 1965, the expulsion of Biermann in 1976).[5] Writers such as Günter de Bruyn, Christoph Hein, Jurek Becker and many others constantly contributed to sometimes veiled debates about the character and shortcomings of the development towards some form of would-be socialist society in the GDR.

It is in some senses too easy to divide the cultural intelligentsia simply into those 'in favour of' and those 'against' the regime. The relationship between intellectuals in one or another area of endeavour and the socialist project was by and large far more ambivalent. Nor was it the case that intellectuals were in any sense expected merely to praise the status quo: criticism of one sort or another was, within limits, part of the very task of 'constructing' the GDR. It is also perhaps a little too easy, perhaps glib, to periodise the cultural production of East German creative writers, poets, artists and film-makers purely according to the ups and downs of official cultural policy. Yet certain overall trends in the character of those public discussions that could take place can nevertheless be perceived.

Relatively early novels such as Brigitte Reimann's *Ankunft im Alltag* (roughly, 'Arrival in Everyday Life', 1961), or Christa Wolf's *Der geteilte Himmel* ('The Divided Heaven', 1962), managed to portray the sheer difficulties of the everyday construction of socialism, both literally – in building sites and industrial plants – and metaphorically, in terms of the social interrelations among very different individuals, all of whom needed in one way or another to work through the tensions of the new society. Despite recognition of the massive difficulties involved in trying to create a better society under the given conditions – including, at the end of Wolf's novel, the brute fact of the Wall and the finalising of German division – these novels were essentially optimistic about the possibility of creating a better society.

Many films of the early 1960s, too, succeeded both in grappling with the very real strains and tensions of the present and yet suggesting ways forward. Somewhat ironically, even those that fell victim to the cultural slaughter unleashed by the Eleventh Plenum portrayed East German society as one in which there were signs that a better future could, or indeed would, eventually be able to triumph. Films such as Kurt Mactzig's *Das Kaninchen bin ich* ('The Rabbit is Me'), Hermann Zschoche's *Karla*, Frank Vogel's *Denk bloß nicht, ich heule* ('Just Don't Think I'm Crying'), all produced in 1965, and the perhaps best-known film of this era, Frank Beyer's 1966 adaptation of Erik Neutsch's novel *Spur der Steine* ('Trail of Stones') were remarkably frank in their portrayals of the shortcomings of East German society. Depictions of the official representatives of the new society – whether in the person of party bureaucrat, prominent judge, trade union official, heavy-handed head teacher or school inspector – were often surprisingly unflattering, given that such films could emerge only after months of internal discussion and adaptation in the light of the reality or perceived threat of censorship. At the same time, however, there were clear glimmerings of hope in each case, such as through the figure of a young protagonist, hovering between critique and commitment, often treated with unexpected kindliness or clemency by an older, somewhat avuncular functionary. Depictions of struggles and tensions in this *Aufbau* period were, then, still conceived as contributions to pointing a constructive way forwards.

Oddly, while the literati of East Germany continued to grapple with the problems of their society, a shift in emphasis or focus of the cultural production of the 1970s and '80s can be discerned that runs parallel to wider shifts in social attitudes and relations. There is – just as in public opinion caught in official reports and surveys – a trend towards bracketing out wider questions about the political whole and its potential future, and an enhanced focus on the individual, or topics to do with personal fulfilment and individual identity in the present. Films and novels to some extent enter the era of the *Alltag* ('everyday life') with debates about daily issues and personal relationships that do not stand for wider issues. Typical of this movement is the contrast between, for example, the role of love triangles in Brigitte Reimann's *Ankunft im Alltag* of 1961 and, just over a decade later, the widely popular film by scriptwriter Ulrich Plenzdorf and director Heiner Carow, *Die Legende von Paul und Paula* of 1973. In this later film, the choice between potential partners for both of the key protagonists is not at the same time a choice between different stances towards the political order as it is for the young heroine Recha in the earlier novel. Many novels of the later 1970s and '80s deal with individual questions of self-fulfilment and personal identity, rather than issues to do with the character of society as a whole, as evident, for example, in the growing literature on women's personal identities in this period, a development echoed, too, in later GDR films.

Film-making depended of course on significant investment of money, equipment and teams of producers and actors. Even films that were in the event made, after months of production, might ultimately be killed off by officially orchestrated criticism after a very short screening. Film production was thus far more easily controlled, and far more dependent on the state than was the more lonely pursuit of writing, where authors could often come to arrangements with censors through a combination of veiled writing and prior self-censorship; and poetry was a form that lent itself particularly well to ambiguity. But in every form of creative endeavour in the GDR there was almost inevitably some form of engagement with the political context, giving rise to multiple possible interpretations. In the visual arts, for example, paintings such as Wolfgang Mattheuer's *Die Flucht des Sisyphos* ('The Flight of Sisyphus', 1972), depicting a working-class figure (represented much on the lines of earlier socialist realism) fleeing down a bleak hillside in a somewhat surreal landscape away from the mammoth boulder he has been condemned to push repeatedly up the hill, or Mattheuer's *Die Ausgezeichnete* (roughly, 'The Award-winner', 1973–4), showing an apparently miserable, resigned and lonely elderly woman – or rather perhaps just a simple member of the working class embarrassed at being singled out for attention? – who has been given flowers in recognition of her contribution to socialist labour, illustrate the ambiguity and scope for cultural critique that was possible within GDR art.[6]

Any sort of writing could in principle, if it could not officially be published, or not published in sufficient quantities to be widely available (another form of semi-censorship), be read aloud in small circles. Some texts were in fact first published in the West; although writers were often to some degree protected by international status and visibility, they might then be pursued by euphemistically framed 'tax' laws, or other unpleasant consequences, particularly for works explicitly engaging with present realities as in the case of Rudolf Bahro's critique of 'actually existing socialism', *The Alternative in Eastern Europe* (1978). The cultural intelligentsia was also riddled through and through with Stasi collaborators and informants – including, briefly, the great 'state poet' Christa Wolf, occasioning a storm of controversy when this revelation followed hard on the heels of her post-1990 publication of a novelette describing a day under Stasi surveillance, *Was bleibt*.[7] Even the allegedly highly dissident 'scene' of Prenzlauer Berg 'alternative poets' in the 1980s had Stasi informants at its heart, most notoriously in the shape of Sascha Anderson.

Thus any notion of a 'public sphere' in any genuine sense was severely circumscribed by the SED's express concerns about giving ammunition to the 'class enemy', about the 'abuse' of critical utterances by the Western media, and about the possibility of fomenting internal unrest. There were always clear limits, many of which were more constant features than the periodic visible ups and downs of cultural policy might suggest. Censorship, while an uncomfortable fact of life, was one that in different ways many writers learnt to circumvent, address, evade and live with. The public image had to be strenuously controlled by the Party, as demonstrated by Honecker's intensive concern with press presentations of himself and Party policies. The restrictions on the extent of any wider public sphere were quite clear, as articulated, for example, by the playwright Heiner Müller in a small circle discussing the controversial statement, signed by key members of the cultural intelligentsia, protesting against the enforced exile of Wolf Biermann:

> The point now is to see what can be made of this situation, how it can used as a chance to talk about the things that we all want to talk about, and that could only

ever be talked about in such circles. I do not think it is possible any more, in the current international context of the GDR, just to define the public sphere as the public sphere in factories, institutions and so on. The press also has finally to open up slowly as a forum for debate. Of course the question of how much is possible here will remain a controversial one.[8]

As far as the SED leadership under Honecker was concerned, the question was not merely controversial: it was closed. The public image of the GDR had to remain without any vestiges of dissent and uncontrolled debate, despite Honecker's desire to present himself as a reformer, encouraging 'dialogue'. For critical members of the cultural intelligentsia, there could in these circumstances be no public sphere in any real sense.

It would, however, be very unwise to over-generalise in this most diverse area. Debates among East German intellectuals in the Kulturbund and in unofficial discussion circles were far more lively than anything that was able to appear in print. The twists and turns of official policy, and of the various alternative 'bohemian' scenes in the GDR, have been traced in detail by cultural scholars, and it would be out of place to try even to begin to summarise the complexities in this context. But by the time the big names of the GDR cultural intelligentsia came out on the metaphorical barricades of the 'gentle revolution', sharing a platform in Berlin's Alexanderplatz at the mass demonstration on 4 November 1989 with such unlikely revolutionaries as the long-term spy Markus Wolf and calling for a 'dialogue', it was clear that such a dialogue had long hence been taking place in far wider quarters than merely among the 'state thinkers and poets'.

Controlled participation in public debate

Public debate was of course always controlled, and nowhere more so than when instigated by the SED itself. Here, however, it is important to distinguish between the undoubtedly often cynical and manipulative aims (on which, incidentally, politicians in the GDR did not have a monopoly) of at least some of those instigating the debates, and the ways in which orchestrated public 'discussions' were experienced and perceived by East Germans.

At certain levels of the political and social hierarchy, a degree of controlled debate was in part actively fostered, in part tolerated – although at certain times more wide-ranging discussions were possible than at others. Both among the technical experts whose input was essential for an advanced industrial society, and in the sphere of (always-censored) cultural production, it was possible for individuals who were not necessarily politically close to the regime to have at least some limited say in the development of their society. As far as broader groups of the population were concerned, one of the SED's favourite slogans was: 'work together, plan together and govern together!' ('Arbeite mit, plane mit, regiere mit!'), and there were continued attempts to put this slogan into well-controlled practice. In certain local settings, programmes for 'voluntary' community action – tidying up the village, constructing a new sports facility – could even generate a degree of spontaneous enthusiasm. Within less mainstream subcultural milieus, people initiated and developed all manner of conversations about the kinds of community life they wanted to practise; sometimes in conscious engagement with or in opposition to official conceptions; sometimes in active development of social and cultural traditions that had long predated East German communism, often by many centuries.

Contributions to internal debates took place at all levels of society. In the 1960s – within the security of the Wall – Ulbricht sought to involve more technical experts in processes of planning and advising as an integral part of political decision-making. Stenographic reports of discussions between Ulbricht and his advisers give the impression that Ulbricht appears to have enjoyed debate, frequently making his own impromptu interventions, and often provoking laughter (the reports note *Heiterkeit*, or mirth) in a way not apparently characteristic of Honecker's rule. But Ulbricht also sought to involve wider circles in what might be considered the GDR equivalent of the 'focus groups' and media manipulations of well-controlled agendas of public debate characteristic of later twentieth-century Western politics, although the latter of course did not impose repressive sanctions on those who chose to disagree vociferously and fundamentally with government policies.

One of the ways in which the East German state actively sought to involve citizens was through well-orchestrated 'discussions' of particular policy statements, issues or developments. Such 'discussions' were of course initiated, controlled and evaluated from above. But their purposes were multiple, and not always purely manipulative or malign. 'Discussions' were very closely related to the practice of 'citizen's petitions' or *Eingaben*, and the opinions thus aired were often taken into account in policy-making processes.

'Discussions' were of course designed to serve a number of functions, the most obvious of which are the 'top-down' political functions for the SED. They were in the first instance a useful means of tapping popular opinion – as an information-gathering exercise on matters affecting people in everyday life, perhaps more important than Stasi general 'situation and information' reports. Secondly, they were designed not merely to record but also – or rather – to influence popular opinion, for example by having functionaries put forward the 'correct' arguments in response to hesitations, doubts, queries and downright 'counter-revolutionary' arguments on the part of the participants. And even if the task of convincing people of the correctness of an unpopular measure proved impossible to achieve (as most blatantly in the case of the building of the Berlin Wall), then at least such discussions could in some measure serve to instruct, by parading what was held to be the 'correct' answer, so that people would know what the current official line was on any given topic. Thus, they served a key educational function. Over time, there is evidence that people began to internalise the categories of discussion, along with some of the underlying concepts and assumptions; they learnt what could or could not be usefully discussed in any given context, and they learnt to deploy – or even, among younger generations, actually internalise – the 'language' of 'actually existing socialism', even if they did not always fully agree with the substance. In an interactive process, popular uses of the language also affected the ways in which those in a position to frame policy thought and responded. Finally, such discussions performed a crucial function in relation to *Kaderpolitik*, or the selection, training and also, where necessary, disciplining of functionaries. Keeping a close eye on who was less than articulate, or who failed to propagate the official line with sufficient energy (to use the favoured expression, those who failed adequately to 'intervene, taking the offensive', or 'offensiv eintreten') was a means towards the identification and weeding out of weak functionaries.

But to recognise these undoubted political functions is not quite to do justice to the place of 'discussions' in the life of the GDR. What such an account leaves out are the ways in which views and voices from below were often (though not always) taken seriously and listened to by those in positions of power. Input from below could, on a rather limited range of matters, even affect the character of policy or the precise formulation of legislation. Of course this was far from always the case, and least of all where the general boundaries of the regime – in all senses – were concerned: the Wall alone is sufficient proof, if such were needed, that where the essential parameters of power were concerned popular opinion mattered not at all. But as far as domestic social policies are concerned, on issues to do with youth or women, for example, there was far greater scope for popular input into policy formation. Over time, people came not exactly to accept but rather (most of the time) to bracket out the Wall or the 'system' as a whole from daily consciousness, and were able to have (at least the sense of) some input into (at least some of) the domestic matters that affected their more immediate existence. They did not, in short, experience the regime as always repressive, in face of which they had to maintain silence or retreat. And in so far as the unwritten rules of the game were internalised, such processes began to appear more ordinary, more 'normal'. It should perhaps be remembered in this context that widespread cynicism about one's own capacity to affect events, or about the motives and morals of politicians, is not unique to communist states. A degree of resignation, or acceptance of one's fate, is common to all those who have had to develop a folk wisdom of 'you have to make the best of it', 'you've only got one life', and similar sentiments, whatever the political system.

The Wall itself was of course a non-negotiable issue for the regime. Thus 'discussions' about the 'National Document' of March 1962, which inevitably raised issues relating to the inner-German border, could only be 'educational' in intent. Yet the mere fact of the Wall's existence led to changes in the character and possibilities of debate within a GDR whose labour supply was now – for the worst of reasons – more secure. Thus the second decade of Ulbricht's rule saw a wide range of public 'discussions'. There were frequent well-orchestrated 'discussions' around particular political events, such as Party conferences and important anniversaries such as the fiftieth anniversary of the Russian Revolution in 1967 or the twentieth anniversary of the GDR itself in 1969. Probably the most genuinely open in purpose were the 'discussions' about specific social policies, designed both to inform citizens of what they were about to receive, and to anticipate and possibly negotiate or deflect potentially critical reactions where concessions, compromises and modifications could readily be made. So for example, in 1965 the Council of Ministers decided that there should be (controlled) public discussion of the new Family Law (Familiengesetzbuch). The process of discussion was inaugurated on 14 April, and by 30 September 1965 a staggering total of 33,973 meetings had been arranged to discuss the proposed legislation. Discussions were also conducted in the press, on radio and television, and in 'readers' and listeners' circles'. Editors of local and national newspapers had the duty of sending on all letters to *Bezirk* law courts and to the Ministry of Justice. Arising from these communications, 23,737 specific suggestions were made, of which around half concerned the proposed legislation directly; and, on the basis of these 'discussions', it has been estimated that perhaps 230 changes were made to specific details of the new family code.[9]

The 1968 constitution, which explicitly enshrined the 'leading role' of the SED, was also the focus of extensive 'discussions' in the lead-up to a plebiscite that was to give the new constitution the seal of popular legitimation. For a variety of reasons, 1968 was a turning point in a large number of both capitalist and communist states, with political and cultural clashes over a range of issues, linking matters of international war and peace (notably Vietnam) to individual lifestyles and gender roles ('hippies', bra-burning, rethinking sexuality) under slogans such as 'make love not war', and seeking to redefine politics in a wide variety of ways (workers marching with students in Paris, young Germans challenging the roles of their parents' generation under Nazism, Alexander Dubček's reform policies in Czechoslovakia). Even had 1968 not been so notable for such a cluster of internationally significant developments, including not least the suppression of Dubček's reforms – the 'Prague spring' – by Warsaw Pact troops, the new constitution in the GDR might have aroused little general attention. It was in large part merely registering the realities of GDR politics nearly two decades after the state's foundation; it reflected more accurately the existing political system than had the constitution of 1949, drafted at a time when the division of Germany was viewed as merely temporary and provisional. Thus in terms of any really fundamental constitutional issues, the views of ordinary East Germans were not likely to make much of a dent.

Yet in a number of respects the public discussions surrounding the introduction of the new constitution have to be taken seriously. In general, it seems that by the spring of 1968 in the GDR, most people were capable of living a double-track life: on the one hand perfectly aware of the outer constraints on their freedom, on the other hand prepared to participate in channelled discussions about the detail of domestic policies and arrangements that would affect their everyday lives. This is a form of 'coming to terms with the present' – or, to adapt the words of an old prayer, people having the courage to try to change the things that they could change, the patience to accept those that they could not change, and the wisdom to know the difference.

From FDGB reports of the discussions, it is clear that some questions were debated more intensively and with greater interest than others.[10] Two questions were of course particularly contentious: that of why there was no right to strike contained in the draft of the constitution; and the question of freedom of travel to West Germany, alongside the right to emigration and freedom more generally. Members of the intelligentsia, in particular, seem to have focused on this wider political picture: questions of the relations between the two German states, the status of Berlin, the right to strike, to travel and to emigrate, figured alongside searching questions concerning individual articles, such as those dealing with the right to defence in court, the meaning of *Dringlich-keitsfall* (case of emergency) that would allow the Council of State to have the final decision, and whether 'it will still be possible to hold opposing opinions'. But what is also striking about this report is the way in which – bracketing out these wider questions of freedom – people appear to have been not merely engaged by, but also clearly felt their input could have some impact on, domestic issues that closely affected their own lives.

Thus women, for example, are reported as debating in detail the implications of having not only the constitutional right, but also the duty to work, given problems with how this could be realised in practice if there were insufficient childcare facilities (including for children who were unwell). They also welcomed the fostering of women's chances of obtaining further qualifications, as well as their right to accommodation, and in particular the suggestion that elderly single women should be re-housed in favour of making large flats available for families with children. Somewhat less welcome was the proposal to raise the school leaving age, extending compulsory schooling to the tenth class, which appears to have met considerable hostility from parents of large families who felt they could not afford to have a child delaying the start of work for so long, and from those who were concerned that their child might not have the mental aptitude to meet the demands of the tenth grade. The close and detailed engagement of women and parents with these questions that would affect their daily lives is echoed, if less positively, in the reactions of young people to the draft constitution. Here, what was euphemistically termed 'lack of clarity' (*Unklarheiten*) – in other words, disagreement with official views – seems to have been more widely prevalent, including criticism of the restrictions on freedom if one could not listen freely to Beat music; criticism of the ways in which social background rather than (only) school achievement was taken into account when under consideration for higher and further education; criticisms of the proposal that all young people should have to learn a trade or profession, even if skills were not really needed as a manual worker; criticisms of having to stay at school for more than eight years; and criticisms of restrictions on being able to choose one's own profession or area of apprenticeship due to lack of appropriate training places. It is nevertheless still very striking that these young people seem to have bracketed out (or perhaps had learnt that it was not worth explicitly raising) wider questions, and were, rather, intensively engaged with issues that affected their daily lives.

A local study of the constitutional 'discussions' in Thuringia confirms this general picture in more detail.[11] There appears to have been extraordinarily extensive coverage in this area: no fewer than 716,077 (57 per cent) of Bezirk Erfurt's citizens attended meetings or events within one week alone, from 28 March to 3 April. Yet at the same time, even functionaries sometimes appear to have had difficulty explaining the individual articles or the reasons behind some of the constitutional changes. A further feature of note is the fact that, by 1968, the general parameters of the political system and the 'leading role' of the SED were not widely discussed or directly criticised, while attention was focused primarily on more specific policies that affected everyday life, including freedom of movement and socio-economic reforms. Questions concerning religion (particularly in Catholic areas) and education also appear to have been the subject of considerable controversy. Perhaps the most interesting aspect to emerge from the Thuringian example is the extent to which popular views on religion were actually taken into account by the authorities, leading – in the context also of massive input by the Churches – to revisions and modifications of the draft.[12] In the event, for a variety of reasons the plebiscite delivered the required level of support: when the votes were cast on 6 April 1968, just under 95 per cent of the population who voted proved willing to give their formal assent to the new constitution.

This interlude reveals that by the late 1960s, many East Germans abstained from explicitly challenging the existence, character and continuity of the GDR as a separate state – about which they rightly felt they could do very little – and concentrated rather on making their voices heard with respect to those issues where they could hope to effect changes in a desired direction. A later oppositionalist, Freya Klier, commented how at the time of these discussions she was still naive enough to believe that her voice counted for something, and that as a young person she took the discussion very earnestly (although she was also highly ambivalent about the GDR at the time, for a variety of reasons).[13] Given that Klier was a politically sophisticated and highly intelligent person, her experience of trust and active engagement in the discussions at the time must have been rooted in a wider culture and shared by many less politically sensitive individuals. Another 'discussion' of the same year, on proposed reforms of higher education, similarly appears to have been taken very seriously by contemporaries.[14]

Similarly, the draft Youth Law of 1974 was circulated widely for consultation before the final version was produced. A study by the ZIJ analysed around 1,200 responses, including 2,400 suggestions, in order to be able 'better to evaluate the character, strength and spread [among the population] of these arguments and also to provide tips for answers'.[15] Those whose comments were considered came from 'the widest circles', ranging from 'Christian citizens right through to political functionaries'. The character of the SED regime as a 'listening state' is well illustrated by this evaluation, which rightly drew attention to the fact that 'many of the problems raised here will continue to determine the character of discussions in the near future'.[16] Interestingly, around three-quarters of all suggestions relating to the Preamble and the first section of the proposed Youth Law came from Christian circles.[17]

The suppression of Dubček's reforms in Czechoslovakia with the invasion of Warsaw Pact troops in August 1968, and the rapid repression by the security forces of any signs of protest about this in the GDR, obviously underlines the point that there should be no illusions about the extent of real democracy in East Germany in this middle period. Nevertheless, this did not preclude a degree of continued popular input into matters of domestic policy formation where the ultimate aims were roughly in line with those of the regime and where there was no risk to the external security or political character of the GDR.

The key point here is not so much that the SED retained ultimate control of policy formation – a point that has been made often enough – but rather that, at least from the mid-1960s to the mid-1970s, citizens were involved, in however controlled and circumscribed a fashion, in officially orchestrated discussions of domestic policy. Thus many of them at least had the experience of being able to participate actively in discussions on domestic matters that directly affected them, so long as these issues were not politically highly sensitive.

Subcultural variations and distinctive milieus

Discussions, debates and alternative ways of living co-existed also in a wide variety of subcultural milieus that developed and changed in a variety of ways throughout the lifetime of the GDR. Different religious and cultural traditions, regional accents and habits, persisted – as the many jokes about Walter Ulbricht's Saxon speech readily attest (to speak in a Saxon accent even has a verb of its own in German: *sächseln*). New regional variations developed in part as a result of new economic developments, with changing patterns of settlement, as in the socialist new towns.[18] There were also a variety of subcultural milieus based in more long-standing cultural, social and religious traditions.

Members of the tiny remaining Jewish community – numbering only in the hundreds, among whom the religiously committed community were ageing and dwindling – found themselves in an ambivalent position, privileged and fostered on the one hand, subjected to a degree of constraint on the other.[19] The SED's policies towards Jews were always somewhat double-edged: Jews were passive 'victims' of fascism, rather than active 'fighters against' fascism, as communists had been; and the SED was extremely anti-Zionist as far as foreign policy was concerned. Higher pensions for having been 'persecuted' by the Nazi regime were counter-balanced by constraints; the Jewish community in the GDR only gained a degree of leeway and support, for example for the renovation of the Berlin synagogue, accompanied by the appointment of an American rabbi, in the later 1980s. The situation on the ground, in terms of daily experiences, was equally ambivalent. Those who survived persecution within the Third Reich, or returned from exile abroad, often had rather uncomfortable experiences in a German society that had been exposed to, passively condoned or actively carried out Hitler's anti-Semitic policies. Even the children of survivors had ambivalent experiences with respect to their identity and heritage. Anetta Kahane, for example, recounts the difficulties of being 'different' in school, and of being treated with hostility by the parent of a schoolfriend when she came to her house wearing a Star of David on a necklace. She was utterly shocked when, on wandering around the former Jewish quarter of Berlin where her father's family had lived, she asked an elderly resident who it was who had formerly lived here and received the reply: 'Riff-raff. Just scum. Tarts and Jews! Today only decent people live here.'[20] There are numerous other instances of everyday anti-Semitism in this and in other accounts of life in the GDR: not quite so headline grabbing as the major incidents, such as the periodic daubing of swastikas, the desecration of graves in the Weissensee Jewish cemetery, or racist physical attacks on individuals, but indicative of a combination of philo-Semitism and anti-Semitism that made Jews feel never completely at home among their German compatriots. This ambivalence is caught well in a scene, based apparently on an autobiographical incident, in Jurek Becker's novel *Bronsteins Kinder* (1986), where the young protagonist, having punched a schoolmate in the showers after swimming, is effectively exonerated by the teacher on spurious grounds relating to his Jewish identity.

The Christian community formed a very much larger, and indeed initially a majority, 'subculture' in the GDR. At the end of the war, in eastern Germany between 90 per cent and 95 per cent of the population belonged to a Christian church, whether Catholic or one of the Protestant regional church organisations in this area of Germany, which was historically predominantly Protestant. The Christian Churches, while subjected to a combination of political attacks and more subtle infiltration, nevertheless continued to play a major role in East German society in all manner of ways, including making a significant contribution to the health and welfare system of the GDR. They also provided a quite distinctive environment and alternative value system for some families and individuals. Catholic communities – totalling somewhere in the region of one million people – were particularly concentrated in certain areas such as the Eichsfeld in Thuringia, lending a quite different flavour to these rural communities, which proved more resistant to processes of secularisation than did the wider Protestant society.[21] Those who remained active in the various Protestant Churches of the GDR, with eight different regional Churches (*Landeskirchen*), although scattered more sparsely and widely across the GDR than the generally more concentrated Catholic communities, nevertheless inhabited small metaphorical islands forming a very different milieu from that of the dominant and increasingly secular culture. For most of the GDR's history, people with religious commitment found themselves discriminated against and under more or less active attack from the atheist state. With processes of industrialisation and population movements, particularly in urban centres, Christian beliefs began to decline – although with some notable variations, and not without efforts on the part of the Churches to counter this tide. The original figure of around 15 million Protestants at the time of the foundation of the GDR had shrunk to a mere quarter or so of that total by the 1980s. But in the wake of the 1978 Church–State agreement – an agreement in which the SED in effect sought to co-opt the Church as a long arm of the state, beholden to and ultimately under the control of the dominant SED, which could withdraw its privileged status at any time – the Protestant Churches began to take on renewed political significance in the 1980s. If anywhere, it was within the context and under the protective umbrella of the Protestant Churches that a public sphere of sorts really began to develop in the GDR. Unofficial discussion groups allowed people to explore major issues of the day in a period of heightened international tension and increasingly palpable economic decline without needing constantly to pay obeisance to the official rhetoric or ideology of the SED. It was from within this context that the first unofficial peace movements, and environmentalist and human rights groups began to be formed, which in the later 1980s found the courage to break out from the confines of the church environment. In the revolutionary autumn of 1989, nevertheless, the influence of the Church was still evident in the insistence on non-violent demonstrations, prayer meetings and the use of candles to symbolise the peaceful protests. Without the discipline and spirit infused by the religious penumbra, it is arguable that the demonstrations of September and October 1989 might not have proceeded with such little bloodshed; the history of the end of the GDR might have been far more violent. Religious institutions and the renewed significance of alternative views of life, morality and political responsibility were to prove immensely important in the history of the GDR.[22]

More regionally based were the linguistically and culturally distinct communities of the Sorbs, who had mixed experiences in the GDR – although infinitely better than their previous experiences under Nazi repression. The Sorbish or Wendish peoples (the terms *Sorben* and *Wenden* are used interchangeably), speaking dialects of a Slavic language with, variously, similarities to Polish and Czech, had inhabited a (shrinking) area of Central Europe for many centuries; subjected to increasing Germanisation in the nineteenth century, in 1912 Sorbs founded a political body to represent their interests, the Domowina. This was abolished in 1937 by the Nazis, who sought ruthlessly to erase Sorbian language and culture; but it was refounded after the end of the war. From the foundation of the GDR, the creative development of Sorb cultural traditions was both constrained and at the same time fostered by the SED regime.[23] The Sorbs' representative body, the Domowina, could of course only operate within the wider political constraints of conformity to SED policies. Nevertheless, active steps were taken to preserve the culture and language. In the areas of Sorb residence in the Upper and Lower Lausitz, around Cottbus, Hoyerswerda and Bautzen, Sorbs had their own Sorb-language schools or were able to attend German-language schools in which Sorbian (in its variant dialects) was also taught. Dual-language signs were put up in towns and villages, and Sorbian theatre, literature and customs – including the colourful traditional costumes and seasonal festivals, particularly around Easter – were fostered. It was scarcely under SED control that younger Sorbs themselves chose no longer to wear the distinctive and varied costumes (*Trachten*) that many of the older generation still wore, either on a daily basis or on occasions such as weddings and seasonal festivals.

But, for all the official support of Sorbian language, culture, traditions and customs, SED economic policies tended in two ways to undermine (even literally) the continued existence of a viable Sorbian community. Sorb settlements were very severely affected by the devastating impact of extensive shallow brown-coal mining and the village clearances necessitated by the switch to reliance on brown-coal energy in the 1980s. Even before this, Sorb communities had begun to disintegrate as younger members not merely became disaffected with the religious beliefs and apparently old-fashioned habits of their grandparents, but also discovered they would be disadvantaged in the search for employment if they did not speak German as their first language; and there was considerable migration of young Sorbs from villages to cities in search of work. By the 1980s, Sorb culture was essentially fostered as a somewhat fossilised tourist attraction in the Spreewald area, with its old-world charms and winding rivers; but despite Kurt Hager's proclamation on the occasion of the Sixth Festival of Sorbian Culture in June 1985 that 'the Sorbian culture is a firm and at the same time independent constituent part of the socialist national culture of the GDR', the preconditions for a genuine living Sorb community were slipping away.[24] In this respect, the situation was not so very different from that of other minority languages and cultures in Western European states, such as Gaelic in Ireland; the success of the resurrection of Welsh as a living language is perhaps a remarkable exception.

Pockets of linguistic and ethnic difference existed also, on a rather different basis, among the many immigrants and foreigners who lived, studied and worked for longer or shorter periods of time in the GDR.[25] While some were kept well segregated in special hostels and expected to return to their home-lands within a relatively short period of time, others became sufficiently integrated to develop close personal relationships with East Germans. Mixed marriages were not uncommon, but they could, however, prove highly problematic when it came to a desire for residence outside the GDR. Many experienced not only official hostility and difficulties at the hands of authori-ties, but also racism in everyday life. Reports of troubles in the workplace involving foreign workers also crop up quite frequently in FDGB files.

There were many other subcultures within the variegated mix that made up the ever-changing kaleidoscope of GDR society. Musical tastes, clothing and lifestyles often served to distinguish different youth subcultures – from the rock 'n' roll fans of the 1950s, through the Beat groups of the 1960s, to the punks, grufties, and others of the 1970s and '80s. Whether forced into a category of political relevance by an over-censorious regime, or whether simply entering some kind of a refusal by the decision to 'drop out', or whether through one or another sort of non-conformist behaviour being designated an 'asocial', people who pursued alternative lifestyles in this highly politicised state inevitably appeared to make some kind of political statement. But these subcultures were, on the whole, far less politically relevant than either the paranoid Stasi at the time, or subsequent accounts of their expressions of disaffection, have sometimes made them out to be.

Conclusion

For large numbers of ordinary East Germans the experience at the time of relative stabilisation of the GDR in the later 1960s and early '70s was not one of constant repression under a distant and malevolent dictatorship, but rather one of being able to participate in limited ways, even to help build for the future, and also to be able to speak out critically on at least certain issues. The experience of being able to speak one's mind, even if what was said was subsequently ignored by the powers that be, was crucial to the sense of being an active participant in shaping one's future; and not that of being an 'accom-plice' in evil or a passive victim of constant oppression. The immense frustra-tion experienced by many ordinary East Germans in the later 1980s, when Gorbachev was calling for greater 'openness' and discussion in the Soviet Union, was in part because of the sense that even the semblance of dialogue was no longer on Honecker's agenda. This is why so many East Germans can see no dissonance between their critiques of the GDR at the time of its fall and their capacity to live within its boundaries and make a critical, even active and positive, contribution to its development in earlier years: rather than making a startling jump from allotted role as 'complicit accomplice of evil' to later 'passive victim' or 'hero of opposition', many East Germans simply registered the combination of rising problems and declining willingness on the part of the regime even to admit, let alone discuss, these problems at precisely the time the opposite development was taking place in the Soviet Union. Meanwhile, vast numbers of East Germans made use of far more individual channels for the expression of their views.

Chapter Thirteen

The people's own voices?
The culture of complaint and the privatisation of protest

There were many ways in which East Germans could moan. People complained to each other, in a daily 'community of solidarity'; they cracked jokes about the shortcomings of daily life and made fun of their political leaders; they operated practices of idling on the job, taking time off during working hours to shop for sudden supplies of otherwise scarce goods; and on occasion they downed tools and went on unofficial strike. Oddly, they were even encouraged to complain through official channels, a feature of the dictatorship that has received little explicit coverage in analyses focusing on the organisational structure and formal political system. Over time, the character of complaints changed subtly, reflecting the changing character of perceptions and experiences of everyday life in the GDR.

Every aspect of life, from the quality of coffee on the breakfast table to the question of whether one even had a home in which to enjoy a breakfast table, was a matter of concern for the very top, in a state in which the SED claimed responsibility for meeting popular demands. Many areas of domestic politics and policies were also the subject of well-orchestrated 'discussions', in which widespread popular discussion and criticism were actively elicited. The fact that the bottom line did not add up – that a very wide range of demands could never, in principle, be met – added to the ways in which criticisms of specific deficiencies ultimately amounted to a critique of the system as a whole.

Reflecting on the (stifled, controlled) channels of communication in the GDR, several important developments can be discerned. On the one hand, the state fostered, even encouraged, a climate of complaint – sometimes dismissed as a *Meckerkultur*, a culture of constant grumbling and dissatisfaction – that, while underlining the regime's paternalistic concern for the welfare of individual citizens, could ultimately only serve to draw attention to the GDR's many shortcomings. On the other hand, the channels of complaint were intended to be individual, rather than collective, in character: in the form of individual 'petitions' rather than based in collective organisations for interest representation and conflict resolution. And, even where complaints drew attention to shortcomings rooted in the system as a whole – and hence had, even if only implicitly, the effect of speaking on behalf of a wider community – the complaints were constrained to address individual issues or shortcomings that, it was at least posited, could in principle be rectified without querying the deeper systemic roots.

The institutional channels legitimised not only the demands but even the very voicing of these demands. In this way, citizens were often active protagonists in seeking to improve their circumstances, and the authorities often genuinely sought to respond to complaints, at least where there was a congruence of aims or where it was actually possible to satisfy demands perceived as legitimate. But the most major and pressing complaints and demands could never be satisfied, and some areas were totally off limits for critique and discussion. Questions concerning the Wall, the West, and freedom of movement (or lack of it), were taboo; and, as far as consumer satisfaction was concerned, the economy could neither deliver the goods, nor keep pace with changing expectations and desires, not least in the light of comparisons with the increasingly affluent West.

So a state claiming paternalistic responsibility for just about everything created an absurd situation, in which it simultaneously both encouraged widespread complaints and could in principle never satisfy popular demands and desires; and a population that knew, in principle, that there were absolute limits to its capacity to influence policy, nevertheless had the experience, which was not always purely illusory, that there was real space for individual and collective voices in processes of policy formation and change.

This situation was thus riddled with internal contradictions. But it is significant for several reasons. First, many of those representing the 'state' were genuinely trying to meet what they identified as legitimate needs; there was thus more overlap in aims and values between 'regime' and 'people' than is often noted. Secondly, many of those often lumped by historians into the category of 'society', and conceived merely as the passive object of policies received from on high, were in fact often active participants in processes of shaping at least the details if not the overall direction of wider policies, and, often even more importantly, in seeking to negotiate the parameters of their own individual lives. Finally, and not least in importance: even if the actual capacity of individuals to effect real changes was severely restricted (and some areas, as indicated, were totally out of bounds), people did at least experience a degree of freedom to express their anger, frustration, desires; and many were able to hope for some real improvements or fulfilment of their requests – however justified a degree of cynicism and irony may also have been.

The ambivalent balance between limited freedom of expression and complaint, between experienced limits and hope of the capacity to shape one's own future, shifted constantly over time; and the shifts register wider changes in the political and socio-economic context. These avenues of complaint and discussion thus help to explain why, in the changing circumstances of the Gorbachev era, it was so easy – at all levels of the hierarchy – for complaints about details to expand into critiques of the whole. But for the vast majority of people – those who did not become members of the tiny dissident groups of the 1980s – familiarity with individual channels of complaints meant also the search for individual solutions: escaping across the border to the West, to improve one's own position and that of one's immediate family, rather than seeking to change the conditions for the whole. Here, as in so many other areas of GDR life, patterns of individualisation arguably emerged that were at odds with the official collective goals of the regime, and which, in the end, played an important part in its ultimate undoing.

Citizens' communications (*Eingaben*)

Citizens' voices were actively elicited through the practice of *Eingaben*. Cumulatively, these, too, informed the character and direction of the domestic political agenda, as well as giving many individual East Germans some sense that they could make their views heard.

The word *Eingaben* is generally translated as 'petitions', although this is not actually a very good translation, given the rather different connotations of the word 'petition' in English, where it is more frequently used to refer to a document with many signatories making a collective appeal on behalf of a significant number of people. In the longer-term German background – in the very different political systems of eighteenth- and nineteenth-century German states – *Eingaben* arguably underlined a somewhat deferential political culture of reliance on the almost arbitrary bestowal of individual favours on the part of rulers. While rooted in this long-term tradition, the character and implications of the practice inevitably changed in the very different political circumstances of the GDR. 'Citizens' communications' might perhaps be more appropriate than 'petitions', though it is simpler to stay with the German word since there is no exact equivalent in English.

Eingaben actively encouraged a form of popular participation in the domestic politics of the GDR at the most immediately relevant level of the political hierarchy. They allowed the ventilation of grievances, which were then to be speedily and efficiently dealt with by the relevant authorities, with an oral or written answer to be delivered within four weeks (leaving aside the substantive differences, the sort of 'quality assurance procedures' that have crept like a rash across the Western bureaucratic landscape were well in place at a much earlier stage in the GDR). *Eingaben* were indeed explicitly conceived to be an integral part of 'socialist democracy', 'which includes a variety of forms of democratic participation and ever more consciously realised collective responsibility'.[1]

Eingaben were embedded already in Article 3 of the 1949 constitution. In Article 103 of the constitutions of 1968 and 1974, *Eingaben* were defined as follows:

(1) Every citizen may turn to the representative bodies of the people, their individual members, or state and economic organisations, with *Eingaben* (suggestions, tips, requests, or complaints). This right is also available to social organisations and citizens' communities. Exercise of this right should not bring any disadvantages to them.

(2) Those organs that are responsible for the decision are required to address the *Eingaben* of citizens or communities within the time period laid down by law and to report back the outcome to the petitioners.

(3) The way in which *Eingaben* are dealt with is determined by law.[2]

An advantage, from the citizen's point of view, is that one could complain to higher authorities about the incompetence of lower or more immediate authorities. But one could not always go very much higher, however popular it may have been to write directly to the President in the lifetime of Wilhelm Pieck, or, following his death, to the Chair of the Council of State (Staatsrat) who was also generally the First Secretary (from May 1976 redesignated General Secretary) of the SED; hence Ulbricht and Honecker in one or another capacity.[3] However, in practice, if citizens did not actually direct their complaint to the closest relevant level – the state or economic authorities, the factory or collective farm – then it would simply be sent 'back down' the hierarchy from wherever it had been initially directed.[4] In principle this all sounds remarkably like a form of genuine grass-roots political participation, providing a real avenue for every citizen to voice their opinions and express their feelings and wishes.

There was, of course, more to it than that, however. The underlying remit and function of *Eingaben*, including their hidden political agenda, is well described – if unwittingly so – in a comment on the experience of the District Council of Klötze, in Bezirk Magdeburg, from 1966:

The primary emphasis of the *Eingaben* process [is] above all about improving the working and living conditions of people, as well as deepening the relationship of trust between citizens and their state through the further development of socialist leadership activities [that are closely] connected to life.[5]

This nicely encapsulates the characteristic interplay of paternalistic concern with the well-being of citizens and the achievement of real social improvements on the one hand, and the preservation and propagation of the leading role of the Party on the other.

The system in the GDR, unlike comparable Western practices, ultimately prioritised autocratic decision-making with no chance for further appeal once a decision had been pronounced. Jokes prevalent after 1990 suggest that former GDR citizens treated their earlier constitutional entitlement to complain with a pinch of salt.[6] One joke (which unfortunately only works well in the original German) contrasted East and West Germany: while in the capitalist West everything worked on a system of 'income and expenditure' ('Einnahmen und Ausgaben'), the communist GDR had operated on a system of 'petitions and exceptions' ('Eingaben und Ausnahmen'). This is not a bad summary of one of the key drawbacks of this system. While expression of grievances and wishes could be guaranteed, it was often said that the answers depended not on the predictable and just application of an impartial system of written rules, but rather on individual and political considerations. This criticism is in part justified, but perhaps needs some qualification, since, although the rules were unwritten and often only implicit, the underlying principles and guidelines appear to have been fairly predictable, widely understood, and repeatedly applied: the productive, the politically committed and active, the needy – and best of all, anyone with all these attributes in combination – took priority over those whose presumed needs and contribution to socialist society were deemed to be less. Thus the art of writing a successful letter in part entailed demonstrating high scores on these aspects; but the authorities would also make appropriate enquiries about the individual complainant in other places, to see what level of 'deserving customer' they were dealing with. Further criticisms included the fact that when a particular petitioner achieved a positive outcome with respect to their own complaint, the grievance was addressed only at a personal level; there was no guarantee that conditions would be similarly eased for others in a similar situation. This, too, had to do with the acute scarcity of relevant resources, entailing severe rationing of desired outcomes, whether these were a flat, a holiday, or children's clothing in a particular size. The fault lay less in the system of *Eingaben* than in the very real problems about which people were complaining. Finally, although *Eingaben* could be passed up the hierarchy, any decision taken at whatever was the highest appropriate level was considered to be final; there was no possibility of independent legal appeal, or even, after a change of law in 1975, of further complaint against the decision to the local authority dealing with *Eingaben*.[7]

Eingaben fulfilled a variety of functions, which differed somewhat depending on perspective. As far as individual petitioners were concerned, these functions included ventilation of specific grievances with or without much hope of redress, a channel for informing 'denen da oben' (roughly 'them lot up there') of more general frictions and miseries on the ground, and a means of articulation of particular requests, a significant proportion of which had a real hope of some success. As far as the authorities were concerned, *Eingaben* were a means of involving citizens in the political process; of engaging in a dialogue over what was and what was not realistic or possible at any time; a means of identifying widespread concerns; and a means of seeking ways forward where there was a genuine congruence of concerns, although under economic conditions that made it remarkably difficult to provide any kind of real solution to the multiple difficulties of everyday life. Much of the evidence suggests that, far from being merely cynical and manipulative, East German authorities were very often driven by a genuine desire to improve conditions for ordinary people – not least because such improvements were often tied in with state goals such as improvements in productivity, as well as increased popular support. Thus any one-sided perspective is not going to do full justice to the range of motives for and functions fulfilled by *Eingaben* among different groups in the GDR.

Eingaben took a variety of forms in the GDR: letters to functionaries at all levels of the hierarchy, up to and including Walter Ulbricht and Erich Honecker; discussions in person at 'open surgeries' (*Sprechstunden*) held by relevant authorities; informal communications or formal letters to magazines, newspapers, radio and television programmes; complaints to doctors, shop assistants or political committees; even investigations of a particular area, industry or problem instigated by a committee of the Volkskammer. Although the latter were concerned with general and collective issues, and were initiated from 'on high', the vast majority of *Eingaben* came spontaneously 'from below' and related to individual requests or grievances. Some were clearly written out of sheer desperation, as in the innumerable cases of desperate pleas for better housing. Many letters and oral communications were, however, not originally intended as *Eingaben*, though the authorities chose to classify and treat them as such; from 1961, for example, readers' letters to GDR newspapers pointing out problems, criticising individuals or institutions, or making suggestions for improvements, had officially to be treated as *Eingaben* whether intended as such or not. So too did any suggestions or criticisms raised in public meetings, radio or television as soon as they had come to the attention of the relevant state authorities. In 1969 this was extended to any such complaints and suggestions as soon as they had come to the attention of economic organs, socialist factories, combines and state institutions.[8]

All of this was not so very different from specific functional equivalents in many democratic capitalist societies. The range of similar practices in Western democracies would include correspondence and personal appointments with local councillors, members of parliament (or equivalent) and other political representatives, grievance procedures at work, complaints to manufacturers about consumer goods, letters to the editors of newspapers and journals, appeals against the decisions of bodies concerned with pensions or medical care, consumer satisfaction surveys and comments in the 'suggestions boxes' of supermarkets, or internal correspondence between members and organising committees of political and social organisations. Of course, such practices in democratic societies take place in a very different wider political context. What is, therefore, perhaps most remarkable is simply the mere fact that similar practices operated at all under the dictatorial political system of the GDR. Even more surprising – given all due regard for the incapacity of the system to meet all the citizens' desires and demands – is the fact that this practice was not only tolerated, but actively encouraged; that so many Eingaben were taken so seriously; and that at least some were met with a degree of success.

Most Eingaben in the GDR were essentially individual complaints and appeals, with a view to achieving specific aims. If written by a functionary, or perhaps jointly by the executive committee of an organisation, a letter might be on behalf of a whole group, as for example when the Institute for Post and Telecommunications wrote to the Ministry for Environmental Protection concerning the dangers to children's health posed by the polluted waters at the Ernst-Thälmann holiday camp of the German Postal Service.[9] If, however, an individual wrote on behalf of others without the appropriate representative function, then the response might include some form of reprimand: in 1986 Frau Ingeborg R., for example, felt that in the subsequent face-to-face discussion of her letter she was treated like an 'enemy of the state, who is trying to shake the chair legs from under the government' for having raised the concerns of many women across a range of matters, including difficulties with income, pensions, lack of fresh fruit and vegetables, children's clothes, doctors, housing and childcare; dissatisfied with this treatment at the time, she resigned from the DFD in protest, but gained the courage to raise her concerns again in the more open climate of discussion in the autumn of 1989.[10] Sometimes several people might write in on the same matter, or supporters might add their voices to that of the main individual complaining, as in the case of Herr

Falk J., whose housing problem (being threatened with eviction following his wife's miscarriage) prompted not merely a letter from his brigade leader and his department leader, but also the trade union branch chair and the collective of his trade union group at the VEB Kombinat Robotron where he worked.[11] When instigated from above, as in the parliamentary committees' inquiries, there was a form of investigative commission or audit, with a view to achieving collective improvements.

Unlike the more variable procedures generally surrounding similar practices in Western societies, the practice in the GDR was highly regulated, controlled and monitored, with quarterly reports detailing absolute numbers, percentages dealing with different issues, processes and outcomes.[12] Once again, the paper trail from the East German dictatorship was collected with remarkable efficiency and thoroughness, unintentionally leaving excellent collections of material for historians. Even a brief sampling of this material reveals the care that was generally taken to deal promptly, efficiently, and often with great courtesy, with citizens' complaints, even where there was no obvious solution to the problem. Even seriously difficult customers who would try the patience of any bureaucrat appear to have been answered with remarkable goodwill, as in the case of the more or less professional complainant Herr Heinz H., 'who is well-known in most central offices (including the District Central Office of the SED) on account of his many *Eingaben*'.[13] Many responses started with a standard formula along the lines of 'We thank you for the trust you have put in our organisation' and indicated that the letter had been passed on to the appropriate further authorities to be dealt with.[14] The extent of effort that was put into either trying to deal with a case to the complainant's satisfaction, or explaining that it was not possible to provide a solution, is also on occasion quite remarkable; just how much bureaucratic time would have been freed up if the economy had been stronger and citizens less dependent on the state hardly bears thinking about. There was also a standard procedure for indicating that the case was closed, the *Eingaben* treated as *erledigt* ('dealt with').

It has been estimated that there are well over a million letters from individual citizens extant in the various archives of the GDR. Given the fact that some individuals were responsible for more than one letter (in complex and doggedly pursued cases, there might be a string of letters from the same person), it is less easy to estimate precisely how many GDR citizens participated in the *Eingaben* process. Some estimates suggest that around half of the adult population, or perhaps two thirds of households, at one time or another had experience of sending such a letter.[15] On other estimates, the total numbers may even have averaged out at one per head of the population as a whole.[16] Even non-letter-writers might perhaps have been participants in an investigation by a parliamentary committee of inquiry. Although there are methodological problems with calculating overall numbers, the quantity of letters sent to the highest political levels appears to have risen significantly; certainly the numbers of letters received by Honecker in the later 1980s – as many as 100,000 in 1988 – appear to have risen to the levels received by Ulbricht in the early 1960s, following a decline in the intervening years.[17] The interpretation of such figures also gives rise to methodological problems. Wilhelm Pieck, President until his death in 1960, appears to have taken some pride in his role as paternalistic father figure, and actively welcomed large quantities of *Eingaben* as a means of keeping in direct touch with the concerns of the people; so too, it appears, did Ulbricht, who saw the high numbers as a sign of faith in the state to redress all ills. On taking office in 1971, Honecker by contrast interpreted the *decline* in numbers as an indicator of increasing satisfaction, while rising numbers later in his period of office were seen as indicative of rising levels of dissatisfaction. Thus, while for Ulbricht high levels of *Eingaben* were to be welcomed, for Honecker, perhaps more realistically, they posed a less welcome challenge to the regime's legitimacy. Whatever the precise figures and most appropriate interpretation, it is clear that *Eingaben* were a well-known conduit in the GDR for dialogue between individual citizens and the state authorities at levels ranging from the most local right up to the very highest reaches of the political structure.

Causes for complaint: Congruence of aims?

The character of complaints seems to have shifted somewhat over time, reflecting both the changing balance of concerns and contexts of discussion. Interestingly, within a circumscribed area, there was remarkable consensus over what was a justifiable basis for critique.

Some policies were obviously beyond the bounds of permissible discussion, although it was clearly important that local representatives of Party and state should present these policies in a politically 'constructive' manner when faced with citizens' complaints. This was particularly the case with respect to the borders of the GDR, although not all functionaries appear to have served equally well in this capacity. As one report complains, 'the lack of understanding for the security measures in border areas is strengthened further by the mode of argument of certain members of the People's Police'.[18] Similar lack of understanding was evident with respect to requests to leave the GDR for the West. In the early to mid-1960s, scarcely surprisingly, a major issue was that of travel to the West (or rather lack of it), and receipt of packets from the West. *Eingaben* relating to the desire to move to the Federal Republic or West Berlin appear to have declined somewhat following the conclusion of *Ostpolitik*.[19] In 1977, Willi Stoph even decreed that petitions seeking permission to relocate to the West were not '*Eingaben* within the meaning of the law on *Eingaben* of the GDR' because there was no provision in GDR law for a right to move to 'non-socialist states and West Berlin'.[20] From 1982 onwards, however, there was a rise in *Eingaben* relating to travel to the West – a topic that became particularly a focus of discussion throughout the 1980s, as visa restrictions were somewhat relaxed in the context of Honecker's own attempted visit of 1984, and then his actual official visit to the West in 1987. The percentage of *Eingaben* requesting permission to travel or move to the West increased significantly in the later 1980s, as did threats of making such an application in *Eingaben* in which the primary focus was some other matter.[21] Nor, apparently, did the authorities follow Stoph's directive and cease to treat such *Eingaben* as such; even Erich Honecker responded, with his characteristic signature following a laconic '*Einverstanden*' ('agreed'), to selected pleas from significant persons that came his way.[22]

Concern about the West was in the early 1960s closely followed by concerns over housing – which soon became the predominant cause for complaint – and foodstuffs.[23] Conditions with respect to housing are brought home in some of the individual cases: one woman, for example, reported that her family of seven was living in a flat consisting of one bedroom and a kitchen; only three beds could be accommodated in the bedroom so that, while one child had to sleep in its pram, an older boy had to sleep alongside his aunt in one bed, while she herself slept in another bed along with two of her children.[24] Presumably her husband – or whoever the unidentified seventh member of the family was – had the other bed to himself. A report for the community of Großschönau in March 1964 lists innumerable cases of four-person families having to live in one room.[25] In May 1967, for example, 49 per cent of *Eingaben* to the Council of State were to do with housing problems; in 1976, despite the attention devoted to housing under Honecker, housing complaints still made up 44 per cent of the total.[26] These relative statistics have to be treated with something of a broad brush, given that the totals of which they formed a percentage also fluctuated; there was, for example, an overall rise of 16 per cent in numbers of *Eingaben* in 1976 compared to 1975; after Honecker became the Chairman of the Council of State, the numbers of *Eingaben* to this body rose by 40 per cent compared with previous months.[27] But nevertheless it is clear that housing remained a constant problem. Alongside such issues as lack of cement and bathtubs, underwear and batteries, or the eighteen-year wait for a car, housing still appears to have been a top priority in *Eingaben* as late as the autumn of 1988.[28] And this was an area to which the government had devoted a great deal of energy and resources.[29]

Apart from housing, there were of course many other general causes for complaint. Summary reports had to deal with just about every area of life in a state in which there were innumerable potential sources of dissatisfaction. Workers continually complained about a whole gamut of work-related problems, including problems with new work regulations, wage levels, premiums, productivity agreements, working hours, holiday entitlement, taxation and insurance issues, lack of appropriate cloakroom and toilet facilities in the workplace, kitchen and refectory conditions, and conflicts between whatever was envisaged in the annual plan and what was actually feasible with available resources.[30] Music-lovers complained about the proportions of different types of music played on particular radio channels, chafing in particular against the regulation that the popular music station DT64 was to have a 60:40 ratio of 'politically correct' communist-produced music versus the more genuinely popular Western product. Residents complained about the cost of building, lack of garages, air pollution caused by industrial emissions, and noise nuisance caused by overflights of aeroplanes at high speed. Pensioners complained about levels of state pensions, or sought to achieve the coveted status of heroic veterans and 'anti-fascist resistance-fighters' to improve their own pension entitlements.[31] Parents in the Berlin suburb of Pankow complained in the summer of 1971 about the lack of usable toilets in their children's school, the Wilhelm-Pieck Upper School, and threatened to keep their children away from school until the situation was rectified; in response, they were informed that a change in the situation had not been envisaged in the plan, and that no new toilet bowls would be available until the following year.[32] 'Small animal holders' in Guben complained about the lack of appropriate fodder for 'egg-producing small animals'; other Guben residents complained about the irregularity of buses and the fact that pavements in new residential areas had not been completed on time.[33] Consumer dissatisfaction was continually expressed over issues such as inadequate supplies of particular foodstuffs; costs and prices; imbalances in supplies, even between cream cakes and 'ordinary' cakes, and increases in size of cake slices entailing related price increases without consulting the customer; the ludicrous shapes and sizes of certain clothing, including the cessation of subsidies for children's clothing already at small children's sizes, for fear that small adults might also benefit; and lack of appropriate spare parts for repairs.[34]

Social-policy questions, particularly those raised by single parents, pregnant women and working mothers, rose dramatically in the mid- to later 1970s, at precisely the time when one might think most improvements were being introduced in this area. Thus expectations that had been raised by the high profile given to social policy by Honecker were evidently not easily fulfilled. Numbers of *Eingaben* relating to environmental problems also increased in the mid-1970s.[35] There was a rise of 25 per cent in numbers of complaints about the measures and decisions taken by state lawyers and 'investigative organs' in 1977 compared with 1976.[36] A further theme that appears to have gained in significance in the 1980s was that of health.[37] From the mid-1980s, there was a rise in numbers of complaints about just about everything: not merely questions about travel to the West, but also about perceived deterioration in the quality of 'consumer socialism', ranging from inadequate supplies of spare parts for washing machines, through the increased waiting times for cars, to the availability or otherwise of other long-life consumer goods. Increasing numbers of people also included demands for more participation, more democratic discussion and more genuine information in the later 1980s, reflecting the changed mood of the Gorbachev period.

Although there are occasional sharp comments when citizens' communications overstep the boundaries of the taboo, the overwhelming tone of the official documents relating to these petitions is one of paternalistic concern. One notable feature of official analyses of *Eingaben* is thus the frequency with which the authorities agreed with the complainants and felt that they were fully justified in raising their concerns. Analysing widespread complaints about housing, for example, the Committee for Citizens' Communications in Kreis Zittau of March 1964 concluded that there was 'justified cause for complaint. A completely inadequate overview of the available accommodation, the lack of plans for distribution of housing, reassurances and the failure to keep promises are significant causes of *Eingaben*.'[38] Similarly, in 1966 the story of the extraordinary lengths to which a citizen from Jena had to go to find a spare part for his motorbike, taking a day off work to travel first to Gera, then Weimar, and eventually Eisenach before finding the requisite item, led to the general moral that 'the fully justified criticisms of citizens' should give occasion for the Ministry for Trade and Supplies, in conjunction with the relevant trade and finance organs, to develop appropriate measures to deal with such complaints.[39]

This thorough response to *Eingaben* was not least because many of the felt needs of citizens corresponded closely to perceived needs on the part of officials with an interest in improved productivity and more effective living and working conditions. Here, the goals of policy makers and the aspirations of ordinary people actually coincided and there was a genuine rather than forced 'congruence of aims'. Thus, for example, complaints and petitions from particular areas of industrial production were often seen as a means of improving relations between workers and managers, and ensuring a more effective channel of communication. This was particularly important when introducing changes into the structure and functioning of industry to ensure the informed input and subsequent cooperation of workers rather than mere 'administrative' imposition by managers. Given the particular difficulties consequent on the transformation of formerly small or craft-like enterprises into modernised larger concerns with concomitant rationalisation and the introduction of new technology, it was all the more important to ensure good relations between managers and workers and open discussion in the work-place.[40] But a main aim was the fostering of discussion between management and workers, to ensure enhanced efficiency and smoother functioning and development of economic enterprises. With respect to the cases of two VEBs in Berlin and Stralsund, one report points out that workers felt a high degree of responsibility for their factory, and that their ideas and suggestions should be taken into account as early as possible.[41] Similarly, when introducing structural changes in industry it was important to involve the affected workforce fully.[42]

If the conditions of life – transport, housing, childcare, shopping – could be made easier, then productivity as well as worker satisfaction would also be enhanced. There were even attempts to anticipate, 'prophylactically', the views and needs of people to such a degree that, as one report put it, 'many causes of *Eingaben* could be avoided in advance'. This required 'the permanent, timely consideration of the suggestions and criticisms of citizens', and 'constantly taking into account the opinions of citizens in reaching decisions and in the thorough explanation of decisions to citizens'.[43] Thus parliamentary committees of inquiry were sent in, for example, to investigate the implications of shift work and other relevant issues in Kreis Döbeln in 1978.

If a culture of complaint was to some extent encouraged, so too was at least a degree of what might be called quality control over 'customer care' – although this appears to have been severely limited in its success rate in practice. Nevertheless, it is worth noting the relative frequency of criticisms of failure to deal sensitively or appropriately with complaints.[44] This was not merely out of concern for the feelings of the recipients of curt or inappropriate responses. It was also seen to damage the image of the Party, and indeed to destroy the desired atmosphere of 'trust' in the paternalistic Party that the system of *Eingaben*, as so much else, was supposed to bolster. As one report put it, 'Despite all progress, state functionaries frequently deal with citizens in a heartless and bureaucratic manner. Often promises are given lightly, which cannot then be kept, so that the citizen's relationship of trust in the organs of state is significantly damaged.'[45] Or, as Dr Fritz Rösel, FDGB functionary and

Chair of the Committee for Work and Social Policy put it when reprimanding one of his subordinates for having dealt, as he saw it, inappropriately with one particular case:

> I would like to emphasise once again: *Eingaben* from the citizens of our Republic are a matter to be taken seriously, and every state and economic organ, as well as every societal organisation, has a duty to examine the citizen's request conscientiously, to make a decision, and to reply. In this process it is the contents that matter, not the form ... I am sure you will agree with me that the state, economy and societal organisations are there for the people and not the other way round.[46]

The authorities were often much exercised by the fact that they were not able to meet all the demands and needs that they felt were fully justified. One report that had emphasised the importance of ensuring good working relationships in the workplace through satisfactory handling of *Eingaben* and the way in which this assisted in a relationship of trust between workers and management, went on to regret the fact that many causes of complaint – such as low wages – were not ones to which solutions could be found at a local level.[47]

In face of all this, the political leadership at the very top was often faced with an almighty mountain of popular dissatisfaction and heightened expectations. Multiple complaints about the apparently most trivial matters – supplies of candles for Christmas trees, colour film for cameras – thus could lead to major political actions at the highest level.[48] Shortages of coffee, and of the hard currency required to buy high-quality Colombian and Brazilian coffee beans, for example, led to top level discussions in the Politburo in the late 1970s and early '80s about the introduction of an almost undrinkable *Mischkaffee*, a 'coffee mixture' that included minimal percentages of ground coffee alongside chicory, rye and other grains. This bitter brown mixture masquerading as coffee occasioned innumerable letters of complaint from citizens about both the taste and the unmentionable effects on the digestive system of the new brew. Attempts to vary the proportions of the ingredients were unsuccessful. Continuing protests about the quality of 'coffee' led ultimately to the secret trading of weapons for coffee beans with Ethiopia, Angola and other 'new nations' such as Vietnam, Laos and the Philippines, thus nicely balancing the interests of the 'class struggle' across the world with the resolution of conflicts over the breakfast table in the GDR. Eventually Western brands of coffee such as Tschibo and Jacobs were introduced at a price in Delikat shops and other special outlets for those with spare cash. Alexander Schalck-Golodkowski, head of the euphemistically termed Bereich Kommerzielle Koordinierung (Koko, or Office for Commercial Coordination), was involved not only in the weapons-for-coffee trade, but also in many similar deals responding to popular dissatisfaction, ranging from vital medical equipment to the more mundane matter of supplies of raisins for the traditional German Christmas cakes, *Stollen*.

Interestingly, citizens of the GDR came increasingly to know what rhetoric to use, and what appeals to make to official ideals, in order to achieve maximum effect; in short, they learnt how to deploy a particular form of discourse in pursuit of their ends. This may not have been a question of genuine internalisation of 'official-speak', but rather one of (metaphorical) bilingualism, or a capacity to play the system in a manner appropriate to achieving certain aims. Letters in the 1980s to the relatively popular GDR television programme *PRISMA*, for example, tended to conform to a particular form of discourse.[49] The most successful versions would begin by establishing the letter writer's own credentials as a worthy and committed member of socialist society, sharing in a broad consensus about wider ideals and goals. The specific complaint or request, drawing attention to a particular shortcoming, might be accompanied by a threat of some sort – bringing it to the attention of a yet higher authority, refusing to go and vote, and, at the most extreme, putting in an application for an exit visa. Thus the citizen, having first located him- or herself as a fully committed member of GDR society, was in effect threatening to withdraw some or indeed all of that commitment, by refusing either to participate in certain ritual acts of 're-commitment' or demonstrative support (such as casting a vote where there was in fact no real choice) or indeed taking the further step of rejection of the system as a whole by seeking to leave. Finally, letters might legitimate the protest by a choice quotation from Honecker or other high political authority, thus implying that rectifying the currently inadequate state of affairs would serve to reinstate the status quo as desired by the highest political or ideological authorities. But equally remarkable about the mountains of letters produced by the citizens of the GDR is the sheer variation in style and appearance, from the arduously hand-written on squared pieces of children's exercise-book paper, through the scribbled notes on plain paper, to flowing prose over several pages of typewritten or beautifully hand-written composition. Moreover, it is far from clear when reading these letters whether the professions of faith in the system and active commitment to the society are really to be read in the ironic mode of post-1990 academic scholarship, reading into these phrases some form of tongue-in-cheek manipulation of official discourse, or whether they genuinely reflect the way in which people experienced and saw their own situation at the time. Given the sheer range of writers and issues over the decades, one begins to suspect that at least a significant proportion genuinely believed in what they were saying (the ironic treatment of *Eingaben* in Wolfgang Becker's 2003 film *Goodbye Lenin!* notwithstanding).

Seen in this light, *Eingaben* were at least to some extent 'system-sustaining'. They confirmed the possibility of drawing attention to shortcomings in a system that, while imperfect in practice, was nevertheless developing on the right lines and could in principle be improved. To critique, within this framework, was thus not to criticise in the sense of attack but rather positively to contribute to the improvement of the system. Sufficient numbers of people were satisfied, for the most part either by simply having let off steam and then understood why their request could not be met, or indeed by having achieved some real improvement with respect to their own personal problems, for the practice to be widely supported. The sense one gets is that – in stark contrast to the closing stages of the Third Reich, when very minimal criticisms of the regime could land an individual in prison or in receipt of a death sentence – very large numbers of East Germans did not, for the most part, have the feeling that it was impossible to voice their criticisms. This, too, forms part of the complex set of reasons why the dictatorship was not for many people much of the time experienced as such.

For some, of course, the outcome was far from happy. The attention of the authorities might be drawn to someone expressing opinions that went beyond the constrained limits of acceptable complaints; surveillance on the part of the Stasi and possible malign intervention in the individual's life, with knock-on adverse effects for the lives of family members, might follow in certain cases. Putting in an application for an exit visa might result in two years' imprisonment before the exit visa was granted; and while the end result might be the desired one, the exit to the West might be bought at the expense, not merely of two extremely unpleasant years of incarceration, but related physical and psychological damage to the individual. To point to the relatively system-sustaining effects of the *Eingaben* system in that majority of cases that played by the (mainly unwritten) rules does not preclude the reality and severity of difficulties when implicit boundaries were transgressed and taboos broken. But even analysis of the disturbing developments when *Eingaben* challenged the boundaries serves to demonstrate just how much scope there was for participation in a wider 'conversation' about possible improvements to the system within these boundaries, so long as the system itself was not put seriously in question.

Conflicts, communities and individual interests

Analysis of *Eingaben* serves to underline the fact, which is repeatedly evident in the material but inadequately reflected in many theoretical models of the

GDR, that not all conflicts were along the simple lines of the 'people' versus the 'state'. Conflicts were more complex, cross-cutting this easy dichotomy. Some involved lower-level functionaries appealing on behalf of individual 'constituents' to higher authorities; some involved higher-level functionaries agreeing with the complaints of individual letter-writers about incompetence on the part of lower-level functionaries; others involved conflicts between one area of the state and another. Many involved agreement on broad aims, and common frustrations concerning the wider (often economic) reasons why these aims could not be achieved, or desires fulfilled.

Some scholars have critiqued the GDR-specific practice as essentially a sham, revealing more about the shortcomings of the system than the good intentions of the rulers. On one interpretation, while *Eingaben* provided the SED with a rich source of information about popular opinion, the SED effectively 'filtered out' or 'repressed' critical signals and 'pleas for help' from the population.[50] Others have taken a more differentiated view, while also poking gentle fun at the sometimes quite absurd responses of the authorities. On this view, the practice reveals the way in which East Germans actively used 'self-irony, gallows humour, sarcasm and sometimes also cynicism' to negotiate conflicts and reassert shared goals and values.[51] While the system of *Eingaben* functioned, even while critiquing the shortcomings of the GDR, people were nevertheless at the same time implicitly affirming the essential viability and capacity for improvement of an 'as yet' imperfect GDR.

As with any mechanism for conflict articulation and resolution, the system of *Eingaben* clearly had innumerable shortcomings, and is readily open to criticism. Most obviously, the status of the GDR and the leading role of the Party could never be denounced or compromised in any way. But there is a degree of urgency about attempts to involve citizens and engage in a process of consultative decision-making that goes beyond the merely indoctrinatory, manipulative, cynical or sloganising. The overwhelming impression gained from a reading of these files is one of very real concern on the part of many functionaries for bringing about improvements in the well-being of the people against all the odds and despite incredible difficulties in seeking to realise these improvements in practice. One has the sense of an advanced form of a Western-style consumerist 'customer care and quality assurance system' without the affluence required to back it up and deliver the goods. It is hardly surprising, then, that many of those who struggled under virtually impossible circumstances to improve the lives of their fellow citizens should feel a shade aggrieved at being denounced, after 1990, as having been 'fellow-travellers', duplicitous manipulators and the like. Here again, the realities were simply more complex. While there were undoubtedly attempts to cover up shortages or deny the grounds for criticism, there were also genuine channels for listening, investigating, responding. Degrees of consultation and institutional channels for the articulation and negotiation of conflicts were greater than usually thought in areas concerning people's daily lives – but not where complaints amounted to challenging the existence or character of the GDR as the SED-state.

Was there a process of 'individualisation' involved here, despite the official emphasis on collectives? It is possible to present an argument along these lines. Thus, some scholars have pointed to the fact that forms of collective defence of interests, such as strikes or unofficial work stoppages, declined over time, while individual forms of interest representation rose in relative importance.[52] It is undoubtedly the case that the numbers of workers involved in strikes became smaller and total numbers of strikes overall declined over the decades. While in 1971 there were 48 strikes, and in 1972 there were 39 strikes, there were only 14 in 1981, one in 1983, six in 1972, and none at all in 1984.[53] Analysis of the 'besondere Vorkommnisse' or 'special incident' reports of the FDGB also reveals that the numbers of work conflicts that did not develop into full-blown work-stoppages also declined over this period. One could thus suggest there was a shift from collective interest representation to individual forms of intervention. However, the relationship is a little difficult to disentangle, for several reasons. For one thing, strikes involved relatively few individuals compared to the large numbers writing *Eingaben*, or making complaints that the authorities chose to treat as *Eingaben*, in any given year. Moreover, those doing the striking and those putting forward *Eingaben* may well have come from different quarters of society. Strikers were (almost by definition) predominantly working-class, at least in terms of the occupation in the course of which they chose to down tools in protest. Without a more accurate analysis of the social profile of those millions involved in the *Eingaben* process, it is impossible to generalise; but even a general overview reveals that the writers of letters came from across the full social spectrum, including also retired members of society. Secondly, the relatively steady decline in numbers and scope of strikes over time was not related in any simple way to a rise in overall numbers of individual *Eingaben*, as might be suggested by a notion of displacement of collective protest by individualised complaint. As noted above, the fluctuating numbers of *Eingaben*, and particularly the highs in the early 1960s and late '80s, can be variously interpreted as indicative of either confidence in, or critique of, the system as a whole. Thirdly, it might even be misplaced to see *Eingaben* as purely an individualised form of protest. Although the immediate occasion for a specific request or complaint was in a majority of cases a purely individual matter, on occasion collective (and sometimes also anonymous) *Eingaben* were submitted on the part of a group; and very often the individual cause for complaint was one shared by a very much larger group suffering from the same general shortage, injustice, difficulty, sense of dissatisfaction, or whatever else the occasion prompting the complaint might have been. Complaints were therefore often implicitly predicated on a notion along the lines of 'improve or rectify this situation for me, and you will have improved the GDR as a whole'. Thus even when couched in individual terms, *Eingaben* still related to systemic shortcomings that the complainant hoped might be dealt with for the good of the wider community – a not dissimilar situation to that of workers going on strike for fair wages or better working conditions that might, if successful, be achieved not only for themselves but for the wider comparable working community.

If the thesis of the rising individualism of protest is a little hard to sustain in these terms, however, there is one way in which it may be highly relevant. A constant background refrain of complaint about shortages of consumer goods, spare parts, or adequate housing, was augmented at times of crisis by far more politicised complaints about freedom of movement and freedom of speech. Thus, as indicated, the West was an issue in the early 1960s, following the construction of the Berlin Wall, and again in the changed international context of the 1980s; and the questions of 'restructuring' and open discussion of problems rose to the surface in the era of *perestroika* and *glasnost*. But in contrast to June 1953, when workers downed tools in mass protest, the vast majority of East Germans in the later 1980s sought multiple individual solutions to societal problems. Only tiny numbers participated in the collective protests of the oppositional groups of the 1980s; many thousands voted with their feet, on an essentially individual basis, once the border to the West became more porous in the summer of 1989. The rhetoric of supporting in principle a GDR that was 'still' open to improvement, if only certain failings and shortcomings could be rectified, was rapidly abandoned in favour of a personal dash for freedom and material plenty.

What, then, are we to make of all this? Several features appear to be particularly worthy of note. The sheer honesty and widespread willingness to complain in a state where, on some models, one should be too afraid to want to draw attention to critical views, is a striking feature both of state organised 'discussions' and of *Eingaben*. So too is the choice (or unthinking internalisation) of appropriate rhetoric – the appeals to the official slogans, ideals and language of the state – to highlight the gap between allegedly shared goals and the shortcomings experienced in reality. It may be the case that a proportion of (but by no means all) official responses left a lot to be desired, retreating into absurd arguments to seek to defend the indefensible.[54] But a further feature that is quite remarkable to Western observers, particularly those of a cynical disposition, is the way in which there is often real evidence of genuine attempts to deal appropriately with at least some requests. The degree of sympathy of responses varied dramatically according to both the character of the complaint and the significance of the policy area, however. As far as purely domestic issues are concerned, there is often a startling resonance with the kinds of complaint and request familiar to local politicians in inner-city areas of Western Europe. The tales of domestic strife, overcrowding and desire for re-housing would be on a different scale, but not of a dramatically different nature, from comparable miseries expressed in local councillors' ward surgeries by many of the council tenants in inner-city boroughs in the UK, for example. The sheer ordinariness, if not of the character and extent of the complaints, then at least of the process of complaining or the culture of complaint, is perhaps the most extraordinary feature of this aspect of life in the participatory dictatorship.

Conclusion

Chapter Fourteen

Conclusion: From Nazis to Ossis?

Hitler came to power not quite on a tidal wave of popular enthusiasm – even in March 1933 the NSDAP still did not score an absolute majority – but at least with widespread consent. He was constitutionally appointed Chancellor of a mixed cabinet by the President of the Weimar Republic, Paul von Hindenburg. Whatever the undoubted role of violence in Hitler's rise to power, it was only after his appointment that the structures of democracy were systematically dismantled and replaced by the Nazi dictatorship. Through the peace-time years, and even into the first two years or so of the war, Hitler was able to count on a great deal of genuine, if fluctuating, enthusiasm among certain sections of the population, with his own personal popularity a key ingredient in the character of Nazi rule. The Nazi regime was based on a combination of consent and coercion, charisma and terror. It was only a minority of the population who sought, against horrendous repression, to oppose Nazi rule; and for the millions of victims of the regime, opposition in high places was far too little, and far too late.

The GDR was a very different kind of dictatorship. Imposed from above, and from without, it was certainly not rooted in anything that could be described as either popular enthusiasm or the widespread consent of elites. The population was defeated, demoralised, disorientated; the elites of Nazi Germany were destroyed, and only those left-wing groups who had the backing of the Soviet Military Administration were in any kind of position even to try seriously to take their place. But the GDR, from these artificial beginnings, lasted forty years: long enough to produce new elites, and a very new kind of society.

Why should it be controversial to point out that, by the 1970s, this society included significant numbers of people who were in large measure products of the system, had learnt to play by its rules, and were even committed to many of its ideals (if critical of a lack of realisation in practice)? To point out that there were Nazi supporters in Hitler's Germany does not automatically make a historian an apologist for Nazism; yet to suggest that there was any degree of consensus, as well as coercion, in the GDR seems to be grounds for accusations of being in some way a fellow-traveller or a simple dupe of SED propaganda. It is vital, then, to spell out as clearly as possible the argument developed in this book.

First: the Wall was essential to the viability of the GDR. Without it – as became obvious in 1989–90 – the GDR could not survive as a separate state. In this sense, of course the GDR lacked intrinsic legitimacy. That the GDR had an ever more extensive, frightening and malign apparatus of power and internal repression is also beyond question. To point to a degree of internal consensus is not to pretend that the GDR was a rosy bed of freedom and democracy.

But secondly, and equally importantly: the character of the regime within these outer parameters was very much more complex than is often depicted. The vast majority of East Germans were caught up in a system in which they had to participate; and by virtue of their participation, they were themselves changed. It was thus, in the end, a dictatorship sustained by the actions and interactions of the vast majority of the population. This was a system that was more like a honeycomb full of criss-crossing little cells than a simple homogeneous pot of 'the people' with a repressive lid, the 'regime', clamped down on it to keep the contents from boiling over. It is crucial to understand the changing roles and relationships within this honeycomb, in which there were so very many functionary positions, both official and honorary, and in which, to get anywhere and make anything of one's life, one had to play by the emergent rules. As in every social system, some people were more malleable or ambitious than others, some more willing to adapt, make compromises and commitments, or see things differently than others; and every system has its misfits, its opponents and its casualties. This particular system allowed fewer deviations from its ordained worldview, and was more committed to a vision of what people should believe, how society should develop, than Western democracies; and the penalties for deviance were far greater. But that should not blind us to the extent to which, at the same time, very large numbers of people did not merely 'come to terms with' the system, but were actually in some sense constituted by it, their attitudes informed by it; and by their actions they also sustained, reproduced and changed it. To write this into the history of the GDR is neither easy nor uncontroversial; but in the interests of a comprehensive and hence more adequate picture of this society, it is essential.

To point to wide areas of consensus is not to suggest that all was well with the GDR. The honeycomb structure of the participatory dictatorship allowed those within, and more specifically those who were prepared to use the structures and play by the rules, to make their own lives, with a sense at least of some autonomy; but clamped over it all was, to expand the metaphor and adapt a phrase from Max Weber, effectively a 'steel-hard cage' ('stahlhartes Gehäuse', more often translated as 'iron cage'). In Weber's use, this referred to the system founded on the secularised spirit of modern capitalism, within which, to survive, without ever having been convinced by the early Puritan notion of a vocation, people are nevertheless invisibly 'forced' to abide by the hidden rules or be cast by the wayside as failures. The rules of the communist system were not so invisible, not so hidden from the naked eye; and the system's casualties were far more evident. If anyone hit against the literal or metaphorical margins of the dictatorship, the degrees of freedom within the honeycomb came to an abrupt and often violent end.

It is a false dichotomy to suggest that states are based either on coercion, or on consent, and that to point to areas of the latter is to deny the former. Far greater differentiation is needed if we are to understand the people's paradox. There were varying mixtures at different times, and for different people in different areas of their lives. To speak of the ways in which the vast majority of East Germans felt they could live what they saw as 'perfectly ordinary lives', at least for most of the time, is not to deny the acts of brutality, repression and fear experienced by others. Such repression was perhaps most evident in the early phase of radical social revolution, when very large numbers of Germans experienced the coercive transformation of post-Nazi society into a communist mould as exceedingly brutal, with virtually no regard either for capitalist property rights or for individual human rights more generally. Repression also became more visible in the later 1980s, in no small part as a result of growing and ever more organised popular dissatisfaction: without being able to tackle the root causes, the SED leadership and its 'sword and shield', the Stasi, could only lash out at the symptoms. The economy was in such a state of terminal decline by the mid- to late 1980s that it was evident to increasing numbers of people that the situation was unsustainable in the long term. Rising consciousness of environmental disaster, a deteriorating food supply and growing fears about world peace, combined to produce an atmosphere of escalating unrest, even before Mikhail Gorbachev took over as leader of the Soviet Union and identified precisely the same bundle of problems. It was because of the frustrations building up within this system, ever more visible with the progressive collapse of the economy in the 1980s, that so many were willing to go out on the streets to demonstrate and to demand more dialogue in the changing circumstances of autumn 1989.

People were, in short, never blind to the undoubted and highly obvious problems of the GDR. The restrictions on Western contacts and Western travel, and on freedom of association and expression, were a continued, constant source of deep-rooted discontent, much more among some groups than others. Difficulties with the supply of material goods, facilities and food-stuffs, from cars and telephones to road repairs and fresh fruit, were a constant source of extremely widespread irritation. The housing problem was never adequately solved, despite the best efforts of the government. Undoubtedly the advantages of Western-style affluence and unrestricted travel (for those who could afford it) were appealing.

Yet at the same time, East Germans had become used to a society in which they were assured of childcare places and cheap holidays; of education, training and guaranteed employment; of a degree of comradeship among workplace colleagues, and relaxation in work-based sporting and social activities, on outings and anniversaries. Until these features of everyday life disappeared with unification and the introduction of what was widely denigrated as the capitalist 'elbow society', many Germans – both East and West – had been almost unaware of just how different East German society was from the more individualistic, competitive, personal achievement-oriented society of the Federal Republic. It was these aspects of their past that East Germans, in a situation of rising unemployment and in some areas increasing depopulation, began to hanker after the most. Much may have been seen in a far more positive light of nostalgia than it was experienced at the time; but there was a real basis for this nostalgia.

How then should we re-conceive GDR history? The ruling communist party of East Germany, the Socialist Unity Party (SED), claimed always to rule in the best interests of the people: one of its key slogans was 'everything for the benefit of the people' ('Alles zum Wohle des Volkes!'), with a linguistic allusion to of the customary drinking toast, 'zum Wohl', or 'your health!' Large numbers of East Germans treated this with a hefty degree of cynicism at the time. Yet in the upheavals and uncertainties of the 1990s, 'Ostalgia' (*Ostalgie*), or a degree of nostalgia for an East German past that had irretrievably disappeared, became ever stronger in some quarters, particularly among those groups who were less well placed to benefit from the new freedoms. Fond memories of the 'the good old days' always accompany periods where losses are registered along with rapid changes, however positive some of these may be.

But 'Ostalgia' alone is not a sufficient explanation of the ways in which people did not 'recognise their own pasts' in the history textbooks outlining the structures of power and repression. The paradox of the realities of repressive structures and yet widely prevalent positive memories is in part rooted in the fact that repressive institutions and practices were not all there was to life in the GDR. The history books that have focussed primarily on the institutions and practices of coercion are not necessarily wrong; but they are to some degree incomplete, and are predicated on an over-simplistic model of the ways in which the GDR system worked, and the ways in which it changed over time. In exploring the people's paradox in more detail, we can come to a far more complex and historically adequate picture of life in the GDR, beyond the mere condemnation of dictatorial political structures. Several points seem to me of particular importance in developing a more adequate and nuanced approach.

First, the 'state' and the 'centres of power' were not at all the same thing. The real centres of power encompassed only very few people – a matter of dozens, hundreds at most – whereas the extended 'state' was a far wider phenomenon, in which huge numbers of 'perfectly ordinary' citizens were involved in ways that seemed to them at worst harmless, at best actually helpful and directed towards the common good. Literally millions of people were involved in one way or another with the activities of the state institutions, parties and mass organisations. This huge area of overlap between what are conventionally distinguished as 'state' and 'society', the lack of a clear dividing line in a massive margin of popular involvement, and the sheer extent of participation in the functioning of the structures of power on the ground, make it very difficult for a significant percentage of East Germans to adopt the black-and-white condemnation of the 'evil regime' beloved of theorists of totalitarianism. For this would mean casting themselves in the roles of 'perpetrators' and 'accomplices' and hence condemning themselves.

Nor could most East Germans be happy with allotted roles of passive 'victim' or 'dupe', mere 'object' rather than 'subject' of history. Secondly therefore, and perhaps equally significant, it is important to recognise the fact that 'the people' more generally – and not merely those who participated actively either in the formal structures of power or as dissidents and political opponents – played an active role in shaping their own lives, and taking initiatives to shape their own futures in the circumstances in which they found themselves. To paraphrase Marx: people made their own history, but they made it not in conditions of their own choosing.

A static and ahistorical conception of a somehow 'frozen' society, in which all 'sub-areas' of life were coordinated and controlled from above, has therefore to be rejected out of hand. People did not, by and large, sit for forty years in a state of frightened inner emigration, or find themselves coerced into some form of obedience; nor did those who participated in upholding the structures of power necessarily engage in some form of reprehensible pact with the Devil. A few did, of course: at one end of the spectrum, there were those who never came to terms with the regime, and lived their lives in conscious retreat and withdrawal into alternative lifestyles, or who actively tried to oppose and alter the structures of power; at the other, there were those who came to collude in acts that by virtually any standards have to be seen as inherently immoral, manipulative, deceitful and utterly antipathetic to any notion of human rights. But the vast majority of the population fit neither of these categories, highly important though they are.

Large number of East Germans actively devised strategies for seeking to improve their own personal situations, and for navigating the rules, procedures and constraints of their circumstances. Nor were they afraid to speak up and speak out; most learnt the unwritten rules of what to say where and in what form; many internalised the norms and discourse of the regime, or at least spoke and acted as if they had. People were prepared to argue at public meetings and 'discussions'; to refuse their signatures on declarations of support for one or another development or action of the regime; to use the individual system of letters and complaints to try to obtain better housing or childcare places, scarce goods, or improvements in some area of their lives. And such 'pressures from below' were in part supported and carried upwards by functionaries of the regime, who thus also played at times a genuinely representative role. Popular pressures, whether collective or individual, also, very importantly, had a significant impact on the responses of those in positions of genuine power. So although real power remained concentrated in a few hands at the top, and there were certain issues that were totally beyond negotiation, there still remained large areas in which people's input could make a practical difference to their lives. 'Top-down' accounts thus need to be complemented by accounts that reinsert 'ordinary people' as active participants in making themselves and their own history.

Thirdly, just as 'all that glitters is not gold', so too all that is communist is not intrinsically or inherently 'bad': all that the regime did and was aiming for was not necessarily reprehensible and repressive. It may be the historian's task not to condemn but to try to understand, represent, explain; nevertheless, so much writing on the GDR has been so explicitly either condemnatory or exculpatory that it seems to need pointing out explicitly that, in the GDR as in any society, there was a wide spectrum of aims and practices. A great deal more of what the SED was trying to do was comparatively 'normal', or at least comparable to the aims and policies of Western polities of the time, than some accounts would appear to recognise. It is indeed remarkable just how 'ordinary' many of the wider assumptions and policies – to do with housing, education, health, the status of women, faith in scientific and technological progress – actually appear in comparison with developments in Western capitalist societies in the later twentieth century. And many of the SED's goals were also shared by significant numbers of the population – or, to put it the other way round, the goals of significant numbers of the population were not merely shared and represented by the SED, but there was also a kernel of truth in their paternalistic claim to be trying, however unsuccessfully in the end, to realise these goals in the genuine interests of 'the well-being of the people'.

It has, of course, to be remembered that this 'normality', or relatively wide spectrum of consensus, was played out within a context that was anything other than 'normal': behind the watchtowers and death strip of the Wall, and under the hidden surveillance and malign, manipulative intervention of the Stasi. It was only when citizens hit up against these literal and metaphorical margins that the boundaries of 'normality' became painfully evident. For those active opponents of repression who fought and suffered, and for those who lived in fear or whose lives were deformed by the constraints of the system, the repressive aspects of the regime were terrifyingly obvious; but it is important also to notice just how many people never had occasion to hit against these boundaries, and genuinely felt that they were able to lead 'perfectly ordinary lives'. In this book, it is the history of the latter that I have sought to raise to a greater degree of consciousness than is often the case in accounts focusing on the more central political topics of dictatorship and opposition.

Finally, there are many individual stories that could be told, each of which is in some way a tiny strand in that vast multiplicity of people's lives that, together, constitute the wider story of East German society: stories of love, stories of pain and struggle, stories of happiness and achievement, stories of boredom and gloom. There is a great deal more to social history than can be encompassed in accounts focusing primarily on repressive institutional structures, central policy formation, and the effects of or resistance to politically driven policies. The memories of East Germans are filled with personal experiences, events and activities that – though inevitably shaped and channelled by their political and historical context, as are all individual lives wherever and whenever they are lived – cannot be reduced to these. In addition, wider structural changes, of which contemporaries may have been entirely unaware, in part shaped both peoples' experiences and their perceptions, in turn shaping the kinds of stories that could be told. The character of East German society changed in relation to the changing environment. Lifestyles rooted in particular forms of rural or urban society changed as patterns of settlement and leisure activity changed; cultural currents and social trends affected aspirations and activities. The curious combination of constructive griping, utopian visions and brutal limits altered in balance over time; but while society evolved within the GDR borders, the outer boundaries remained beyond contradiction. This complexity, too, is integral to the people's paradox: that the experience of a degree of freedom, constructive participation in, and facilitation by, the socialist project, was authentically possible at the very same time as the knowledge of outer political constraints.

This complexity, difficult though it is to grasp and express, has to be written into GDR history. It is this multifaceted and complex character of East German social history that helps to explain the paradox of conflicting histories and memories, of undoubtedly repressive structures and genuine nostalgia for lived experiences.

Notes

Chapter 1

1 For overviews of the historiography, see, for example, Mary Fulbrook, *Interpretations of the Two Germanies, 1945–1990*, 2nd edn (Basingstoke: Macmillan, 2000); Corey Ross, *The East German Dictatorship: Problems and Perspectives in the Interpretation of the GDR* (London: Arnold, 2002) and Mary Fulbrook, 'Approaches to German contemporary history since 1945: Politics and paradigms', *Zeithistorische Forschungen* 1, no. 1 (January 2004), pp. 31–50. I have sought here to keep footnote references to historiographical debates to a minimum.

2 For a clear overview, see A. James McAdams, *Judging the Past in Unified Germany* (Cambridge: Cambridge University Press, 2001).

3 Deutscher Bundestag (ed.), *Materialien der Enquete-Kommission 'Überwindung der Folgen der SED-Diktatur im Prozeß der deutschen Einheit'* (Baden-Baden: Nomos-Verlag, 1999).

4 See, for example, Anna Funder, *Stasiland* (London: Granta, 2003); John O. Koehler, *Stasi: The Untold Story of the East German Secret Police* (Boulder, Colo.: Westview Press, 1999); Timothy Garton Ash's ruminations on his own rather tangential brushes with Stasi informers in *The File: A Personal History* (London: HarperCollins, 1997); and Anthony Glees's rather more substantial academic analysis in *The Stasi Files: East Germany's Secret Operations against Britain* (London: Simon & Schuster, 2003).

5 I shall of course be looking at communist policies throughout this book; the point here is that this is not all there is to the domestic history of the GDR. Both those arguing in favour of and those arguing against the concept of totalitarianism focus not merely on regime policies but also on resistance to them, and explore the areas in which regime aims were not achieved. However, such arguments are effectively irrelevant, both as a defence and as a critique of 'totalitarian' theories: the point here is that there is a great deal more to the complexities of people's involvement in the history of the GDR than is captured either by the categories of regime policies on the one hand, and effects or resistances on the other, or by a narrative that is structured only to tell the story in terms of 'the regime acts, the people react'.

6 See, for example, Jeffrey Kopstein, *The Politics of Economic Decline in East Germany, 1945–1989* (Chapel Hill: University of North Carolina Press, 1997).

7 These developments are currently the subject of an AHRC-sponsored collaborative research project based at UCL (University College London). Part of this project includes a comparison with the Third Reich, which – quite apart from other major differences in respect particularly of racist and genocidal ideology and aggressive military aims – was, of course, a far less stable regime, lasting a mere dozen years.

8 For example, the clearly written, well-balanced and highly informative account by Mike Dennis, *The Rise and Fall of the German Democratic Republic, 1945–1990*

(Harlow: Pearson, 2000), explicitly seeks to develop a notion of 'post-totalitarianism' with respect to power structures after the early Stalinist phase of terror and repression was over. Yet in Dennis's overview of GDR history, the people rarely appear as actors: the narrative is of high politics, and of social policies, with very little apparent impetus coming 'from below' with the exception of occasional popular disturbances, as in 1953, or the Leipzig popular riots of 1965. I do not wish here to critique this very useful work, but rather to indicate that it leaves one with a sense of something still missing, of social actors who are for the most part only passively present on the historical stage, unless actively engaged in some act of resistance. Similarly, whether one speaks of 'totalitarianism' or of a 'society drenched through with authority' ('durchherrschte Gesellschaft'), there are certain presuppositions built in about presumed relations between distinct spheres of 'state' and 'society'. See particularly, the classic totalitarian account in Klaus Schroeder, *Der SED-Staat: Partei, Staat und Gesellschaft, 1949–1990* (Munich: Carl Hanser Verlag, 1998); see also Klaus Schroeder, 'Die DDR: eine (spät) totalitäre Gesellschaft', in Manfred Wilke (ed.), *Die Anatomie der Parteizentrale: Die KPD/SED auf dem Weg zur Macht* (Berlin: Akademie Verlag, 1998); and Klaus-Dietmar Henke (ed.), *Totalitarismus* (Dresden: Hannah-Arendt-Institut für Totalitarismusforschung, Berichte und Studien Nr. 18, 1999). For early contrasting approaches, see the path-breaking collection of essays on social history in Hartmut Kaelble, Jürgen Kocka and Hartmut Zwahr (eds), *Sozialgeschichte der DDR* (Stuttgart: Klett-Cotta, 1994).

9 This point may need reiterating, blindingly obvious though it is, since proponents of totalitarianism theory seem to fail to realise that to discuss anything more or other than repression and brutality, opposition and the fight for freedom, is not in some way to pretend that those aspects were not important. Of course they were central. But they do not tell the whole story; and in leaving out the rest, such an approach ultimately distorts rather than clarifies the picture.

10 It should be noted that this is not an either/or matter, as it was sometimes conceived in the debates of the 1960s and '70s.

11 See, for example, Alf Lüdtke, *Eigen-Sinn: Fabrikalltag, Arbeiterfahrungen und Politik vom Kaiserreich bis in den Faschismus* (Hamburg: Ergebnisse Verlag, 1993); and Thomas Lindenberger (ed.), *Herrschaft und Eigen-Sinn in der Diktatur: Studien zur Gesellschaftsgeschichte der DDR* (Cologne: Böhlau Verlag, 1999).

12 The notion of 'congruence of aims', applied by some historians to the relationship between certain elite groups and the Nazi regime particularly in the period 1934–38, is perhaps also, if in very different substantive ways, applicable to the GDR – which, it should be remembered, was not committed to expansionist foreign policies culminating in world war, and racist policies culminating in genocide.

13 See also Jeannette Z. Madarász, *Conflict and Compromise in East Germany, 1971–1989: A Precarious Stability* (Basingstoke: Palgrave Macmillan, 2003).

14 See, for similar issues in relation to the social history of the Soviet Union, Sheila Fitzpatrick, *Everyday Stalinism: Ordinary Life in Extraordinary Times: Soviet Russia in the 1930s* (Oxford: Oxford University Press, 1999).

15 On rhetoric and reality with respect to social mobility in the Third Reich, see David Schoenbaum, *Hitler's Social Revolution: Class and Status in Nazi Germany, 1933–1939* (London: Weidenfeld & Nicolson, 1967): and Ian Kershaw, *The Nazi Dictatorship: Problems and Perspectives of Interpretation*, 4th edn (London: Arnold, 2000), ch. 7.

Chapter 2

1 This is scarcely the place for a catch-all footnote about the Nazi regime, on which there is an enormous literature. But for an entry into discussions of the issues mentioned in this paragraph see, for example, Ian Kershaw, *The 'Hitler Myth': Image and Reality in the Third Reich* (Oxford: Oxford University Press, 1987), and Kershaw, *Popular Opinion and Political Dissent in the Third Reich: Bavaria, 1933–1945* (Oxford: Clarendon Press,

1983); Robert Gellately, *Backing Hitler: Consent and Coercion in Nazi Germany* (Oxford: Oxford University Press, 2001); Eric Johnson, *The Nazi Terror: The Gestapo, Jews and Ordinary Germans* (New York: Basic Books, 1999); Saul Friedländer, *Nazi Germany and the Jews*, vol. 1: *The Years of Persecution, 1933–1939* (London: Weidenfeld & Nicolson, 1997); and Omer Bartov (ed.), *The Holocaust: Origins, Implementation, Aftermath* (London: Routledge, 2000). More generally, see Ian Kershaw, *The Nazi Dictatorship: Problems and Perspectives of Interpretation*, 4th edn (London: Arnold, 2000); as well as Kershaw's outstanding biography, *Hitler 1889–1936: Hubris* (London: Allen Lane, 1998), and *Hitler 1936–1945: Nemesis* (London: Allen Lane, 2000). For an excellent selection and discussion of documents in translation, see Jeremy Noakes and Geoffrey Pridham (eds), *Nazism* (Exeter: University of Exeter Press, 4 vols, 1983–98).

2 The classic study was, of course, David Schoenbaum, *Hitler's Social Revolution: Class and Status in Nazi Germany, 1933–1939* (London: Weidenfeld & Nicolson, 1967). For more recent overviews of these wide-ranging debates, see, for example, Pierre Ayçoberry, *The Social History of the Third Reich, 1933–1945*, tr. Janet Lloyd (New York: New Press, 1999); and David F. Crew (ed.), *Nazism and German Society, 1933–1945* (London: Routledge, 1994).

3 For an extraordinarily vivid personal account, see Victor Klemperer, *Ich will Zeugnis ablegen bis zum letzten: Tagebücher, 1942–1945* (Berlin: Aufbau Verlag, 1999), 2:661 ff.

4 Filip Müller, *Eyewitness Auschwitz: Three Years in the Gas Chambers*, ed. and tr. Susanne Flatauer (Chicago: Ivan R. Dee, published in association with the United States Holocaust Memorial Museum, 1979), p. 171.

5 See also the discussion in Richard Bessel, *Nazism and War* (London: Weidenfeld & Nicolson, 2004), ch. 4.

6 Klemperer, *Ich will Zeugnis ablegen bis zum letzten*, p. 773.

7 Anon., *Eine Frau in Berlin: Tagebuchaufzeichnungen vom 20. April bis 22. Juni 1945* (Frankfurt am Main: Eichborn, 2003), pp. 180–81.

8 On rape, see particularly, Norman M. Naimark, *The Russians in Germany: A History of the Soviet Zone of Occupation, 1945–1949* (Cambridge, Mass.: Harvard University Press, 1995).

9 Brigitte Reimann, *Aber wir schaffen es, verlaß dich drauf! Briefe an eine Freundin im Westen* (Berlin: Elefanten Press, 1995), letter of 10 Oct. 1947, pp. 16–17.

10 Imperial War Museum archive, MISC 141 Item 2193, letter of 18 March 1949, f. 2.

11 Dieter Voll's archive, Pastoralkolleg Neuendettelsau: Gertrud Alexandra Sally Kapp, 'Die ersten Jahre nach dem Krieg, 1945–1947' (manuscript, Nov. 1982), appendix containing original letters, f. 27.

12 Imperial War Museum archive, MISC 141 Item 2193, letter of 18 March 1949, f. 1.

13 The classic eye-witness account of this is Wolfgang Leonhard, *Die Revolution entlässt ihre Kinder* (Cologne: Kiepenheuer & Witsch, 1955).

14 The persistence of racist and anti-communist attitudes among large numbers of East Germans is an area requiring far more extensive and systematic exploration than is possible here.

15 I have written about this in more detail in *German National Identity after the Holocaust* (Cambridge: Polity Press, 1999), in which further references can be found.

16 Manfred Uschner, *Die zweite Etage: Funktionsweise eines Machtapparates*, 2nd edn (Berlin: Dietz Verlag, 1995), p. 29.

17 See, for example, Peter Grieder, *The East German Leadership, 1946–1973: Conflict and Crisis* (Manchester: Manchester University Press, 1999); Gary Bruce, *Resistance with the People: Repression and Resistance in Eastern Germany, 1945–1955* (Lanham, Md: Rowman & Littlefield, 2003); and Mike Dennis, *The Stasi: Myth and Reality* (London: Pearson Longman, 2003).

18 For recent debates on the controversial character and consequences of the June 1953 uprising, see, for example, the highly critical overview by Bernd Eisenfeld, Ilko-Sascha

Kowalczuk and Ehrhart Neubert, *Die verdrängte Revolution: Der Platz des 17. Juni 1953 in der deutschen Geschichte* (Bremen: Edition Temmen, 2004).

19 Statistisches Amt der DDR (ed.), *Statistisches Jahrbuch der DDR '90*, vol. 35 (Berlin: Rudolf Haufe Verlag, 1990), p. 17.

20 Ibid., p. 125.

21 The sections and chapters that follow will trace these social policies through in detail with respect to different groups and classes.

22 Heike Solga, *Auf dem Weg in eine klassenlose Gesellschaft?: Klassenlagen und Mobilität zwischen Generationen in der DDR* (Berlin: Akademie Verlag, 1995).

23 See particularly Monika Kaiser, *Machtwechsel von Ulbricht zu Honecker: Funktionsmechanismen der SED-Diktatur in Konfliktsituationen 1962 bis 1972* (Berlin: Akademie Verlag, 1997).

24 On this period of GDR economic history, see, for example, André Steiner, 'Von "Hauptaufgabe" zu "Hauptaufgabe": Zur Wirtschaftsentwicklung der langen 60er Jahre in der DDR', in Axel Schildt, Detlef Siegfried and Karl Christian Lammers (eds), *Dynamische Zeiten: Die 60er Jahre in den beiden deutschen Gesellschaften* (Hamburg: Hans Christians Verlag, 2000).

25 On Apel, Kaiser (*Machtwechsel*) sets up a plausible case that Apel's death was not actually suicide but possibly murder instigated by the KGB; at this distance, as Kaiser concedes, there is no way of conclusively closing this question.

26 See, for example, Theo Pirker *et al.* (eds), *Der Plan als Befehl und Fiktion: Wirtschaftsführung in der DDR: Gespräche und Analysen* (Opladen: Westdeutscher Verlag, 1995), pp. 64–5.

27 See particularly the insights from a variety of quarters in Pirker *et al.*, *Plan als Befehl und Fiktion*.

28 See Pirker *et al.*, *Plan als Befehl und Fiktion*, pp. 52–4.

29 Manfred Schmidt, 'Grundlagen der Sozialpolitik in der Deutschen Demokratischen Republik', in Bundesministerium für Arbeit und Sozialordnung und Bundesarchiv (eds), *Geschichte der Sozialpolitik in Deutschland seit 1945*, vol. 1: *Grundlagen der Sozialpolitik* (Baden-Baden: Nomos Verlag, 2001), pp. 733–4; Pirker *et al.*, *Plan als Befehl und Fiktion*, pp. 73–5.

30 See, for example, the ZIJ study: SAPMO-BArch, FDJ/5868, Leonhard Kasek, 'Zum Ökologiebewußtsein junger Werktätiger und Studenten' (June 1983), ff. 7–8.

31 See Dorothee Wierling, *Geboren im Jahr Eins: Der Jahrgang 1949 in der DDR: Versuch einer Kollektivbiographie* (Berlin: Chr. Links Verlag, 2002).

32 See particularly, Annette Kaminsky, *Wohlstand, Schönheit, Glück: Kleine Konsumgeschichte der DDR* (Munich: C. H. Beck, 2001).

33 DA 1 13848, 'Stenografisches Protokoll: Sitzung des Ausschusses für Eingaben der Bürger am 15.11.1978', p. 18.

34 ZIJ F84/15, 'Zum Gesundheitsverhalten Leipziger Schüler 7.–10. Klassen', p. 4.

35 Siegfried Grundmann, 'Räumliche Disparitäten in der DDR', in Lothar Mertens (ed.), *Soziale Ungleichheit in der DDR: Zu einem tabuisierten Strukturmerkmal der SED-Diktatur* (Berlin: Duncker & Humblot, 2002), p. 165.

36 DA 1 13848, Stenografisches Protokoll, pp. 23–5.

37 See in particular, Kaminsky, *Wohlstand, Schönheit, Glück*.

38 On the consumer culture of the 1960s see particularly, Ina Merkel, *Utopie und Bedürfnis: Die Geschichte der Konsumkultur in der DDR* (Cologne: Böhlau, 1999).

39 The notion of being 'laid to rest' (*stillgelegt*), which provided the starting point for much theoretical debate in the 1990s, was coined by Sigrid Meuschel.

40 On the relations between East German politics and socio-economic development, see, for example, Mike Dennis, *Social and Economic Modernisation in Eastern Germany: From Honecker to Kohl* (London: Pinter, 1993); Jeffrey Kopstein, *The Politics of Economic Decline in East Germany, 1945–89* (Chapel Hill: University of North Carolina

Press, 1997); and Charles Maier, *Dissolution: The Crisis of Communism and the End of East Germany* (Princeton N.J.: Princeton University Press, 1997).

Chapter 3

1   SAPMO-BArch, DY 30 / vorl. SED 36878, 'Information über Probleme und Aufgaben zur weiteren Stärkung der Staatsmacht in den kreisangehörigen Städten und Gemeinden', 19.4.82, Bl. 4.
2   See further chapter 13, below.
3   According to the memory of a worker interviewed in 1989, quoted in Dagmar Semmelmann, 'Neue Heimat Stalinstadt: Eine Collage aus Interviews', in Evemarie Badstübner (ed.), *Befremdlich anders: Leben in der DDR* (Berlin: Karl Dietz Verlag, 2000), p. 126. Even if Ulbricht did not make exactly such a remark, in exactly these words, it is significant that he is remembered in this way.
4   Anon., 'Ein Programm und sein Maß: Bauen in der DDR', in Hans Modrow (ed.), *Das große Haus von außen* (Berlin: edition ost, 1996).
5   Figures from Statistisches Amt der DDR (ed.), *Statistisches Jahrbuch der DDR '90*, vol. 35 (Berlin: Rudolf Haufe Verlag, 1990), p. 51.
6   See, for example, Wolfgang Engler, *Die Ostdeutschen* (Berlin: Aufbau Verlag, 2002).
7   ZIJ, F74/7, 'Lebensgestaltung junger Ehen'.
8   Lothar Mertens, 'Ungelöstes gesellschaftliches Problem: Ehescheidungen in der DDR', in Lothar Mertens (ed.), *Soziale Ungleichheit in der DDR: Zu einen tabuisierten Strukturmerkmal der SED-Diktatur* (Berlin: Duncker & Humblot, 2002), p. 30.
9   ZIJ, F80/84, 'Jugend der Stadt Dresden', March 1980, p. 21.
10 ZIJ, F84/16, 'Jugend in der Stadt Leipzig (III)', Oct. 1984.
11 *Statistisches Jahrbuch der DDR '90*, p. 51.
12 Siegfried Grundmann, 'Räumliche Disparitäten in der DDR', in Lothar Mertens (ed.), *Soziale Gleichheit in der DDR* (Berlin: Duncker & Humblot, 2002), pp. 179–81.
13 ZIJ, F84/16, 'Jugend in der Stadt Leipzig (III)', Oct. 1984.
14 Mertens, 'Ungelöstes gesellschaftliches Problem', pp. 20–2.
15 SAPMO-BArch, DY 31/563, letter of 14 December 1962, fol. 11.
16 SAPMO-BArch, DY 31/564, letter of 22 April 1980, fols 13–14.
17 SAPMO-BArch, DY 31/602, fols 44–60.
18 Ibid., letter of 16 December 1988, fols 56–7.
19 SAPMO-BArch, DY 31/564, fols 55–61.
20 SAPMO-BArch, DY 31/602, fols 63–76.
21 SAPMO-BArch, DY 31/602, fols 14–24.
22 SAPMO-BArch, DY 34/25414, 'Information über vorliegende besondere Vorkommnisse im Jahr 1984' (July 1985), p. 2.
23 Ibid., Anlage 6.
24 Andreas Ludwig, 'Kurze Geschichte Eisenhüttenstadts', in Stadtverwaltung Eisenhütt-enstadt (ed.), *Eisenhüttenstadt: Architektur – Skulptur, Stadtbilder* (Eisenhüttenstadt: Fürstenberger Druck and Verlag GmbH, 1998), p. 7.
25 Ibid., pp. 9, 11.
26 See Semmelmann, 'Neue Heimat Stalinstadt', pp. 117–41. Semmelmann carried out interviews with more than sixty 'founding residents' of Eisenhüttenstadt – people who had settled there in the early 1950s – under the auspices of an oral history project based in the GDR Akademie der Wissenschaften, which she then continued on her own initia-tive after the collapse of the GDR and the winding up of this institute. She claims that the narratives uttered in 1989 remained valid even after the end of the GDR; the published snippets from her interviews, with a fairly wide range of sentiments expressed, certainly provide interesting insights into the way in which this first socialist new town was perceived, remembered and represented in the late GDR. I also carried out some interviews with residents of Eisenhüttenstadt aged between fifty and seventy-five in July

2004, and was surprised by the similarity of the sentiments expressed, which were, if anything, even more positive than those of Semmelmann's interviewees – perhaps a consequence of a further decade or so of experience of unified Germany.

27 See particularly the interviews in Semmelmann, 'Neue Heimat Stalinstadt', pp. 134–41.
28 Fulbrook interviews with residents, July 2004.
29 Günter Fromm, 'Eisenhüttenstadt, sein Störsender und die verbotenen Antennen' in Badstübner (ed.), *Befremdlich anders*, pp. 219–32.
30 On Hoyerswerda, see particularly, Joachim Palutzki, *Architektur in der DDR* (Berlin: Dietrich Reimer Verlag, 2000), pp. 148–61.
31 On Paulick, see *Wer war wer in der DDR*, p. 647.
32 See Rita Aldenhoff-Hübinger, 'Die Ausstrahlung der "Halbleiterpflaume": Folgen einer Betriebsgründung in Frankfurt/Oder', in Andreas Ludwig (ed.), *Fortschritt, Norm und Eigensinn: Erkundungen im Alltag der DDR* (Berlin: Chr. Links Verlag, 1999).
33 Fulbrook interviews with residents, July 2004.
34 *Statistisches Jahrbuch der DDR '90*, p. 8.
35 See, for example, the discussion of figures in Alexander von Plato and Almut Leh, *'Ein unglaublicher Frühling': Erfahrene Geschichte im Nachkriegsdeutschland, 1945–1948* (Bonn: Bundeszentrale für politische Bildung, 1997), chapter 1.
36 See particularly Grundmann, 'Räumliche Disparitäten'.
37 Wendelin Strubelt, 'Regionale Disparitäten zwischen Wandel und Persistenz', in Wendelin Strubelt *et al.* (eds), *Städte und Regionen: Räumliche Folgen des Transformationsprozesses* (Opladen: Leske & Budrich, 1996), p. 17.
38 See, for example, Maiken Umbach (ed.), *German Federalism: Past, Present, Future* (Basingstoke: Palgrave, 2002).

Chapter 4

1 Authors' collective under the leadership of Peter Voß (ed.), *Die Freizeit der Jugend* (Berlin: Dietz Verlag, 1981), p. 14.
2 See, for example, the book providing helpful tips and advice for young people: Authors' collective under the leadership of Peter Voß (ed.), *Freie Zeit: Was nun?* (Berlin: Dietz Verlag, 1986).
3 SAPMO-BArch, DY 30/IV A 2/16/123, ZK der SED, Abt. Jugend, collection of essays under the title 'Wie wünsche ich mir meine Eltern?'
4 The issue of generations in the GDR requires more extensive treatment than is possible here.
5 Zentralinstitut für Jugendforschung (ed.), 'Jugend und Freizeit', 1968, manuscript produced in Berlin as a confidential report for the Amt für Jugendfragen beim Ministerrat der Deutschen Demokratischen Republik, p. 36. Although a former member of the ZIJ has recently cast some doubt on the methodological validity of the ZIJ research on free time (oral comment at a conference in Magdeburg, 17–18 June 2004), the findings seem entirely consistent with a wide range of other evidence.
6 Ibid., p. 39.
7 Ibid., p. 40.
8 See figures and discussion in ibid., pp. 52–63.
9 ZIJ, F71/18, 1971, p. 22.
10 ZIJ, F71/18, 1971, p. 25.
11 The '10 Gebote' are reprinted in Klaus Schroeder, *Der SED-Staat: Partei, Staat und Gesellschaft, 1949–1990* (Munich: Carl Hanser Verlag, 1998), pp. 671–2; Walter Ulbricht's comment about teachers' clothing is in SAPMO-BArch, DY 30/IV 2/2.111/8, 'Stenografische Niederschrift der gemeinsamen Sitzung der Jugendkommission beim Politbüro des ZK und der Regierungskommission für die Ausarbeitung des Jugendgesetzes im Plenarsaal des Hauses des Zentralkomitees am Freitag, den 29. März 1963', f. 55.

12 See further chapter 6, below.

13 Quotations from SAPMO-BArch DY 30/IV A 2/16/123, 'Abschrift eines Fernschreibens der Bezirksleitung Potsdam an Abteilung Parteiorgane vom 21. September 1967 (eingegangen in der Kulturabteilung am 22.9.1967)', p. 1. The peremptory haircut was perpetrated on a FDJ member who was on an official FDJ delegation to Rostock in 1967 when he was caught by surprise, arrested and exposed to what he saw as Nazi-style brutality, made to stand against a wall in a police cell for forty-five minutes, and had his head banged against the wall if he complained; incident recounted in Michael Rauhut, *Beat in der Grauzone: DDR-Rock 1964 bis 1972. Politik und Alltag* (Berlin: Basis Druck, 1993), pp. 171–2.

14 ZIJ, F79/25, 'Forschungsbericht über das Verhältnis Jugendlicher zur Mode sowie über Bedingungen und Ausprägung modebezogene Verhaltensweisen', Nov. 1979, p. 4.

15 Ibid., p. 8.

16 ZIJ, F84/16, 'Jugend in der Stadt Leipzig (III)', Oct. 1984, p. 8.

17 Autorenkollektiv unter der Leitung von Kurt Krambach (ed.), *Wie lebt man auf dem Dorf? Soziologische Aspekte der Entwicklung des Dorfes in der DDR* (Berlin: Dietz Verlag, 1985); on youth and leisure in particular, pp. 141–7.

18 BArch Bibliothek, FDJ/6058, H. Süße, 'Zur Entwicklung der Landjugend in der DDR', Nov. 1979, ff. 21–3, f. 24.

19 BArch Bibliothek, FDJ/6059, Werner Holzweissig, 'Jugendliche Arbeitspendler und ihre Freizeit', May 1980, pp. 3, 13–14.

20 BArch, DY 30/vorl. SED 36878, Abt. Staats und Rechtsfragen, 'Information über Probleme und Aufgaben zur weiteren Stärkung der Staatsmacht in den kreisangehörigen Städten und Gemeinden', 19 April 1982, Anlage 1, 'Abschrift einer Eingabe an die Volkskammer der DDR von G. A., 2081 Leussow, von 11/2/82', ff. 1–2.

21 See, for example, the autobiographical account in Günter de Bruyn, *Vierzig Jahre: Ein Lebensbericht* (Frankfurt am Main: Fischer Taschenbuch Verlag, 1998), and novels by Günter de Bruyn, Christoph Hein, Christa Wolf and others.

22 Brigitte Reimann and Christa Wolf, *Sei gegrüßt und lebe: Eine Freundschaft in Briefen, 1964–1973* (Berlin: Aufbau Verlag, 1993), letter of 13 March 1969, p. 36.

23 Christa Wolf's letter of 23 February 1969, in ibid.

24 See particularly Esther von Richthofen's rather surprising findings on the relative lack of SED members among cultural functionaries in the 1970s: Esther von Richthofen, UCL 2005 PhD thesis on 'Bringing Culture to the Masses' in Bezirk Brandenburg (part of the wider AHRC-sponsored project on the 'normalisation of rule').

25 ZIJ F84/27, 'Leipzig – Grünau im Bild – Fotomappe zum Bericht Freizeitgestaltung der Jugend unter den Bedingungen einer sozialistischen Großstadt'. See also ZIJ F84/23 for the accompanying hundred-page report on youth and leisure in this new housing estate area.

26 Figures on theatres from Dieter Voigt, Werner Voss and Sabine Meck, *Sozialstruktur der DDR* (Darmstadt: Wissenschaftliche Buchgesellschaft, 1987), p. 234. On culture and the intelligentsia, see also chapter 12, below.

27 SAPMO-BArch, DY/30 IV A2/2.024/30, 'Information über den Stand und die Entwicklung der Besucherzahlen in Theatern, Filmtheatern und der Fernsehanmeldungen in den Länder des RGW', f. 6.

28 Ibid., f. 8.

29 Figures quoted in Uta Poiger, *Jazz, Rock, and Rebels: Cold War Politics and American Culture in a Divided Germany* (Berkeley, Calif.: University of California Press, 2000), p. 85.

30 BArch Bibliothek, FDJ/5997, Dieter Wiedemann, 'Forschungsbericht zur Studie: "Kino DDR 82 – Zur Rezeption des Films *Märkische Forschungen*" ', Leipzig, Aug. 1982, f. 2.

31 Ibid., ff. 2, 15.

32 See, for example, Joshua Feinstein, *The Triumph of the Ordinary: Depictions of Daily Life*

in the East German Cinema, 1949–1989 (Chapel Hill: University of North Carolina Press, 2002); and Manfred Krug, *Abgehauen* (Düsseldorf: Econ Taschenbuch Verlag, 1998).

33 On popular reactions to, and indeed almost faith in, *PRISMA* as a channel for consumer opinion, see Ina Merkel, ' "… in Hoyerswerda leben jedenfalls keine so kleinen viereckigen Menschen": Briefe an das Fernsehen der DDR', in Alf Lüdtke and Peter Becker (eds), *Akten, Eingaben, Schaufenster: Die DDR und ihre Texten* (Berlin: Akademie Verlag, 1997); and Ina Merkel (ed.), *'Wir sind doch nicht die Meckerecke der Nation': Briefe an das DDR-Fernsehen* (Cologne: Böhlau Verlag, 1998).

34 Examples taken from *Das Magazin*, Sept. 1961, Oct. 1962, Nov. 1968, Dec. 1975 and Aug. 1978. See also, more generally, Simone Barck, Martina Langermann, Siegfried Lokatis (eds), *Zwischen 'Mosaik' und 'Einheit': Zeitschriften in der DDR* (Berlin: Chr. Links Verlag, 1999).

35 SAPMO-BArch, DY 30/IV 2/17 9, fol. 82.

36 SAPMO-BArch, DY/34 10262, 'Eingabenanalyse des Jahres 1974', 10 February 1975.

37 See, for example, SAPMO-BArch DY 34/12668, letter of 23 January 1983.

38 SAPMO-BArch, DY 34/12668, letter of 12 March 1986.

39 SAPMO-BArch, DY/34 14617, response to letter from Herr Reinhard G. of 1 July 1989.

40 SAPMO-BArch, DY 34/12668, letter of 16 March 1982.

41 SAPMO-BArch, DY 34/12668, letter of 3 June 1983.

42 SAPMO-BArch, DY 34/11032, letter of 28 April 1978.

43 SAPMO-BArch, DY 34/12668, letter of 26 January 1982.

44 SAPMO-BArch, DY 34/12668, letter of 25 May 1982.

45 SAPMO-BArch, DY 30/IV A 2/16/123, 'Information über Urlaubsreisen ausgewählter Bevölkerungsgruppen 1966'.

46 Günter Manz, *Armut in der 'DDR'-Bevölkerung: Lebensstandard und Konsumtionsniveau vor und nach der Wende* (Augsburg: Maro Verlag, 1992), p. 56.

47 Voigt, Voβ and Meck, *Sozialstruktur*, p. 235.

48 Manz, *Armut*, pp. 56–7.

49 BArch DY/12668, letter of 16 March 1982.

50 See, for example, Grit Hartmann, *Goldkinder: Die DDR im Spiegel ihres Spitzensports* (Leipzig: Forum Verlag, 1997).

51 Statistisches Amt der DDR (ed.), *Statistisches Jahrbuch der DDR '90*, vol. 35 (Berlin: Rudolf Haufe Verlag, 1990), p. 335.

52 Voigt, Voss and Meck, *Sozialstruktur*, p. 234.

53 See the rich material on this question in Daniel Wilton's UCL 2005 PhD thesis, 'Regime versus People? Public opinion and the Development of Sport and Popular Music in the GDR, 1961–1989'.

54 SAPMO-BArch, DY/34 25471, 'Einschätzung des gemeinsamen Sportprogramms des DTSB der DDR, des FDGB und der FDJ', 15 May 1981, p. 2.

55 Ibid., p. 3.

56 SAPMO-BArch, DY/34 25471, 'Information über die Entwicklung der FDGB-Pokalwettbewerbe mit massensportlichem Charakter 1980', p. 3.

57 BArch Bibliothek, FDJ/5803, Wolfgang Netzker, 'Bereit und fähig zur Verteidigung des Sozialismus. GST-Mitglieder', Leipzig, July 1986, f. 66.

58 Ibid., ff. 15, 39.

59 SAPMO-BArch, DY 30/IV 2/19/20, 'Der Stand der Vorbereitungen auf die Olympischen Sommerspiele 1964 und Massnahmen zur weiteren Entwicklung der Leistungen in den olympischen Sportarten', Vorlage an das Sekretariat des ZK der SED, 28 November 1962, fol. 8.

60 SAPMO-BArch, DY 30/IV 2/2.106/20, 'Kurzinformation über Stimmungen und Meinungen der Bürger zu aktuell-politischen Ereignissen', 31 August 1972.

61 Ibid., 'Kurzinformation' of 6 September 1972, fol. 4.

62 Cf. also Norman Naimark, *The Russsians in Germany: A History of the Soviet Zone of Occupation, 1945–1949* (Cambridge, Mass.: Harvard University Press, 1995); and David Pike, *The Politics of Culture in Soviet-Occupied Germany, 1945–1949* (Stanford: Stanford University Press, 1992).

63 See *Handbuch der gesellschaftlichen Organisationen in der DDR. Massenorganisationen, Verbände, Vereinigungen, Gesellschaften, Genossenschaften, Komitees, Ligen* (Berlin: Staatsverlag der Deutschen Demokratischen Republik, 1985); and Rüdiger Henkel, *Im Dienste der Staatspartei: Über Parteien und Organisationen der DDR* (Baden-Baden: Nomos Verlag, 1994).

64 Wilhelm Bleek, 'Kleingärtner, Kleintierzüchter und Imker' in Dieter Voigt and Lothar Mertens (eds), *Minderheiten in und Übersiedler aus der DDR* (Berlin: Duncker & Humblot, 1992), pp. 67, 71, 82.

65 I have discussed this at greater length in Mary Fulbrook, *Anatomy of a Dictatorship: Inside the GDR, 1949–1989* (Oxford: Oxford University Press, 1995).

66 See further the discussion in chapter 7, below.

67 SAPMO-BArch, DY IV 2/17/89, 'Bericht über die Arbeit des DFD seit der Veröffentlichung des Kommuniqués des Politbüros "Die Frau – der Frieden und der Sozialismus" ', Anhang 12 April 1962, f. 250.

68 Ibid., f. 245.

69 Ibid.

70 SAPMO-BArch, DY IV 2/17/89, DFD Bundesvorstand, 'Einschätzung der Arbeit des Demokratischen Frauenbundes Deutschlands', 7 December 1962, f. 257.

71 See further chapter 6 on youth, below.

72 As Klaus Schroeder puts it, the mass organisations 'fulfilled ... the task of a comprehensive control of the population': *Der SED-Staat*, p. 416.

73 According to Schroeder, 'because they could not evade the pressure for conformity' ('weil sie dem Konformitätsdruck nicht ausweichen konnten'): ibid., p. 417.

74 See the discussion in Dan Wilton, "Regime versus people?"; also Esther von Richthofen, UCL PhD thesis.

75 On the notion of a niche society, see particularly Günter Gaus, *Wo Deutschland liegt* (Munich: Deutscher Taschenbuch Verlag, 1986).

Chapter 5

1 Annette Kaminsky, *Wohlstand, Schönheit, Glück: Kleine Konsumgeschichte der DDR* (Munich: C. H. Beck, 2001), p. 18.

2 Brigitte Reimann, *Aber wir schaffen es, verlaß dich drauf! Briefe an eine Freundin im Westen* (Berlin: Elefanten Press, 1995), pp. 7–8, 10–11.

3 See, for example, SAPMO-BArch, FDGB DY 34/20624, protocol of a discussion on 7 September 1949, involving a catalogue of complaints by a worker protesting against conditions in the Wismut mines, p. 4.

4 See, for example, Robin Ostow, *Jews in Contemporary East Germany: The Children of Moses in the Land of Marx* (Basingstoke: Macmillan, 1989), pp. 2–3.

5 Gunnar Winkler (ed.), *Geschichte der Sozialpolitik der DDR, 1945–1985* (Berlin: Akademie Verlag, 1989), p. 60.

6 Annette Timm, 'Guarding the Health of Worker Families in the GDR', in Peter Hübner and Klaus Tenfelde (eds), *Arbeiter in der SBZ-DDR* (Essen: Klartext, 1999), p. 485; see also Norman M. Naimark, *The Russians in Germany: A History of the Soviet Zone of Occupation, 1945–1949* (Cambridge, Mass.: Harvard University Press, 1995), ch. 2.

7 Statistisches Amt der DDR (ed.), *Statistisches Jahrbuch der DDR*, vol. 1 (Berlin: VEB Deutscher Zentralverlag, 1955), p. 8.

8 Donna Harsch, 'Society, the State and Abortion in East Germany, 1950–1972', *American Historical Review* 102, no. 1 (February 1997), pp. 53–84.

9 Ibid., p. 61.

10 On the denazification of the medical profession, see further chapter 9 below.

11 Timm, 'Guarding the health'.

12 P. C. Ludz (ed.), *DDR-Handbuch*, 2nd edn (Cologne: Verlag Wissenschaft und Politik, 1979), pp. 474–85.

13 *Statistisches Jahrbuch 1990 für die Bundesrepublik Deutschland* (Stuttgart: Metzler-Poeschel, 1990), Anlage: Deutsche Demokratische Republik und Berlin (Ost), p. 662.

14 Ibid.

15 Ludz, *DDR-Handbuch, loc. cit.*

16 See, for example, the pamphlets targeted at Western visitors; see also the rosy report by a British academic who was subsequently revealed as a Stasi informer and communist fellow-traveller, Gwynne Edwards, *GDR Society and Social Institutions* (London: Macmillan, 1985), parts of which have the unmistakable whiff of a thinly disguised digest of GDR propaganda.

17 Christian Münter, 'Das Gesundheitswesen der DDR: Ein großes Konzept, das jedoch nicht aufging', in Hans Modrow (ed.), *Das große Haus: Insiderberichten aus dem ZK der SED* (Berlin: edition ost, 1994).

18 Bundesarchiv, DQ1 10731, 'Niederschrift über eine Beratung im Kreiskrankenhaus Pasewalk am 18.4.1974', Bl. 7.

19 Linde Wagner, 'Polikliniken – ein gesundheitspolitisches Modell', in Stefan Bollinger and Fritz Vilmar (eds), *Die DDR war anders: Eine kritische Würdigung ihrer sozialkulturellen Einrichtungen* (Berlin: edition ost, 2002), p. 226.

20 Ibid., p. 231.

21 See Bernhard Meyer, 'Gesundheitspolitik', in Andreas Herbst, Gerd-Rüdiger Stephan and Jürgen Winkler (eds), *Die SED: Geschichte – Organisation – Politik: Ein Handbuch* (Berlin: Dietz Verlag, 1997).

22 Bundesarchiv, DQ1 10425, Ministerium für Gesundheitswesen, 'Information über den im Jahre 1979 erreichten Stand der medizinischen und sozialen Betreuung der VdN-Kameraden', p. 1.

23 Maxie Wander, *Tagebücher und Briefe* (Berlin and Weimar: Aufbau Verlag, 1990), p. 33.

24 Brigitte Reimann and Christa Wolf, *Sei gegrüßt und lebe: Eine Freundschaft in Briefen, 1964–1973* (Berlin: Aufbau Verlag, 1993).

25 SAPMO-BArch, DY 30/IV 2/17 9, Bl. 78.

26 Bundesarchiv, DQ1 11623, 'Säuglingssterblichkeit'.

27 See also chapter 7 below.

28 Timm, 'Guarding the health', p. 493.

29 Bundesarchiv, DQ1 11623, 'Information über Schwerpunktprobleme auf dem Gebiet der Krippen und Heime (insbesondere Entwicklung des Netzes der Krippen und Heime, Leitungstätigkeit, Aus- und Weiterbildung der Mitarbeiter und leitenden Kader, Erhöhung der Qualität der Arbeit) mit Schlussfolgerungen zur Durchsetzung des Beschlusses des Präsidiums des Ministerrates vom 22.3.1979 "… über den gegenwärtigen Versorgungsgrad mit Krippenplätzen und sich daraus ergebende Aufgaben" ' (n.d.).

30 See, for example, Bundesarchiv, DQ1 10790, 'Einschätzung der Wirksamkeit finanzieller Zuwendungen an schwerstgeschädigte Bürger sowie an Familien mit einem geschädigten Kind', 16 December 1980, p. 1.

31 Klaus-Peter Schwitzer, 'Behinderte in der DDR', in Dieter Voigt and Lothar Mertens (eds), *Minderheiten in und Übersiedler aus der DDR* (Berlin: Duncker & Humblot, 1992).

32 Sabine Gries, ' "Sie haben doch gesunde Kinder, da stört das Behinderte nur": Vom wissenschaftlichen und staatlichen Umgang mit behinderten Kindern in der DDR', in Lothar Mertens and Dieter Voigt (eds), *Humanistischer Sozialismus? Der Umgang der SED mit der Bevolkerung, dargestellt an ausgewählten Gruppen* (Münster: Lit Verlag, 1995).

33 Ibid.

34 Schwitzer, 'Behinderte in der DDR', pp. 134–5.

35 See, for example, Bundesarchiv, DQ1 10789, 'Einschätzung der Zusammenarbeit mit der Volkssolidarität', 16 December 1980.

36 Bundesarchiv, DA1 7541, 'Stenografisches Protokoll. Beratung des Auschusses für Eingaben der Bürger der Volkskammer am 11.3.1971 im Hause der Volkskammer zu Berlin', p. 8.

37 Bundesarchiv, DQ1 11613, 'Bericht zum Sterben in den Einrichtungen des Gesundheitswesens und zum Leichenwesen', 11 February 1982.

38 Ibid., Bl. 2–3.

39 Ibid., Bl. 6.

40 ZIJ F84/15, 'Zum Gesundheitsverhalten Leipziger Schüler 7.–10. Klassen', p. 5.

41 Young-sun Hong, 'Cigarette Butts and the Building of Socialism in East Germany', *Central European History* 35, no. 3 (2002): 327–344, p. 334.

42 For details of these quite vociferous debates, see ibid., *passim*.

43 For the following details and figures on smoking in the UK, see Virginia Berridge, 'Postwar Smoking Policy in the UK and the Redefinition of Public Health', *Twentieth-century British History* 14, no. 1 (2003): 61–82, pp. 62–3.

44 ZIJ F84/15, 'Zum Gesundheitsverhalten Leipziger Schüler 7.–10. Klassen', p. 6.

45 According to a 1982 study ('Diss B') by Günter Heichel of the Martin-Luther-Universität Halle-Wittenberg, cited by Lothar Mertens, ' "Sozialistische Lebensweise" bei Schülern? Gesundheitsverhalten und -wissen von Kindern in der DDR', in Mertens and Voigt, *Humanistischer Sozialismus*, p. 198.

46 Ibid., pp. 201–5.

47 Deutsches Institut für Wirtschaftsforschung Berlin (ed.), *Handbuch DDR-Wirtschaft*, 4th edn (Hamburg: Rowohlt, 1984), p. 285.

48 Wissenschaftlicher Beirat für Kriminalitätsforschung beim General-Staatsanwalt der DDR, 'Probleme der Bekämpfung der Alkoholkriminalität und des Alkohol-mißbrauchs' (1967), Sekretariat des Leiters, Büro Ministerrat, Bundesarchiv, DQ 00163.

49 Ibid., p. 2.

50 Ibid., p. 4.

51 Ibid., p. 9.

52 Ibid., p. 7.

53 See, for example, SAPMO-BArch, FDGB reports, 15/1470/6447, 'Schriftwechsel über besondere Vorkommnisse (AK) der Bezirksvorstände des FDGB (1961)', reports of 13 December 1960, 23 November 1961, 15 November 1961, 11 November 1961; and FDGB 3023, AK(S), 25 September 1964.

54 See, for example, FDGB 3023, AK(S), reports of 20 July 1967 and 27 February 1969.

55 FDGB 3023, AK(S), report of 29 July 1969, where the work stoppage was in protest at being sold beer bottles in ten-packs rather than twelve-packs.

56 Landolf Scherzer, *Der Erste: Eine Reportage aus der DDR* (Cologne: Kiepenheuer & Witsch, 1989), p. 162.

57 Bundesarchiv, DQ1 12952, Ministerium für Jugend, Familie, Frauen und Gesundheit, Abteilung Recht.

58 SAPMO-BArch, DY 31/564, f. 55.

59 This paragraph is largely based on Matthias Zeng, *'Asoziale' in der DDR* (Münster: Lit Verlag, 2000); the figure of 12 per cent is given on p. 76.

60 ZIJ F84/15, 'Zum Gesundheitsverhalten Leipziger Schüler 7.–10. Klassen', p. 10.

61 Ibid., p. 14.

62 ZIJ F84/48, 'Zum Gesundheitsverhalten Leipziger Schüler 7.–10. Klassen'.

63 Emile Durkheim, *Suicide* (London: Routledge, 2002).

64 See, for example, Bundesarchiv, DQ1 11617, which contains a letter from Mecklinger dissuading someone from doing a *Habilitation* or second (post-doctoral) dissertation ('Diss. B') on the topic of suicide. Cf. also Bundesarchiv, DQ1 12952, Ministerium für Jugend, Familie, Frauen und Gesundheit, Abteilung Recht, where the section under the

heading 'Sterbehilfe und Suizid' – 'assisted death' (a euphemism for 'euthanasia') and suicide – is empty, suggesting that at some point the documents relating to these questions were removed from the file.

65 Dieter Voigt, Werner Voss and Sabine Meck, *Sozialstruktur der DDR* (Darmstadt: Wissenschaftliche Buchgesellschaft, 1987), p. 233.

66 Udo Grashoff and Christian Goeschel, 'Der Umgang mit Selbstmorden in den beiden deutschen Diktaturen', in Günther Heydemann and Heinrich Oberreuter (eds), *Diktaturen in Deutschland: Strukturen, Institutionen und Verhaltensweisen im Vergleich* (Bonn: Bundeszentrale für politische Bildung, 2003), pp. 476–503.

67 Edeltraud Schulze (ed.), *DDR-Jugend: Ein statistisches Handbuch* (Berlin: Akademie Verlag, 1995), pp. 76–7.

68 SAPMO-BArch, FDGB Bundesvorstand, 5414, 'Bericht der Einsatzgruppe des Bundesvorstandes des FDGB zum Explosionsgeschehen am 11. Juli 1968 im PVC-Betrieb des VE Elektrochemischen Kombinates Bitterfeld', 8/8/1968'.

69 Cf. Münter, 'Das Gesundheitswesen', p. 231.

70 Bundesarchiv, DQ1 11763, 'Information über die arbeitshygienischen Sanierungsschwerpunkte der Volkswirtschaft', 1984.

71 Ibid., Mecklinger's letter, no pagination.

72 Ibid., letter of 25 July 1985. The urgency and unambiguity of the quotation are hard to render well in English: 'zu Schwerpunkten in der Volkswirtschaft, die für eine nicht geringe Anzahl von Werktätigen gleichbedeutend mit einer unmittelbaren schwerwiegenden gesundheitlichen Schädigung sind.'

73 Bundesarchiv, DA 1/13848, 'Zusammenfassender Bericht über den Einsatz von zwei Arbeitsgruppen des Volkskammerausschusses für Eingaben der Bürger vom 10.–12.10.1978 im Kreis Döbeln', p. 43.

74 Hans Günter Hockerts, in Hartmut Kaelble, Jürgen Kocka and Hartmut Zwahr (eds), *Sozialgeschichte der DDR* (Stuttgart: Klett-Cotta, 1994), p. 540, n. 36.

75 On environmentalist movements in the GDR, see, for example, Mary Fulbrook, *Anatomy of a Dictatorship* (Oxford: Oxford University Press, 1995), ch. 8.

76 Bundesarchiv, DQ1 11638, 'Beschluß zum Stand des Umweltschutzes auf bestimmten Gebieten', 25 January 1982, quotation p. 16.

77 Bundesarchiv, DQ1 11638.

Chapter 6

1 Herausgeberkollektiv (eds), *Wörterbuch zur sozialistischen Jugendpolitik* (Berlin: Dietz Verlag, 1975), p. 249.

2 Ibid., pp. 249–50.

3 The institutional developments and particularly the early decades of the GDR have been very well served in these respects. See, for example, Ulrich Mählert and Gerd-Rüdiger Stephan, *Blaue Hemden, rote Fahnen: Die Geschichte der Freien Deutschen Jugend* (Opladen: Leske & Budrich, 1996); Peter Skyba, *Vom Hoffnungsträger zum Sicherheitsrisiko: Jugend in der DDR und Jugendpolitik der SED, 1949–1961* (Cologne: Böhlau, 2000); Marc-Dietrich Ohse, *Jugend nach dem Mauerbau: Anpassung, Protest und Eigensinn (DDR 1961–1974)* (Berlin: Chr. Links Verlag, 2003); and Alan McDougall, *Young East Germans and the Free German Youth (FDJ) during the Ulbricht Era, 1952–68* (Oxford: Oxford University Press, 2004).

4 Cf. the brief sketch in Klaus Schroeder, *Der SED-Staat: Partei, Staat und Gesellschaft, 1949–1990* (Munich: Carl Hanser Verlag, 1998), pp. 585–6.

5 Herausgeberkollektiv, *Wörterbuch zur sozialistischen Jugendpolitik*, p. 250.

6 'Gesetz über das einheitliche sozialistische Bildungssystem', in Kanzlei des Staatsrates der Deutschen Demokratischen Republik (ed.), *Unser Bildungssystem – wichtiger Schritt auf dem Wege zur gebildeten Nation. Materialien der 12. Sitzung der Volkskammer der DDR und das Gesetz über das einheitliche sozialistische Bildungssystem* (Berlin: Staatsverlag der DDR, 1965), p. 87.

7   Alexander Abusch, 'Unser Bildungssystem entspricht der nationalen Mission der Deutschen Demokratischen Republik', in Kanzlei des Staatsrates der Deutschen Demokratschen Republik, *Unser Bildungssystem,* p. 29.

8   Lothar Mertens, 'Ungelöstes gesellschaftliches Problem. Ehescheidungen in der DDR', in Lothar Mertens (ed.), *Soziale Ungleichheit in der DDR: Zu einem tabuisierten Struk-turmerkmal der SED-Diktatur* (Berlin: Duncker & Humblot, 2002), pp. 22–3, 12–13.

9   Ibid., p. 21.

10 Hans-Joachim Maaz, *Behind the Wall: The Inner Life of Communist Germany* (New York and London: W.W. Norton, 1995), p. 28.

11 Dorothee Wierling, *Geboren im Jahr Eins: Der Jahrgang 1949 in der DDR: Versuch einer Kollektivbiographie* (Berlin: Chr. Links Verlag, 2002), pp. 329–34.

12 See, for example, Jörn Mothes *et al.* (eds), *Beschädigte Seelen: DDR-Jugend und Staatssicherheit* (Rostock: Edition Temmen, 1996); and Klaus Behnke and Jürgen Wolf (eds), *Stasi auf dem Schulhof: Der Missbrauch von Kinder* (Berlin: Ullstein, 1998).

13 See, for example, BArch, DY 34/25404 for (not actually very informative) information and planning reports on various *Messe der Meister von Morgen* in the 1980s.

14 See, for example, the ongoing research by Emmanuel Droit: paper delivered at a conference of the Centre Marc Bloch, Berlin, March 2005.

15 SAPMO-BArch, DY 30/IV 2/9.05/103, 'Bericht aus dem Kreis Salzwedel', f. 177.

16 See, for example, the various documents in SAPMO-BArch, DQ1 10731; the quotation is from the speech delivered to *Jugendweihe* recipients at the Nikolai-Ostrowski Oberschule in Berlin in 1974, p. 9.

17 SAPMO-BArch, DY 30/IV 2/9.05/105, 'Zusammenfassung der Bezirksberichte (Woche vom 29.1. bis 3.2.62)', ff. 110, 115.

18 SAPMO-BArch, DY 30/IV B 2/9.05/42, 'Wie weiter in der Kirchenpolitik?'

19 I have discussed Church/state relations and the growth of political activism far more extensively in Mary Fulbrook, *Anatomy of a Dictatorship: Inside the GDR, 1949–1989* (Oxford: Oxford University Press, 1995), and will therefore not pursue these issues further here.

20 SAPMO-BArch, DY 30/IV 2/9.05/105, 'Zusammenfassung der Bezirksberichte (Woche vom 29.1. bis 3.2.62)', f. 114.

21 SAPMO-BArch, DY 30/IV 2/9.05/68.

22 SAPMO-BArch, DY 30/IV B 2/9.05/65, 'Problemmaterial. Betrifft: Zu Entwicklungs-tendenzen im Bewußtsein und in der Haltung der Jugend' (n.d., *c.* 1977), pp. 6, 8, 10, 12.

23 See, for example, SAPMO-BArch, DY 30/IV B 2/9.05/42, 'Ergebnisse bei der Erfüllung des Beschlusses des Politbüros von 11.12.1979 (Militärische Nachwuchsgewinnung) und Schlußfolgerungen für die weitere Arbeit', 3 November 1980; and 'Zu Problemen der Gewinnung des Nachwuchses für militärische Berufe'.

24 BArch Bibliothek, FDJ/5802, Günter Roski, ' "Bereit und fähig zur Verteidigung des Sozialismus": Jugendliche zum bevorstehenden Dienst in der Nationalen Volksarmee', Leipzig, July 1986, f. 17.

25 Ibid., ff. 23–4.

26 Ibid., f. 22.

27 But see recently Hans Ehlert and Matthias Rogg (eds), *Militär, Staat und Gesellschaft in der DDR* (Berlin: Chr. Links Verlag, 2004).

28 SAPMO-BArch, DY 24/14521, FDJ-Zentralrat, 'Diskussionsbeitrag Prof. Walter Friedrich auf der Tagung des Wissenschaftlichen Rates für Jugendforschung am 14.10.1987', f. 78.

29 On the FDJ, see Ulrich Mählert and Gerd-Rüdiger Stephan, *Blaue Hemden, rote Fahnen: Die Geschichte der Freien Deutschen Jugend* (Opladen: Leske & Budrich, 1996).

30 Cf. Dorle Zilch, *Millionen unter der blauen Fahne: Die FDJ: Zahlen – Fakten – Tendenzen* (Rostock: Norddeutscher Huchschulschriften Verlag, 1994).

31 The GST was technically a separate mass organisation, at times in some tension with the FDJ.
32 Herausgeberkollektiv, *Wörterbuch zur sozialistischen Jugendpolitik*, pp. 123–4.
33 For a wide range of post-unification personal accounts, see, for example, Barbara Felsmann (ed.), *Beim Kleinen Trompeter habe ich immer geweint: Kindheit in der DDR – Erinnerungen an die Jungen Pioniere* (Berlin: Lukas Verlag, 2003).
34 See particularly Dorothee Wierling, 'Die Jugend als "innere Feind" …', in Hartmut Kaelble, Jürgen Kocka and Hartmut Zwahr (eds), *Sozialgeschichte der DDR* (Stuttgart: Klett-Cotta, 1994).
35 The changing youth policies of the early 1960s, in which the Leipzig incident played a key role, have provoked a range of in part conflicting interpretations. In addition to Wierling, 'Die Jugend als "innere Feind" ', see also: Michael Rauhut, *Beat in der Grauzone: DDR-Rock 1964 bis 1972: Politik und Alltag* (Berlin: Basis Druck, 1993), pp. 137–55; Monika Kaiser, *Machtwechsel von Ulbricht zu Honecker: Funktionsmechanism der SED-Diktatur in Konfliktsituation 1962 bis 1972* (Berlin: Akademie Verlag, 1997), pp. 178 ff.; Mark Fenemore, *Machismo: Rebellion and Reaction in East Germany* (Oxford: Berghahn, forthcoming); Mark Fenemore, 'The Limits of Repression and Reform: Contradictions in the SED's Youth Policy in the early 1960s', in Patrick Major and Jonathan Osmond (eds), *Ulbricht's Germany: State and Society in the SBZ/GDR, 1945–1971* (Manchester: Manchester University Press, 2001), p. 171–89; Ohse, *Jugend nach dem Mauerbau*; Alan McDougall, *Young East Germans*, ch. 4; Daniel Wilton, 'Regime versus People? Public Opinion and the Development of Sport and Popular Music in the GDR 1961–1989', UCL PhD thesis, 2005; and more generally Wierling, *Geboren im Jahr Eins*.
36 For details of the power struggles at the top, see particularly Kaiser, *Machtwechsel*, pp. 167 ff.; the Honecker quotations are at p. 174. On the exaggeration of youth 'criminality', see Rauhut, *Beat in der Grauzone*, p. 125.
37 See Kaiser, *Machtwechsel*, p. 180; Rauhut, *Beat in der Grauzone*, pp. 137–55. According to Dan Wilton's research, it also seems probable that the crackdown on youth 'Rowdytum' was actively supported by a not insignificant proportion of members of the local population, particularly among the older generation, providing a supportive context for the harsher turn in SED policies. See Wilton 'Regime versus People?'.
38 SAPMO-BArch, DY 30/IV 2/17 37, 'Veranstaltungen der Jugendklubhäuser', 1956 programme, ff. 13–14.
39 SAPMO-BArch, DY 30/IV A 2/16/123, Abteilung Jugend des ZK der SED, 'Erfahrungen bei der Bildung und Arbeit des Jugendklubs des Rostocker Volkstheaters, 29.11.1963', pp. 3–4, 5.
40 SAPMO-BArch, DY 30/IV A 2/16/123, ZK der SED – Jugend, 'Information zu einigen Fragen der Entwicklung des geistigen Lebens der Jugend in der Stadt Potsdam', 3 December 1963.
41 SAPMO-BArch, DY 30/IV A 2/16/123, ZK der SED – Jugend, 'Einschätzung zu einigen Fragen der Entwicklung des geistigkulturellen Lebens in den Wohngebieten der Stadt Potsdam nach den Volkswahlen 1963'.
42 SAPMO-BArch, DY 30/IV A 2/16/123, ZK der SED – Jugend, 'Analyse Jugendklubs: Stadtbezirk Prenzlauer Berg, 12.5.65'.
43 SAPMO-BArch, DY 30/IV A 2/16/123, ZK der SED – Jugend, 'Jugendclub "Friedrich Ebert", Berlin, 29.11.64'.
44 SAPMO-BArch, DY 30/IV A 2/16/123, ZK der SED – Jugend, report to Kurt Turba from Arne Rehahn, 10 November 1965, on a meeting in the Jugendklub Berlin-Grünau.
45 SAPMO-BArch, DY 30/IV A 2/16/123, ZK der SED – Jugend, 'Bericht über die Aussprachen zu den Problemen des Jugendklubs in Rathenow, Bezirk Potsdam'.
46 SAPMO-BArch, DY 30/IV A 2/16/123, ZK der SED – Jugend, Rathenow. 'Information' from Kurt Turba to Ulbricht, Honecker, Hager and Norden, 13 November 1965.

47 SAPMO-BArch, DY 30/IV A 2/16/123, ZK der SED – Jugend, 'Abschrift eines Fernschreibens der Bezirksleitung Potsdam an Abteilung Parteiorgane vom 21. September 1967'.
48 For the following summary, see in more detail, Wilton, 'Regime versus People?'; Rauhut, *Beat in der Grauzone*; Michael Rauhut, *Schalmei und Lederjacke: Udo Lindenberg, BAP, Underground: Rock und Politik in den 80er Jahren* (Berlin: Schwarzkopf & Schwarzkopf, 1996); R. Galenza, H. Havemeister, *Wir wollen immer artig sein ... Punk, New Wave, Hip-Hop, Independent-Szene in der DDR, 1980–1990* (Berlin: Schwarzkopf & Schwarzkopf, 2000).
49 SAPMO-BArch, DY 30/J IV 2/9.06/2, Kurt Hager, 'Information über den Verlauf der Aktion "Rock für den Frieden" 1985', 17 April 1985, p. 2.
50 This incident, too, is the subject of some controversy.
51 SAPMO BArch, DY 24/14088, letter of 31 March 1988 from Eberhard Aurich to Egon Krenz. See also 'Interner Standpunkt des Sekretariats des Zentralrats der FDJ zu den Vorkommnissen am Brandenburger Tor / Unter den Linden zu Pfingsten 1987' in the same file.
52 See, for example, Christoph Dieckmann, *My Generation: Cocker, Dylan, Honecker und die bleibende Zeit*, 2nd edn (Berlin: Chr. Links Verlag, 1999).
53 According to the account given by Arnold Pinther and Jochen Schreiber, 'Mein Jugendklub', in Authors' collective under the leadership of Peter Voß, *Freie Zeit: Was nun?* (Berlin: Dietz Verlag, 1986), p. 195.
54 SAPMO-BArch, vorl. SED 18029/1, 'Einige ausgewählte statistische Angaben zur Entwicklung und den Ergebnissen der Jugendpolitik in der DDR', 3 February 1973, p. 13.
55 BArch Bibliothek, FDJ/6125, Wolfgang Geier, 'Jugendklubs in der DDR 1979. Forschungsbericht', ff. 5–6.
56 Authors' collective under the leadership of Peter Voß, *Die Freizeit der Jugend* (Berlin: Dietz Verlag, 1981), pp. 11–12.
57 BArch Bibliothek, FDJ/6017, Ute Karig, 'Jugendklubs als spezifische Möglichkeit der Freizeitgestaltung Jugendlicher', Leipzig, April 1985, f. 4.
58 Ibid., f. 12.
59 SAPMO-BArch, DY 24/14521, 'Thesen zur ideologischen Entwicklung im Jugendalter', Dr Guenther Lange, 12 April 1988, ff. 108–9.
60 SAPMO-BArch, DY 24/14521, Vortrag von Dr Peter Förster, 12 April 1988, f. 131.

Chapter 7

1 For a range of interpretations and discussion of controversies over women and gender in Nazi Germany, see, for example: Gisela Bock, 'Antinatalism, Maternity and Paternity in National Socialist racism', in Ian Kershaw and Moshe Lewin (eds), *Stalinism and Nazism: Dictatorships in Comparison* (Cambridge: Cambridge University Press, 1997); Claudia Koonz, *Mothers in the Fatherland: Women, the Family and Nazi Politics* (London: Jonathan Cape, 1987); Mary Nolan, 'Work, gender and everyday life: reflections on continuity, normality and agency in twentieth-century Germany', in Kershaw and Lewin, *Stalinism and Nazism*; Eve Rosenhaft, 'Women in modern Germany', in Gordon Martel (ed.), *Modern Germany Reconsidered: 1870–1945* (London: Routledge, 1992); Adelheid von Saldern, 'Victims or perpetrators? Controversies about the role of women in the Nazi state', in David Crew (ed.), *Nazism and German Society, 1933–45* (London: Routledge, 1994); Jill Stephenson, *Women in Nazi Society* (London: Croom Helm, 1975); idem., *The Nazi Organisation of Women* (London: Croom Helm, 1981); and most recently the overview of relevant debates in Jill Stephenson, *Women in Nazi Germany* (London: Pearson, 2001).
2 In addition to the literature cited above, see also Michael Burleigh and Wolfgang

Wippermann, *The Racial State: Germany 1933–1945* (Cambridge: Cambridge University Press, 1991).

3   The production of healthy progeny even took precedence over conventional notions of the family as a social unit, as illustrated by the 'Lebensborn' institutions for the antenatal care of pregnant women, and after birth the appropriate care or placement of their offspring, irrespective of marital status, so long as the pregnant women and the presumed fathers were deemed to be producing 'healthy stock'.

4   Reasons included 'congenital feeblemindedness'; conditions considered to be hereditary such as epilepsy, deafness or blindness; 'asocial' behaviour, which was held to have some genetic basis; schizophrenia; a range of physical deformities; and so on.

5   As Schoenbaum pointed out long ago in his classic analysis of Hitler's proclaimed 'social revolution', the 'modernising' trends of previous decades appear to have continued, irrespective of Nazi ideology, even in the peacetime years. David Schoenbaum, *Hitler's Social Revolution* (London: Weidenfeld & Nicolson, 1967). See also Ian Kershaw, *The Nazi Dictatorship*, 4th edn (London: Arnold, 2000).

6   See Nolan, 'Work, gender and everyday life', p. 311, from which these and the following figures are taken.

7   See particularly von Saldern, 'Victims or perpetrators?'.

8   See also Graf von Krockow, *Die Stunde der Frauen* (Stuttgart: Deutsch Verlags-Anstalt, 1988).

9   Statistisches Amt der DDR (ed.), *Statistisches Jahrbuch der DDR*, vol. 1 (Berlin: VEB Deutscher Zentralverlag, 1955), p. 8.

10 This and the profile for males only in Figure 1 were compiled from the statistics given in *Statistisches Jahrbuch der DDR* (1955).

11 See also the discussion of the family in the previous chapter.

12 The full text is reproduced in Kirsten Thietz (ed.), *Ende der Selbstverständlichkeit? Die Abschaffung des §218 in der DDR* (Berlin: BasisDruck, 1992), pp. 70–5.

13 Ibid., p. 71.

14 Ibid., p. 75.

15 'Die Frauen – Der Frieden und der Sozialismus', in *Dokumente der Sozialistischen Einheitspartei Deutschlands*, vol. 8 (Berlin: Dietz Verlag, 1962).

16 Ibid., p. 505.

17 Ibid., pp. 506–7.

18 Ibid., p. 506.

19 Ibid., p. 507.

20 See particularly Christina Onnasch, 'Der Einfluss von Frauen in politischen Führungspositionen der DDR: Das Beispiel Inge Lange', *Deutschland Archiv* 32, no. 3, pp. 419–30.

21 See the discussion in the previous chapter.

22 See particularly the detailed reconstruction in Donna Harsch, 'Society, the State and Abortion in East Germany, 1950–1972', *American Historical Review* 102, no. 1 (February 1997), pp. 53–84; see also Atina Grossmann, ' "Sich auf ihr Kindchen freuen." Frauen und Behörden in Auseinandersetzungen um Abtreibungen, Mitte der 1960er Jahren', in Alf Lüdtke and Peter Becker (eds), *Akten, Eingaben, Schaufenster: Die DDR und ihre Texte* (Berlin: Akademie Verlag, 1997), p. 246.

23 See the figures reproduced in Thietz, *Ende der Selbstverständlichkeit*, p. 218.

24 Ibid.

25 SAPMO-BArch, DY 30/IV 2/17 37, 'Bericht über die Arbeit der FDJ unter den Mädchen und jungen Frauen im Kreis Greiz', 3 September 1955, Bl. 5.

26 Ibid., Bl. 6.

27 Ibid., Bl. 7.

28 SAPMO-BArch, DY 30/IV 2/17 37, 'Einschätzung über die Entwicklung der Stellung der weiblichen Jugend in unserer Gesellschaft' (n.d.), Bl. 42.

29 SAPMO-BArch, DY 30/IV 2/17 37, 'Richtlinien des Büros des Zentralrates der FDJ für die Arbeit mit den Mädchen und jungen Frauen' (n.d., *c.* 1957), Bl. 15.

30 Ibid., Bl. 17.

31 SAPMO BArch, DY 30/IV 2/17 37, 'Einschätzung zu einigen Problemen der Lage der jungen Arbeiterinnen in der Textilindustrie', 5/5/1061, Bl. 99.

32 Ibid., Bl. 102.

33 Ibid., Bl. 106.

34 Ibid., Bl. 110.

35 SAPMO-BArch, DY 30 / Vorl. SED 36878, 'Sofortinformation über die Durchführung einer Bevölkerungsbefragung zum Kinderwunsch von Frauen und zur Lebensweise von Familien', Akademie der Wissenschaften der DDR, Institut für Soziologie und Sozialpolitik, 30 October 1982, Bl. 7.

36 SAPMO-BArch, DY/30 IV 2/2.042/2, 'Enschätzung der Umfrage über Probleme der Frau in unserer Gesellschaft', Institut für Meinungsforschung beim ZK der SED, 9 October 1968, Bl. 43–4.

37 Ibid., Bl. 44.

38 SAPMO-BArch, DY/30 IV 2/2.042/2, 'Ergebnisse der Umfrage zur Stellung der Frau in Familie und Gesellschaft von November 1970', Bl. 69, 73.

39 SAPMO-BArch, DY 30 / Vorl. SED 16714, 'Information über Ergebnisse der vom Institut für Marktforschung Leipzig im Jahre 1970 durchgeführten Befragung über den Zeitaufwand für hauswirtschaftliche Tätigkeiten in den Haushalten der DDR', 14 June 1972, p. 2.

40 SAPMO-BArch, DY 30 IV 2/2.042/34, Institut für Marxismus-Leninismus beim ZK der SED, 'Einschätzung der Umfrage zur Rolle der Frau in Familie und Gesellschaft', September 1975, Bl. 64, 65.

41 SAPMO-BArch, DY 30 / Vorl. SED 36878, 'Sofortinformation über die Durchführung einer Bevölkerungsbefragung zum Kinderwunsch von Frauen und zur Lebensweise von Familien', Akademie der Wissenschaften der DDR, Institut für Soziologie und Sozialpolitik, 30 October 1982, Bl. 5.

42 See Leonore Ansorg, 'Der Fortschritt kommt aufs Land: Weibliche Erwerbstätigkeit in der Prignitz', in Gunille-Friederike Budde (ed.), *Frauen Arbeiten: Weibliche Erwerbstätigkeit in Ost- und Westdeutschland nach 1945* (Göttingen: Vandenhoeck & Ruprecht, 1997), on which this paragraph is based.

43 See the Volker Koepp film *Wittstock, Wittstock.*

44 See Annegret Schüle, 'Industriearbeit als Emanzipationschance? Arbeiterinnen im Büromaschinenwerk Sömmerda und in der Baumwollspinnerei Leipzig', in Budde, *Frauen Arbeiten.*

45 Petra Clemens, 'Die "Letzten": Arbeits- und Berufserfahrungen einer Generation Niederlausitzer Textilarbeiterinnen', in Jürgen Kocka (ed.), *Historische DDR-Forschung: Aufsätze und Studien* (Berlin: Akademie Verlag, 1993).

46 SAPMO-BArch, DY 30/IV 2/17 37, 'Einschätzung zu einigen Problemen de Lage der jungen Arbeiterinnen in der Textilindustrie', 5 May 1961, f. 104.

47 Christel Panzig, 'Hin zum eigenen Beruf: Frauen in den landwirtschaftlichen Produktionsgenossenschaften der DDR', in Budde, *Frauen Arbeiten.*

48 Lutz Niethammer, Alexander von Plato and Dorothee Wierling, *Die volkseigene Erfahrung* (Berlin: Rowohlt, 1991); see particularly the summary on pp. 44–5.

49 Ibid., p. 118.

50 SAPMO-BArch, DY 30/IV 2/2.042/46, Büro Lange, 'Notiz zur Entwicklung von Frauen in ausgewählten Leitungsfunktionen in der Volksbildung', Edith Spitzer, 19 August 1987, p. 1.

51 SAPMO-BArch, DY 30/IV 2/17 9, report of 19 February 1960, f. 56.

52 Gunille-Friederike Budde, 'Paradefrauen: Akademikerinnen in Ost- und Westdeutschland', in Budde (ed.), *Frauen Arbeiten.*

53 SAPMO-BArch, DY 30/IV 2/2.042/46, Büro Lange, 'Entwurf: Studie über den Stand der Auswahl, Vorbereitung und den Einsatz von Frauen in verantwortlichen Funktionen der Volkswirtschaft, des Staatsapparates sowie in gesellschaftlichen Bereichen', 21 June 1988, p. 28.

54 Ibid., pp. 35–8.

55 Barbara Bertram et al., Adam und Eva Heute (Leipzig: Verlag für die Frau, 1988), p. 10.

56 See, for example, Authors' collective under the leadership of Barbara Bertram, Typisch weiblich – typisch männlich? (Berlin: Dietz Verlag, 1989).

57 See, for example, Zentrum für interdisziplinäre Frauenforschung der Humboldt-Universität Berlin (ed.), Unter Hammer und Zirkel: Frauenbiographien vor dem Hintergrund ostdeutscher Sozialisationserfahrungen (Pfaffenweiler: Centaurus Verlagsgesellschaft, 1995); Gisela Helwig and Hildegard Maria Nickel (eds), Frauen in Deutschland, 1945–1992 (Bonn: Bundeszentrale für politische Bildung, 1993).

58 Matthias Judt (ed.), DDR-Geschichte in Dokumenten: Beschlüsse, Berichte, interne Materialien und Alltagszeugnisse (Berlin: Chr. Links Verlag, 1997), p. 176.

59 BArch, DQ 1 11763, 'Zu Problemen der Homosexualität in der DDR', 23 October 1984.

60 Ibid., Bl. 2.

61 BArch, DQ1 12953, letter of 17 February 1986, Bl. 8–9.

62 Ibid., letter of 2 May 1984, Bl. 2–3.

63 See Bertram et al., Adam und Eva Heute, for a remarkable collection of photos, not only of those challenging employment role stereotypes but also of the 'quasi-pornographic' variety that became prevalent in the 1980s. See also Gunilla-Freiderike Budde, 'Einleitung: Zwei Welten?' in Budde, Frauen Arbeiten; and Ina Merkel, 'Leitbilder und Lebensweisen von Frauen in der DDR' in Hartmut Kaelble, Jürgen Kocka and Hartmut Zwahr (eds), Sozialgeschichte der DDR (Stuttgart: Klett-Cotta, 1994).

64 Kleine Enzyklopädie: Die Frau (Leipzig: VEB Bibliographisches Institut, 1987).

65 Günther Schabowski, Das Politbüro (Hamburg: Rowohlt, 1990), p. 46.

66 SAPMO-BArch, DY 30/IV 2/2.042/46, Büro Lange, 'Information zu Ergebnissen bei der Erhöhung des Anteils der Frauen in Leitungsfunktionen in den zentralen und örtlichen Staatsorganen und die für den Zeitraum bis 1990 vorgesehenen Aufgaben', Edith Spizter, 26 June 1987, p. 1.

67 Ibid., p. 4,

68 Sabine Ross, 'Verhinderte Aufstieg? Frauen in lokalen Führungspositionen des DDR-Staatsapparats der achtziger jahre', in Peter Hübner (ed.), Eliten im Sozialismus: Beiträge zur Sozialgeschichte der DDR (Cologne: Böhlau Verlag, 1999).

69 SAPMO-BArch, DY 30/IV 2/2.042/46, Büro Lange, 'Information zu Ergebnissen bei der Erhöhung des Anteils der Frauen in Leitungsfunktionen in den zentralen und örtlichen Staatsorganen und die für den Zeitraum bis 1990 vorgesehenen Aufgaben', Edith Spizter, 26 June 1987, p. 6.

70 Ibid., p. 6.

71 SAPMO-BArch, DY 30/IV 2/17 9, 'Betr. Konferenz der werktätigen Frauen über die Durchführung des neuen Kurs', 13 October 1953, ff. 11–15.

72 SAPMO-BArch, DY 30/IV 2/17 9, 'Information zu einigen Problemen in Bezug auf die Tätigkeit und den Einsatz der weiblichen Volksvertreter sowie ihren prozentualen Anteil an den Kreistagen, Stadtverordneten- und Stadtbezirksverordnetenversamm-lungen und Gemeindevertretungen' (n.d., late 1950s) f. 47.

73 SAPMO-BArch, DY 30/IV 2/17 63, 'Hinweise aus dem Kreis Jessen zur Durchführung der 1. Kreiskonferenz der Bäuerinnen am 11. Juni 1959', Bl. 102.

74 SAPMO-BArch, DY 30/IV 2/17 9, 'Information zu einigen Problemen in Bezug auf die Tätigkeit und den Einsatz der weiblichen Volksvertreter sowie ihren prozentualen Anteil an den Kreistagen, Stadtverordneten- und Stadtbezirksverordnetenversamm-lungen und Gemeindevertretungen', Bl. 47.

75 Ross, 'Verhinderte Aufstieg?'

76 See also Daphne Berdahl, *Where the World Ended* (Berkeley: University of California Press, 1999) for a sensitive anthropological study of one such small community, Kella, shortly after unification. The long-serving female mayor of this community was a Christian.

77 See also the discussion of the DFD and leisure activities in chapters 4 and 6.

78 See, for example, Vera Wollenberger, *Virus der Heuchler* (Berlin: Elefanten Press, 1992); Samirah Kenawi (ed.), *Frauengruppen in der DDR der 80er Jahre: Eine Dokumentation* (Berlin: Grauzone – Dokumentationsstelle zur nichtstaatlichen Frauenbewegung in der DDR, 1995).

79 In addition to the various individual works of writers such as Christa Wolf, Maxie Wander, Irmtraud Morgner, Brigitte Reimann, Gabriele Eckart and others, see also, for selections of women's writing in translation, Nancy Lukens and Dorothy Rosenberg (eds), *Daughters of Eve: Women's Writing from the German Democratic Republic* (Lincoln and London: University of Nebraska Press, 1993).

80 SAPMO-BArch, DY 34/14617, *Eingaben* to the Ministerium für Volksbildung, letter of 15 September 1988.

81 Ibid., letter of 22 November 1989.

82 Ibid., letter of 29 October 1989.

83 For the complexity of women's attitudes, and hopes and fears connected with unification, see Gunnar Winkler, *Frauenreport '90* (Berlin: Verlag Die Wirtschaft, 1990), p. 202.

84 For example, Klaus Schroeder rather emphatically and one-sidedly puts it thus: 'Women could not autonomously articulate their interests in society, since this would have contradicted the totalitarian understanding of politics and society of the SED. The official organs for the representation of women primarily represented the interests of state and Party . . . SED policies towards women and family remained primarily oriented to economic and demographic frameworks. They totally abstained from any emancipatory impulse, did not challenge men's understanding of their roles, and expected of women a double burden and a lack of equality of opportunity in career and society.' *Der SED-Staat: Partei, Staat and Gesellschaft, 1949–1990* (Munich: Carl Hanser Verlag, 1998), p. 529.

Chapter 8

1 Even residents were aware of this joke: cf. Lamberz in Manfred Krug, *Abgehauen* (Düsseldorf: Econ Taschenbuch Verlag, 1998), p. 63.

2 For insiders' views by former members of the Wandlitz staff, see Thomas Grimm (ed.), *Das Politbüro privat: Ulbricht, Honecker, Mielke & Co. aus der Sicht ihrer Angestellten* (Berlin: Aufbau Verlag, 2004).

3 On Goering, see Richard Overy, *Goering: The 'Iron Man'* (London: Routledge & Kegan Paul, 1984).

4 Günther Schabowski, *Das Politbüro* (Hamburg: Rowohlt, 1990), p. 46.

5 See for details Gerd Meyer, *Die DDR-Machtelite in der Ära Honecker* (Tübingen: A. Francke Verlag, 1991).

6 See, for example, Ulrich Mählert, *Kleine Geschichte der DDR* (Munich: C. H. Beck, 1998); and Hermann Weber, *Geschichte der DDR*, revised edn (Munich: dtv, 1999).

7 See the classic insider account by Wolfgang Leonhard, *Die Revolution entlässt ihre Kinder* (Cologne: Kiepenheuer & Witsch, 1955).

8 See, for example, Peter Grieder, *The East German Leadership, 1946–1973: Conflict and Crisis* (Manchester: Manchester University Press, 1999).

9 For interpretations of the context and character of the 1953 Uprising, which has seen an enormous amount of historical attention devoted to it in recent years, see for example, Gary Bruce, *Resistance with the People: Repression and Resistance in Eastern Germany, 1945–1955* (Lanham, Md: Rowman & Littlefield, 2003); and Bernd Eisenfeld, Ilko-Sascha Kowalczuk and Ehrhart Neubert, *Die verdrängte Revolution: Der Platz des*

17. Juni 1953 in der deutschen Geschichte (Bremen: Edition Temmen, 2004). On the wider problems with the functionary system of rule at this time, see, for example, Corey Ross, *Constructing Socialism at the Grass-Roots: The Transformation of East Germany* (Basingstoke: Macmillan, 2000).

10 Monika Kaiser, *Machtwechsel von Ulbricht zu Honecker: Funktionsmechanismen der SED-Diktatur in Konfliktsituationen 1962 bis 1972* (Berlin: Akademie Verlag, 1997), p. 39.

11 For an early, perceptive (over-)statement of the significance of what was seen as a new 'counter-elite', see P. C. Ludz, *The Changing Party Elite in East Germany* (Cambridge, Mass.: MIT Press, 1972). While the strong thesis of a 'counter-elite' no longer appears tenable, the increased proportion of specialist cadres with higher educational qualifications in positions of political importance remains an indubitable fact.

12 Kaiser, *Machtwechsel*, pp. 45–7.

13 On Honecker's rise to power, see particularly the excellent analysis of Kaiser, ibid.

14 Cf. ibid.; Grieder, *East German Leadership*; and the forthcoming results of in-depth studies of particular policy areas and developments on the ground, such as the current work of Jeannette Madarász. See also Chapter 2, above.

15 On Hitler's charismatic leadership position, see particularly Ian Kershaw, *Hitler* (London: Longman, 1991, 'Profiles in Power' series) and Kershaw's definitive two-volume biography of *Hitler* (London: Penguin, 2000–02).

16 For clear general overviews of the Stasi, see, for example, Mike Dennis, *The Stasi: Myth and Reality* (London: Pearson, 2003); and Jens Gieseke, *Mielke-Konzern: Die Geschichte der Stasi, 1945–1990* (Munich: Deutsche Verlags-Anstalt, 2001).

17 See the excellent overview by Manfred G. Schmidt, 'Grundlagen der Sozialpolitik in der Deutschen Demokratischen Republik', in Bundesministerium für Arbeit und Sozialordnung und Bundesarchiv (ed.), *Geschichte der Sozialpolitik in Deutschland seit 1945* (Baden-Baden: Nomos Verlag, 2001), p. 723. On GDR social policy see also, for a GDR perspective, Gunnar Winkler (ed.), *Lexikon der Sozialpolitik*, 2 vols (Berlin: Akademie Verlag, 1987); Gunnar Winkler, *Geschichte der Sozialpolitik der DDR, 1945–1985* (Berlin: Akademie Verlag, 1989).

18 See Peter Hübner, 'Einleitung: Anti-elitäre Eliten?', in Hübner (ed.), *Eliten im Sozialismus: Beiträge zur Sozialgeschichte der DDR* (Cologne: Böhlau Verlag, 1999), p. 34.

19 On the alleged experience of growing up as the son of a top Stasi officer, see the surreal parody by Thomas Brussig, *Helden wie Wir* (Berlin: Volk und Welt, 1995).

20 Markus Wolf, *Im eigenen Auftrag* (Munich; Schneekluth Verlag, 1991); on Seidowsky, Merrilyn Thomas, *Communing with the Enemy: Covert Operations, Christianity and Cold War Politics in Britain and the GDR* (Bern, Berlin, Frankfurt: Peter Lang, 2005).

21 See the detailed analysis by Helga Welsh, 'Kaderpolitik auf dem Prüfstand: Die Bezirke und ihre Sekretäre, 1952–1989', in Hübner, *Eliten*.

22 See the current work of Jeannette Madarász on the AHRC normalisation project.

23 See the very useful analysis in Heike Solga, *Auf dem Weg in eine klassenlose Gesellschaft?: Klassenlagen und Mobilität zwischen Generationen in der DDR* (Berlin: Akademie Verlag, 1995), p, 69.

24 Manfred Uschner, *Die zweite Etage: Funktionsweise eines Machtapparates*, 2nd edn (Berlin: Dietz Verlag, 1995), p. 19.

25 Ibid., p. 22.

26 Ibid., pp. 31–2.

27 'Innovation – nur gegen den Plan. Gespräch mit Prof. Dr. Claus Krömke', in Pirker *et al.* (eds), *Plan als Befehl und Fiktion: Wirtschaftsführung in der DDR* (Opladen: Westdeutscher Verlag, 1995), p. 58.

28 Erhard Meyer, 'Der Bereich Günter Mittag' in Hans Modrow (ed.), *Das große Haus: Insider Berichten aus den ZK der SED* (Berlin: edition ost, 1994). There is, of course, a

methodological problem with all these post-*Wende* accounts, namely that of attempted self-justification and shifting of blame. But the supreme control of the economy by Mittag, his ultimate power in final decision-making, is confirmed again and again, including in contemporary documents with respect to different policy areas.

29 Cf. Ross, *Constructing Socialism*.

30 See particularly Daniel Wilton, 'Regime versus People? Public Opinion and Development of Sport and Popular Music in the GDR, 1961–1989', UCL PhD thesis, 2005, with respect to functionaries in the areas of mass sports and popular music, and also that of Esther von Richthofen (in preparation, 2005) concerning cultural functionaries.

31 Landolf Scherzer, *Der Erste: Eine Reportage aus der DDR* (Cologne: Kiepenheuer & Witsch, 1989).

32 Hans-Dieter Fritschler, 'Die Kreisleitung als verlängerter Arm des Politbüros?', in Hans Modrow (ed.), *Das große Haus von außen* (Berlin: edition ost, 1996), pp. 49–52.

33 See, with particular respect to female mayors, Sabine Ross, 'Verhinderter Aufstieg? Frauen in lokalen Führungspositionen des DDR-Staatsapparats der achtziger Jahre', in Hübner, *Eliten*; see also the post-*Wende* anthropological account of a border village by Daphne Berdahl, *Where the World ended: Re-unification and Identity in the German Borderland* (Berkeley: University of California Press, 1999).

34 Ross, 'Verhinderter Aufstieg', pp. 160, 150, 154.

35 SAPMO-Barch, DY 30/IV 2/2.106/21, Agitationskommission beim Politbüro, 'Information' of 26 March 1973, Bl. 14 (ff. 78–9).

36 Cf. Hübner's 'Selbstisolation' of these groups: 'In beiden Fällen wurden die Loyalität gegenüber der SED-Führung und die Bereitschaft zur Abgrenzung gegenüber anderen Bevölkerungsgruppen durch eine soziale Privilegierung erreicht'. Peter Hübner, 'Einleitung: Anti-elitäre Eliten?', in Hübner, *Eliten*, p. 34.

Chapter 9

1 See, for example, the theoretical doubts raised in Anna-Sabine Ernst, *'Die beste Prophylaxe ist der Sozialismus.' Ärzte und medizinische Hochschullehrer in der SBZ/DDR, 1945–1961* (Münster, New York, Munich, Berlin: Waxmann, 1997), pp. 16–20.

2 See, for example, Manfred Lötsch, 'Zur Entwicklung der Intelligenz in der Deutschen Demokratischen Republik', in Authors' collective (eds), *Die Intelligenz in der sozialistischen Gesellschaft* (Berlin: Dietz Verlag, 1980).

3 According to Rudi Weidig's analysis of 1988, quoted in Siegfried Grundmann, 'Zur Sozialstruktur der DDR', in Evemarie Badstübner (ed.), *Befremdlich anders: Leben in der DDR* (Berlin: Karl Dietz Verlag, 2000), p. 22.

4 On the occupation period, see particularly Norman Naimark, *The Russians in Germany: A History of the Soviet Zone of Occupation, 1945–1949* (Cambridge, Mass.: Harvard University Press, 1995).

5 For a detailed analysis of the confusions and complexities of this process, which was in practice by no means as straightforward as it may sound in brief summary, see Frank Ebbinghaus, *Ausnutzung und Verdrängung: Steuerungsprobleme der SED-Mittelstandspolitik, 1955–1972* (Berlin: Duncker and Humblot, 2003).

6 Brigitte Hohlfeld, *Die Neulehrer in der SBZ/DDR, 1945–1953: Ihre Rolle bei der Umgestaltung von Gesellschaft und Staat* (Weinheim: Deutscher Studien Verlag, 1992), pp. 11, 44.

7 Ibid., p. 56.

8 Ibid., p. 11; Lothar Mertens and Ulrich Spiekerkötter, 'Austausch der Lehrerschaft in der SBZ: Die Neulehrer 1945–1949', in Lothar Mertens and Sabine Gries (eds), *Arbeit, Sport und DDR-Gesellschaft* (Berlin: Duncker & Humblot, 1996), p. 116.

9 Hohlfeld, *Neulehrer*, p. 70

10 Ibid., pp. 71–2.
11 Ibid., p. 417.
12 SAPMO-BArch, DY 30/IV 2/9.05/103, 'Die Lage im Schulwesen'.
13 SAPMO-BArch, DY 34/21500, Gewerkschaft Unterricht und Erziehung, n.d., c. 1960–61.
14 Brigitte Reimann, *Aber wir schaffen es, verlaß dich drauf! Briefe an eine Freundin im Westen* (Berlin: Elefanten Press, 1995), letters of 11 June 1947, pp. 5–6, and 10 October 1947, pp. 15–17.
15 Ibid., letters of 21 May 1950, pp. 29–33, and 13 June 1950, pp. 36–7.
16 Ibid., letter of 7 July 1950, pp. 38–9.
17 H. Müller-Enbergs and J. Wielgohs (eds), *Wer war wer in der DDR?* (Bonn: Bundeszentrale für politische Bildung, 2001).
18 Hohlfeld, *Neulehrer*, pp. 417–18.
19 SAPMO-BArch, DY 30/IV 2/9.05/105, 'Zusammenfassung der Bezirksberichte (Woche vom 29.1. bis 3.2.62', f. 112.
20 SAPMO-BArch, DY 34/21500, 'Die zeitliche Belastung der Lehrer', n.d.
21 SAPMO-BArch, DY 30/IV B 2/9.05/42, 'Zur Entwicklung der Parteikader im Bereich des Volksbildungswesens', pp. 2–3; and 'Einige Bemerkungen zu Kaderentwicklung', p. 1.
22 SAPMO-BArch, DY 30/IV B 2/9.05/42, 'Information über das Anlaufen des Studienjahres 1980/81 an den Pädagogischen Hochschulen, Instituten für Lehrerbildung und Pädagogischen Schulen für Kindergärtnerinnen', 29 September 1980, p. 8.
23 For a somewhat subjective view of education in the GDR as being along the lines of George Orwell's *1984*, and written largely on the basis of anecdotal evidence acquired after 1990, see John Rodden, *Repainting the Little Red Schoolhouse* (New York and Oxford: Oxford University Press, 2002).
24 Imperial War Museum archive, MISC 141 Item 2193, f. 3.
25 For a brief overview and summary of the current state of research in this area, see Hermann Wentker, 'Justiz und Politik in der DDR', in Rainer Eppelmann, Bernd Faulenbach and Ulrich Mählert (eds), *Bilanz und Perspektiven der DDR-Forschung* (Paderborn: Ferdinand Schöningh, 2003), pp. 126–32. Important studies include Roger Engelmann and Clemens Vollnhals (eds), *Justiz im Dienste der Parteiherrschaft: Rechtspraxis und Staatssicherheit in der DDR* (Berlin: 1999); and Karl Wilhelm Fricke, *Politik und Justiz in der DDR: Zur Geschichte der politischen Verfolgung, 1945–1968* (Cologne: Wissenschaft und Politik, 1979).
26 SAPMO-BArch, DY 34/21500, 'Informationsbericht über den Einsatz in der Universität Jena zur Untersuchung der Situation unter der Intelligenz', 16 January 1961, p. 3.
27 Ernst, '*Die beste Prophylaxe ist der Sozialismus*', p. 339.
28 Ibid., p. 150.
29 SAPMO-BArch, DY 30/IV 2/19/66, 'Bericht über die Lage in der medizinischen Intelligenz', 10 December 1959, Bl. 5.
30 Christoph Klessmann, 'Relikte des Bildungsbürgertums in der DDR', in Hartmut Kaelble, Jürgen Kocka and Hartmut Zwahr (eds), *Sozialgeschichte der DDR* (Stuttgart: Klett-Cotta, 1994), p. 258.
31 Ibid., p. 259.
32 Schmidt, 'Grundlagen der Sozialpolitik in der Deutschen Demokratischen Republik', in Bundesministerium für Arbeit und Sozialordnung und Bundesarchiv (ed.), *Geschichte der Sozialpolitik in Deutschland seit 1945*, vol. 1: *Grundlagen der Sozialpolitik* (Baden-Baden: Nomos Verlag, 2001), p. 751; Ernst, '*Die beste Prophylaxe ist der Sozialismus*', pp. 54–5.
33 SAPMO-BArch, DY 34/21500, letter of 27 January 1962 from the Gewerkschaft Gesundheitswesen, Kreisgewerkschaftsgruppe Zahnärzte, Meissen, to the FDGB Executive in Berlin.

34 SAPMO-BArch, DY 30/IV 2/19/58, 'Vorlage für das Sekretariat des Zentralkomitees der SED. Betr.: Durchführung einer Aussprache mit Angehörigen der medizinischen Intelligenz', 11 October 1956, Bl. 3–4.

35 SAPMO-BArch, DY 34/21500, 'Bericht über den Einsatz an der Universität Halle am 10., 11., u. 12.1.61', p. 3.

36 SAPMO-BArch, DY 30/IV 2/19/58, 'Zur politisch-ideologischen Entwicklung der medizinischen Fakultäten und Akademien' (n.d.; *c.* late 1950s), Bl. 4.

37 Ibid., Bl. 8.

38 Ibid., Bl.11.

39 Ernst, '*Die beste Prophylaxe ist der Sozialismus*', p. 338. See also Sonja Süß, *Politisch mißbraucht? Psychiatrie und Staatssicherheit in der DDR* (Berlin: Chr. Links Verlag, 1998).

40 See, for example, Maxie Wander, *Tagebücher und Briefe*, 3rd edn (Berlin and Weimar: Aufbau Verlag, 1990), letter of 9 September 1976 to her brother, pp. 9–10; Reimann, *Aber wir schaffen es, verlaß dich drauf!*, letter of 21 April 1972, p. 185.

41 Ralph Jessen, 'Professoren im Sozialismus: Aspekte des Strukturwandels der Hochschullehrerschaft in der Ulbricht-Ära', in Kaelble, Kocka and Zwahr, *Sozialgeschichte*, pp. 223–5.

42 SAPMO-BArch, DY 34/21500, 'Informationsbericht über den Einsatz in der Universität Jena zur Untersuchung der Situation unter der Intelligenz, 16.1.1961', p. 3.

43 SAPMO-BArch, DY 34/21500, 'Aktennotiz über die Aussprache mit Kollegen Prof. Dr. Grümmer von der Universität Greifswald am 18.1.1961'.

44 SAPMO-BArch, DY 34/21500, 'Informationsbericht über den Einsatz an der Universität Halle am 10., 11., u. 12.1.61', p. 2.

45 SAPMO-BArch, DY 34/21500, 'Bericht über den Einsatz am 3. und 4. 8. 1961 in Magdeburg', pp. 3, 6.

46 SAPMO-BArch, DY 34/21500, 'Bericht der Brigade des Zentralvorstandes der Gewerkschaft Wissenschaft zur Untersuchung der Intelligenz-Politik an der Universität Greifswald, 16. Jan. 1960'.

47 Ibid., p. 2.

48 See the exhaustive analysis of the early post-war years by Wolfgang Tischner, *Katholische Kirche in der SBZ/DDR: Die Formierung einer Subgesellschaft im entstehenden sozialistischen Staat* (Paderborn: Ferdinand Schöningh, 2001).

49 On the activities of Catholics in the Eichsfeld, see, for example, Mark Allinson, *Politics and Popular Opinion in East Germany, 1945–1968* (Manchester: Manchester University Press, 2000).

50 I have discussed this in more detail in Mary Fulbrook, *Anatomy of a Dictatorship: Inside the GDR, 1949–1989* (Oxford: Oxford University Press, 1995), where further references may be found.

51 Manfred Krug, *Abgehauen* (Düsseldorf: Econ Taschenbuch Verlag, 1998).

52 SAPMO-BArch, DY 30/IV A 2/11/7, 'Information zu einigen Fragen der kadermäßigen Zusammensetzung des Mitteldeutschen Verlages', 2 July 1970, f. 5.

53 SAPMO-BArch, DY 30/IV A 2/11/7, 'Information über einige Probleme der politisch-ideologischen und kaderpolitischen Situation in der Philharmonie Dresden', f. 55.

54 SAPMO-BArch, DY 30/IV A 2/11/7, 'Bericht zur politisch-ideologischen und kaderpoltischen Situation der Dresdener Philharmonie mit Schlußfolgerungen', f. 71.

55 SAPMO-BArch, DY 30/IV A 2/11/7, 'Information über die Kaderprobleme im Bereich des staatlichen Komitees für Fernsehen beim Ministerrat der DDR', 18 April 1969, f. 45.

56 SAPMO-BArch, DY 30/J IV 2/9.06/32, 'Bericht über den V. Kongress des Filmverbandes der UdSSR, Moskau, Mai 1986, Kremlin'.

57 See, for example, SAPMO-BArch, DY 30/J IV 2/9.06/32, 'Informationsbericht des Kulturbundes der DDR über Stimmungen, Meinungen und Haltungen – vor allem der

Intelligenz – zu aktuellen politischen und kulturellen Fragen', Kurt Hager, 12 December 1986.

58 SAPMO-BArch, FDGB DY 34/21500, 'Informationsbericht über den Einsatz in der Universität Jena zur Untersuchung der Situation unter der Intelligenz', 16 January 1961, p. 2; and 'Einschätzung über den Stand der Arbeit mit der künstlerischen-wissenschaftlichen Intelligenz im Bereich der Gewerkschaft Kunst', 17 January 1961, p. 5.

59 For the official portrayal of workers and intellectuals in DEFA films, see Ina Merkel, 'Arbeiter und Konsum im real existierenden Sozialismus', in Peter Hübner and Klaus Tenfelde (eds), *Arbeiter in der SBZ-DDR* (Essen: Klartext, 1999). The role and identity of the technical intelligentsia will be explored further in the work of Renate Hürtgen. For a very early analysis of the political role of the technical intelligentsia, see Thomas Baylis, *The Technical Intelligentsia and the East German Elite: Legitimacy and Social Change in Mature Communism* (Berkeley: University of California Press, 1974).

Chapter 10

1 Brigitte Reimann, *Franziska Linkerhand* (Munich: dtv, 1977) pp. 243–4.

2 On the related notion of an 'Arbeitsgesellschaft', see Martin Kohli, 'Die DDR als Arbeitsgesellschaft? Arbeit, Lebenslauf und soziale Differenzierung', in Hartmut Kaelble, Jürgen Kocka and Hartmut Zwahr (eds), *Sozialgeschichte der DDR* (Stuttgart: Klett-Cotta, 1994).

3 This definition loosely combines aspects of both Marxist and Weberian approaches to class; it is, however, the combination that seems to me most useful.

4 Heika Solga, 'Aspekte der Klassenstruktur in der DDR in den siebziger und achtziger Jahren und die Stellung der Arbeiterklasse', in Renate Hürtgen and Thomas Reichel (eds), *Der Schein der Stabilität: DDR-Betriebsalltag in der Ära Honecker* (Berlin: Metropol Verlag, 2001), p. 41.

5 C. Boyer, 'Arbeiterkarrieren? Zur sozialen Herkunft der zentralen Staatsbürokratie der SBZ/DDR, 1945–1961', in Peter Hübner and Klaus Tenfelde (eds), *Arbeiter in der SBZ-DDR* (Essen: Klartext, 1999), p. 679.

6 See, for example, Alexander von Plato, 'Arbeiter-Selbstbilder in der DDR', in Hübner and Tenfelde, *Arbeiter in der SBZ-DDR*; and Alf Lüdtke, ' "Helden der Arbeit" – Mühen beim Arbeiten: Zur mißmutigen Loyalität von Industriearbeitern in der DDR', in Kaelble, Kocka and Zwahr (eds), *Sozialgeschichte der DDR*.

7 See Solga, 'Aspekte', p. 50.

8 For summaries of the large historiography in this area, see, for example, P Ayçoberry, *A Social History of the Third Reich, 1933–1945* (New York: New Press, 1999); and Ian Kershaw, *The Nazi Dictatorship*, 4th edn (London: Arnold, 2000).

9 See also chapter 7, above.

10 Peter Hübner, 'Arbeiter und sozialer Wandel im Niederlausitzer Braunkohlenrevier von den dreißiger Jahren bis Mitte der sechziger Jahre', in Hübner (ed.), *Niederlausitzer Industriearbeiter 1935 bis 1970: Studien zur Sozialgeschichte* (Berlin: Akademie Verlag, 1995), p. 25.

11 See chapter 3, above.

12 See also Ralf Engeln, 'Betriebliche Arbeitsbeziehungen bei der AG Wismut und in der volkseigenen Industrie in Vergleich, 1946–1953', in Hübner and Tenfelde (eds), *Arbeiter in der SBZ-DDR*.

13 See, for example, Imperial War Museum archive, Misc 141 Item 2193, letter to 'Marjorie' from 'Hellmut', Chemnitz, 18 March 1949.

14 This paragraph is largely based on reports and letters dating from June 1947 to September 1950, in SAPMO-BArch, FDGB DY/34 20624.

15 SAPMO-BArch, FDGB DY/34 20572, reports from January to November 1955.

16 SAPMO-BArch, DY/34 5159, 'Bericht zur Lage', 11 November 1965, pp. 5–7.

17 This paragraph is largely based on the outstanding work in this area of Arnd

Bauerkämper, *Ländliche Gesellschaft in der kommunistischen Diktatur: Zwangs-modernisierung und Tradition in Brandenburg, 1945–1963* (Cologne, Weimar, Vienna: Böhlau Verlag, 2002); and Arnd Bauerkämper, 'Von der Bodenreform zur Kollektivierung: Zum Wandel der ländlichen Gesellschaft in der sowjetischen Besatzungszone Deutschlands und DDR 1945–1952' in Kaelble, Kocka, Zwahr (eds), *Sozialgeschichte der DDR.*

18 Bauerkämper, 'Von der Bodenreform zur Kollektivierung', in Kaelble, Kocka and Zwahr, *Sozialgeschichte der DDR*, p. 131.

19 See, for example, Andreas Kapphan, 'Wandel der Lebensverhältnisse im ländlichen Raum', in Wendelin Strubelt *et al.* (eds), *Städte und Regionen: Räumliche Folgen des Transformationsprozesses* (Opladen: Leske & Budrich, 1996), p. 220.

20 For an in-depth case study of the process of 'normalisation' of agricultural life in the Erfurt region in the 1960s and '70s, see particularly the UCL 2006 PhD thesis by George Last.

21 André Steiner, 'Von "Hauptaufgabe" zu "Hauptaufgabe": Zur Wirtschaftsentwicklung der langen 60er Jahre in der DDR', in Axel Schildt, Detlef Siegfried and Karl Christian Lammers (eds), *Dynamische Zeiten: Die 60er Jahre in den beiden deutschen Gesellschaften* (Hamburg: Hans Christians Verlag, 2000), p. 239.

22 Kapphan, 'Wandel der Lebensverhältnisse', p. 223.

23 Von Plato, 'Arbeiter-Selbstbilder in der DDR', p. 876.

24 See Lutz Niethammer, Alexander von Plato and Dorothee Wierling, *Die volkseigene Erfahrung* (Berlin: Rowohlt, 1991), pp. 44–5.

25 Solga, 'Aspekte', p. 41.

26 See, for example, the useful summary and discussion in Ralph Jessen, 'Mobility and Blockage during the 1970s', in Konrad Jarausch (ed.), *Dictatorship as Experience* (Oxford and New York: Berghahn, 1999); for a more detailed analysis, see Heike Solga, *Auf dem Weg in eine klassenlose Gesellschaft? Klassenlagen und Mobilität zwischen Generationen in der DDR* (Berlin: Akademie Verlag, 1995).

27 Thomas Reichel 'Die "durchherrschte Arbeitsgesellschaft": Zu den Herrschaftsstruk-turen und Machtverhältnissen in DDR-Betrieben', in Hürtgen and Reichel, *Schein der Stabilität*, pp. 91–4.

28 In fact, since it included people working for the Stasi who did not figure in official employment statistics, the membership of the FDGB could amount to more than 100 per cent of those officially designated as employed.

29 Sebastian Simsch, 'Aufgeschlossenheit und Indifferenz: Deutsche Arbeiterinnen und Arbeiter, Deutsche Arbeitsfront und Freier Deutscher Gewerkschaftsbund, 1929–1962', in Hübner and Tenfelde, *Arbeiter in der SBZ-DDR.*

30 See chapter 4, above.

31 Peter Hübner, *Konsens, Konflikt und Kompromiß: Sozialer Arbeiterinteressen und Sozialpolitik in der DDR, 1945–1970* (Berlin: Akademie Verlag, 1995), p. 215.

32 See, for example, Jörg Roesler, 'Das Brigadetagebuch – betriebliches Rapportbuch, Chronik des Brigadelebens oder Erziehungsfibel?' in Evemarie Badstübner (ed.), *Befremdlich anders. Leben in der DDR* (Berlin: Karl Dietz Verlag, 2000), pp. 151–66.

33 Jörg Roesler, 'Die Produktionsbrigaden in der Industrie der DDR. Zentrum der Arbeitswelt?', in Kaelble, Kocka and Zwahr, *Sozialgeschichte der DDR.*

34 See, for example, Alf Lüdtke, 'Alltag "in unserer Ebene": Anfragen zu den Perspektiven auf die 1970er und 1980er Jahre in der DDR', in Hürtgen and Reichel, *Schein der Stabilität*, p. 299; Thomas Lindenberger, 'Everyday History: new approaches to the history of the post-war Germanies', in Christoph Klessmann (ed.), *The Divided Past: Rethinking Post-war German History* (Oxford and New York: Berg, 2001), p. 56.

35 See Peter Hübner, 'Die Zukunft war gestern: Soziale und mentale Trends in der DDR-Industriearbeiterschaft', in Kaelble, Kocka and Zwahr, *Sozialgeschichte der DDR*, pp. 235–9.

36 As pointed out by Reichel, 'Die "durchherrschte Arbeitsgesellschaft" ', p. 90.
37 See particularly Jeffrey Kopstein, *The Politics of Economic Decline in East Germany, 1945–1989* (Chapel Hill: University of North Carolina Press, 1997).
38 See chapter 13, below.
39 Cf. the interesting essay by Jens Gieseke, 'Die Einheit von Wirtschafts-, Sozial- und Sicherheitspolitik: Militarisierung und Überwachung als Probleme einer Sozialgeschichte der Ära Honecker. Christoph Kleßmann zum 65. Geburtstag', *Zeitschrift für Geschichtswissenschaft* 11 (2003), pp. 996–1021.
40 Solga, 'Aspekte', in Hürtgen and Reichel, *Schein der Stabilität*, pp. 47–8.
41 Boyer, 'Arbeiterkarrieren?', pp. 74–5
42 See Lothar Mertens (ed.), *Soziale Ungleichheit in der DDR* (Berlin: Duncker & Humblot, 2002), pp. 130 ff.
43 Cf. also Wolfgang Engler, *Die Ostdeutschen* (Berlin: Aufbau Verlag, 2002).
44 Arnold Sywottek, 'Gewalt – Reform – Arrangement: Die DDR in den 60er Jahren', in Axel Schildt, Detlef Siegfried and Karl Christian Lammers (eds), *Dynamische Zeiten: Die 60er Jahre in den beiden deutschen Gesellschaften* (Hamburg: Hans Christians Verlag, 2000), p. 70.

Chapter 11

1 Thomas Ammer, 'Strukturen der Macht – Die Funktionäre im SED-Staat' in Jürgen Weber (ed.), *Der SED-Staat: Neues über eine vergangene Diktatur* (Munich: Olzog Verlag, 1994), pp. 5–7.
2 SAPMO-BArch, DY 34/21500, 'Die zeitliche Belastung der Lehrer', p. 12.
3 SAPMO-BArch Bibliothek, FDJ/6163, Zentralinstitut für Jugendforschung, 'Zum demographischen und politischen Profil der ehrenamtlichen Funktionäre der FDJ', Leipzig, May 1980, pp. 4, 16, 26–31.
4 SAPMO-BArch, DY/34 10262.
5 SAPMO-BArch, DY/34 10262, letter of 28 August 1975.
6 SAPMO-BArch, DY/34 10262, letter of 13 November 1975.
7 SAPMO-BArch, DY/34 11032, letter of 11 June 1978.
8 SAPMO-BArch, DY/34 12668, letter of 5 October 1983.
9 SAPMO-BArch, DY 34/12668, letter of 16 March 1982.
10 SAPMO-BArch, DY/34/14617, letter of 9 October 1989.
11 Mike Dennis, *The Stasi: Myth and Reality* (London: Pearson, 2003), p. 4. On the Gestapo, see particularly Robert Gellately, *The Gestapo and German Society* (Oxford: Oxford University Press, 1990). See also Gisela Diewald-Kerkmann, 'Vertrauensleute, Denunzianten, geheime und inoffizielle Mitarbeiter in diktatorischen Regimen', in Arnd Bauerkämper, Martin Sabrow and Bernd Stöver (eds), *Doppelte Zeitgeschichte: Deutsch-deutsche Beziehungen, 1945–1990* (Bonn: Dietz, 1998).
12 See particularly H. Müller-Enbergs, *Inoffizielle Mitarbeiter des Ministeriums für Staatssicherheit. Teil 1: Richtlinien und Durchführungsbestimmungen*, 3rd edn (Berlin: Chr. Links Verlag, 2001).
13 See particularly Jens Gieseke, *Mielke-Konzern: Die Geschichte der Stasi, 1945–1900* (Munich: Deutsche Verlags–Anstalt, 2001) pp. 112–13.
14 Müller-Enbergs, *Inoffizielle Mitarbeiter*, pp. 150–1.
15 Gieseke, *Mielke-Konzern*, p.121.
16 See particularly the overviews and discussion in ibid., ch. 4; and H. Müller-Enbergs, 'Warum wird einer IM?', in Klaus Behnke and Jürgen Fuchs (eds), *Zersetzung der Seele: Psychologie und Psychiatrie im Dienste des MfS* (Hamburg: Rotbuch Verlag, 1995). See also for examples based on oral history interviews with ten former informants in the 1990s, Barbara Miller, *Narratives of Guilt and Compliance in Unified Germany* (London: Routledge, 1999); and the more impressionistic, journalistic approach in Anna Funder, *Stasiland* (London: Granta, 2003).

17 See the devastating personal testimony in Vera Wollenberger, *Virus der Heuchler* (Berlin: Elefanten Press, 1992).

18 I have discussed the Stolpe case at greater length in Mary Fulbrook, *Anatomy of a Dictatorship: Inside the GDR, 1949–1989* (Oxford: Oxford University Press, 1995), where further references may be found.

19 Brigitte Reimann, *Ich bedauere nichts: Tagebücher, 1955–1963* (Berlin: Aufbau Verlag, 1997), p. 73, entry of 28 September 1957.

20 Ibid., p. 83, entry of 25 January 1958.

21 See, for example, the contributions to Hans Joachim Schädlich (ed.), *Aktenkundig* (Berlin: Rowohlt, 1992). The literature in this area is by now very extensive, and it would be inappropriate to try to give full bibliographical references here.

22 A somewhat sensationalist account of particular cases can be found in John O. Koehler, *Stasi: The Untold Story of the East German Secret Police* (Boulder, Colo.: Westview Press, 1999).

23 See, for example, Peter Wensierski, 'DDR-Schriftsteller Jürgen Fuchs an Folgen der Stasi-Bestrahlung gestorben?', *Der Spiegel* 20 (17 May 1999), pp. 42–4.

24 Sonja Süß, *Politisch mißbraucht? Psychiatrie und Staatssicherheit in der DDR* (Berlin: Chr. Links Verlag, 1998), pp. 58–69.

25 Claudia Rusch, *Meine freie deutsche Jugend* (Frankfurt am Main: Fischer, 2003), pp. 16–17.

26 Ibid., p. 113.

27 Lutz Rathenow, 'Teile zu keinem Bild oder das Puzzle von der geheimen Macht', in Schädlich, *Aktenkundig*, p. 78.

28 Manfred Schmidt, 'Grundlagen der Sozialpolitik in der Deutschen Demokratischen Republik', in Ministerium für Arbeit und Sozialordnung und Bundesarchiv (ed.), *Geschichte der Sozialpolitik in Deutschland seit 1945* (Baden-Baden: Nomos Verlag, 2001), vol. 1, pp. 716–17.

Chapter 12

1 On dissidence and opposition, which have received very widespread attention since the fall of the GDR, there are numerous works. See, for example, Gary Bruce, *Resistance with the People: Repression and Resistance in Eastern Germany, 1945–1955* (Lanham, Md: Rowman & Littlefield, 2003); Erhart Neubert, *Geschichte der Opposition in der DDR, 1949–1989* (Berlin: Chr. Links Verlag, 1997); Ulrike Poppe, Rainer Eckert and Ilko-Sascha Kowalczuk (eds), *Zwischen Selbstbehauptung und Anpassung: Formen des Widerstandes und der Opposition in der DDR* (Berlin: Chr. Links Verlag, 1995); and my own early take on these issues in Fulbrook, *Anatomy of a Dictatorship: Inside the GDR, 1949–1989* (Oxford: Oxford University Press, 1995).

2 Victor Klemperer, *So sitze ich denn zwischen allen Stühlen*, vol. 2: *Tagebücher, 1950–1959* (Berlin: Aufbau Verlag, 1999), p. 680.

3 Ibid., vol, 2, p. 681.

4 Ibid., p. 682.

5 Among the many works on these themes, see, for example, Günter Agde (ed.), *Kahlschlag: Das 11. Plenum des ZK der SED* (Berlin: Aufbau Taschenbuch Verlag, 1991); David Bathrick, *The Powers of Speech: The Politics of Culture in the GDR* (Lincoln and London: University of Nebraska Press, 1995); Wolfgang Emmerich, *Kleine Literaturgeschichte der DDR* (Berlin: Aufbau Taschenbuch Verlag, 2000); Manfred Jäger, *Kultur und Politik in der DDR, 1945–1990* (Cologne: Deutschland Archiv, 1995); Jeannette Z. Madarász, *Conflict and Compromise in East Germany, 1971–1989: A Precarious Stability* (Basingstoke: Palgrave Macmillan, 2003); and for an intriguing insight from an insider's perspective, Günter de Bruyn, *Vierzig Jahre: Ein Lebensbericht* (Frankfurt am Main: Fischer Taschenbuch Verlag, 1998).

6 It is clearly impossible to do any kind of justice to this topic in a couple of sentences

here. But see for further discussion and a wide range of examples the excellent catalogue of a retrospective exhibition of GDR art: *Kunst in der DDR: Eine Retrospektive der
Nationalgalerie* (Berlin: G+H Verlag, 2003).

7 There is an extensive literature on the Stasi and culture: see, for example, Hans Joachim
Schädlich (ed.), *Aktenkundig* (Berlin: Rowohlt, 1992); and Joachim Walther,
*Sicherungsbereich Literatur: Schriftsteller und Staatssicherheit in der Deutschen
Demokratischen Republik* (Berlin: Chr. Links Verlag, 1996). On the Christa Wolf case,
see, for example, Hermann Vinke (ed.), *Akteneinsicht Christa Wolf: Zerrspiegel und
Dialog* (Hamburg: Luchterhand, 1993).

8 Heiner Müller, in Manfred Krug, *Abgehauen* (Düsseldorf: Econ Taschenbuch Verlag,
1998), p. 69.

9 Ellen Bos, *Leserbriefe in Tageszeitungen der DDR: Zur 'Massenverbundenheit' der Presse,
1949–1989* (Opladen: Westdeutscher Verlag, 1993), p. 119.

10 FDGB, 1201.2684; FDGB Bundesvorstand, Abteilung Organisation, '5/68: Sonder-
information über die Diskussion der Werktätigen zur Ausarbeitung einer sozialistischen Verfassung in der Deutschen Demokratischen Republik', 29 February 1968.
Sywottek sees the discussions as rather artificial and manipulative in character ('breit
inszeniert'): Sywottek in Axel Schildt, Detlef Siegfried and Karl Christian Lammers
(eds), *Dynamische Zeiten: Die 60er Jahre in den beiden deutschen Gesellschaften*
(Hamburg: Hans Christians Verlag, 2000), p. 67; but what matters here is less the
cynical intentions of the rulers than the ways in which such discussions were actually
experienced on the ground.

11 Mark Allinson, *Politics and Popular Opinion in East Germany, 1945–1968* (Manchester:
Manchester University Press, 2000), pp. 140–6.

12 As Allinson suggests, 'the minor modifications cost the party little but greatly improved
sentiment among those upon whom the system relied for support, and were exemplary
in foreign relations as a sign of a more liberal approach to human rights ... The amend-
ments also achieved much greater support from the religious communities than might
have been achieved had Christians not believed they had achieved a victory along the
way.' Ibid., p. 144.

13 See Dorothee Wierling, *Geboren im Jahr Eins: Der Jahrgang 1949 in der DDR: Versuch
einer Kollektivbiographie* (Berlin: Chr. Links Verlag, 2002), p. 302 n.352.

14 Ibid., p. 303, n.355.

15 ZIJ, F 74/3, 'Auswertung der Vorschläge zum Entwurf des Jugendgesetzes 1974'.

16 Ibid., p. 2.

17 Ibid., p. 3.

18 See chapter 3, above.

19 For fuller discussions of SED policy towards Jews and the development of Jewish religious communities in the GDR, see for a range of differing perspectives in what
remains a highly sensitive area, Robin Ostow, *Jews in Contemporary East Germany: The
Children of Moses in the Land of Marx* (Basingstoke: Macmillan, 1989); Lothar Mertens
(ed.), *Davidstern unter Hammer und Zirkel: Die jüdischen Gemeinden in der SBZ/DDR
und ihre Behandlung durch Partei und Staat, 1945–1990* (Hildesheim: Georg Olms
Verlag, 1997); and Mario Keßler, *Die SED und die Juden – Zwischen Repression und
Toleranz: Politische Entwicklungen bis 1967* (Berlin: Akademie Verlag, 1995).

20 Anetta Kahane, *Ich sehe was, was du nicht siehst: Meine deutschen Geschichten* (Berlin:
Rowohlt, 2004), p. 51.

21 On the early re-adjustment of Catholic institutional structures, arguably positioning
the Catholic community for survival through the atheist regime, see the detailed study
by Wolfgang Tischner, *Katholische Kirche in der SBZ/DDR: Die Formierung einer
Subgesellschaft im entstehenden sozialistischen Staat* (Paderborn: Ferdinand Schöningh,
2001).

22 Religion, and particularly the curiously ambivalent position of the Protestant

Churches, has attracted a great deal of attention from historians: relations between Church, Stasi and state, and the role of the Churches in what was sometimes dubbed the 'Protestant revolution' of 1989, were the focus of major historical attention particularly in the early 1990s. I have analysed this in greater detail in *Anatomy of a Dictatorship*. For more recent references to the by now very extensive material in this area, see, for example, the suggested reading in Rainer Eppelmann, Bernd Faulenbach and Ulrich Mählert (eds), *Bilanz und Perspektiven der DDR-Forschung* (Paderborn: Ferdinand Schöningh, 2003). See also, on religion and young people, chapter 6, above.

23 See for more detail, Peter Barker, 'The Birth of Official Policy towards the Sorbian Minority in the Soviet Zone of Occupation in Germany', in *German History* 14, no.1 (1996); and Peter Barker, *Slavs in Germany: The Sorbian Minority and the German State since 1945* (Lampeter: Edwin Mellen Press, 2000); see also my article on 'Democratic centralism and regionalism in the GDR', in Maiken Umbach (ed.), *German Federalism: Past, Present, Future* (Basingstoke: Palgrave Macmillan, 2002), pp. 146–71. For a publication from a GDR perspective, giving a flavour of the policy, see *Die Sorben: Wissenswertes aus Vergangenheit und Gegenwart der sorbischen nationalen Minderheit*, 3rd edn (Bautzen: VEB Domowina-Verlag, 1970). Sorbian costumes, furniture, literature and paintings, children's books, bibles, musical instruments, colourful Easter eggs, and photos of festivals and scenes from daily life going back a century or so, can be seen in the Wendisches Museum in Cottbus.

24 SAPMO-BArch, DY 30/J IV 2/9.06/2, 'Kurzinformation über die Durchführung des VI. Festivals der sorbischen Kultur', 6 June 1985, p. 2.

25 See particularly Damian mac con Uladh, UCL PhD thesis, 2005; see also, for an account based on interviews carried out in the early 1980s, Landolf Scherzer, *Die Fremden* (Berlin: Aufbau Verlag, 2002).

Chapter 13

1 *Kleines Politisches Wörterbuch* (Berlin: Dietz Verlag, 1978), p. 188.

2 Siegfried Mampel (ed.), *Die sozialistische Verfassung der Deutschen Demokratischen Republik* (Frankfurt am Main: Alfred Metzner Verlag, 1982), p. 1312.

3 For a brief period, from his ousting as First Secretary of the SED by Honecker in 1971 until his death in 1973, Ulbricht retained the function of Chair of the politically relatively unimportant Staatsrat. From 1973 until October 1976, Willi Stoph was Chair of the Council of State; the function was then taken over by Honecker.

4 Mampel, *Die sozialistische Verfassung*, p. 1319.

5 SAPMO-BArch, DQ4 00163, 'Information über die Eingabenarbeit im IV. Quartal 1966', Bl. 21.

6 See also the lampooning of the system of complaint letters in Wolfgang Becker's satirical film *Goodbye Lenin!* (2003), in which the mother, who is highly loyal to the Party, is portrayed as writing letters on behalf of aggrieved constituents; in this film, which captures an extraordinary flavour of authenticity, some of the phrases used are taken from genuine *Eingaben*.

7 *DDR Handbuch*, 2nd edn (Cologne: Verlag Wissenschaft und Politik, 1979), p. 292.

8 See Ellen Bos, *Leserbriefe in Tageszeitungen der DDR: Zur 'Massenverbundenheit' der Presse, 1949–1989* (Opladen: Westdeutscher Verlag, 1993), pp. 114–17.

9 SAPMO-BArch, DY 34/10262, series of letters from July to December 1974.

10 SAPMO-BArch, DY 31/602, letter of 13 October 1989, f. 14; the whole correspondence going back to 1986 is at ff. 14–24.

11 SAPMO-BArch, DY 34/10262, letters of 20 October 1975.

12 See, for example, SAPMO-BArch, DY 31/603, Eingaben-Analysen 1983–88.

13 SAPMO-BArch, DY 34/12668, Aktennotiz of 5 May 1983, and letter of 18 March 1983.

14 SAPMO-BArch, DY 31/563, letter of 9 July 1962.

15 See Jochen Staadt, *Eingaben: Die institutionalisierte Meckerkultur der DDR* (Working

paper of the Forschungsverbund SED-Staat, Free University, Berlin, December 1996), p. 2. I am very grateful to Jochen Staadt for making a copy of this paper available to me.

16 See, for example, Ina Merkel and Felix Mühlberg, 'Eingaben und Öffentlichkeit', in Ina Merkel (ed.), 'Wir sind doch nicht die Meckerecke der Nation': Briefe an das DDR-Fernsehen (Cologne: Böhlau Verlag, 1998), pp. 9–32.

17 Staadt, Eingaben, p. 17.

18 SAPMO-BArch, DQ 4/00163, Bl. 19.

19 SAPMO-BArch, DA 5/1062, 'Bericht über den Hauptinhalt der an die Volkskammer und den Staatsrat gerichteten Eingaben im 1. Quartal 1974', p. 11.

20 Quoted in Staadt, Eingaben, pp. 22–3.

21 Ibid., p. 34.

22 Cf. also Monika Deutz-Schroeder and Jochen Staadt (eds), Teuerer Genosse! Briefe an Erich Honecker (Berlin: Transit, 1994).

23 See, for example, SAPMO-BArch, DQ 4/00163, 'Information über die Eingabenarbeit im IV. Quartal 1966'.

24 SAPMO-BArch, DA 1/6482, 'Sprechstunde Dr. Holland am 7. Juli 1964 im VEB Baumwollweberei und Veredlung, Werk II, Neusalza-Spremberg', p. 3.

25 SAPMO-BArch, DA 1/6480, 'Material für die Untersuchungen in Wohnungsfragen in der Gemeinde Großschönau am 12.3.1964'.

26 SAPMO-BArch, DQ 4/00163, 'Information über Probleme aus den im 2. Vierteljahr an den Ministerrat gerichteten Eingaben der Bürger', '3. Wohnungswirtschaft'; SAPMO-BArch DA 5/1138, 'Bericht über die an den Staatsrat gerichteten Eingaben im Jahre 1976', p. 42.

27 SAPMO-BArch, DA 5/1138, 'Bericht über die an den Staatsrat gerichteten Eingaben im Jahre 1976', p. 41.

28 SAPMO-BArch DA 1/17301, 'Stenografisches Protokoll. Sitzung des Ausschusses für Eingaben der Bürger vom 25. bis 27. Oktober 1988 in Dessau'.

29 See also Chapter 6, above.

30 See, for example, SAPMO-BArch, DA 1/6482, VEB Baumwollweberei und Veredlung Neusalza/Spremberg, 'Konzeption für den Einsatz einer Arbeitsgruppe des Eingabenausschusses der Volkskammer, 6. und 7.7.1964 (Kreis Löbau)'; SAPMO-BArch, DA 1/6476, 'Information über Eingaben zum neuen Handwerkssteuergesetz'; and the snappily entitled 'Einschätzung einiger Konflikte und offener Fragen bei der Durchsetzung des Gesetzbuches der Arbeit, die sich wiederholt als Ursache für Eingaben an den Staatsrat erweisen' (1966).

31 See, for example, SAPMO-BArch, DQ 4/00163, 'Information über die Eingabenarbeit im II. Quartal 1966'; on veterans see, for example, SAPMO-BArch, DY 30/IV A 2/11/15; on cadre questions in other areas see also SAPMO-BArch, DY 30/IV A 2/11/7.

32 SAPMO-BArch, DA 1/7541, 'Stenografisches Protokoll. Beratung des Ausschusses für Eingaben der Bürger der Volkskammer am 11.3.1971 im Hause der Volkskammer zu Berlin'.

33 Ibid., p. 33.

34 See, for example, on children's clothing Ina Merkel, ' "… in Hoyerswerdaleben jedenfalls keine so kleinen viereckigen Menschen." Briefe an das Fernsehen der DDR', in Alf Lüdtke and Peter Becker (eds), Akten, Eingaben, Schaufenster: Die DDR und ihre Texte (Berlin: Akademie Verlag, 1997); on cakes, SAPMO-BArch, DA 1/6480, 'Konzeption für den Einsatz des Vorstandes und einiger Mitglieder des Ausschusses für Eingaben der Bürger in Kreis Zittau vom 12.3–14.3.1964', p. 5; and material in DA 1/6482.

35 SAPMO-BArch, DA 5/1138, 'Bericht über die an den Staatsrat gerichteten Eingaben im Jahre 1976', pp. 47, 53.

36 SAPMO-BArch, DA 5/1153, 'Bericht an den Staatsrat der DDR über die Arbeit der Staatsanwaltschaft mit den Eingaben im Jahre 1977', p. 14.

37 Renate Hürtgen, 'Entwicklung in der Stagnation? Oder: was ist so spannend am

Betriebsalltag der 70er und 80er Jahre in der DDR?', in Renate Hürtgen und Thomas Reichel (eds), *Der Schein der Stabilität: DDR-Betriebsalltag in der Ära Honecker* (Berlin: Metropol Verlag, 2001), pp. 28–9, 31–2.

38 SAPMO-BArch, DA 1/6482, 'Konzeption für den Einsatz des Vorstandes und einiger Mitglieder des Ausschusses für Eingaben der Bürger in Kreis Zittau vom 12.3–14.3.1964', p. 3.

39 SAPMO-BArch, DQ 4/00163, 'Information über die Eingabenarbeit im IV. Quartal 1966', Bl. 9.

40 SAPMO-BArch, DQ 4/00163, Bl. 19, 20.

41 SAPMO-BArch, DQ 4/00163, 'Information über Probleme aus den im 2. Vierteljahr 1967 an den Ministerrat gerichteten Eingaben der Bürger', pp. 1, 3.

42 SAPMO-BArch, DQ 4/00163, 'Vorbereitung und Durchführung der Zusammenlegung oder Auflösung bzw. Neuzuordnung von volkseigenen Produktionsbetrieben', p. 1.

43 SAPMO-BArch, DA 1/6480, 'Einschätzung der Arbeit des Rates des Kreises Zittau mit den Eingaben der Bürger', p. 5.

44 See also, for example, SAPMO-BArch, DA 1/6480, 'Material für die Untersuchungen in Wohnungsfragen in der Gemeinde Großschönau am 12.3.1964', pp. 4–5.

45 SAPMO-BArch, DA 1/7541, 'Stenografisches Protokoll. Beratung des Ausschusses für Eingaben der Bürger der Volkskammer am 11.3.1971 im Hause der Volkskammer zu Berlin', p. 26

46 SAPMO-BArch, DY 34/10262, 1975.

47 SAPMO-BArch, DA 1/6482, 'Bericht über den Einsatz einer Arbeitsgruppe des Eingabenausschusses der Volkskammer, 6. und 7.7.1964 (Kreis Löbau)', pp. 4–5.

48 See Staadt, *Eingaben.*

49 See the analysis by Ina Merkel and Felix Mühlberg, 'Eingaben und Öffentlichkeit', in Ina Merkel (ed.), *'Wir sind doch nicht die Meckerecke der Nation'*: *Briefe an das DDR-Fernsehen* (Cologne: Böhlau Verlag, 1998), pp. 24–7.

50 See Staadt, *Eingaben,* p. 5. Staadt summarises the suppression of what he calls 'Notrufe' as a 'phänomenale Verdrängungsleistung'. Although much of his own material, on which I draw below, then goes on to provide evidence against this interpretation, this remains the underlying tenor or implicit moral of Staadt's article.

51 Merkel and Mühlberg, 'Eingaben und Öffentlichkeit', p. 10.

52 See, for example, Renate Hürtgen, 'Der Streik in der DDR: Wie viel Widerstand gab es in den DDR-Betrieben?', lecture delivered in the series *DDR-Geschichte* in the Berlin Haus der Demokratie und Menschenrechte, 2 June 2003; printed version in *Horch und Guck* 43 (2003), 'Ökonomie in der Ära Honecker', pp. 7–11.

53 SAPMO-BArch, DY 34/25414.

54 See, for example, Ina Merkel, ' "... in Hoyerswerda leben jedenfalls keine so kleinen viereckigen Menschen" '.

Select bibliography

Research on the history of the GDR has developed massively with the opening of the archives in the 1990s. This bibliography lists a relatively small selection of the many recent books on aspects of GDR society and social history. It also includes a few collections of published primary sources, and some pre-1989 GDR publications of continuing interest that may not be widely known. A small number of autobiographies, biographies and works on political history have also been included, but the temptation has been resisted to list too many works on topics that are well covered elsewhere in the secondary literature. Many of the works listed below contain detailed suggestions for further reading.

References to archival sources, individual book chapters and journal articles will be found in the endnotes above, and are not included again here. With the reorganisation of the archival legacy of the GDR, many files have been re-catalogued; source references to primary material have been given with the reference number at the time I did the research (so, for example, studies carried out by the Leipzig Central Institute for Youth Research have been cited with the ZIJ reference if I read them while they were still in Leipzig, and the number prefixed with FDJ if I read them following their transfer to the library of the Bundesarchiv in Berlin).

Johannes Abele, Gerhard Barkleit and Thomas Hänseroth (eds), *Innovationskulturen und Fortschrittserwartungen im geteilten Deutschland* (Cologne: Böhlau Verlag, 2001)

Günter Agde (ed.), *Kahlschlag: Das 11. Plenum des ZK der SED* (Berlin: Aufbau Taschenbuch Verlag, 1991)

Mark Allinson, *Politics and Popular Opinion in East Germany, 1945–1968* (Manchester: Manchester University Press, 2000)

Leonore Ansorg, *Kinder im Klassenkampf: Die Geschichte der Pionierorganisation von 1948 bis Ende der fünfziger Jahre* (Berlin: Akademie Verlag, 1997)

Authors' collective under the leadership of Kurt Krambach, *Wie lebt man auf dem Dorf? Soziologische Aspekte der Entwicklung des Dorfes in der DDR* (Berlin: Dietz Verlag, 1985)

Authors' collective under the leadership of Manfred Lötsch, *Ingenieure in der DDR* (Berlin: Dietz Verlag, 1988)

Authors' collective under the leadership of Peter Voß, *Die Freizeit der Jugend* (Berlin: Dietz Verlag, 1981)

Evemarie Badstübner (ed.), *Befremdlich anders: Leben in der DDR* (Berlin: Karl Dietz Verlag, 2000)

Simone Barck, Martina Langermann and Siegfried Lokatis (eds), *Zwischen 'Mosaik' und 'Einheit': Zeitschriften in der DDR* (Berlin: Chr. Links Verlag, 1999)

David Bathrick, *The Powers of Speech: The Politics of Culture in the GDR* (Lincoln and London: University of Nebraska Press, 1995)

Theresia Bauer, *Blockpartei und Agrarrevolution von oben* (Munich: Oldenbourg Wissenschaftsverlag, 2003)

Arnd Bauerkämper, *Ländliche Gesellschaft in der kommunistischen Diktatur: Zwangsmodernisierung und Tradition in Brandenburg, 1945–1963* (Cologne, Weimar, Vienna: Böhlau Verlag, 2002)

—— *et al.* (eds), *Gesellschaft ohne Eliten? Führungsgruppen in der DDR* (Metropol, 1997)

——, Martin Sabrow and Bernd Stöver (eds), *Doppelte Zeitgeschichte: Deutsch-deutsche Beziehungen, 1945–1990* (Bonn: Dietz, 1998)

Franziska Becker, Ina Merkel and Simone Tippach-Schneider (eds), *Das Kollektiv bin ich: Utopie und Alltag in der DDR* (Cologne, Weimar, Vienna: Böhlau Verlag, 2000)

Klaus Behnke and Jürgen Wolf (eds), *Stasi auf dem Schulhof: Der Missbrauch von Kinder* (Berlin: Ullstein, 1998)

Richard Bessel and Ralph Jessen (eds), *Die Grenzen der Diktatur: Staat und Gesellschaft in der DDR* (Göttingen: Vandenhoeck & Ruprecht, 1996)

Stefan Bollinger and Fritz Vilmar (eds), *Die DDR war anders: Eine kritische Würdigung ihrer sozialkulturellen Einrichtungen* (Berlin: edition ost, 2002)

Ellen Bos, *Leserbriefe in Tageszeitungen der DDR: Zur 'Massenverbundenheit' der Presse, 1949–1989* (Opladen: Westdeutscher Verlag, 1993)

Beatrix Bouvier, *Die DDR – ein Sozialstaat?: Sozialpolitik in der Ära Honecker* (Bonn: Verlag J. H. W. Dietz Nachf., 2002)

Gary Bruce, *Resistance with the People: Repression and Resistance in Eastern Germany, 1945–1955* (Lanham, Md: Rowman & Littlefield, 2003)

Günter de Bruyn, *Vierzig Jahre: Ein Lebensbericht* (Frankfurt am Main: Fischer Taschenbuch Verlag, 1998)

Gunille-Friederike Budde (ed.), *Frauen Arbeiten: Weibliche Erwerbstätigkeit in Ost- und Westdeutschland nach 1945* (Göttingen: Vandenhoeck & Ruprecht, 1997)

David Childs, *The Fall of the GDR: Germany's Road to Unity* (Harlow: Longman, 2001)

—— and Richard Popplewell, *The Stasi* (London: Macmillan, 1996)

Mike Dennis, *Social and Economic Modernisation in Eastern Germany: From Honecker to Kohl* (London: Pinter, 1993)

——, *The Rise and Fall of the German Democratic Republic, 1945–1990* (Harlow: Pearson Longman, 2000)

——, *The Stasi: Myth and Reality* (London: Pearson, 2003)

Hans-Ulrich Deppe, Hannes Friedrich and Rainer Müller (eds), *Gesundheitssystem im Umbruch von der DDR zur BRD* (Frankfurt: Campus Verlag, 1993)

Deutscher Bundestag (ed.), *Materialien der Enquete-Kommission 'Überwindung der Folgen der SED-Diktatur im Prozeß der deutschen Einheit'* (Baden-Baden: Nomos-Verlag, 1999)

Monika Deutz-Schroeder and Jochen Staadt (eds), *Teuerer Genosse! Briefe an Erich Honecker* (Berlin: Transit, 1994)

Christoph Dieckmann, *My Generation: Cocker, Dylan, Honecker und die bleibende Zeit*, 2nd edn (Berlin: Chr. Links Verlag, 1999)

Dokumentationszentrum Alltagskultur der DDR (eds), *Fortschritt, Norm und Eigensinn: Erkundungen im Alltag der DDR* (Berlin: Chr. Links Verlag, 1999)

Hans Ehlert and Matthias Rogg (eds), *Militär, Staat und Gesellschaft in der DDR* (Berlin: Chr. Links Verlag, 2004).

Bernd Eisenfeld, Ilko-Sascha Kowalczuk and Ehrhart Neubert, *Die verdrängte Revolution: Der Platz des 17. Juni 1953 in der deutschen Geschichte* (Bremen: Edition Temmen, 2004)

Thomas Elkeles *et al.* (eds), *Prävention und Prophylaxe* (Berlin: Rainer Bohn Verlag, 1991)

Wolfgang Emmerich, *Kleine Literaturgeschichte der DDR* (Berlin: Aufbau Taschenbuch Verlag, 2000)

Wolfgang Engler, *Die Ostdeutschen* (Berlin: Aufbau Verlag, 2002)

Rainer Eppelmann, Bernd Faulenbach and Ulrich Mählert (eds), *Bilanz und Perspektiven der DDR-Forschung* (Paderborn: Ferdinand Schöningh, 2003)

Anne-Sabine Ernst, 'Die beste Prophylaxe ist der Sozialismus.' Ärzte und medizinische Hochschullehrer in der SBZ/DDR, 1945–1961 (Münster, New York, Munich, Berlin: Waxmann, 1997)

Joshua Feinstein, The Triumph of the Ordinary: Depictions of Daily Life in the East German Cinema, 1949–1989 (Chapel Hill: University of North Carolina Press, 2002)

Barbara Felsmann (ed.), Beim Kleinen Trompeter habe ich immer geweint: Kindheit in der DDR – Erinnerungen an die Jungen Pioniere (Berlin: Lukas Verlag, 2003)

Peter Förster, Walter Friedrich, Harry Müller and Wilfried Schubarth, Jugend Ost: Zwischen Hoffnung und Gewalt (Opladen: Leske & Budrich, 1993)

Arnold Freiburg and Christa Mahrrad, FDJ: Der sozialistische Jugendverband der DDR (Opladen: Leske & Budrich, 1982)

Walter Friedrich and Hartmut Griese (eds), Jugend und Jugendforschung in der DDR: Gesellschaftliche Situationen, Sozialisation und Mentalitätsentwicklung in den achtziger Jahren (Opladen: Leske & Budrich, 1991)

R. Galenza and H. Havemeister, Wir wollen immer artig sein ... Punk, New Wave, Hip-Hop, Independent-Szene in der DDR 1980–1990 (Berlin: Schwarzkopf & Schwarzkopf, 2000)

Günter Gaus, Wo Deutschland liegt (Munich: Deutscher Taschenbuch Verlag, 1986)

Gert Geissler and Ulrich Wiegmann, Schule und Erziehung in der DDR: Studien und Dokumente (Neuwied and Berlin: Luchterhand, 1995)

——, Pädagogik und Herrschaft in der DDR (Frankfurt: Peter Lang, 1996)

Jens Gieseke, Die hauptamtlichen Mitarbeiter der Staatssicherheit: Personalstruktur und Lebenswelt, 1950–1989/90 (Berlin: Chr. Links Verlag, 2000)

——, Mielke-Konzern: Die Geschichte der Stasi, 1945–1990 (Munich: Deutsche Verlags-Anstalt, 2001)

Helga Gotschlich (ed.), 'Links und Links und Schritt gehalten . . .' Die FDJ: Konzepte – Abläufe – Grenzen (Berlin: Metropol Verlag, 1994)

Tilmann Grammes (ed.), Staatsbürgerkunde in der DDR: Quellen und Dokumente (Opladen: Leske & Budrich, 1999)

Peter Grieder, The East German Leadership, 1946–1973: Conflict and Crisis (Manchester: Manchester University Press, 1999)

Thomas Grimm (ed.), Das Poltibüro privat: Ulbricht, Honecker, Mielke & Co. aus der Sicht ihrer Angestellten (Berlin: Aufbau Verlag, 2004)

Sonja Häder, Schülerkindheit in Ost-Berlin: Sozialisation unter den Bedingungen der Diktatur (Cologne: Böhlau Verlag, 1998)

—— and Heinz-Elmar Tenorth (eds), Bildungsgeschichte einer Diktatur (Weinheim: Deutscher Studien Verlag, 1997)

Handbuch Gesellschaftlicher Organisationen in der DDR: Massenorganisationen, Verbände, Vereinigungen, Gesellschaften, Genossenschaften, Komitees, Ligen (Staatsverlag der Deutschen Demokratischen Republik, 1985)

Erich Hasemann, Soldat der DDR (Berlin: Verlag am Park, 1997)

Julia Hell, Post-fascist Fantasies: Psychoanalysis, History and the Literature of East Germany (Durham, N.C.: Duke University Press, 1997)

Gisela Helwig and Hildegard Maria Nickel (eds), Frauen in Deutschland, 1945–1992 (Bonn: Bundeszentrale für politische Bildung, 1993)

Klaus-Dietmar Henke (ed.), Totalitarismus (Dresden: Hannah-Arendt-Institut für Totalitarismusforschung, Berichte und Studien Nr. 18, 1999)

Rüdiger Henkel, Im Dienste der Staatspartei: Über Parteien und Organisationen der DDR (Baden-Baden: Nomos Verlag, 1994)

Walter Hennig and Walter Friedrich (eds), Jugend in der DDR: Daten und Ergebnisse der Jugendforschung vor der Wende (Weinheim and Munich: Juventa Verlag, 1991)

Andreas Herbst, Winfried Ranke and Jürgen Winkler (eds), So funktionierte die DDR (Reinbek bei Hamburg: Rowohlt, 1994)

Andreas Herbst, Gerd-Rüdiger Stephan and Jürgen Winkler (eds), *Die SED: Geschichte –
Organisation – Politik: Ein Handbuch* (Berlin: Dietz Verlag, 1997)
Brigitte Hohlfeld, *Die Neulehrer in der SBZ/DDR, 1945–1953: Ihre Rolle bei der
Umgestaltung von Gesellschaft und Staat* (Weinheim: Deutsche Studien Verlag, 1992)
Peter Hübner, *Konsens, Konflikt und Kompromiß: Soziale Arbeiterinteressen und Sozialpolitik
in der SBZ/DDR, 1945–1970* (Berlin: Akademie Verlag, 1995)
—— (ed.), *Niederlausitzer Industrie-Arbeiter 1935 bis 1970: Studien zur Sozialgeschichte*
(Berlin: Akademie Verlag, 1995)
—— (ed.), *Eliten im Sozialismus: Beiträge zur Sozialgeschichte der DDR* (Cologne, Weimer,
Vienna: Böhlau Verlag, 1999)
—— and Klaus Tenfelde (eds), *Arbeiter in der SBZ-DDR* (Essen: Klartext, 1999)
Johannes Huinink *et al.*, *Kollektiv und Eigensinn: Lebensverläufe in der DDR und danach*
(Berlin: Akademie Verlag, 1995)
Antonia Maria Humm, *Auf dem Weg zum sozialistischen Dorf? Zum Wandel der
dörflichen Lebenswelt in der DDR und BRD 1952–1969* (Göttingen: Vandenhoeck &
Ruprecht, 1999)
Renate Hürtgen and Thomas Reichel (eds), *Der Schein der Stabilität: DDR-Betriebsalltag in
der Ära Honecker* (Berlin: Metropol Verlag, 2001)
Manfred Jäger, *Kultur und Politik in der DDR, 1945–1990* (Cologne: Deutschland Archiv,
1995)
Konrad Jarausch (ed.), *Dictatorship as Experience* (Oxford and New York: Berghahn, 1999)
Ralph Jessen, *Akademische Elite und kommunistische Diktatur: Die Ostdeutsche Hochschul-
lehrerschaft in der Ulbricht-Ära* (Göttingen: Vandenhoeck & Ruprecht, 1999)
Matthias Judt (ed.), *DDR-Geschichte in Dokumenten: Beschlüsse, Berichte, interne
Materialien und Alltagszeugnisse* (Berlin: Chr. Links Verlag, 1997)
Hartmut Kaelble, Jürgen Kocka and Hartmut Zwahr (eds), *Sozialgeschichte der DDR*
(Stuttgart: Klett-Cotta, 1994)
Monika Kaiser, *Machtwechsel von Ulbricht zu Honecker: Funktionsmechanism der SED-
Diktatur in Konfliktsituationen 1962 bis 1972* (Berlin: Akademie Verlag, 1997)
Annette Kaminsky, *Wohlstand, Schönheit, Glück: Kleine Konsumgeschichte der DDR*
(Munich: C. H. Beck, 2001)
Mario Keßler, *Die SED und die Juden – zwischen Repression und Toleranz: Politische
Entwicklungen bis 1967* (Berlin: Akademie Verlag, 1995)
Christoph Klessmann (ed.), *Zwei Staaten, eine Nation: Deutsche Geschichte, 1955–1970*
(Göttingen: Vandenhoeck & Ruprecht, 1988)
—— (ed.), *The Divided Past: Rethinking Post-War German History* (Oxford and New York:
Berg, 2001)
—— and Georg Wagner (eds), *Das gespaltene Land: Leben in Deutschland 1945 bis 1990:
Texte und Dokumente* (Munich: C. H. Beck, 1993)
Freya Klier, *Lüg Vaterland: Erziehung in der DDR* (Munich: Kindler Verlag, 1990)
Jürgen Kocka (ed.), *Historische DDR-Forschung: Aufsätze und Studien* (Berlin: Akademie
Verlag, 1993)
—— and Martin Sabrow, *Die DDR als Geschichte: Fragen, Hypothesen, Perspektiven* (Berlin:
Akademie Verlag, 1994)
John O. Koehler, *Stasi: The Untold Story of the East German Secret Police* (Boulder, Colo.:
Westview Press, 1999)
Jeffrey Kopstein, *The Politics of Economic Decline in East Germany, 1945–1989* (Chapel Hill:
University of North Carolina Press, 1997)
Sandrine Kott, *Le Communisme au quotidien: Les enterprises d'etat dans la société est-alle-
mande* (Paris: Belin, 2001)
Manfred Krug, *Abgehauen* (Düsseldorf: Econ Taschenbuch Verlag, 1998)
Marianne Krüger-Potratz, *Anderssein gab es nicht: Ausländer und Minderheiten in der DDR*
(Münster: Waxmann, 1991)

Jürgen Kuczynski, *Ein Leben in der Wissenschaft der DDR* (Münster: Westfälisches Dampfboot, 1994)
Jürgen Lemke (ed.), *Gay Voices from East Germany* (Bloomington: Indiana University Press, 1991)
Wolfgang Leonhard, *Die Revolution entlässt ihre Kinder* (Cologne: Kiepenheuer & Witsch, 1955)
Achim Leschinsky, Petra Gruner and Gerhard Kluchert (eds), *Die Schule als moralische Anstalt: Erziehung in der Schule: Allgemeines und der 'Fall DDR'* (Weinheim: Deutscher Studien Verlag, 1999.
Thomas Lindenberger, *Volkspolizei: Herrschaftspraxis und öffentliche Ordnung im SED-Staat, 1952–1968* (Cologne: Böhlau Verlag, 2003)
—— (ed.), *Herrschaft und Eigen-Sinn in der Diktatur: Studien zur Gesellschaftsgeschichte der DRR* (Cologne: Böhlau Verlag, 1999)
Jan Lorenzen, *Erich Honecker: Eine Biographie* (Hamburg: Rowohlt, 2001)
Alf Lüdtke and Peter Becker (eds), *Akten, Eingaben, Schaufenster: Die DDR und ihre Texte* (Berlin: Akademie Verlag, 1997)
Andreas Ludwig (ed.), *Fortschritt, Norm und Eigensinn: Erkundungen im Alltag der DDR* (Berlin: Chr. Links Verlag, 1999)
Hans-Joachim Maaz, *Behind the Wall: The Inner Life of Communist East Germany* (New York and London: W. W. Norton, 1995)
A. James McAdams, *Judging the Past in Unified Germany* (Cambridge: Cambridge University Press, 2001)
Jeannette Z. Madarász, *Conflict and Compromise in East Germany, 1971–1989: A Precarious Stability* (Basingstoke: Palgrave Macmillan, 2003)
Ulrich Mählert, *Kleine Geschichte der DDR* (Munich: C. H. Beck, 1998)
—— and Gerd-Rüdiger Stephan, *Blaue Hemden, rote Fahnen: Die Geschichte der Freien Deutschen Jugend* (Opladen: Leske & Budrich, 1996)
Patrick Major and Jonathan Osmond (eds), *The Workers' and Peasants' State* (Manchester: Manchester University Press, 2002)
Siegfried Mampel (ed.), *Die sozialistische Verfassung der Deutschen Demokratischen Republik* (Frankfurt am Main: Alfred Metzner Verlag, 1982)
Günter Manz, *Armut in der 'DDR'–Bevölkerung: Lebensstandard und Konsumtionsniveau vor und nach der Wende* (Augsburg: Maro Verlag, 1992)
Ludwig Mecklinger, Horst Kriewald and Rolf Lämmer (eds), *Gesundheitsschutz und soziale Betreuung der Bürger* (Berlin: Staatsverlag der Deutschen Demokratischen Republik, 1974)
Ina Merkel, *Utopie und Bedürfnis: Die Geschichte der Konsumkultur in der DDR* (Cologne: Böhlau Verlag, 1999)
—— (ed.), *'Wir sind doch nicht die Meckerecke der Nation': Briefe an das DDR-Fernsehen* (Cologne: Böhlau Verlag, 1998)
Lothar Mertens, *Wider die sozialistische Familiennorm: Ehescheidungen in der DDR, 1950–1989* (Opladen: Westdeutscher Verlag, 1998)
—— (ed.), *Davidstern unter Hammer und Zirkel: Die jüdischen Gemeinden in der SBZ/DDR und ihre Behandlung durch Partei und Staat 1945–1990* (Hildesheim: Georg Olms Verlag, 1997)
—— (ed.), *Soziale Ungleichheit in der DDR: Zu einem tabuisierten Strukturmerkmal der SED-Diktatur* (Berlin: Duncker & Humblot, 2002)
—— and Sabine Gries (eds), *Arbeit, Sport und DDR-Gesellschaft* (Berlin: Duncker & Humblot, 1996)
—— and Dieter Voigt (eds), *Humanistischer Sozialismus? Der Umgang der SED mit der Bevölkerung, dargestellt an ausgewählten Gruppen* (Münster: Lit Verlag, 1995)
Gerd Meyer, *Die DDR-Machtelite in der Ära Honecker* (Tübingen: A. Francke Verlag, 1991)
Ingrid Miethe, *Frauen in der DDR-Opposition* (Opladen: Leske & Budrich 1999)

Barbara Miller, *Narratives of Guilt and Compliance in Unified Germany: Stasi informers and their impact on society* (London: Routledge, 1999)

Armin Mitter and Stefan Wolle, *Untergang auf Raten: Unbekannte Kapitel der DDR-Geschichte* (Munich: C. Bertelsmann Verlag, 1993)

Hans Modrow (ed.), *Das große Haus: Insider berichten aus dem ZK der SED* (Berlin: edition ost, 1994)

—— (ed.), *Das große Haus von außen* (Berlin: edition ost, 1996)

Jörn Mothes *et al.* (eds), *Beschädigte Seelen: DDR-Jugend und Staatssicherheit* (Rostock: Edition Temmen, 1996)

H. Müller-Enbergs, *Inoffizielle Mitarbeiter des Ministeriums für Staatssicherheit*, vol 1: *Richtlinien und Durchführungsbestimmungen*, 3rd edn (Berlin: Chr. Links Verlag, 2001)

—— and J. Wielgohs (eds), *Wer war wer in der DDR?* (Bonn: Bundeszentrale für politische Bildung, 2001)

Norman M. Naimark, *The Russians in Germany: A History of the Soviet Zone of Occupation, 1945–1949* (Cambridge, Mass.: Harvard University Press, 1995)

Erhart Neubert, *Geschichte der Opposition in der DDR, 1949–1989* (Berlin: Chr. Links Verlag, 1997)

Heinz Niemann, *Meinungsforschung in der DDR: Die geheimen Berichte des Instituts für Meinungsforschung an das Politbüro der SED* (Cologne: Bund-Verlag, 1993)

——, *Hinterm Zaun: Politische Kultur und Meinungsforschung in der DDR: Die geheimen Berichte an das Politbüro der SED* (Berlin: edition ost, 1995)

Lutz Niethammer, Alexander von Plato and Dorothee Wierling, *Die volkseigene Erfahrung* (Berlin: Rowohlt, 1991)

Alan Nothnagle, *Building the East German Myth: Historical Mythology and Youth Propaganda in the German Democratic Republic, 1945–1989* (Ann Arbor: University of Michigan Press, 1999)

Marc-Dietrich Ohse, *Jugend nach dem Mauerbau: Anpassung, Protest und Eigensinn (DDR 1961–1974)* (Berlin: Chr. Links Verlag, 2003)

Robin Ostow, *Jews in Contemporary East Germany: The Children of Moses in the Land of Marx* (Basingstoke: Macmillan, 1989)

Joachim Palutzki, *Architektur in der DDR* (Berlin: Dietrich Reiner Verlag, 2000)

David Pike, *The Politics of Culture in Soviet-Occupied Germany, 1945–1949* (Stanford: Stanford University Press, 1992)

Theo Pirker *et al.* (eds), *Der Plan als Befehl und Fiktion: Wirtschaftsführung in der DDR* (Opladen: Westdeutscher Verlag, 1995)

Plato, Alexander von, 'The Hitler Youth generation and its role in the two post-war German states' in Mark Roseman (ed.), *Generations in Conflict* (Cambridge: Cambridge University Press, 1995)

—— and Wolfgang Meinecke (eds), *Alte Heimat – neue Zeit: Flüchtlinge, Umgesiedelte, Vertriebene in der Sowjetischen Besatzungszone und in der DDR* (Berlin: Verlags-Anstalt Union, 1991)

Uta Poiger, *Jazz, Rock, and Rebels: Cold War Politics and American Culture in a Divided Germany* (Berkeley: University of California Press, 2000)

Detlef Pollack, *Kirche in der Organisationsgesellschaft* (Stuttgart: Kohlhammer, 1994)

Ulrike Poppe, Rainer Eckert and Ilko-Sascha Kowalczuk (eds), *Zwischen Selbstbehauptung und Anpassung: Formen des Widerstandes und der Opposition in der DDR* (Berlin: Chr. Links Verlag, 1995)

Michael Rauhut, *Beat in der Grauzone: DDR-Rock 1964 bis 1972: Politik und Alltag* (Berlin: Basis Druck, 1993)

——, *Schalmei und Lederjacke: Udo Lindenberg, BAP, Underground: Rock und Politik in den 80er Jahren* (Berlin: Schwarzkopf & Schwarzkopf, 1996)

Brigitte Reimann, *Aber wir schaffen es, verlaß dich drauf! Briefe an eine Freundin im Westen* (Berlin: Elefanten Press, 1995)

——, *Ich bedauere nichts: Tagebücher, 1955–1963* (Berlin: Aufbau Verlag, 1997)

—— and Christa Wolf, *Sei gegrüßt und lebe: Eine Freundschaft in Briefen, 1964–1973* (Berlin: Aufbau Verlag, 1993)

David Rock (ed.), *Voices in Times of Change* (New York and Oxford: Berghahn, 2000)

John Rodden, *Repainting the Little Red Schoolhouse* (Oxford: Oxford University Press, 2002)

Mark Roseman (ed.), *Generations in Conflict* (Cambridge: Cambridge University Press, 1995)

Corey Ross, *Constructing Socialism at the Grass-Roots: The Transformation of East Germany* (Basingstoke: Macmillan, 2000)

——, *The East German Dictatorship: Problems and Perspectives in the Interpretation of the GDR* (London: Arnold, 2002)

Maria Elisabeth Ruban, *Gesundheitswesen in der DDR* (Berlin: Verlag Gebr. Holzapfel, 1981)

Claudia Rusch, *Meine freie deutsche Jugend* (Frankfurt am Main: Fischer, 2003)

Günther Schabowski, *Das Politbüro* (Hamburg: Rowohlt, 1990)

Hans Joachim Schädlich (ed.), *Aktenkundig* (Berlin: Rowohlt, 1992)

Helmut Schelsky, *Die skeptische Generation* (Frankfurt am Main: Ullstein, 1975)

Landolf Scherzer, *Der Erste: Eine Reportage aus der DDR* (Cologne: Kiepenheuer & Witsch, 1989)

——, *Die Fremden* (Berlin: Aufbau Verlag, 2002)

Axel Schildt, Detlef Siegfried and Karl Christian Lammers (eds), *Dynamische Zeiten: Die 60er Jahre in den beiden deutschen Gesellschaften* (Hamburg: Hans Christians Verlag, 2000)

Manfred Schmidt, 'Grundlagen der Sozialpolitik in der Deutschen Demokratischen Republik', in Bundesministerium für Arbeit und Sozialordnung und Bundesarchiv (eds), *Geschichte der Sozialpolitik in Deutschland seit 1945*, vol. 1: *Grundlagen der Sozialpolitik* (Baden-Baden: Nomos Verlag, 2001), pp. 685–798

Klaus Schroeder, 'Die DDR: eine (spät-)totalitäre Gesellschaft', in Manfred Wilke (ed.), *Die Anatomie der Parteizentrale: Die KPD/SED auf dem Weg zur Macht* (Berlin: Akademie Verlag, 1997)

——, *Der SED-Staat: Partei, Staat und Gesellschaft, 1949–1990* (Munich: Carl Hanser Verlag, 1998)

Elmar Schubbe (ed.), *Dokumente zur Kunst-, Literatur- und Kultur-Politik der SED*, vol. 1: 1946–1970 (Stuttgart: Seewald Verlag, 1972)

Eberhard Schulze (ed.) *DDR-Jugend: Ein statistisches Handbuch* (Berlin: Akademie Verlag, 1995)

Annette Simon and Jan Faktor, *Fremd im eigenen Land?* (Giessen: Psychosozial-Verlag, 2000)

Peter Skyba, *Vom Hoffnungsträger zum Sicherheitsrisiko: Jugend in der DDR und Jugendpolitik der SED, 1949–1961* (Cologne: Böhlau Verlag, 2000)

So lachte man in der DDR: Witze und Karikaturen (Munich: Eulenspiegel, 1999)

Heike Solga, *Auf dem Weg in eine klassenlose Gesellschaft? Klassenlagen und Mobilität zwischen Generationen in der DDR* (Berlin: Akademie Verlag, 1995)

Die Sorben: Wissenswertes aus Vergangenheit und Gegenwart der sorbischen nationalen Minderheit, 3rd edn (Bautzen: VEB Domowina-Verlag, 1970)

Statistisches Amt der DDR (ed.), *Statistisches Jahrbuch der DDR* (Berlin: VEB Deutscher Zentralverlag, 34 vols, 1955–1989; Rudolf Haufe Verlag, vol. 35, 1990)

André Steiner, *Von Plan zu Plan* (Munich: DVA, 2004)

Gerd-Rüdiger Stephan (ed.), *'Vorwärts immer, rückwärts nimmer!': Interne Dokumente zum Zerfall von SED und DDR, 1988–89* (Berlin: Dietz Verlag, 1994)

Carola Stern, *Ulbricht: Eine politische Biographie* (Cologne: Verlag Kiepenheuer & Witsch, 1964)

Raymond Stokes, *Constructing Socialism: Technology and Change in East Germany, 1945–1990* (Baltimore, Md: Johns Hopkins University Press, 2000)

Wendelin Strubelt *et al.* (eds), *Städte und Regionen: Räumliche Folgen des Transformationsprozesses* (Opladen: Leske & Budrich, 1996)

Sonja Süß, *Politisch mißbraucht? Psychiatrie und Staatssicherheit in der DDR* (Berlin: Chr. Links Verlag, 1998)

Walter Süss, *Staatssicherheit am Ende: Warum es den Mächtigen nicht gelang, 1989 eine Revolution zu verhindern* (Berlin: Chr. Links Verlag, 1999)

Heinz-Elmar Tenorth, Sonja Kudella and Andreas Paetz, *Politisierung im Schulalltag der DDR: Durchsetzung und Scheitern einer Erziehungsambition* (Weinheim: Deutscher Studien Verlag, 1996)

Kirsten Thietz (ed.), *Ende der Selbstverständlichkeit? Die Abschaffung des §218 in der DDR* (Berlin: Basis Druck, 1992)

J. K. A. Thomaneck and James Mellis (eds), *Politics, Society and Government in the GDR: Basic Documents* (Oxford and New York: Berg, 1989)

Heiner Timmermann (ed.), *Diktaturen in Europa im 20. Jahrhundert – der Fall DDR* (Berlin: Duncker & Humblot, 1996)

Wolfgang Tischner, *Katholische Kirche in der SBZ/DDR: Die Formierung einer Subgesellschaft im entstehenden sozialistischen Staat* (Paderborn: Ferdinand Schöningh, 2001)

Heike Trappe, *Emanzipation oder Zwang?: Frauen in der DDR zwischen Beruf, Familie und Sozialpolitik* (Berlin: Akademie Verlag, 1995)

Manfred Uschner, *Die zweite Etage: Funktionsweise eines Machtapparates*, 2nd edn (Berlin: Dietz Verlag, 1995)

Michael Veester, Michael Hofman and Irene Zierke (eds), *Soziale Milieus in Ostdeutschland* (Cologne: Bund-Verlag, 1995)

Dieter Voigt (ed.), *Die Gesellschaft der DDR* (Berlin: Duncker & Humblot, 1984)

—— and Lothar Mertens (eds), *Minderheiten in und Übersiedler aus der DDR* (Berlin: Duncker & Humblot, 1992)

——, Werner Voss and Sabine Meck, *Sozialstruktur der DDR* (Darmstadt: Wissenschaftliche Buchgesellschaft, 1987)

Clemens Vollnhals and Jürgen Weber (eds), *Der Schein der Normalität: Alltag und Herrschaft in der SED-Diktatur* (Munich: Olzog Verlag, 2002)

Joachim Walther, *Sicherungsbereich Literatur: Schriftsteller und Staatssicherheit in der Deutschen Demokratischen Republik* (Berlin: Chr. Links Verlag, 1996)

Maxie Wander, *'Guten Morgen, Du Schöne': Frauen in der DDR: Protokolle* (Darmstadt: Luchterhand, 1980)

——, *Tagebücher und Briefe* (Berlin and Weimar: Aufbau Verlag, 1990)

Hermann Weber, *Geschichte der DDR*, revised edn (Munich: dtv, 1999)

Jürgen Weber (ed.), *Der SED-Staat: Neues über eine vergangene Diktatur* (Munich: Olzog Verlag, 1994)

Harald Welzer, Sabine Moller and Karoline Tschuggnall, *'Opa war kein Nazi': Nationalsozialismus und Holocaust im Familiengedächtnis* (Frankfurt am Main: Fischer, 2002)

Dorothee Wierling, *Geboren im Jahr Eins: Der Jahrgang 1949 in der DDR: Versuch einer Kollektivbiographie* (Berlin: Chr. Links Verlag, 2002)

Gunnar Winkler (ed.), *Lexikon der Sozialpolitik*, 2 vols (Berlin: Akademie Verlag, 1987)

—— (ed.), *Geschichte der Sozialpolitik der DDR, 1945–1985* (Berlin: Akademie Verlag, 1989)

—— (ed.), *Frauenreport '90* (Berlin: Verlag Die Wirtschaft, 1990)

Stefan Wolle, *Die heile Welt der Diktatur: Alltag und Herrschaft in der DDR, 1971–1989* (Berlin: Chr. Links Verlag, 1998)

Vera Wollenberger, *Virus der Heuchler* (Berlin: Elefanten Press, 1992)

Matthias Zeng, *'Asoziale' in der DDR* (Münster: Lit Verlag, 2000)

Zentrum für interdisziplinäre Frauenforschung der Humboldt-Universität Berlin (ed.), *Unter Hammer und Zirkel: Frauenbiographien vor dem Hintergrund ostdeutscher Sozialisationserfahrungen* (Pfaffenweiler: Centaurus Verlagsgesellschaft, 1995)

Dorle Zilch, *Millionen unter der blauen Fahne: Die FDJ: Zahlen – Fakten – Tendenzen* (Rostock: Verlag Jugend und Geschichte, 1994)

Index

Note: Page references in italics indicate tables.